Our Voices II: *the de-colonial project*

ORO Editions
Publishers of Architecture, Art, and Design
Gordon Goff: Publisher

www.oroeditions.com
info@oroeditions.com

Published by ORO Editions

Graphic Layout and Design: Pablo Mandel of Circular Studio
Text and Images: Indigenous Architecture and Design Publishing Collective 2021
ORO Project Coordinator: Kirby Anderson

10 9 8 7 6 5 4 3 2 1 First Edition

Library of Congress data available upon request. World Rights: Available

ISBN: 978-1-943532-56-8

Color Separations and Printing: ORO Group Ltd.
Printed in China.

International Distribution: www.oroeditions.com/distribution

ORO Editions makes a continuous effort to minimize the overall carbon footprint of its publications. As part of this goal, ORO Editions, in association with Global ReLeaf, arranges to plant trees to replace those used in the manufacturing of the paper produced for its books. Global ReLeaf is an international campaign run by American Forests, one of the world's oldest nonprofit conservation organizations. Global ReLeaf is American Forests' education and action program that helps individuals, organizations, agencies, and corporations improve the local and global environment by planting and caring for trees.

Our Voices II: *the de-colonial project*

By Rebecca Kiddle, luugigyoo patrick stewart, and Kevin O'Brien

ORO
EDITIONS

Table of Contents

Foreword: Frontier Conflict

Fiona Foley
Badtjala

In Bruce Pascoe's most recent publication titled, *Salt*, he states, **"Any nation's artists and thinkers set the tone and breadth of national conversation."** That national conversation at some point must take into account the invasion and subsequent frontier wars of Australia and reparations to the sovereign Aboriginal nations of this continent.

As a five-year old child, I remember looking across to Fraser Island and experiencing a deep sense of loss. It was a loss for my country, for my culture and for my old people. From an early age I wanted to know more because I have an intellect and am curious. That is not a crime. I became a racialised person – not from my family, but by other's, when I entered the school gates at Urangan, Hervey Bay. My parents faced much racism in the 1970s and at one point were forced to leave Hervey Bay and move to Mt. Isa to escape the pressures of race hatred because of their mixed marriage. By then I was in third grade.

Racism in this country is a topic we like to avoid discussing but it manifests itself everywhere, including in architectural process and practice, the focus of this book. It is a societal burden I've learned to carry. That gaze wrapped up in judgment from a white society and white individuals. For me it manifests itself in everyday educational environments, including my present-day status as an academic at Griffith University, with "Dr" in front of my name.

As an adult, I reflect on the fact that many in Australia carry deep psychological scars from what Judy Atkinson terms intergenerational trauma. Aboriginal people were not allowed to bury our dead after massacres had taken place. I believe this country carries deep wounds from the trauma of these frontier wars. We carry it inside our souls whether we are conscious of it or not. This brutality, in turn, has also affected the perpetrators and their descendants.

I did not know I was destined to be an artist in life but that has sustained me for the past 35 years. While studying in the sculpture department at Sydney College of the Arts I created a sculpture in 1986 *Annihilation of the Blacks* that speaks to this trauma. I was told about a massacre on my country along the Susan River by my late mother, Shirley Foley. Indeed, many such oral histories are carried, in the living memory, of Aboriginal people. That image stayed with me, the image of the Badtjala people being maimed, killed or fleeing on foot. It was a powerful history to carry and to make of it – something. A kind of decolonial act.

Art and politics have had an uneasy relationship in this country. Many years later after the initial purchase of my sculpture, *Annihilation of the Blacks* courted controversy from the conservative, John Howard government. The sculpture, and what it symbolised played a role in the history wars unfolding nationally contributing to the non-renewal of Dawn Casey's contract as the Director of the National Museum of Australia, as a case in point. Dawn Casey, an Indigenous Australian, oversaw the "democratisation of museums" and fore fronted Indigenous challenges, working under a regime that was antagonistic to Indigenous worldviews.

Fast forward to another Canberra institution, the National Gallery of Australia. People may be familiar with my work titled, *Dispersed*. This work was created after reading a number of publications by historians such as Rosalind Kidd, Jonathan Richards, Raymond Evans and Tony Roberts. Reading about what really took place in Queensland has been a lifetime passion of mine to find out the truth, attitudes held by the colonial man and woman, a guerrilla war with strategic and repeated attacks on the invader. We were not passive in the take-over of our country despite the fact that some have said to me on occasion, "Australia had been settled peacefully." Let's remember that every inch of Queensland soil has been fought over and bloodied.

Finding the true history of Queensland was a slow process of reading and piecing together an epic jigsaw puzzle one piece at a time. No one taught me in a classroom setting about the history of Queensland and its race politics. Only through the simple act of reading books I taught myself about the true counter narrative. In 1984, the first book I bought on this subject was by C.D. Rowley, titled The *Destruction of Aboriginal Society*. Then it was a slow grind reading book after book after book, unfolding over decades. Australia has an uneasy relationship with our history as we keep running into a stock standard conservative, revisionist pathology.

My life has been about the fight for justice for Aboriginal people and telling the true history of Australia.

My platform has been through the visual arts. Visual arts, architecture, landscape design ... it all has power to provoke and inch by inch move us towards decolonisation in sometimes subtle and other times overt ways.

I will end here with a quote by the writer Toni Morrison – she says, **"facts CAN exist without human intelligence – but truth cannot."**

A collaborative team has made a valuable contribution to the research not currently known before in Queensland. Taking shape through the discipline of archaeology and Indigenous knowledge from Aboriginal descendants of frontier conflict they have been able to join forces to bring this information to the general public. This research was funded through an Australian Research Council Discovery Project grant (DP160100307, The Archaeology of the Queensland Native Mounted Police) from 2016–2020. It was a joint project conducted by researchers from Flinders University, the University of Southern Queensland, the University of Notre Dame Australia, the University of New England and James Cook University.

Mayem *[welcome]*: Introduction

The Ethics of writing and producing a book on De-colonisation

This book picks up where *Our Voices: Indigeneity and Architecture* left off. It continues in the same vein of Indigenous authorship and collaboration to maintain space for our voices within the built environment. We must speak into the contexts that directly affect ourselves, our communities and the cultural impacts the modern world has brought us. This collaboration includes editors and authors of Indigenous heritage from Australia, Aotearoa New Zealand (NZ), Turtle Island Canada and the United States. The diversity of contributions reflects an acute awareness of the effects of colonisation and how we might move beyond the continued trauma and violence. It includes works from the perspectives of artists, academics, designers, architects, planners, urban designers and policy strategists.

Our Voices: The DE-colonial Project showcases works that seek to confront the limitations of the colonial built environment. The land, towns and cities on which we live have always been Indigenous places yet, for the most part our Indigenous value sets and identities have been disregarded or appropriated. Indigenous Peoples continue to be gentrified out of the places to which they belong and both neo-conservative and neo-liberal systems work to continuously subjugate Indigenous involvement in decision-making processes in differing, but equally effective ways. However, we are not, and have never been cultural dopes. Rather, we have, and continue to, subvert the colonial value sets that overlay our places in important ways.

Between July 4-6 of 2019, the *Our Voices: The DE-colonial Project* open conference brought together many of the contributors to the University of Sydney. For three days, presentations and discussions considered not just the colonising effects of those wo/man made things that surround us (i.e. architecture and the city) but also the colonising effects on the Indigenous body. From identity, to fashion and to homelessness, it was made clear that our skin (i.e. colour), what we put on (i.e. clothes) and how we might be in public space (i.e. act) is invariably viewed through a colonial filter as an "Indigenous problem." It reminded us all that the presence of Indigenous Peoples in our cities and Countries begins (and arguably ends) with the human experience. The resulting framework for this book was deliberately broadened to enable a variety of interpretations and contributions that have come together as a demonstration of the depth and breadth of thought around de-colonising practices and projects.

Another word on Indigenous

The use of the word Indigenous, with a capital "I" extends its application in *Our Voices: Indigeneity and Architecture* as an ongoing editorial position to move beyond the colonial origins of the word. This move continues the assertion from the first book that the inherent importance of the notion of Indigenous (and Indigeneity) as a shared identity with a related set of knowledges and experiences.

It does, however, remain a genuine paradox to recondition a collective word that is acceptable and respectful to the various origins of the contributors. The reframing and reclaiming of this and other words that might describe our greater collective is consistent with cultural, political and philosophical change.

Other words such as native, aborigine, aboriginal and indigenous are used throughout the world to identify Indigenous Peoples on general terms as "other." Indeed, these words are present even in this book as a sign of the underpinning political sentiment and ideology surrounding the contributor's unique experience and position and the fields in which they operate. However, where in Aotearoa New Zealand "Native" has been rejected in favour of "Māori," and in Turtle Island Canada, Indigenous is becoming the norm and Australia "Aborigine/Aboriginal" has become accepted, there is no substitute for the more precise tribal identity that is delivered through nation, language, totemic or clan names. Identity is complex and many things define and, most importantly, unite us.

De-colonisation/de-colonising/de-colonise

The focus of this book is bound to the Indigenous origins of the contributors and therefore specifically addresses those moves to counter the destructive legacies of European colonisation in Australia, Aotearoa New Zealand (NZ), Turtle Island Canada and the United States today. These counter moves are the de-colonial projects presented in this book. However, it must also be understood that these de-colonial projects are part of much larger intellectual, theoretical and political fields that reach deep into global history and stretch well beyond the remit of this book.

Linda Tuhiwai Smith's *Decolonizing Methodologies: Research and Indigenous People* published by Zed Books Ltd, London and New York, and the University of Otago Press, Dunedin, in 1999 is considered a seminal text critiquing euro-centric concepts of research to articulate a new research agenda from an Indigenous position. It is frequently referenced and highly influential in this part of the world. Presented in two parts, the first part (amongst other points) identifies research classification as a weapon used to subjugate the minds of Indigenous people. In the second part, the suspicion of research in Māori communities was argued as an active form of colonisation that sought to remove agency from Indigenous people. These two points are in no way a summary of a much more comprehensive text, rather, they have struck thematic chords in this book where "freedom of mind" leads to cultural engagement, and "agency" leads to self-determination.

The Ethics of Production

In this book we have continued the ambition of the Indigenous voice to guide both content and process set out in *Our Voices: Indigeneity and Architecture.* Beginning with the shared Indigenous culture of our editorial group of Rebecca Kiddle (Ngāti Porou and Ngā Puhi, urbanist and academic), luugigyoo patrick stewart (Nisga'a, architect and academic) and Kevin O'Brien (Kaurereg and Meriam, architect and academic), it was extended to include sub-editors Rau Hoskins (Ngāti Hau and Ngā Puhi, architect, and academic), David Fortin (Métis, architect, and academic) and Michael Mossman (kuku yalanji, architect and academic). As a group, it was possible to maintain a forum where process and intent could be discussed around the questions arising from such a general term as "Indigenous." Thankfully, the first book tested and set our original framework for ensuring a safe cultural space for all contributors. This book not only extends the intention to make it even more accessible to all those with something to say, but also to feel safe in saying it in their own way.

Each contribution has been peer reviewed in an open manner by at least two members of the broader editorial group; in many cases, especially the academic contributions, also by many others prior to being included here. It is worth reminding that in support of Indigeneity, we wanted to privilege Indigenous knowledges and research/writing methodologies as being central to our process. Authors were encouraged to seek peer review from those in their communities whom they respected. This review process was set out in *Our Voices: Indigeneity and Architecture* and predicated on the work of the National Collaborating Centre on Aboriginal Health (NCCAH) in Canada who developed an Indigenous peer review framework for a journal publication they had developed. We again thank them for this seminal work.

The NCCAH set out a number of goals that have been duplicated and taken on board for this publication given their relevance. These assert that this publication will:

- Create a place of respect and safety where Indigenous writing and wisdom is valued and acknowledged;
- Provide a new model of publication that creates access for Indigenous scholars;
- Provide a place of dialogue and sharing;
- Promote Indigenous Peoples academic research and writing;
- Promote and mentor Indigenous talent;
- Reclaim our voice;
- Showcase best Indigenous practice; and,
- Encourage cultural competence and congruence through research and making connections to administration, policy and practice (NCCAH:2007).

This has meant there are contributions that range from song and poetry, to opinion pieces in addition to more architectural profession and academic pieces that in total represent a broad spectrum of thought and position. Across this spectrum, one concept unites us all, that of the need for the Indigenous voice in guiding our changing environments.

The arrangement and format

This book is hosted in Australia and for that reason, the first words emanate from Fiona Foley, a Badtjala woman and internationally acclaimed artist. Fiona Foley has kindly contributed an opening foreword outlining her experiences as presented in her keynote address at the *Our Voices: The DE-colonial Project* in July 4-6, 2019. This is followed by this introduction and concluded with the last words led by co-editor, Kevin O'Brien of Kaurereg and Meriam descent. There are four sections, each co-titled in Meriam (in honour of Kevin O'Brien's maternal line) and English languages.

kopat [everybody together] (section 1): People and Community reminds us that the de-colonial project starts with our lived experience and originates in our bodies. The section begins with the lyrics of a song from Earth feather (aka Josephine Clarke) describing how language, when plucked out from a community, has a devastating effect on culture and the identity of a people. An invitation is extended to simply read the lyrics aloud and listen to the sounds. These sounds, and the associated rhythms intimate how language, and therefore people, belong to the land. This work sets the theme for this section and is followed by Linda Lavallee's ongoing work in fashion where the positive expression of cultural identity in public spaces can attract unwanted negative behaviours from the non-indigenous community. luugigyoo patrick stewart and Diane Menzies writings independently discuss the need to support the de-colonising process with our children and through our communities. Keri

Whaitiri, Daniel J. Glenn, and Richard Begay continue the discussion and extend the notion of community into built conditions of urban recovery, contemporary village and cultural relevancy respectively.

meta [house] dewer [to build] (Section 2): Architecture and Building begins with a searing poem by Timmah Ball that laments the injustice of a land title system supporting the beguile of its planning and architectural representatives. Blak Box, a travelling pavilion for the telling of stories by Kevin O"Brien, suggests that identity begins in thought, transpires as sounds and ends in an aesthetic. Reuben Friend's writing takes us from the physical to the virtual and introduces questions around how cultural knowledge might be stored, accessed and most importantly enabled through guardianship. Elisapeta Hinemoa Heta's story outlines a way into space and placemaking as a matter of agency. Eladia Smoke and Krystel Clark separately discuss how agency informs the building through cultural ideation and healing respectively. This section is brought together through Eladia Smoke, David Fortin and Wanda Dalla Costa's co-written piece addressing the challenges and ambitions of a significant cultural building located at the contested intersection of politics, culture, history and identity.

meriba ged [our land] (Section 3): Country and City considers a larger scale of context in which the previous two sections sit. Jason De Santolo introduces the idea of Country as a living entity that people belong to and care for in a cycle of renewal. A way into designing with Country is further explored by Dillon Kombumerri and Daniele Hromek's co-written piece. This is followed by Daniele Hromek's stand-alone piece addressing the nature of contested ground in the city; and also a further piece co-written with siblings Michael Hromek and Sian Hromek that demonstrates the potency of uncovering latent narratives in urban contexts. Amanda Yates ends this section examining de-colonisation as a social-cultural-political process. One that proposes that Indigenous urbanism grounded on agricultural activism is a powerful urban decolonising practice.

dirsir [to prepare, fix, make] (section 4): Principles and Action invites us to think and act. Kristi Leora Gansworth's poem beautifully expresses the spirit as a source of knowledge informed by a principled view of the planet, introducing an inclusive start to the section. Michael Mossman's explanation of a design studio of 25 projects worked in close collaboration with community demonstrates an inclusive approach to teaching non-indigenous students about engagement and culture specificity. Fleur Palmer dissects the prevalent Eurocentric system of architectural education and calls for a rethinking that addresses the interconnected-ness of all things. Desna Whaanga-Schollum and Ngā Aho's paper continues this view to describe a large network of design professionals who meet, discuss and act on issues enabling leadership in their creative disciplines and working contexts. Jade Kake's paper, and Brian Martin

and Jefa Greenaway's co-written paper, both contribute to the complex and dynamic discussion around the specificity and application of Indigenous design principles and guidelines in practice and in institutions respectively. The final paper by Rebecca Kiddle summarily shares some friendly advice around how we might engage with the principles and actions previously outlined so as not to undermine nor dilute Indigenous leadership and knowledge.

Our Voices: The DE-colonial Project draws together a broad spectrum of voices to address issues confronting Indigenous peoples in Australia, Aotearoa New Zealand, and Turtle Island Canada and the United States of America. Although comprehensive in its global reach, it is by no means a claim to a definitive position on the de-colonial project. Rather, this is a space for the active concerns and endeavours of multiple indigenous voices at this point in time.

References

Smith, L.T. (1999). *Decolonizing Methodologies: Research and Indigenous People.* Dunedin: The University of Otago Press; London and New York: Zed Books Ltd.

National Collaborating Centre on Aboriginal Health (NCCAH) (2007). *Developing an Indigenous Peer Review Framework and process for an online child, family and community focused journal,* re-retrieved 4 February 2020, from https://fncaringsociety.com/sites/default/files/docs/Developing_Indigenous_Framework_Process_OnlineJournal_2007.pdf.

Chapter 1.0: E KO

Josephine Clarke – Te Rarawa, Te Aupōuri, Ngāpuhi and Ngāti Porou

*Josephine is a creative, poet, singer songwriter and artist.
She is on the Ngā Aho Executive committee, a member
of Te Tau-a-nuku, and on the Māori Advisory Committee
for the Unitec Landscape Architecture Department.
Josephine specialises in several fields of landscape
architecture and urban design particularly in cultural
expressive design and integrated design for the public
and private sector in Auckland and wider Waikato Region.
Josephine's professional goals focus on the inclusion of
Te Ao Māori values as an approach to design.*

E KŌ

Singer songwriter: Earthfeather aka Josephine Clarke

[Chorus]
E kō, e kō ana te rangatira (x2)

Ū Ū Ū Ū

(V1)
Hutia mai te rito o te harakeke
Kei whea te kōmako
E kō ana

(V2)
[Ko te ira tangata
i ngaro mai te pūkaki
ki te ūkaipō o te
ao mārama] x2

[Chorus]
E kō, e kō ana te rangatira (x2)

Ū Ū Ū Ū

(Bridge)
Mai i te oro o te manu
kō te Kurawaka o te Ū
A Hine-tītama mai i
a Hine-ahu-one

Tihei,Tihei,Tihei mauri -o- ra.

[Chorus]
E kō, e kō ana te rangatira.
Me kō, me kō ana ngā mokopuna.
Me kō, me kō ana te reo rangatira.

E kō, e kō ana te rangatira. *(x2)*

Ū Ū Ū Ū

E kō -lyric translation

To sing (of birds), the chief sings.
To sing (of birds), the chief sings.

*If the heart of the harakeke was removed, where
will the bellbird sing? (the heart in this context is
the language, if the language is plucked out of our
culture where would we sing)*

*The human element has lost the stream, source of
sustenance, to the world of light.*

To sing (of birds), the chief sings.
To sing (of birds), the chief sings.

*From the voice of the bird, lies
the Kurawaka (Kurawaka is the name of the
place in our māori creation narratives where the
first woman was created) the landing place, from
Hine-tītama (the dawn) daughter of Hine-ahu-one
(the first woman/human being formed by Tāne-
Mahuta from the red earth, the fertile soil of Papa-
tū-a-nuku).*

*The sneeze, the sneeze, the sneeze of life (the
first breath of Hine-ahu-one)*

*To sing (of birds), the chief sings. Let us sing,
the descendants sing. Let us sing, the chiefly
language (te reo māori) sings. To sing (of birds),
the chief sings.*

Kaupapa of this waiata. (Meaning of this song)

I wrote this waiata for Māori Language Week years ago. In a nutshell the rangatira (chief) I'm referring to is our reo and it is calling us to speak.

The whakatauki (proverb) at the top refers to our reo as the rito. If the rito (our language) is plucked out of us, our heart is plucked out, where is our culture, where are we as people. The bridge of the waiata talks about how our reo (language) connects us to our whakapapa (lineage). In my perspective when reo was created it was formed around the time of Hine-ahu-one and Hine-tītama. This is our creation story and connection to Papa-tū-a-nuku (Mother Earth). Using our language connects us to our land. It was formed from us studying the oro of manu. Kupu (words) were formed from the sounds around us. They are our breath of life. They are the familiarity, the essence that calls us and guides us home. This song connects us to the integrity of our being. To the integrity that lies in the sounds of our language. E kō ana te Rangatira!

CON.TRUST
EARTHFEATHER

Chapter 1.1: Sacred Superwoman

Linda Lavallee – Montreal Lake Cree Nation in northern Saskatchewan

Abstract

The Human Rights Commission of the Province of Ontario in Canada has broadly defined racial profiling as any action undertaken for reasons of safety, security, or public protection that relies on stereotypes about race, color, ethnicity, ancestry, religion, or place of origin rather than on reasonable suspicion, to single out an individual for greater scrutiny or different treatment. The discriminatory practice of racial profiling has resulted in an over-representation of Indigenous people being incarcerated across the country. For example, in my home province of Saskatchewan, more than 90% of incarcerated males and females are Indigenous while only making up 15% of the population.

As a Cree woman, I too know the violence, pain, and humiliation of being racially profiled. As a fashion designer, I wondered what I could do about it. I found that when I dressed in traditional clothing, I was treated with respect. I started my 365 ribbon skirt campaign. This chapter will outline this ribbon skirt campaign.

My name is Linda Lavallee of the Montreal Lake Cree Nation in northern Saskatchewan in what we call Turtle Island, also now known as Canada. Through my mother, we are what is known as Woodland Cree. My great grandmother's family on my mother's side originated near present-day La Ronge Saskatchewan. On my father's side, his great grandmother originated from present-day Manitoba. No information about her has survived except that she was Cree. She had a son with one Louis Lavallee, who had arrived from France. Her son, my dad's grandfather, also known as Louis Lavallee, traveled as a small boy from his home in Manitoba to Fort QuAppelle (established in 1864) in Saskatchewan to live with his uncles. He was what is known in Canada, as Metis, a mixed blood of French and Indian. As a young man, he traveled northwest and settled before 1885 in the area that was to become Prince Albert National Park in 1927 in northern Saskatchewan. It was there that he met a local Cree woman, Marguerite, and had ten children including my grandfather Moise. It was Moise's son Joseph, my dad, who met my mom, Marion, a Cree woman from Montreal Lake Cree Nation. In Canada, the government has blood distinctions of Indigeneity. Since Confederation

in 1867, the federal government has tried to manage legal theft of the land through genocide. In 1876, they passed the Indian Act which stated that an Indian woman who marries a non-Indian man loses her status as an Indian under the Act. My mom lost her status when she married my Dad, a Metis. The federal government tried to fix what they had done by passing another law that gave back the status to those women and children who had their status taken away. Though when they did this, they created a tiered system that labeled those same people with second-class status. This has affected my parents, myself, my children, and grandchildren.

With my introduction I hope you begin to understand how colonialism has affected my family and my culture. It is definitely complex. My family and I still struggle to find our place in this country. Though to settlers, our skin color still sets us apart, as they derogatorily continue to refer to us as Indian.

As I have learned, it is proper protocol to introduce one's self to begin a relationship with another; whether in person or on the page. So, *tansi (*hello)!

Dress for Success

In the psychology of fashion, there has long been a movement of dressing for success. Hutson and Rodriguez (2016) have written that clothes impact both the wearer and the people around them. When my husband and I got married we had a photo session. (Fig. 1)

Complete strangers came up and took photos of us. We did seem to impact the crowds of people around the site in Las Vegas, where we had the photo shoot. We dressed in cultural fashions that reflected my husband's Nisga'a heritage (Fig. 2). Why would they want photos of strangers? Sure, we looked good, but what did our clothes say to onlookers?

Even on workdays when my husband wears our fashion, he is often approached and asked where he got the shirt, or his boots. Not to put down other fashion designers but shirts by Ralph Lauren or Perry Ellis (and my husband has shirts from these other designers as well) do not garner that type of attention. Of course, such fashions have to be handled with care. Our daughter tries to navigate the malls and streets unnoticed but has

Figure 1. Wedding day photo (Linda Lavallee and Luugigyoo Patrick R. Stewart, designers. Used with permission.)

Figure 2. Wedding day photo (Linda Lavallee and Luugigyoo Patrick R. Stewart, designers. Used with permission.)

told us it is impossible when she wears our clothes, so she does not wear our fashion unless she is with us. As we experience these reactions, we wonder if it is the culture that our fashions portray that attracts people. What is it about our cultures as Indigenous to this land that attracts people? Is it something lacking in their own culture that they have lost? Whatever the answer we wear our fashions with pride knowing that they impact people around us. By extension when we impact people, we impact the space we as people inhabit.

All of this to say that people do make snap judgments based upon appearances, both through clothing and ethnicity. It was with this in mind as an Indigenous woman that I started to de-colonize my appearance.

Skirt Journey

I started this journey out of hurt, anger, and humiliation. Whenever I would go out by myself it seemed as if I was profiled more than when I went out with my husband. That is racism! I was getting afraid to go out by myself. It was getting to point where I worried for my own children and grandchildren on their own treatment when they went out. We took the treatment we received living in Prince Albert (Saskatchewan) as just part of life. You either survived the town or you did not go there. You had to take it and just shake it off. But I am now over 50, living in British Columbia and enough is enough. My children

go through it and their children, my grandchildren will go through it. But why? So, my journey is just starting. Some days I just want to give up and continue as it is, but then I remembered why I am doing what I am doing. I said to myself, "If you are going to judge me for my skin color, then I will dress my culture, but with pride and dignity! Ribbon skirt on!" When I put a ribbon skirt on it feels like my ancestors are there walking with me and I hold my head high and feel no fear. I have the confidence that I am protected. (Fig. 3)

At first, the skirts were just that. Protection skirts for me. I designed and sewed short ones, long ones, sexy, and plain skirts. And some skirts I loved so much. I could wear them day after day. My husband would always ask me what each particular skirt represented. Some days it was just a skirt I wore to protect myself and then there are other skirts that mean so much. Some remind me of my mother and father and all the stuff they had done to influence my life and how much I miss them.

Weaving was something that I had heard my mom talk about and how they would go pick willows and weave. I never did learn from her or even wanted to learn. Now I am regretting how much I did not learn from her and how this is so important. Luckily my dad taught me how to make my first moss bag with red willows. He had so much to teach me, but I was so full of myself and did not think it was important. Now I constantly try to remember what he taught me. I wish I could go back in time. He did

Figure 3. Linda in ribbon skirt and Patrick in boots and shirt (Linda Lavallee, designer. Used with permission.)

Figure 4. Installation in the Royal Alberta Museum, Edmonton Alberta (Linda Lavallee, designer. Used with permission.)

force me learn how to bead and work with moccasins. He wanted me to have a skill that would feed my babies. The force that my dad had is what drives me today. Never to be afraid to do something, do anything to learn something. I am trying to teach my children, nieces, and soon my grandchildren.

Ribbon Skirts[1]

Traditional Cree skirts were made from deer hide and decorated with plant pigment. With the introduction of European trade goods, cotton calico and ribbons were then used to carry the meanings and teachings. The silhouette shape of the skirt itself comes from a sacred place, and it follows the outline of the *mikiiwaap* (Cree), or *tipi* (Dakota). The bottom of the skirts would touch the earth's medicines, and as the women walked they said, "Mother Earth would always know who it was that was making their presence felt on her back," and her prayers were answered accordingly.

Those of us who know the teachings and cherish the ways of the old people, choose to honor ourselves as women by putting skirts on. We know that there's a

___

1. Ribbon is a narrow strip or band of fabric finished at the edges and used for trimming, tying, or finishing. Woven-edge ribbons are common to the textile industry; they are narrow pieces of fabric with two selvedges or woven edges. Ribbon is classified by the textile industry as a narrow fabric ranging in various widths. Ribbons have been used for centuries as ornamentation. Once called ribands, they were narrow strips of fabric attached to garments (*Columbia Electronic Encyclopedia,* 6th ed.)

sacred teaching for our children when they see us being proud of who we are as women, and I think that is the greatest gift.

Ribbonwork is a rainbow tradition of color and beauty. Although the present base materials are of non-Indigenous manufacturing, the fundamental styles and motifs are from Indigenous knowledge handed down from generation to generation. My inspiration comes from knowledge handed down from my mother, her mother and her mother before her. (Fig. 4)

First Nations artists and makers have been using ribbons in garments for generations since the colonizers arrived in this country. The use of ribbonwork today is spectacular and the intricacy of the planning, cutting, folding, and sewing of its manufacture clearly demonstrates the sophistication and skill of Indigenous arts. A colonial scholar developed a ribbonwork classification system. Donna Abbass (1979) developed a typology, or a system of notation for classifying ribbonwork based on techniques and structural characteristics of ribbonwork samples of tribes from Oklahoma. These same characteristics have application here among our own peoples' designs. Abbass described specific construction techniques based on four developmental styles of ribbonwork:

1. *Developmental stage* - simple geometric design and construction (Fig. 5)
2. *Style I* - shingled ribbonwork where the pattern is repeated with multiple layers of ribbon (Fig. 6)
3. *Style II* - negative ribbonwork formed with pairs of ribbon; the top ribbon is cut away and the bottom ribbon is revealed, an example is reverse appliqué (Fig. 7)
4. *Style III* - positive ribbonwork where the top ribbon forms a design (Fig. 8)

Figure 5. Geometric ribbon skirt design and construction (Linda Lavallee, designer. Used with permission.)

Figure 7. Negative ribbon skirt design and construction (Linda Lavallee, designer. Used with permission.)

Figure 6. Shingled ribbon skirt design and construction (Linda Lavallee, designer. Used with permission.)

Figure 8. Positive ribbon skirt design and construction (Linda Lavalle, designer. Used with permission.)

Figure 9. Simple ribbon design and construction (Linda Lavallee, designer. Used with permission.)

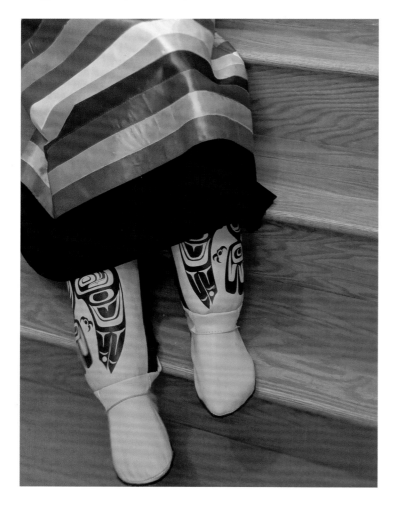

Figure 10. Appliqué design and construction (Linda Lavallee, designer. Used with permission.)

Abbass's (1979) classification system was developed for the description of technical aspects and chronological stages of styles of ribbonwork. She also made the distinction in the technique called appliqué, the use of cut cloth to form medallions or motifs, as opposed to "ribbonwork" using lengths of cut and sewn selvedge edged ribbons. (Fig. 9)

However, the appliqué technique as well as the use of simple ribbons to decorate garments was omitted from her classification system. (Fig. 10)

Finally, her study was limited to ribbonwork from her own classification system and her study was limited to ribbonwork from Native American culture groups from Oklahoma. As more and more Indigenous Nations explore their own design knowledge, there will be many more exciting designs to come.

Sharing Cree and Nisga'a designs with the world results in amazing opportunities for designers of all ages. Figure 11 shows my niece, Gia, from Saskatchewan in Canada participating in our photoshoot at the Sydney Opera House in 2019. It's been an amazing personal journey so far (Fig. 12). I would never have imagined myself as a young woman from down a dirt road in a remote northern community in Canada attending fashion shows and photoshoots in Toronto, New York, Vancouver, Melbourne, and Sydney. My fashion will continue to impact our everyday lives and those of others and the spaces we move through. Tansi.

References

Abbass, Donna (1979). *Contemporary Oklahoma Ribbonwork: Styles and Economics.* Southern Illinois University: Department of Anthropology.

Hutson, Matthew and Tori Rodriguez (2016). "Dress for Success." *Scientific American 27*. Retrieved March 23, 2020. https://www.scientificamerican.com/article/dress-for-success-how-clothes-influence-our-performance/

Figure 11. Gia dressed in Cree and Nisga'a designs on the steps of the Sydney Opera House, Sydney Australia (Photo by Patrick Stewart. Used with permission.)

Figure 12. Linda and Patrick brought nine youth from Canada to the University of Sydney to present at a conference and a photoshoot (Linda Lavallee, designer. Used with permission.)

Chapter 1.2: decolonizing one child at a time

luugigyoo patrick stewart – Killerwhale House of Daaxan of the Nisga'a Village of Gingoix

Dr Stewart's name in Nisga'a is Luugigyoo. He has a PhD from the University of British Columbia and a MArch from McGill University and, most recently, an adjunct professor at the McEwen School of Architecture at Laurentian University. He is Chair of the Indigenous Task Force of the Royal Architectural Institute of Canada and Chair of the Provincial Aboriginal Homelessness Committee in British Columbia on Canada's west coast. He continues his architectural practice since 1995.

ABSTRACT

there are more children living in foster care of all levels of government in what is now known as c\a\n\a\d\a in 2019 than attended "indian" residential schools at their height between 1896 and 1996 over 150,000 children were forced to attend   over 50% of foster children in c\a\n\a\d\a under the age of 14 are indigenous despite being only 8% of the total population

in my home province of b\r\i\t\i\s\h c\o\l\u\m\b\i\a where i was born homeless and raised in care   68% of children in care are indigenous   in the province of m\a\n\i\t\o\b\a 90% of the childrenincare are indigenous and in the northern territory of n\u\n\a\v\u\t 100% of the childrenincare are indigenous

there is one northern indigenous nation in b\r\i\t\i\s\h c\o\l\u\m\b\i\a wanting to stop the "stealing" of their children   the matrilineal gitxsan nation   the gitxsan child and family services society (gcfss)   that serves the nation   want to bring their children and youth home   they estimate there are more than 130 gitxsan childrenincare   living outside the traditional territory of their nation   for the past few years gcfss hosted a summertime "welcome home" ceremony on their traditional lands   in 2018 over 300 people   including children youth and their caregivers came "home" for a visit   this was the impetus for gcfss executive director   cheryl williams   needed to implement a project called "bringing our children home"   in a move to de-colonize child welfare   gcfss is planning to build a "longhouse" in each of its six gitxsan communities each longhouse is based on the traditional building form of the nation and will house ten childrenincare   two youth agingoutofcare and three singleparentsandchildren

fleeing violence   this project is based on traditional ceremony   protocols and language of the gitxsan nation in the face of genocide

simgigat[1]   sigadum haanak̲' (pronounced sim/gig/gat   sig/a/dum   han/ak) [translated: honourable men and honourable women]   luugigyoothl waẏ (pronounced loo/gig/e/o/thl/why)   gisk'ahaast n̓iiẏ (pronounced gis/gas/knee)   wilp daax̲an n̓iiẏ (pronounced will/p/dack/an//knee)   nisgaa n̓iiẏ (pronounced nis/ga/knee)   git gingolx (pronounced git/gin/goal/th)   luu-am'aamhl gagoodim wilgaa'sim (pronounced lou/am/th/l/ga/god/dim/will/gaa/a/sim)

in my language i said my name is luugigyoo |calm waters| of the killerwhale house of daax̲an of the nisgaa village of gingolx [translated as kincolith |place of skulls| and that i am glad to be here [literally, means my heart is glad to be here]   meaning that i am glad to be present my name   luugigyoo   situates me close to my village

i want to acknowledge the traditional   ancestral unceded territory of the indigenous peoples upon where you happen to be reading this chapter just as i acknowledge the traditional unceded territory of the **ts'elxwéyeqw [pronounced chill quay ick]** nation where i have written this chapter

the elders of the nisgaa nation teach that introducing oneself is to start a relationship off in a good way and that is what i attempt to do each time i write   if you have read or heard this opening multiple times in different settings   then you will be familiar with the protocol

this is the traditional formal oral introduction to an audience that i privilege as the readers of this chapter in this way   i write as i speak and i am speaking to each of you

---

1. a note about my writing style   since i defended my dissertation   *indigenous architecture through indigenous knowledge:* (Stewart 2015)   i have added another layer of meaning to my use of the nisgaa language   where i use nisgaa   i provide plain english phonetic pronunciation to assist in reading the language   i use plain english because nisgaa is not represented by the international phonetic alphabet (ipa) symbols so i am using a phonetic system based on plain english (as a non linguist)

stolen generations

*growing up in foster care   feeling powerless   life out of control
coping day-to-day   not knowing family   not living within the nation
feeling scared   feeling abandoned   loss of nation   loss of
culture   loss of language   loss upon loss   and this is the
foundation for a life?*

what is this   if not genocide?

characterizing foster care experiences as genocide
is the only response that make sense in the face of
federal and provincial governments in this country still
legislating colonialism   i understand that colonialism
in this country called c\a\n\a\d\a[2] is not unique   that
indigenous peoples elsewhere on this planet also live
under genocide   native hawaiians of the a\m\e\
r\i\c\a\n state of hawaii have recently begun a public
campaign to bring attention to the genocide   and so
i acknowledge that   i am nisgaa by birth but c\a\n\a\
d\i\a\n by force[3]   this chapter is at once personal
because it reflects my life   and political   because
68% of the childrenincare in my home province of what is
now known as b\r\i\t\i\s\h c\o\l\u\m\b\i\a are indigenous
despite only representing less than 8% of all the children
in the province?

what is the matter with this picture?   judith
butler has coined a concept of the un-grieving life[4]
indigenous children in care are ungrieving   why are
indigenous children in care considered ungrievable?
indigenous children are commodities   pawns or human
resources to be traded   essentially 'bought and sold'
these colonial governments are traffickers of children
in light of the systemic genocide of indigenous peoples
worldwide   how can newborn babies be taken into
foster care in front of her/his parents?   these babies
are not allowed to know the caring touch of their mother
why?   because there is a policy that former foster
children pose a risk as parents and need to have their
children immediately apprehended and i would add that
former students of residential schools were similarly
branded as unfit because as a former student of a
residential school my mother lost me the moment i was
born   how is it that social workers are taught to be
judge and jury by professors who are being paid with

public money to racially profile parents?   as my
mother might say   this is not a scene out of george
orwell s   1984   first published in 1949   but a tragedy
that transpired in b\r\i\t\i\s\h c\o\l\u\m\b\i\a in 2019
this deficit-based profiling is 'race-based genocide'[5]
orwell s novel presents an imaginary dystopian society
that is dehumanizing and as unpleasant as possible
there is nothing imaginary about what is happening right
now in this country and there needs to be significant
changes to child welfare policies in 2019 in b\r\i\t\i\s\h
c\o\l\u\m\b\i\a   if anyone is being neglectful it is the
federal government in their mission to erase indigenous
peoples from the land   to carry out the genocide
childwelfare agencies are by extension guilty of neglect
that allows them to steal the children   as social work
professor and activist cindy blackstock wrote in her 2011
paper   wanted: *moral courage in canadian child welfare*
(Seucharan, Morgan, Hyslop and Sherlock, 2019)
whether yesterday or seventy years ago   the
foster care system in c\a\n\a\d\a continues to enslave
childrenincare   childrenincare are homeless
they live in places that are not their homes   not the
homes of their families   only those with lived
experience of the foster system know such feelings of
homelessness   insecurity/uncertainty   living with
the daily issues of abandonment   abuse   alienation
anxiety   depression and more   creates a maelstrom
that many children are unable to navigate   certainly
not the academics that are hired to research and narrowly
define homelessness
apprehension of indigenous children continues at
unprecedented rates   all the while this country narrowly
defines   as do governments   the stealing of children
in the past tense   as in the "sixties scoop"   not
acknowledging their role in the genocide

bringing the children home

federal and provincial governments in this country
have been offloading their fiduciary responsibilities as
devolution[6]   it is not a surprise to see the provincial
government legalize indigenous organizations with
delegated powers to act as local governments among
first nations across this country   in one effort by
indigenous nations to strengthen their roles   based on

---

2. i refer to colonizing countries (and their provinces/states)
such as the one in which i live   c\a\n\a\d\a   written with
the backward slash   considered grammatically wrong   as
analogous to the wrongfulness of these countries in their treatment
of indigenous peoples   and is a daily reminder to me of the
injustices in the country within which i live   reminding me i can
never stop fighting   advocating   resisting   protesting
3. after strong apparel (2019)   "hawaiian by birth   american by
force"   retrieved from https://strongapparelhawaii.com/
4. for a full discussion on the un-grieving life, see the many
writings of berkeley professor judith butler

5. https://aptnnews.ca/2019/06/27/birth-alerts-are-raced-based-
genocide-says-mikmaw-lawyer/
6. devolution is an attempt by the federal government to diffuse
discontent by bringing decision-making closer to the governed
while still retaining central authority   having the responsibility
for making decisions without the authority has been contentious
and will continue to be so

indigenous peoples voices and beliefs as a guide for their work   three documents have helped define the scope of work that needs to be done : (1) indigenous resilience, connectedness, and reunification-from root causes to root solutions: a 2016 report on indigenous child welfare in british columbia by grand chief ed john; (2) canadian human rights tribunal, specifically, jordan's principle (*canadian human rights tribunal 2*, 2016) and; (3) 2015 aboriginal policy and practice framework in british columbia by the ministry of children & families (gornicki, p.4)

the b\r\i\t\i\s\h c\o\l\u\m\b\i\a government constituted delegated indigenous agencies for child welfare around the province   currently there are twentyfour agencies with various delegated powers one such indigenous agency with delegated authority is the gitxsan child & family services society (gcfss) their mandate is to work on-reserve with member communities of the gitxsan nation   they currently provide child welfare services to five of the six gitxsan communities including   gitanyow   gitsegukla   glen vowel   kispiox and kitwanga

the vision of gcfss is to embrace and strengthen the gitxsan *ayookw* |gitxsan laws| it is through the ayookw that the nation will ensure the health   safety and well-being of the *majagalee* |children| and *wil naa tahl* |families| their mission is to provide culturally-sensitive support   prevention and protection services to gitxsan children and their families by attaining the necessary level of knowledge   capacity and delegation to ensure success

in march 2019 gcfss updated their strategic plan based upon the above vision and mission including goals for children and families   staff and administration community and culture

governance (board   chief & council) and jurisdiction and politics plus the following principles which provides the context for their operational plan

1. gitxsan children are precious and deserve to be protected; they are the future of the gitxsan nation
2. the gitxsan *ayookw* carries timeless values and wisdom, which will guide service delivery and program development
3. the gitxsan family provides natural protection for children
4. we will respect ourselves, each other and all that walk through our doors
5. we will work cooperatively and collaboratively as a team
6. we will be accountable for our actions
7. we will work in an environment that benefits from the positive energy created by humor
8. we will operate with a high level of commitment
9. we will embrace equality recognizing that together we are stronger

as an "indigenous apprehension-prevention consultant"   because federal funding would not allow them to hire me as an architect   i facilitated community input into the project scope and definition   this important first step in the design process occurred with every chief and council of the nation   chief and council invited who they felt necessary from their community to provide input   typically it was the community council members   community social workers   the local gcfss board member   youth workers elders and community members

these first meetings within the five communities introduced the project team and the project itself   it was at these meetings that communities first learned that the provincial housing crown corporation (b\c housing) had capital dollars available for housing and for the first time in the history of b\c housing   the projects could be on and off reserve   not that b\c housing had not funded projects on reserve in the past   as an example i had designed the sto:lo elders lodge in 2005 located on federal property (see figure 1) funded by b\c housing their first on-reserve housing project   (fig. 1)

it was at these first meetings that gcfss explained that over 130 gitxsan childrenincare that they know of   (which is an issue in itself given the history of governments stealing children   they do not readily acknowledge to the nation when they have scooped one of their children) lived outside the traditional territory of the nation and their vision and mission was for these children to return home   for that to happen all six communities agreed to equally participate to host a longhouse   with six longhouses containing ten childrenincare each totalling sixty plus another twelve youth agingoutofcare   gcfss has put an operational plan in place that accounts for the childrenincare and youthagingoutofcare   plus they will offer to house children and youth from other nations   based on need this is within the context that 700 youth ageoutofcare in this province every year   though there is now support for former foster youth of any age who want to pursue postsecondary education   once a youth agesoutofcare they are on their own   this has resulted in a high correlation between youth agingoutofcare and homelessness   almost 50% of the 681 homeless youth counted in 2018 were former foster kids   in the largest urban area in this province over 40% of people experiencing homelessness are indigenous as of the 2018 homeless count in metro vancouver   despite making up only 4% of the population

as a nation-fighting colonization   it is important that housing for childrenandyouth consider the needs of the community   part of this needs analysis can be through a "critical inequity lens" (Gornicki, 2018) that considers cultural   social   environmental and economic determinants

in more than one community meeting over the last year the question was asked   why are the trends so negative for indigenous children and families?   the best answer is   colonialism   federal and provincial governments continue to enact laws and policies

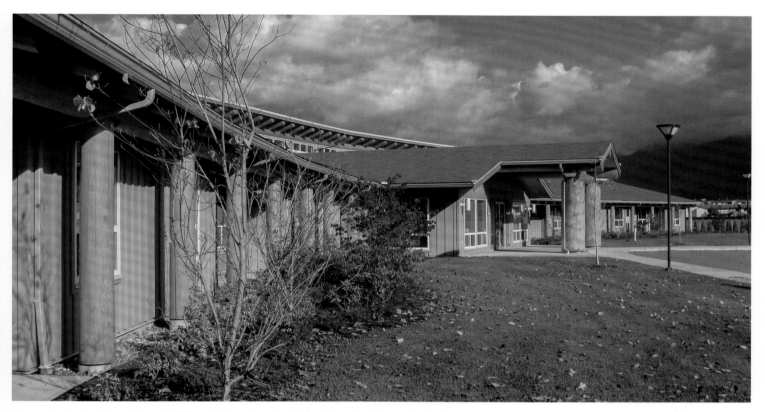

figure 1. sto:lo elders lodge (2005) patrick r stewart architect (used with permission)

that breakdown families   culture and language
moving into the future   first nations communities
organizations and individuals need to focus on strength-
based approaches based upon indigenous knowledges
        working within the structure of colonial policies
first nations are not free to do as they wish   for
gitxsan child & family services looking to provide housing
for childrenincare onreserve   the governing legislation
in c\a\n\a\d\a is the indian act   since its enactment
in 1876 there have been some seventeen amendments
though it retains most of its original provisions   in
order for gcfss to move forward in its desire to build
and operate housing for childrenincare in each reserve
community   they first need to secure tenure in each
community   this necessitates a land lease   you read
that right   the federal government requires first nations
to lease back their own land because the land is held in
right of the queen
        in order to legally use the land for their own
purpose   first nations must follow the process that
indigenous services c\a\n\a\d\a (i\s\c) must oversee in
order to ensure outcomes benefit the federal government
i know that i\s\c thinks it is working to protect first nations
but they say the land is not ours   at least not within
their western colonial minds   nevermind there has never
been a treaty signed with the gitxsan nation   anyway
there is an onerous process that must be followed in

order for housing to be built and operated by gcfss
        it has been almost two years since gcfss was
allocated a $5M dollar capital grant to design and
build the first longhouse in a gitxsan community   to
date a phase 1 environmental assessment has been
completed   a land appraisal has been completed   a
civil assessment of water and wastewater treatment has
been completed   certifying that the designated lands
are appropriate for the proposed longhouse construction
at the time of this writing the schedule is for the first
longhouse to open september 2021 but the land lease is
not yet in place which necessitates a referendum vote by
all community members living both on and off reserve
        before the vote can take place   i\s\c sends out an
information package and designation document to all
members   once this happens 49 days must lapse
before the referendum vote can take place   as of
this writing   the global pandemic of COVID-19 has
shut most federal government department work down
including this referendum   once the pandemic threat
has ended and work resumes   the 49-day count will
begin   within this 49-day window an information
meeting is held with community members between 12
days after the information package has been mailed out
and no later than the day before the referendum vote day
at least 42 days before the vote day the community
posts the notice of referendum and voters list and i\s\c

completes the mailout to all community members   the mailout contains the information documents   designation document   notice of referendum   ballot   instructions to voters   voter declaration form   ballot envelope and restore envelope   the referendum vote needs 50% plus one to pass   once the vote takes place   i\s\c will notify chief and council whether or not the vote supports the land lease for the longhouse project   if the vote is in support   then design can begin in earnest

design with indigenous knowledge

the design of the longhouse is based upon the traditional form of the gitxsan nation though containing the modern building programme to house childrenincare traditionally a longhouse was multigenerational and multifamily (in the modern sense) though all of one wilp or house within the clan system of the nation   being matrilineal everyone followed their mother and it was that family/wilp that lived together   this is not being proposed for this project as the culture has been so fractured by colonization and many of the childrenincare do not know of which family/wilp they belong   this is one of the cultural elements   along with language and ceremony that this project will incorporate into its programming

based upon a modern day interpretation of the use of traditional form   there will be six bedrooms each two sharing one threepiece washroom   there will be common amenity spaces such as a communal dining room   commercial kitchen   living/lounge/ cultural amenity area   offices for staff   meeting rooms tutorial room   family room   first aid/medical room assisted bathing room and a common bathing room plus services spaces   this building program has been written in conjunction with gcfss staff and board with input by community members at community forums held in each community the first week of june 2019   see proposed floor plan layout in figure 2

attached to the longhouse will six studio type units for youthagingoutofcare plus three threebedroom family units for singleparentsandchildrenfleeingviolence the youthagingoutofcare will continue to receive supports from staff as they adjust to living on their own   the singleparentsandchildrenfleeingviolence will also receive supports from staff and community   the basic form of the longhouse is depicted in figure 3

as the team begins design development on the first longhouse   an operational plan is being drafted that will account for the staffing and staff training needs for the longhouse which will operate twentyfour hours a day threehundredandsixtyfive days a year   in tandem with operational planning   licensing needs to be in place on opening day   in this province licensing is under the purview of the community care and assisted living act (2018)   this act takes effect when more than three nonrelated children under the age of thirteen reside

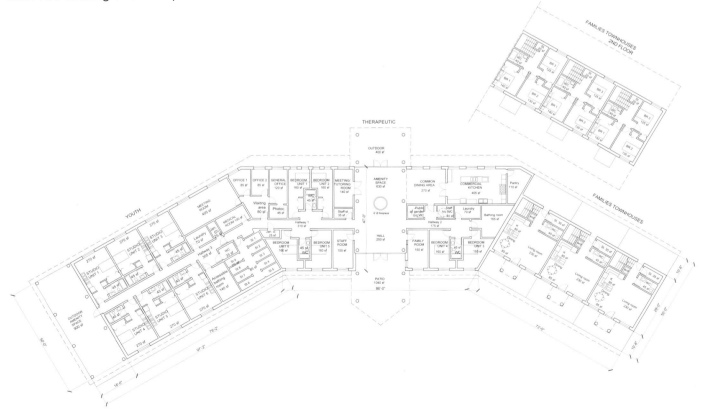

figure 2. gcfss longhouse floorplan (2020) patrick r stewart architect (used with permission)

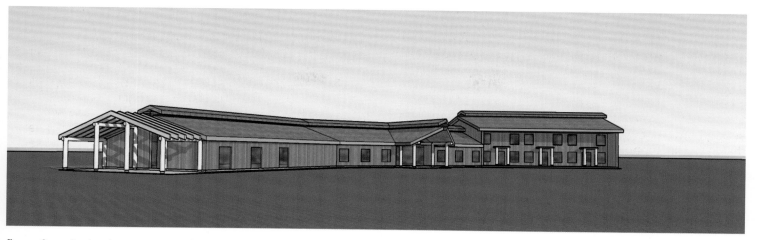

figure 3. gcfss longhouse concept (2020) patrick r stewart architect (used with permission)

together which will be the case in these longhouses licensing can take up to a year to complete so gcfss has begun the process of obtaining a provincial license to operate

key milestones

with all efforts being currently put into the design and construction of the first longhouse to be operational by september 2021   planning has begun on the other four longhouses   it is anticipated that the other longhouse will be operational on the following timeline

- second longhouse constructed by 2022
- third longhouse constructed by 2023
- fourth longhouse constructed by 2023
- fifth longhouse constructed by 2024

at the time of this writing the location and sequence of the other five longhouses has yet to be determined there has also been some discussion as to whether the longhouses may provide specialized housing/supports for example one longhouse may provide services to childrenincare under the age of thirteen   while another may provide services to teenagers   while yet another may provide services to youth struggling from severe trauma   all this is in discussion and as of yet no resolution has been made

next steps

in each of the five other communities   sites have yet to be selected by the community and due diligence needs to be completed including a phase 1 environmental assessment   land appraisal   geotechnical assessment civil assessment for water availability   pressure and quality   plus a civil assessment of wastewater treatment staff availability and training need to be

assessed in the five other communities over the same timeframe as the proposed longhouse occupancies

conclusion

being involved in this project has not been easy we are all dealing with significant issues that affect each of us in different ways   as parents we see the need of childrenincare who live without family and that is heartwrenching   as former childrenincare we see the positives that this project can bring to young lives   it would have made a world of difference in my life

as former youthintransition we see the precariousness which face the youth as they leave care   with all my wordly belongings in my little $300 car i left the relative stability of a rented room after i left foster care and found myself scared and alone when my plans to attend post-secondary did not immediately come about   all i could think about was   what now? i was not given the benefit of an exit interview so i had no idea which nation i was from   who and where my family was   (i later found out that everyone aging out of care is supposed to receive an exit interview)

the plan is for the longhouses to provide a safe healthy environment for childrenincare   youthagingoutofcare and singleparentsandchildrenfleeingviolence and the supports necessary for better outcomes in their lives   this is the community's vision for this project

references

Blackstock, Cindy (2011) wanted: "Moral Courage in Canadian child welfare." *First Peoples Child & Family Review*, Volume 6, Number 2, pp. 35-46.

Brendtro, L., Brokenleg, M., & Van Bockern, S. (2012). *Reclaiming youth at risk: Our hope for the future.* Place of publication not identified: Solution Tree.

BC Aboriginal Child Care Society. (2010). *Bringing Tradition Home: Aboriginal Parenting in Today's World Facilitator's Guide* (1st ed.). West Vancouver: BC Aboriginal Child Care Society.

Child, Family, and Community Service Act 1996 (BC) s. 13 (CA.). Retrieved from http://www.bclaws.ca/civix/document/id/complete/statreg/96046_01.

Gitxsan Child & Family Services Society (2019). *Operational Plan 2019-2023.* Hazelton: GCFSS Report.

Gornicki, Paulina (2018). child welfare practice comparison: early intervention and prevention for aboriginal children and families: a report for the ministry of children and family development.

John, Ed (2016). Chief Ed John. Indigenous Resilience, Connectedness and Reunification – From Root Causes to Root Solutions: A Report on Indigenous Child Welfare in British Columbia. Final Report of the Special Advisor on Indigenous Children in Care. Retrieved from http://fns.bc.ca/wp-content/uploads/2017/01/Final-Report-of-Grand-Chief-Ed-John-re-Indig-Child-Welfare-in-BC-November-2016.pdf

Macvean, M., Shlonsky, A., Mildon, R., & Devine, B. (2017). "Parenting interventions for indigenous child psychosocial functioning: A scoping review." *Research on Social Work Practice, 27*(3), 307-334. doi:10.1177/1049731514565668

Ministry of Children and Family Development. (2015). *Aboriginal Policy and Practice Framework in British Columbia* (Publication). British Columbia: The Government of British Columbia. Retrieved from https://www2.gov.bc.ca/assets/gov/family-and-social supports/child-care/aboriginal/abframework.pdf.

Ministry of Children & Family Development, Government of British Columbia. (2017, March 1). *Multi-Year Action Plan 2017-2020.* Retrieved from http://www.frpbc.ca/media/uploads/files/MCFD_MYAP_Final_Mar_1_1.pdf.

Ministry of Children and Family Development. (2018). *2018/19 – 2020/21 Service Plan*. Victoria: British Columbia, Ministry of Children and Family Development.

Seucharan, Cherise, Brielle Morgan, Katie Hyslop and Tracy Sherlock (2019). B.C.'s focus on foster care neglects need to support struggling families, experts say in *Vancouver Star,* June 13, 2019.

Stewart, Patrick Robert Reid (2015). *Indigenous Architecture through Indigenous Knowledge: dimsagalts'apkw nisim (together we will build a village).* (Doctoral dissertation).

Chapter 1.3: Island Child and Heroic Work for Homeless Families

Diane Menzies – Rongowhakaata, Aitanga-a-Mahaaki

Dr Diane Menzies, ONZM, Rongowhakaata, Aitanga-a-Mahaaki, is a consultant and researcher on cultural landscape and Indigenous issues for Landcult Ltd. She has worked for district, city, regional and central governments, and universities, and is now in private practice. She was Director of Communications for Ministry for the Environment, an elected local government representative, and Commissioner of the New Zealand Environment Court for eleven years, contributing to judgements throughout Aotearoa NZ, and conducting some 300 mediations. Her PhD. is in Resource Management, and she also has academic qualifications in horticulture, landscape architecture, business and mediation. Diane is a member of Ngā Aho and Kahui Whetu, a past President of the International Federation of Landscape Architects, and a member of ICOMOS Cultural Landscape Committee and ICOMOS New Zealand. She received the New Zealand Order of Merit for services to the environment. Her interests are in Indigenous values and social justice. She lives in Auckland and has four grandchildren.

This story is about Island Child, a charitable trust for emergency housing led by Danielle Bergin, who for 15 years has helped homeless young Māori women and their children find more secure homes. Young Māori women with babies are particularly vulnerable to housing pressure. Unaffordable housing rents and costs (Darroch, 2012) as well as intersecting post-colonial issues such as poverty, continually reinforcing traumatic stress (Reid, 2017.), limited employment, domestic violence, fractured homes and education, substance abuse, and fragmented communities (Walker, 2019.) have all exacerbated instability. Māori families in New Zealand are usually the most affected by this current housing nightmare.

This chapter considers how *whānau* have come to be homeless through the stories of four women. Each new family moving into Island Child is given breathing space and guidance through bureaucratic application making to achieve social housing. This is the first step towards greater security of tenure. While staying with the trust, the women and children live in a nurturing, healing place which helps to turn their lives around. Island Child has recently opened new accommodation and those who have found purpose and passion in their lives after

receiving help from Island Child were there to tell their stories.

The new accommodation is a house with small cottages for sleeping in the rear yard, privacy for a family, together with communal cooking and living so that the families are not isolated. This simple expansion step has retained its small grassroots family culture. From here, women can start to reclaim their lives, and also help others in the community. The chapter also addresses systemic housing issues, and considers options for a better future.

Island Child is based in Glen Innes, Auckland. Tamaki Regeneration Company, which is part owned by the Auckland Council and Government, is undertaking major redevelopment of Glen Innes and is also providing some support for Island Child.

The aim of placemaking is to develop better community connections. Glen Innes and community connections have been the focus of the placemaking research project. The Whai Rawa research project has examined the impact of colonisation and continuing economic structures, such as those relating to land and access to finance, which reinforce and exacerbate the Māori housing crisis. This chapter was supported by Building Better Homes, Towns & Cities National Science Challenge research projects, placemaking, and Whai Rawa.

Island Child and Heroic Work for Homeless Families

1. Introduction

People in colonised countries may be familiar with the housing issues that Indigenous peoples face. Many live in impoverished cities, overcrowded and poor quality housing (Groot et al., 2011; Lysnar et al., 2016), affected by past cultural trauma (Reid et al., 2017.), family fragmentation, and low incomes. Māori homelessness is endemic to experiences of colonialism (Groot and Peters 2016, p.323) with Māori having been rendered out of place in their own homelands. Homelessness, notes Groot and Peters, has been a feature of urban life in New

Figure 1. Homes in Glen Innes demolished to make way for more intensive development.

Zealand for over a century. Availability of what is termed *affordable housing* – lower-cost owned housing, or affordable rentals through social or public housing – has decreased in Aotearoa, New Zealand. While there is much evidence to indicate that home ownership has positive socio-economic outcomes (Waldegrave and Urbanova, 2016), Māori currently have only 28% home ownership (NZ Stats 2016).

A survey conducted under the Native Housing Act 1935 found that Māori were living in the worst conditions of any group in the country. As a result, the Labour Government passed the Native Housing Act 1935 which enabled Māori to take up loans on more generous terms than other State Advances loans. However, although eligible for state-assisted loans, many Māori were not in the skilled and semi-skilled brackets, and few were living in urban situations. As Ferguson surmised: poverty and prejudice effectively barred many Māori, both urban and rural, from the mainstream housing market (Mills et al., 2015).

The government intervention in 1935 did help some Māori families, but by 1945, with many returned servicemen starting families, the waiting list for state housing had expanded to 30,000. In 1948, state housing access for Māori people was put on the same basis as for non-Māori – removing previous policy discrimination (Schrader, 2005). The story of social (state) housing is one of continually changing policies with Māori, generally being most disadvantageous. In 1950, tenants were invited to buy their houses but many Māori were unable to raise the deposit. The sell down policy stopped in 1975, but started again in 1980 with the required deposit lowered,

and more state houses were sold. As a consequence of the "mother of all budgets" as described by the then government, which adopted a user pays/full market rental policy and unemployment support in 1991 (Reid et al., 2019), many Māori have faced inter-generational poverty and Māori homelessness has increased. This continued so that in 1997 a 20% rent rise saw half of tenants' wages required for rent, with a response of overcrowding and increased health costs for the 51% Māori in this situation (Schrader 2005, p.77).

Research indicates that the socio-economic status of many Māori is now similar (or worse) to that identified in 1935 (Walker et al., 2019).

Figure 2. New houses which have yet to reflect the spirit of the community.

Eaqub (2017) contended that central government had maintained an effective interventionist policy, building houses to provide for affordable state rental housing and providing ownership assistance programmes since the 1930s. This assistance ended in New Zealand in the 1980s. Had government home construction continued at the previous rate, he argues that there would not have been a housing shortage. However, government policy changes to sell down the government stock of public rental housing led to adopting a market incentivised ideology. This assumed that supply and demand would enable appropriate rental accommodation availablity and pricing (Eaqub, 2017), and encourage private rental housing and self-sufficiency. As land and housing have increased in price, well beyond affordability for those on low incomes (because housing supply was not being encouraged), the supply of social housing has decreased.

Some poorly maintained government rental houses in Glen Innes have been demolished, areas redeveloped for private housing, and other houses have been sold. There is a documented shortage of housing stock in Auckland, as well as construction workers to build them (Coleman and Karagedikli, 2018). Some of those without accommodation have been put into motels as temporary measures by government social workers. Other families have lived in their cars or couch "surfed."

This narrative is not about home ownership, but about those whānau, young solo Māori women with children, who have struggled to find any home, and have been homeless or in temporary, often crowded homes for a number of years. It is a story about those who have obtained respite and help through an emergency housing provider in Glen Innes, Island Child (ICCT), while seeking a longer-term solution.

Danielle, is the leader of Island Child (ICCT), a grassroots trust which has supplied healing and respite for 15 years. From the young women's stories, systemic local and national issues of housing are considered to better understand how affordable housing for Māori families in New Zealand can be achieved. The whānau who told their stories had survived painful and traumatic experiences, and perhaps recounting their stories helped to purge some of that trauma. Their aim though was to explain the difference Danielle had made to their lives, and in doing so had helped the whānau to make changes for the better. They told these stories to highlight the need for more effective financial support for Island Child, and for other homeless families.

The story is based on a literature review and interviews with the mothers, Danielle, and other community members who have participated in government funded research programmes. In addition Tamaki Regeneration Company have shared the findings of their regular community surveys and have held meetings to discuss their focus group findings with researchers. MadAve, a community grass roots organisation, has also shared the work they are doing with youth, schools, and in their

Figure 3. Danielle Bergin of Island Child Charitable Trust, Glen Innes, Auckland.

neighbourhoods by inviting researchers to community meetings. The Building Better Homes, Towns & Cities National Science Challenge research project investigating this issue is called *Whai Rawa*. The aim of Whai Rawa is to examine the economic, administrative, policy, legal, land ownership, and governmental structures of housing that have created and reinforce the Māori housing crisis. A placemaking research project, initiated earlier by the National Science Challenge, enabled contacts with the community of Glen Innes Auckland to be developed and links to be made between the two investigations.

2. Whānau stories

Some of the mothers who were staying or who had been with Island Child after being homeless generously gave their time to recount their stories. Some were keen to be identified as a memory for their grandchildren while others preferred not to be identified. They all were still affected by the traumatic experience of homelessness.

2.1 Hezy's story

Hezy arrived at Island Child late in the year with her five-

Figure 4. New emergency housing for whanau at Island Child Glen Innes.

year-old son. She had been moving from place to place, living in her car, with no home of her own for almost four years – she estimated she had moved some nine times. She travelled between families after her first pregnancy, putting ideas of training for a career on hold. At the start of the second year, she found a a small private rental flat in Auckland with two bedrooms for herself and her (then) two-year-old son for $375 per week. She had no clothes line or dryer in the flat, or a car, needing to take taxis to the laundromat and supermarket. Realising that she couldn't keep up with weekly payments, she left the rental apartment to avoid further debt.

Hezy found staying with families expensive as well. It was uncomfortable in crowded conditions, and staying with families who had different ways. Hezy spoke of two-bedroom houses with sometimes six children, and multiple adults. While mobile, she also found early childhood learning difficult to maintain and was devastated that her son could not enroll for Māori language emersion learning. While she was moving from home to home, he had not spent enough time learning Te Reo Māori. Recognising that instability was a barrier to learning, she was planning to wait until her son was six and in a more secure home, before putting him into schooling.

While a house with affordable rental was her aim, Hezy was advised that she would not qualify for a social housing waiting list because she was not able to provide evidence that she had been doing enough house searching for private rental properties. The government social services policy required that she search newspaper notices, websites, agencies, and visit possible properties, with her two sons, by bus and train. She found being rejected by agents at every visit depressing. Hezy said:

> The only thing everyone ever wants is just a home, a home for their kids so that their children can start on their future. I was pretty much living in a lot of pain, a lot of struggle. Mostly just trying to ignore how depressing the situation was that I was living in, but also thankful that I had a room to live in. At the same time I was struggling financially. You know who wants to show they are struggling? It brings embarrassment. I felt scared, I didn't know what to do, I just know I needed a home.

The loss of spiritual home lands and physical connections to whānau can also be regarded as an aspect of homelessness. This loss includes, "a profound sense of whakamā (shame and humiliation)," as expressed by Hezy (Groot and Peters, p. 326-327).

Hezy was exhausted after searching for homes during two pregnancies. Eventually after viewing twelve houses through an agent she learnt that she was rejected by private rental agencies because she had "bad credit." With that evidence, and the confidence to ring the government social services department, she was able to qualify for the state housing list. Hezy wondered whether the understanding social worker who listened to her difficulties and called Island Child on her behalf, had done so because that social worker was herself Māori, as this was the first sympathetic assistance she had received from a social services government staffer.

Danielle offered Hezy help when she had nothing except blankets and clothes in her car. Island Child also offered Hezy rest and healing. Danielle is working hard to find a suitable state rental house, while helping Hezy with courses and advice. Island Child provides food and all the materials that women with young children need. Hezy commented:

> I'm just glad that I am here at Island Child because I can finally look up. I don't have to struggle as much as I did.

Hezy now has a state rental home to embark on a more secure future for her children.

2.2 Josephine's story

Josephine has two children, and has also faced major financial issues. She had been homeless since her mother, with whom she was staying while working, died. Her mother had provided childminding for her older son, but when she died Josephine was evicted from the social rental and found that the utilities which had all been in Josephine's name had large debts. She was assigned a budget adviser but was unable to work for two years because a "no-asset" bankruptcy procedure had been put in place in response to her debts, and thus had very limited financial means. Even so, social service staff who had the authority to provide social housing insisted that she look for private rental accommodation.

Josephine had given birth to her prematurely born second son and moved from the hospital to a motel for seven nights. Motels were at that time a government solution for emergency housing for vulnerable homeless families, and the motel she had been placed in was funded by government at $780 per week. Josephine struggled being alone with two children in a motel where she knew no one. She tried a women's refuge, but found that was extremely isolating too, tried a boarding house and then moved in with family members in order to live near Tamaki Primary where her son was enrolled. The local tenancy manager threatened eviction of the family to address overcrowding, when she discovered Josephine and her children there, so Josephine was homeless again. Aware that agents for private rental properties were reluctant to let to a single mother with two children, the

Figure 5. Josephine at home in Glen Innes.

government social services staff were still determined that Josephine prove she was unable to find a private rental. This policy direction and dogged inflexibility was pursued even though Josephine was subject to a "no asset bankruptcy procedure."

Josephine was very depressed, still grieving over the loss of her mother and alone with no support, when she finally met Danielle. This occurred after two years constantly moving with her children, trying many housing ideas without success, and neglecting her health. The longer she stayed at Island Child, the more secure Josephine began to feel. Through coaching, taking part in training courses, and encouragement, Danielle helped Josephine improve her health and increase her self-esteem and confidence. An example Josephine gave was of a trip with Danielle to the dentist to replace a front tooth, missing as a result of previous family violence. This enabled Josephine to smile radiantly again.

All of Danielle's family acted as role models for family life and caring – as Josephine explained – for her and other solo mothers and children at Island Child. Danielle encouraged community connections for Josephine through neighbourhood involvement in a food and resourcing scheme called *Pātaka Kai*. Through this,

Figure 6. Natalie's Pataka Kai at Glen Innes.

Josephine made new friends and developed roots in the Glen Innes community. Danielle also introduced her to other support systems, such as the Sisters of Mercy.

Josephine said that she never thought she would have her own home, and she recounted that her son stated how lucky he felt. They were so much better in the house Danielle had helped to find for them. She also said that other mothers at the kindergarten, which her son was now able to attend, knew Danielle and all spoke highly of her.

There are many small steps that Jospehine hoped to achieve, such as getting her driving licence in order to take a greater part in the community, continuing to learn Māori language, and to take up the work she enjoys when her "no asset procedures" period expires. Josephine was inspired by Danielle and has been able to move from "a really dark place" to enjoying having her own home, having breakfast, lunch and dinner daily, and enjoying her boys.

2.3 Natalie's story

Natalie is a solo mother of three boys including one starting at college. She had moved from a smaller town to Auckland to board with her sister because her sons were struggling in the middle-class, largely Pākehā community where she had been living. While she had previously had family in the smaller town they had gradually moved and she found conditions expensive. Although she was boarding and had tried to get on the housing list for a state rental, she was told that since she was not homeless she was not eligible, and since she did not have bad credit she would need to find private rental accomodation. Her sister introduced her to Danielle. Natalie moved there with two of her boys the following week (the third remaining with her sister), and was on the housing list by the next week. Danielle helped Natalie into a home after six weeks.

During her time with Danielle, Natalie gained confidence, and was helped to be a better mother. She loved being with Danielle and she said with a laugh, "If I didn't have to, I wouldn't have moved out." Now she is happy to have her own home and found her boys had settled down. She spoke of Danielle:

> She's just so positive every day, you know? Just her positive words were just really, really nice to hear daily. She made me motivate myself, to get my kids to school and go to these courses and it really helped. It really helped.

Before she moved to Island Child, Natalie had followed instructions from social workers to look for private rental properties, noting that the rental charge per week was USD 680-700 in Glen Innes for a two-bedroom house. She could afford that cost as well as utilities and food. She said that she had looked at so many private rental places, but that agents wanted professional people. "They'd see me turn up with my kids and go, 'Oh nah.' Straight away, pretty much."

As Whittaker has pointed out (Austin-Smith and Martin, 2017) property management companies and landlords are supported by tenancy laws which enable a power imbalance. In such a situation with high demand, discrimination is a consequence for those on limited incomes, and for Māori whānau.

Natalie is now paying USD 111.00 for a social rental home which is affordable. Food parcels are often dropped at her home, through Danielle and others. She is now living close to family members, is starting courses again and doing community volunteer work. Natalie spoke of the Pātaka Kai project which community members supported as a local resource, on a, "Take what you need, and leave what you can," basis. She has a Pātaka Kai in front her her home which she provided and now monitors.

She has been advised by Tamaki Regeneration Company that in one to three years they would be redeveloping her street. Natalie would be rehoused temporarily and then given a new home, to which she was looking forward. Of Danielle, she said, "She's a godsend; love her to bits."

Figure 7. Fleur at Ngati Whatua marae, Orakei.

2.4 Fleur's story

Fleur is a community leader in the Glen Innes area who supports Ruapotaka Marae and her church. Her pastor had also helped those who were homeless but would seek Danielle's help when the support needed became too much for the church. Fleur also has strong roots with Mana Whenua, Māori who have historic and territorial rights over the land. Fleur spoke at the opening of Island Child's new chalets and accommodation from the perspective of a whānau member who had been helped by the Trust. She spoke with confidence and passion, explaining how Danielle had helped her overcome homelessness and challenges. Her presentation moved the large group of supporters, which included Members of Parliament and local government elected representatives. Recently she told me how she had arrived with Danielle.

Explaining how sudden life events can place unexpected demands on Māori families, Fleur told her story of taking responsibility for one of her grandchildren (mokopuna), when his mother was unwell. Three months before the baby arrived, family members had agreed that Fleur would care for the baby when born. On the understanding that this met the requirements of Oranga Tamariki, the Ministry for Vulnerable Children, Fleur left her home to move in with the baby's family. Unfortunately circumstances changed suddenly and as an interim caregiver for the baby, she needed emergency accommodation.

Fleur's circumstances were more complex than that of other whānau of Island Child, as Oranga Tamariki had an interest to separate Fleur from the baby. It seemed that the department had failed to undertake background checks, and having done so after Fleur had been the interim caregiver for several months, determined to intervene. Fleur tells of bullying tactics when social workers would arrive and she would be given tight time frames in which a requirement must be addressed, seemingly designed so that the caregiver would fail. Fleur was transgender and she had wondered whether that was antagonising the government staff, but saw no clear evidence for this. As an example, the social workers expressed concern over possible drug taking that diminished Fleur's ability to care for the baby. Fleur undertook drug tests which were clear, but she wondered whether this testing was standard procedure.

Danielle mediated between the aggressive role taken by the departmental social workers, and Fleur and the baby. After experiencing government staff treatment of young vulnerable mothers, Danielle now required that professional visitors apply for an appointment and provide reasons for their visit.

Fleur had bonded with the baby and as grandmother saw her responsibility to protect the baby within the whānau: to protect her whakapapa. She undertook all necessary training and achieved all the certificates for the courses which the governemnt staff deemed necessary, such as "duty of care," before the department sought evidence of her capability. The advice she needed on detailed safety provisions for the baby was provided by Danielle and Island Child so that Fleur could plan for the future needs of her mokopuna. Danielle also helped intervene working with paediatric and legal experts to challenge the government workers on the threatened uplift of the baby, and after six months assisted Fleur into a home near the heart of her whānau. Her new rental home then passed the safety checks undertaken by the department, such as covers over electrical fittings.

Fleur explained that Danielle was very strategic, working one-on-one with each family that goes to Island Child. The houses she helps find for whānau are within their financial means and are close to peer support groups and other relevant facilities. She explained the emergency housing at Island Child in this way:

> She accepted me into Island Child Charitable Trust, so I became one of her ladies, one of the ladies there. She never accepted any money from me until the benefit had been actually started. And then there was no rent arrears, so it was a hundred and five dollars a week, and that covered food, just everything. When you walk in it's not like walking into an empty house, you're walking in to a cabin with a double bed and everything in it. She removes all the stress from any parent or any mother that's going through that and with the added thing about accommodation or housing. So, she removes all of that stress. So, when you walk in you've actually got a bed there that's fully made with extra sheets and towels and duvets, and you've got food inside there plus kids toys.

Fleur had initially thought that Danielle had welcomed her because of the baby and Fleur's situation but:

> She does that for every person. Everyone that walks through that gate, she'll look after you, she'll take care of you. And she really, really takes care of you. It's good that Danielle is there. She goes over and beyond. Her duty is to help them. And sometimes the gap between stepping stones can be quite a distance, and she's just only too happy to put herself as a stepping stone in between those two stepping stones so you can stand on her to make it to the next stepping stone.

Fleur's mokopuna is now cared for by another grandmother, with Fleur's support. After protecting the bond with her young grandson during the emotional battering by the social workers, Fleur has maintained mental resilience. She is now a confident contributor to cultural events on behalf of her *iwi*, and a passionate supporter of the role of Island Child. In Fleur's words, "Dani brought me home."

3. It shouldn't be so hard.

Danielle Bergin has two children and lives with her partner and family in Glen Innes Auckland. Some 15 years ago, Danielle and her mother started a local opportunity shop selling goods to raise funds for sending medical aid to the Pacific Islands (Hancock, 2018). They realised that families who were homeless were sleeping outside their shop in their cars at night. Danielle invited them into her shop to sleep overnight and from there Island Child Charitable Trust developed by providing emergency housing and preparing families for a more secure home. Danielle tells of the struggle to gain funding to support the families after repeated rejections:

> We just saw a community need. And we just started delivering. We were volunteers for many, many years. We do what we do because it's about people; it's about our people, helping them, helping souls, helping the wairua.

When Danielle and her trustees first started to support those who were homeless, they struck a number of structural and institutional barriers. The first was their status as a trust and the ownership of their home. Although they were using their own resources to house and support those families who were homeless, this was not acceptable to government social services. All resources were expected to be held by the trust, and the range of trustees needed to be more diverse. Danielle and her mother put their home into the trust, expanded the trust and found that grant funding was then possible. Support in the early days, a community friend recounted, was hard to find. Private funders were judgemental and made negative assumptions. Her friend explained that Danielle could understand, communicate, and empathise with the whānau she helped and was motivated to give them support. Initially Danielle needed advice to frame up proposals, and her friend was happy to provide that service. It felt to her friend like a real privilege to help Danielle learn the right language to communicate with grant organisations. Very soon, Danielle understood what was needed, made a calendar to apply to trusts for grants, and formed good relationships. Gradually after gaining success with small grants Danielle's skills grew and with it, greater success with funders. Her friend recounts that Danielle brought strength and passion to the table as well as her entrepreneurial whakapapa.

Island Child Charitable Trust can now accommodate 12 families at a time, generally for up to three months as Danielle works to find housing for them. Danielle describes Island Child's role in this way:

> So, we work with the whānau and they end up into a warm, safe, sustainable home. It is wrap-around services. Comprehensive services where we also identify what is making the person homeless and in what way can we try to remedy or, at least, get them on the right track so that they're never homeless again.

Women may arrive with depression and challenging problems that coaching, counselling and training courses are able to address, while the mother is recovering. Danielle encourages the women to take courses which build their knowledge and self-esteem, while linking them with local friends in the community who might in turn support each other. The courses are run by a variety of agencies including the Sisters of Mercy, MadAve (a Glen Innes commuity support group), and budgeting organisations. The courses include parenting, self esteem, Māori spiritual knowledge, and te reo (Māori language) classes, are generally in short lengths, and transport is provided to the classes. Through this approach Danielle is helping to rebuild the Glen Innes community from a very fractured and changing situation housing those with desperately limited income and health issues, to those who are able to reconnect with wider family relationships, and their tribal roots. Although Danielle is not Māori, her partner is, and she appreciates the strength that Māori culture and spiritual knowledge can provide the young women whose mental health is fragile. This, in turn, is a decolonising process: a means to start addressing the long-term trauma in which the families have been immersed.

Systemic barriers to gaining housing and assistance for homeless families include a number of government policies. For example, Island Child initially tried to obtain funding from Te Puni Kōkiri, the government department for Māori support, as 95% of the families she was then helping were Māori. (Island Child are now getting increasing pleas for help from Pacific Island families as well.) However, after an initial positive and friendly response she was told that Island Child was not "Māori enough," although she was never told how Māori the trust needed to be to receive Te Puni Kōkiri support. She has repeatedly invited that Department to meet her and her mothers, and although Māori Government Ministers have visited her, she has not had Te Puni Kōkiri support. Te Puni Kōkiri may not have the budgeted resources to assist homeless, even though it is mainly Māori who are homeless. Danielle has obtained funding from the private sector through grants as well as other government social services departments.

Her local community board attempted to seek funding on her behalf by writing to the Minister of Social Development, but were rejected. Danielle said:

> We've got her letter of response saying that there is no funding for emergency housing and so therefore, she basically couldn't help.

This occurred while the same department was sending homeless people to motel accommodation as emergency housing. Danielle had disappointing and frustrating experiences with government social support and public housing staff. Their policies prevented open communication with support staff, limited help and support for the Māori families and required intensive form-filling and accounting procedures. If a family had been with Danielle for an extending time, beginning to lose hope of finding a house, and having no housing options to look at, Danielle was unable to check whether there had been a miscommunication on their file which had been the barrier. She had often found after considerable negotiation that notes on the mother's file misrepresented the mother's situation. For instance a note indicating gang affiliations, although incorrect, would limit the mother's house offers. Contracts between the social support agency and Island Child for funding to provide for the families' accommodation were an example. The contracts were inflexible, did not appear to provide for extended Māori families, and maintained tight governmental control. An emergency accommodation contract permitted Island Child to provide emergency housing only to families referred by the Department, whereas some families were brought to Danielle by an auntie or family member who had an overcrowded house themselves. In addition, age barriers created by a perceived policy risk could divide families. Younger homeless are managed by a separate government department, hence divisions, and fragmented policy management. Danielle said:

> We had a situation yesterday where Work and Income referred a young mother with a five-year-old and a two-month-old, siblings. And the young woman came with her 17-year-old sister. And it turned out the 17-year-old is homeless, and she's a month off being 18. Well, she's homeless, but she's not actually linked with the referral from Work and Income. And I said, 'Well, technically, I'm not actually supposed to help you.' And her eyes started to well up with tears. And I thought, 'Oh shit. I can't go down that path of just bouncing her back to the youth provider.'

Institutional racism also seemed to be a barrier to helping homeless families find affordable rental housing. Discrimination in the private rental sector was identified in pre-1948 Auckland, that is before Māori had access to state rentals, when Māori urban migrants were restricted to decrepit workers cottages in industrial zones (Schrader, 2005) (Brown, 2016) and into overcrowded conditions in these small houses. Brown (2016) also describes the violent treatment of Māori by institutions that include health impacts arising from extended families living in poor quality housing. She notes that Māori still face repression and discrimination. Institutional racism was identified as a barrier to obtaining mortgages in a large national study (Houkamau and Sibley, 2015) of self-identified Māori which indicated that the more Māori you look, the less "mortgage worthy" you are perceived to be by banks. However, institutional racism is an even greater concern if it is occurring in government departments and affecting young Māori solo parents who are among their most vulnerable clients. Gabriel's (2015) PhD study of First Nations homelessness in Toronto identified similar concerns. She found severe stereotyping and racial prejudice among service providers. Danielle's whānau and other providers have recounted similar and recurrent experiences. One homeless young Māori woman told the story of being instructed by non-Māori case workers to repeatedly hunt for private rental, only to be rejected each time. She was fortunate to contact a Māori case worker who better understood her desparate situation, had empathy, and suggested the mother contact Island Child. The homeless mother thought it was the case worker's Māori culture and cultural understanding that made the difference for the young mother who then was referred to Danielle and found sanctuary with her.

A further barrier is the inflexibilty of government departments when, for instance, often no staff are available over the Christmas holiday period when a young mother may lose her home.

When Government Departments change policies there is need for new learning, different eligibility requirements, and new relationships to build for emergency housing providers. A friend of Danielle's commented that as soon as one departmental requirement or barrier had been addressed by Danielle, it seemed that the goal posts were changed.

There appears to be only extremely small amounts of discretionary funding in relevant national and local government departments for support of grass roots trusts such as Island Child. The Government's change of housing policies to "market" rental charges and withdrawal of support for social housing construction, made affordable housing much harder to find in Auckland and particularly near family in Glen Innes. Island Child saw an increasing demand for houses but fewer houses were available, and families with young children were staying for longer terms at Island Child than Danielle had seen previously. This put stress on families who saw hope fading, as well as on ICCT who could not locate suitable houses for them. Danielle commented:

> We went from 35 homes a year, to six offers that year. Six houses that year. But we still had had 35 families and all their cousins and relatives, and everyone was saying 'Go to Dani, go to Dani.'

Another reason why housing is scarce in Glen Innes is the failure of successive governments to undertake maintenance of rental housing. The stock in Glen Innes is aging, and cold damp houses have become a health hazard. A local example discussed by whānau was of a government owned rental house where maintenence from a leaking tap had not been addressed and toxic mould had grown, which penetrated a young boy's bedroom. He had major lung tumours, and after heart valve replacements the eight-year-old was a permanent heart patient who could not run or play sports. This was linked by health professionals to the issue of toxic mould. Malva (2017) states that the effect of central and local government policies is the prevention of children's access to high quality housing and a safe physical environment. This is because poorer families have access only to poorly maintained, damp and crowded housing. In the 15 years since 2000, more than 1,180 children died (Oliver et al., 2017) (Anderson et al., 2012) from housing-related illness which he labels "social murder."

An opportunity for Island Child and the homeless whānau was expansion by purchase of a house then for sale, adjacent to Island Child, and development of cottages on the site. Danielle was confident that this would enable much needed additional emergency accommodation, even though Island Child would need to accept the financial risk. Her solution was met with resistance, and even derision from government staff, who doubted Island Child's ability to manage an increased mortgage or even obtain sufficient funding for the purchase deposit, though last minute mortgage assistance was provided. The staff seemed to accept the capabilities and approach of institutional providers such as Churches but not grass roots organisations managed through Māori values of manaaki ("generosity and welcome").

Perceived problems with Island Child have been raised by government staff on a re-occurring basis, all requiring additional policy development for Island Child, and suggesting that Island Child was incapable of providing for homeless families. These challenges by government staff include the requirement for a strategy, a succession plan and new learning. At each apparent obstacle Danielle has wrestled to find a solution, so that she can continue to help the families who contact Island Child.

Island Child searches out financial support from lottery grants, welfare trusts, and generous donations from individuals, as well as volunteer support from local people and those who have been helped by Island Child. More recently, after publicity, discussion directly with departmental heads, having gained a higher profile, the wider support of local and national government polititians, and a recognised track record, she has secured contracts and input from the Ministry of Social Development. Barriers and rules remain though, such as by preventing Island Child addressing errors in whānau housing application forms, through perceived risk to impartiality. The government staff blocked direct communication on the basis that Danielle might achieve unfair advantage for her Māori families by talking directly to staff and checking file notes. It may be that staff also provided the reason of unfair advantage to minimise communication with grass roots organisations. However, more recent monthly meetings with emergency housing providers and Housing New Zealand staff have helped to minimise some of those communication barriers. Danielle said:

> We're not allowed to discuss with Housing New Zealand who we may have, who's in desperate need of a home.

Tamaki Regeneration Company (TRC), jointly governed by Auckland Council and the central government, have been tasked with renewing the housing stock in Glen Innes and Panmure while intensifying development. There are now numerous blocks throughout the area where multiple houses have been removed and redevelopment is underway. TRC provides compassionate and carefully developed social assistance in order to address the social trauma within the community and anticipate the impacts of increased population density. This was observed in meetings with social support staff as well as through interviews. Regular surveys conducted by TRC indicated needs and more in-depth focus groups have indicated key issues for their tenents such as mental health issues and poverty. They have initiated a working group on education and are reviewing a range of other factors in order to provide for the community. TRC have an employment hub to encourage job creation for local people while the community undergoes change and TRC supports Island Child. Tamaki Regeneration Company have funded the revision of admission forms for Island Child required by social service providers, that Danielle fills in with an incoming family; and a booklet on the trust, which will assist funding applications. A staff member of TRC commented:

> Danielle Bergin, she's an amazing operator. It's quite hard for our emergency housing providers to know how to meet the requirements for government procurement processes, so we went in there and just supported them to be able to build their capability, strategic plans and everything else like that so that they could submit to be funded for supply of emergency housing.

TRC are undertaking a range of studies working with Otago University and other social researchers to develop co-designed responses to neighbourhood trauma and the impact of change. They found that 900 whānau or 16% of Tāmaki households are struggling financially on a daily basis. Despite investment in social services in Tāmaki, the system does not work for them. Whānau by Whānau is a social support service designed with the whānau in order to empower the most disadvantaged residents of Tāmaki to make a difference in their lives (TRC, 2019). Their findings echo comments made in interviews by the Island Child whānau.

In early November 2018, Island Child opened their new cottages and extension. The ceremony was well supported by whānau, the community and Government representatives as an indication of fresh hope for homeless families. However, Island Child now has a mortgage to pay as well as the ongoing job of supporting homeless families.

Government initiatives which would enable Island Child and other emergency housing providers to respond to changes in policy or legislation include the provision of adequate and flexible emergency funding for grass roots organisation so that they can manage more effectively. Danielle questions why there was not sound support funding for marae when they are sharing their resources for emergency accommodation. Resources to hire accountancy and administration staff would assist grass root providers as audits and detailed accounting are a consistent demand. There are now many families who have regained their life through Danielle's wisdom, tenacity, staunch family support and compassion, after transitioning from a very bleak period in their lives, but Island Child continues to seek and need support funding.

4. Recurring aspects of homelessness

In 2016, Groot and Peters reported that Māori homelessness emerged from economic and social deprivation, substance abuse, mental illness, and long-term poverty. The whānau who had been with Island Child and were willing to share their story had financial challenges. This was reflected as bad debt recorded by financial monitoring agencies, as well as in one case being part of a bankruptcy "no asset procedure" regime. Similar information was given to Tamaki Regeneration Company through their own research with some 30 whānau. Precarious finances is also reflected in model predictions of home ownership status (Walker et al., 2019) with those with the lowest incomes much less likely to own homes. This report on tenure variables for Māori housing identifies net household income, and welfare dependence between the ages of 21-35 as advantageous/disadvantageous characteristics for home ownership. The most advantaged quintile was 85% likelier to own homes than those most disadvantaged who had 10% likelihood of home ownership (Walker et al., 2019).

Yet the response from government social services is to insist that the mothers provide evidence that they had sought private rental housing before being considered for a state rental property, even though some of the whānau had a record of bad debt. If there was no record of bad debt, that was given as a reason for insistence that a private rental property must be sought. The private rental market in Auckland is beyond the financial ability of those whānau who are welfare-dependent, and others on lower incomes. While government staff have a difficult task when there are few houses, from the stories of whānau, staff seem unwilling to accept that pushing welfare-dependent families into unaffordable private rental will exacerbate their plight of debt.

Many of the whānau supported by Island Child were from families who had similiar financial problems. Effective financial and other support could not be provided long term by extended families, even though there was love and a desire to help. The extended families were often scattered, having limited experience of home ownership and suffered trauma from instability. This also led to high mobility rates among the homeless whānau (also described by Peters and Kern in "Peters and Christensen" about First Nations homeless families). Although homeless whānau helped to pay bills when they are part of the family, be it in New Zealand or staying with First Nations families, tension and lack of privacy jeopardised housing stabilty. Overcrowded housing placed stress on all of the families. Groot and Peters found that Māori cultural values in supporting accommodation for kin often result in overcrowding. While punative action threatened by tenancy managers to address overcrowding and couch "surfing" by family members relieved the stress for resident famiies, it prolonged the trauma for the homeless whānau.

The whānau were sole parents who may have experienced abusive partners and were struggling to provide for their children, as they moved to what they hoped might be more secure, safer places. The need for consistent schooling for their children limited their search for accomodation to places near the schools. The wish to be as close as possible to whānau for support was also important to them. Stable long-term family relationships of more than three years was identified as another predictor of home ownerhip in the tenure study (Whitehead et al., 2019). By contrast, many of the whānau, who had been helped by Island Child had very unstable families and lived in diverse parts of the country, with transitory partners and their own relationships were unstable. The sole parent families were disadvantaged by their relationships.

Depression, low self-confidence, and self-esteem hampered the young mothers from taking effective action for themselves and their children. In early 2009, Johnson found while studying mental health that homelessness affects Māori disproportionately and that health care including mental health needs to be considered with respect to Māori homelessness (Groot et al., 2011). Johnson also found higher rates of physical and mental ill-health among homeless. The young mothers' health deteriorated as they saw their opportunities diminish and their isolation increase. The tenure study (Walker et al., 2019) has identified that over half the Māori cohort of renters had major depression as a health factor in the Christchurch Health and Development Study (CHDS), a longitudinal study of a birth cohort of over 1,200 born over a four month period in 1977. Home owners also exhibited major depression – 42.9% of the cohort. Information from literature reflects the struggle the whānau endured on all measures of well-being undertaken by the New Zealand General Social Survey, Māori have more negative responses for housing measures. Depression and anxiety may be part of long term colonial-induced trauma (Reid, 2017), but are health factors which need to be addressed.

5. The ugly face of Aotearoa/New Zealand

The government policy decisions made in 1991 adopted a neoliberal philosophy to reduce the quantity of state rental housing. The quality of much existing state housing was already aging and in poor repair, having been built relatively solidly, but with the materials, insulating methods and standards of the 60s, with minimal maintenance since then. Other factors have combined to rapidly increase housing costs so neither private rental housing nor "affordable home ownership" is available or attainable for those of the lowest incomes. There is a lack of sufficient affordable housing, and long waiting lists for state housing rental accommodation. The state/social/public rental housing is often overcrowded, families are in stress, and health deterioration and homeless families are the result.

Yet in this distressed situation the experience of homeless families is of prevaricating government staff and lack of compassion. While government leaders aim to overcome the housing capacity issue and encourage government staff to coordinate, from the experiences of the whānau, there remains an entrenched resistance to response. Staff member communications reinforce the trauma of colonisation for Māori families. Colonisation is relevant because the ongoing deprivation and poverty caused by loss of land and cultural connections is reinforced by feelings of worthlessness and lack of cultural empathy communicated by government staff.

Beyond central government departments, local government planning policies also reinforce barriers for Māori, especially those living in cities where costs are higher and Māori land is either in very short and constrained supply, or has multiple barriers to development (Ngā Aho, 2017) (Matunga for Productivity Commission, 2017).

6. Structural changes needed

Government legislation, policy, and planning requires bold change with determination to financially support integrated well-being decision-making and alleviate the well known barriers for Māori. Changes have been timid since the Auditor General conducted the first review of government department responsiveness in 2011 and put forward clear recommendations. While policy, planning, and corporate culture all need to change, the government departmental corporate culture seems entrenched, and should be a focus. This might be addressed by encouraging flexibility and conducting training for staff in

Māori cultural values, communication, and cooperation.

Education on financial literacy has been undertaken by trusts and non government entities and more such training could be mainstreamed. Life skills and parental training has shown beneficial outcomes as well for isolated young families.

Building on Māori land, which assists housing access by lowering the costs, at least theroetically, is a complex and challenging endeavour and there is very limited Māori land in cities.

Supply of housing is not only slow but has been in deficit for a number of years. Therefore urgent work on temporary accomodation is needed that is beyond the very risky approach of sending vulnerable whānau to motels. The legislation does not encourage supply of affordable quality private rental accommodation and whānau have often found only the squalid but high cost options available.

While emphasis has been on private rental accomodation to respond to housing needs, Government taxation and other policies (Coleman, Austen-Smith, and Martin, 2017) have increased inter-generational barriers for rental accommodation. For those who have young families, a low income and are transient with insecure accommodation, life is bleak in Aotearoa/New Zealand.

7. How can we do it better?

Descendants of colonial New Zealanders, particularly those in the middle classes, while also challenged by high housing costs, have higher incomes – often have intergenerational wealth – and greater ability via financial resilience to enter the house owning market. Many are not aware of and do not understand the barriers of poverty, having very limited comprehension of the circumstances in which others in their cities and towns are living. They also have very little understanding of the effects of colonisation on Māori. Much wider and greater understanding of the effects of colonisation and consequent poverty and trauma is essential in order to bring about political change rather than attributing blame for poverty and homelessness on Māori families.

Although much research points to individual, family and national benefit of house ownership as opposed to rental housing (Waldegrave and Urbanova, 2016) the homeless supported by emergency housing providers such as Island Child, do not have their feet on even the first rung of affordable housing, and do not have sufficient income to achieve any equity in house ownership, at least at that stage in their life. Clean safe and culturally appropriate emergency and transitional housing is vital (Kake, 2016) and will continue to be needed, as well as poverty reduction measures to prevent homelessness.

A study by Groot and associates found in 2011, that Indigenous people are more likely to experience poverty and homelessness (Kake, 2016). They advocated for a coordinated national response to homelessness and

Rigby (2017) argues that a firm public commitment to ending homelessness should be undertaken by planning, resourcing and acting. Such policy responses would be extremely helpful but in the meantime, intensive and coordinated social support (Groot and Peters, 2016) is needed to help homeless whānau, as well as to make marked improvement in their circumstances.

A clear vision and plan to change housing trajectories is desparately needed, as well as action. Building in New Zealand has multiple barriers such as high cost. In the category of building costs could be included building material, insufficient trained builders, lack of financial incentives to builders as they follow private funding for commercial building projects (Saville-Smith, 2017). There are also high land costs, which are partly a function of high infrastructure costs, and high local government compliance costs. There are also particular and complex legal and financial barriers to building on Māori land. However, affordable housing is also an international issue and other counties are taking action.

Māori need to be be able to take a lead in resolving this issue. Brown (2018) argues that a long-term solution to Māori housing must address land loss and involve Māori as decision makers. Supporting this, Kake argues that as Māori are over-represented among homeless, Māori values and perspectives are essential in policy formulation. This is not the case at present, as Mills et al., (2015) stated:

> Generally, provision of housing for vulnerable people in New Zealand has tended to be designed and instigated from a mono-cultural perspective, with little attention paid to cultural appropriateness.

Māori are included in the definition of vulnerable. There is optimism though that the new Māori Associate Minister for Māori housing will have sufficient resource and support at her disposal to start making needed and overdue changes to government structures, policy, design, and funding.

Government urgently need to stop using motels and private rental accommodation as short term, unstable solutions for those who are unable to pay for high housing rental fees, for properties which may also be in poor condition. Groot and Peters (2016) have referred to policy-driven homelessness. This is one example.

Integrated department communication including for education, health, and housing as well as iwi/hapū participation is now beginning to produce some local solutions which should be communicated more widely. However, service provision is fragmented and there currently is no coordinated response in New Zealand to homelessness (Groot and Peters, 2016).

We need trained Māori staff to support those in need (Brown et al., 2018). Kake (2016b) reiterated the need for this service, noting that partnerships with mainstream organisations as an interim measure are required to build capacity and relationships. Mainstream organisations are under-resourced and not equipped to deal with cultural disconnections, and support is necessary in cultural competence training for frontline staff. A constructive idea discussed by Rigby (2017) is that Māori therapeutic approaches along with mātauranga Māori, values and perspectives are an opportunity for reciprocal learning for social services, to enable them to provide holistic services for their mainstream clients.

We particularly need flexibility for supporting marae and grass roots organisations, such as Island Child who are working to address these complex issues. New Zealand needs to give strong support to emergency housing providers because, as Te Matapihi, the Māori housing advocate has argued, the need for emergency housing remains (Kake 2016a).

8. Danielle, Island Child and whānau

Rigby (2017) sees homelessness as "the end of resilience." Contrast this with the resilience and tenacity of Danielle Bergin and Island Child to provide 15 years of unwavering support for solo mothers, children, and Māori whānau who are homeless. Substantial financial support would enable them to achieve more for those families, and make an even greater difference in their community.

Such support has rebuilt the confidence and self-esteem of the young solo mothers, enabling them to start to thrive in newly found home-places. Jahnke's (2002) study on Māori womens' identity notes that home-place links are reinforced by physical associations with land, whakapapa, proximity to extended family, experience of te reo and the importance of their marae. Matunga reinforces this by noting, "The ancestral link between people and place is inextricable, indeed fundamental" (Matunga et al., 2018).

Danielle works hard to find rental properties which are close to family, physical, and spiritual associations (marae and whakapapa) while supporting identity aspects such as te reo classes. A small but proliferating aspect of identity expression as well as manaaki is the encouragement Danielle has given to the development of Pātaka Kai, small food stores, like community cupboards, to provide much needed food for those in need. Pātaka Kai are spreading in Glen Innes, supported by Island Child whānau, although much greater support could be given by the commercial community of Auckland.

A friend recounted Danielle's determination to help whānau when she first started the trust, despite being judged critically by others. Danielle now has a strong grass roots track record of success with whānau as well as in building and strengthening the Glen Innes community.

Island Child has impacted many lives and deserves recognition as a model of success. Danielle commented that such support should not be so hard to find. She was right: Aotearoa should pay much greater heed to social justice, to resource those prepared to work at grass roots in our communities. We need to recognise our heroes.

Acknowledgments

Thanks to all those whānau and friends who shared their experiences.

Glossary

Awhi	help/support
Kaupapa	issue
Mana Whenua	Māori with historic and territorial rights over the land
Mokopuna	grandchild
Tohunga	traditional healer
Wairua	spirit
Whānau	family (families)
Whare	house, home

References

Anderson, P. et al.,(2012). "Developing a Tool to Monitor Potentially Avoidable and Ambulatory Care Sensitive Hospitalisations in New Zealand Children." *New Zealand Medical Journal,* vol. 125, no. 1366, In Malva (2017), p. 27.

Austen-Smith, S. and Martin, S. (Eds.) (2017). Progressive Thinking Ten Perspectives on Housing. NZ Public Services Association, Wellington. https://www.psa.org.nz/assets/Uploads/Housing-book-2017-lowres.pdf

Bailey, K. (2017). *Tāmaki Wellbeing.* https://www.tamakiwellbeing.org.nz/single-post/2017/04/28/A-lab-within-a-lab

Brown, D. (2016). "Tūrangawaewae Kore: Nowhere to Stand" in E. J. Peters & J. Christiansen (Eds.), *Indigenous Homelessness: Perceptions from Canada, Australia and New Zealand.* University of Manitoba Press, pp. 331-362.

Brown, D. (2018). "Contemporary Māori Architecture" in Grant. E, Greenop, K. Refiti, R.L. & Glenn, D. (eds). *The Handbook of Contemporary Indigenous Architecture Singapore,* Springer, pp. 303-330.

Coleman, A., & Karagedikli, Ö. (2018). Residential construction and population growth in New Zealand: 1996-2016. DP2018/02, JEL classification: R21, R31, Discussion Paper Series, Reserve Bank, Wellington. www.rbnz.govt.nz/research/discusspapers.

Darroch Ltd. (2010). *Sub-regional Housing Demand in the Northland Region, report prepared for the Centre for Housing Research Aotearoa/New Zealand. Vol 1.,* 146pp. Vol 2., pp. 218.

Eaqub, S. (2017) "Affordable Housing: Tough problems, tougher solutions." *Resource Management Law Journal,* Nov.2017. Resource Management Law Association (pp.13-14). https://www.rmla.org.nz/archive-resource-management-journal/

Faneva, T. (2016). Responding to Homelessness Among Rural Whānau in Northland. Parity, 29(8), 1719.

Gabriel, M. D. (2015). "Indigenous Homelessness and Traditional Knowledge: Stories of elders and outreach support." PhD thesis, University of Toronto, Canada.

Groot, S., Hodgetts, D., Waimarie Nikora, L., Rua, M. (2011). "Māori Homelessness." In T. McIntosh & M. Mulholland. *Māori Social Issues. Huia: Ngā Pae o te Māramatanga,* Vol 1, pp. 235-248.

Groot, S. and Peters, E. J. (2016). "Indigenous homelessness: New Zealand Context" in E. J. Peters & J. Christiansen (Eds.). *Indigenous Homelessness: Perceptions from Canada, Australia and New Zealand.* (pp. 331-362). Minneapolis: University of Manitoba Press.

Habitat for Humanity Annual Report 2018. 2018_HFHNZ_Annual_Report_FINAL (1).pdf

Hancock, Frances (2018). *Island Child The story of a small grassroots organisation with a big heart.* Island Child Charitable Trust and Tamaki Regeneration Company.

HC2A (n.d.) *Guide to Homelessness and Housing Resource.* West, Housing call to Action (2018). file:///D:/Documents/HC2A%20 Guide%20to%20Homelessness%20and%20Housing%20 Resource%20final%20draft%2015.8.18.pdf

Houkamau, C. A. and Sibley, C. G. (2015). Looking Māori predicts decreased rates of home ownership: Institutional racism in housing based on perceived appearance. PloS One, 10(3), e0118540, p. 38.

Jahnke, H. T. (2002). "Towards a secure identity: Māori women and the home-place." *Women's Studies International Forum,* p. 503-513.

Johnson, D. (2009). *Looking past the mess: Māori homelessness and mental health care.* (Unpublished Master's thesis). The University of Waikato, Waikato, New Zealand.

Johnston, A. Howden-Chapman, P., and Eaqub, S. (2018). *A Stocktake of New Zealand's housing.* Wellington. New Zealand Government. https://www.beehive.govt.nz/sites/default/files/2018-02/A%20Stocktake%20Of%20New%20Zealand%27s%20Housing.pdf

Kake, J. (2016a). *Policy response to Māori Urban Homelessness.* Whangarei: Te Matapihi.

Kake, J. (2016b). "Service responses to Māori urban homelessness." *Parity,* 29(8), pp. 15-16.

Malva, S. (2017). "Land, Housing and capitalism: the social consequences of free markets in Aotearoa New Zealand." *Economic and Social Research Aotearoa* (6) https://esra.nz/land-housing-capitalism/

Matunga, H. (2018). "A Discourse on the Nature of Indigenous Architecture," in Grant. E, Greenop, K. Refiti, R.L. & Glenn, D. (eds). *The Handbook of Contemporary Indigenous Architecture Singapore.* Springer, pp. 303-330.

Mills, A., et al. (2015). Meeting the housing needs of vulnerable populations in New Zealand. Auckland: Transforming Cities, University of Auckland.

Ministry of Business, Innovation and Employment. (2014). He Whare Āhuru He Oranga Tāngata – The Māori Housing Strategy. Retrieved from http://www.mbie.govt.nz/info-services/housing-property/maori-housing-strategy. Issue Date: 31/08/2015

New Zealand Productivity Commission (2017). Better urban planning – final report. Wellington.

Ngā Aho (2017). Designing Māori Futures Produced for the Independent Māori Statutory Board Research Report 2017.

New Zealand General Social Survey (2018). http://archive.stats.govt.nz/browse_for_stats/people_and_communities/well-being/nzgss-info-releases.aspx

Office of the Auditor-General. (2011). Government planning and support for housing on Māori land. Retrieved from http://www.oag.govt.nz/2011/housing-on-Māori-land.

Office of the Auditor-General. (2014). Government planning and support for housing on Māori land. Retrieved from http://www.oag.govt.nz/2014/housing-on-maori-land.

Baker, M. et al. (2017). "Risk of Hospitalisation and Death for Vulnerable New Zealand Children." *Archives of Disease in Childhood.* In Malva (2017), p. 4.

Peters, E.J, and Christensen, J. (Eds) (2016) *Indigenous Homelessness Perspectives from Canada, Australia, and New Zealand.* University of Manitoba Press, Winnepeg, Canada.

Reid, J., et al. (2017). *The Colonising Environment: an aetiology of the trauma of settler colonisation and land alienation on Ngāi Tahu Whānau.* University of Canterbury Ngāi Tahu Research Centre, Christchurch, NZ.

Rigby, B. (2017). "Responding to Homelessness in New Zealand: Homelessness and Housing First for Māori: Meaning and Optimisation." *Parity,* Vol. 30(8).

Saville-Smith, K. (2018). Following the money Understanding the building industry's exit from affordable housing production. National Housing Challenge Research Bulletin.

Schrader, B. (2005). *We call it home. A History of State Housing in New Zealand.* Reed, Wellington.

Statistics New Zealand (2016). Changes in home-ownership patterns 1986–2013: Focus on Māori and Pacific people. www.stats.govt.nz.

Waldegrave, C. & Urbanová, M. (2016). Social and Economic Impacts of Housing Tenure. A report for the New Zealand Housing Foundation by family Centre Social Policy Research Unit (FCSPRU).

Whitehead, J. & Walker, G. (2019). Ngā kaihanga, ngā noho, ngā tangata- exploring the factors affecting Māori home ownership. BBHTC National Science Challenge report.

Chapter 1.4: Ngā Whāriki Manaaki[1]: Mending urban fabric with mana wāhine[2]

Keri Whaitiri – Ngāti Kahungunu, Ngāi Tahu, Nederlandse

For the past six years, Keri has worked with Ngāi Tūāhuriri mana whenua cultural engagement organisation, Matapopore, and contributed to urban development in Christchurch (Aotearoa/NZ) through architecture, landscape and public realm design. Keri works with large project teams and mediates between the commercial realm and mana whenua cultural interests. In this role, she has been very fortunate to work with and learn alongside expert Ngāi Tahu traditional weavers, Reihana Parata and Morehu Flutey-Henare. Inspired by these tāua, Keri set out on the whatu (traditional weaving) journey in 2018. This experience now heavily influences her thinking about contemporary design praxis.

This chapter is a personal perspective and is not representative of any wider collective or organisation.

Figure 1. Maumahara - from Ngā Whāriki Manaaki series. (Artwork ©Parata & Flutey-Henare, 2015. Photograph: ©Whaitiri, 2020).

Why use a decolonising approach?

Decolonising approaches a focus on history, colonial processes, ideologies and institutional practices that structure the relations between indigenous people and settler society. These approaches attempt to get under the skin of policy, discourses, knowledge paradigms, and practices that have sustained the myth of New Zealand as a good place for indigenous development. They seek to expose further colonising practices.

(Linda Tuhiwai Smith in Hutchings & Lee, 2016)

Manaaki and Decolonisation: the ethic of "caring for others" and its relevance in urban contexts

The notion of combining urban decolonisation with the ethic of manaaki[3] (a sense of kindness, generosity, empathy, a wider love, respect and care for others) is perhaps a perplexing one.

How might these culturally distinct terms relate to one another?

For mana whenua[4] in their interactions with wider communities and peoples, manaaki is a fundamental responsibility and an effective means of establishing good relations, social cohesion, and mutual trust. Likewise, for wāhine[5] Māori who typically hold a pivotal role in

---

1. Ngā Mahi ā Te Whare Pora: the art of weaving.
2. Mana wāhine: a term that "speaks of the unique power, spiritual essence and mana of women" (Refer to online article by Stacey Morrison (NZ Herald, 2018): https://www.nzherald.co.nz/nz/news/article.cfm?c_id:1&objectid:12124421)
3. Manaaki: to support, take care of, give hospitality to, protect, look out for - show respect, generosity and care for others.
4. Mana whenua: territorial rights, power from the land, authority over land or territory, jurisdiction over land or territory - power associated with possession and occupation of tribal land. The tribes history and legends are based in the lands they have occupied over generations and the land provides the sustenance for the people and hospitality for guests.
5. Wāhine: female, women, feminine.

maintaining equilibrium within a whānau[6] cluster, manaaki is a natural way of keeping whānau safe, loved, and well cared for – strengthening familial bonds and collective resilience. Manaaki is a way of bringing people in and together. It establishes the platform for ongoing good relations and contributes towards the ongoing collective wellbeing. As such, mana whenua and manaaki, as well as mana wāhine and manaaki are terms that go hand-in-hand.

This paper sheds light on two seemingly disparate ideas of manaaki and decolonisation, as brought forward in the recent urban public realm artworks of two tāua, (female elders of Ngāi Tahu descent) within the once-colonial stronghold of Christchurch City. Reihana Parata and Morehu Flutey-Henare are no strangers to advocacy for wāhine and whānau. They lead by example. They enlist manaaki in order to decolonise urban space, casting aside mindsets of exclusivity and privilege, reclaiming a sense of belonging for one and all.

Love and Care in Urban Planning?

It would be fair to say that love and care are not high priority terms in relation to city-making. Western scientific research tends to prioritise quantifiable and objective measures, eschewing these more subjective qualities as unpredictable, irreplicable, and unreliable.

In spatial analysis for urban planning and design, Kevin Lynch introduced generations of spatial professionals to these archetypal terms: paths, edges, nodes, districts, landmarks (Lynch, 1960). By observing these attributes and mapping them within the city, Lynch asserted that we can begin to form the "image" of a city and better understand its underlying character. In this way – for landscape architects, urban designers and the likes – contemporary cities are typically framed as spatial formations that are objective and neutral, thus rendered manageable and plannable. In this framework, cities are comprised of physical structures, public spaces and infrastructure that support urban existence – an impartial system of built-form densification, networks, nodes – interwoven grey, green, and blue infrastructures. Within such a framework, it is easy to assume that cities are distinct from the people that inhabit them, that they are places where all peoples have the same opportunity to make of themselves what they will – without prejudice, impediment or alienation.

But the framing of cities as benign and egalitarian is overly simplistic. Cities possess deep histories that have become manifest in forms, spaces, and monuments that long outlive their makers. These are culturally-loaded

domains established to conform with and reinforce particular social paradigms that have served to privilege some, while actively negating the relevance and presence of others. Colonial cities enshrine such paradigms in stone and mortar; in grand avenues and layers of order and ideology.

Christ Church

Considered by its name alone, Christchurch (New Zealand) is a city that is steeped in colonial ideologies. Christchurch was named after Christ Church, a constituent college of the University of Oxford by a group of men who regularly assembled in the mid-19th century at 22 Whitehall, London. The Canterbury Association, as they were called, met with the explicit purpose of planning out this ideal Anglican city of the colonies. These were men with professional and financial interests staked in the new colony of New Zealand; men with the motivation to ensure the proposed settlement of Christchurch succeeded.

To the English colonial eye, the area under

Figure 2. Tablet in ChristChurch Cathedral (currently in ruins) listing the members of The Canterbury Association. (Photograph: ©Schwede66, 2010). https://commons.wikimedia.org/wiki/File:Canterbury_Association_members.JPG / CC-BY-SA-3.0

---

6. Whānau: extended family, family group, a familiar term of address to a number of people – the primary economic unit of traditional Māori society. In the modern, context the term is sometimes used to include friends who may not have any kinship ties to other members.

consideration for the new township was a swamp – a quagmire, a boggy natural landscape that awaited taming through draining in order to transform it into a useable, marketable, profitable commodity.

In his farewell speech on eventually leaving Canterbury (New Zealand) in 1852, John Robert Godley, the Founder of Canterbury admitted:

> I often smile when I think of the ideal Canterbury of which our imagination dreamed and I am quite sure that without the enthusiasm, the poetry, the unreality, if you will, with which our scheme was overlaid, it would never have been accomplished (Cyclopedia Company Limited, 1903).

But his actual impressions on first arriving on these shores two years earlier had been somewhat to the contrary:

> The first view of these plains is rather disappointing to an English eye. That is, one misses the greenness and luxuriousness which the growth of grass in a country long cultivated and grassed over exhibits (Fitzgerald, 1863).

The underwhelming reality of this imagined city of the colonies is further corroborated by Mr. Warren Adams when he visited the settlement in 1851–2 and recollected:

> The mountains in the distance were completely hidden by the thick rain; and the dreary swampy plain, which formed the foreground beneath our feet, might extend for aught we could see, over the whole island (Cyclopedia Company Limited, 1903).

And the unfavourable first impressions of Lord Lyttelton, a pivotal member of the Canterbury Association, upon first visiting this place in 1868:

> For emigrants of a complaining turn of mind, and fond of the picturesque, [the Canterbury Plains have] at first sight seemed exceedingly repulsive.
> Lord Lyttelton, as quoted in Strongman (1984).

To the contrary, for local Māori – Ngāi Tūāhuriri and wider Ngāi Tahu – the principle waterway, the Ōtākaro, and surrounding area, possessed great value (Tau et al., 2016). Along with its tributaries and fertile soils, the Ōtākaro sustained a vast array of life – terrestrial, aerial and aquatic. It was a place that was known intimately to Ngāi Tūāhuriri for its seasonal, climatic, and diurnal variations. Whakapapa[7] and mātauranga[8] dwelt in the folds of the whenua[9], the trickle of a brook and at the bends of the awa[10]. Despite its natural appearance, to Ngāi Tūāhuriri this was a highly managed landscape – *mahinga kai*[11] – prized for an abundance and diversity of natural resources that thrived in these watery conditions. (Fig. 3)

Figure 3. One of the few remnant areas of unmodified topography in the inner city, sloping down towards Ōtākaro River (in the grounds of St Michaels and All Angels Church and School). (Photograph: ©Whaitiri, 2020).

In 1850, the official plan for the first colonial city of New Zealand was released by the Canterbury Association. A familiar regular grid of property boundary lines and roads was superimposed over pre-existing nohoanga and kāinga (village) – sites of permanent and seasonal Māori occupation that had occupied high and dry ground – dismissing and displacing their well-located presence with newly allotted sites for civic buildings. This geometric planar form would effectively compress, suppress, and largely reject the fluid, undulating mosaic of wetlands, streams, sandbanks, and land that existed before European intervention. The city grid had the dual effect of establishing cultural dominion over nature, as well as over traditional practices of local peoples that were contingent on the natural qualities of this place – mahinga kai.

The emergent city of the mid-19th century was planned to reflect a civic orderliness that harked back to ancient Greece and to attract a better class of English immigrant – a familiar, planned transformation that had its precedents in other colonial cities. All of this served to relocate the vision of an affluent English town to a landscape that, to the English eye, was an unkempt bog on the opposite side of the globe.

Auspicious Anglican names and modified landscapes introduced northern hemisphere plantings that displaced

---

7. Whakapapa: genealogy, genealogical table, lineage, descent.
8. Mātauranga: knowledge, wisdom, understanding, skill.
9. Whenua: land, ground, country, land, nation, state, territory, domain.
10. Awa: river, stream, creek, canal, gully, gorge, groove, furrow.
11. Mahinga kai: The knowledge and values associated with customary food-gathering places and practices.

native flora and fauna, architectural styles, materials, and details distinctive of 'home' (Burke & Burke, 1848; Matunga, 2000). These highly political and deliberate civic representations intentionally played to aesthetic sensibilities grounded in English soil, effectively cementing Christchurch as, "the most English city outside of England" (Priestley, 1990, p.3). Almost fifty years later in 1897, when American writer Mark Twain visited Christchurch, it would appear that this planned Anglicisation had taken effect:

> It was Junior England all the way to Christchurch in fact, just a garden. And Christchurch is an English town, with an English-park annex, and a winding English brook just like the Avon – and named the Avon. If it had an established Church and social inequality it would be England again with hardly any lack (Twain, 1897).

The original plan for Christchurch appealed directly to ambitions for improved social status that were perhaps more elusive to attain in the entrenched social hierarchies of the English motherland. Needless to say, local Māori were absent from the colonial promotional material of the 1800s. Christchurch's status as the exemplary colonial city of New Zealand was secured through the appropriation of familiar English city characteristics and the increasing "invisibility" of local Māori communities from this rapidly changing setting (Matunga, 2000).

> Englishness has mostly defined the city as a place, and that sense of place… has been the main way the city has been imagined (Cookson 2000, p. 13).

English civic identity became the key imagining that Christchurch traded on consistently over time.

This transformation, as first initiated by The Canterbury Association, set the stage for urban development that was to become visually and ideologically driven by Eurocentric masculine rhetoric. It was a plan that was reinforced by subsequent waves of civic decision-makers that guided the city's form and growth.[12]

Given the singular nature of the narrative embedded in the establishment of a colonial city:

> *Is it futile to conceive of decolonisation within the densely woven urban fabric of colonial cities in the 21st century?*

Tragically, in Christchurch it took a natural event of catastrophic proportions to catalyse an ideological shift. No one caused it. Few could have anticipated it. All reeled

Figure 4. Paepae Pounamu (Ngā Whāriki Manaaki series) – greenstone paving detail. (Artwork ©Parata & Flutey-Henare, 2015. Photograph: ©Whaitiri, 2020).

at the loss of life and the sheer scale of devastation caused by the massive earthquakes of 2010 and 2011. Gaps in the pavement opened up large city blocks of unstable and crumbling building material, cleared with little discrimination or warning. The sky burst through with an eerie blue brilliance to dominate the urban areas where densely packed built-form had once stood. No one relished it. All stumbled through, disorientated by the loss of landmarks, and dumbfounded by the speed with which change – expedited by emergency legislation in the name of civic safety and urban recovery – had been thrust upon its already traumatised inhabitants.

In the re-emerging city, mana whenua presence has begun to reseed within interstitial urban "gaps" and through opportunities that have arisen as the city is woven back together. This presence leverages the values of ancestors, longstanding associations with place, and a spirit and vibrance that have always been here, but were previously neglected from the official civic narrative.[13] Within this emergent urban public realm, mana wāhine (a distinctly Māori female presence and influence) has sought to embrace the complexities of Christchurch city and its various peoples.

Mana wāhine embedded in the contemporary public realm can begin to reframe who we are as equal citizens of a future bicultural city through compassion, empathy and the elevation of the principle of care for others. This is all captured in one word – **manaaki**. (Fig. 4)

---

12. While there have occasionally been singular female Christchurch City Councillors over time, women have only become increasingly involved in local government in recent years, particularly since the 1990s (Vicki Buck was Christchurch's first female Mayor from 1989 to 1998; Lianne Dalziel from 2013).

13. The ideological preoccupation of the civic narrative can be surveyed in key publications dedicated to the history of Christchurch (Ansley, 2011; Christchurch City Council & Boffa Miskell Limited, 2007; Cookson, 2000; Dunstall & Cookson, 2000; Gorman, 2013; Priestley, 1990; Rice, 2008, 2014; Wilson, 1989, 2005).

Colonisation

The words colonial and colonisation share etymological roots in Latin from *colere* («to till, cultivate, promote growth"), *colonia* ("land attached to a farm»), *colonus* («farmer, cultivator tiller"). As an important bastion of the purport and intent of current English language terms, the Oxford English Dictionary extends this forward into present day. The OED frames colonisation in similarly innocuous, almost genial terms:

> **colonisation**
> NOUN
> 1. The action or process of settling among and establishing control over the indigenous people of an area.
> 1.1 The action of appropriating a place or domain for one's own use.
> 1.2 *Ecology.* The action by a plant or animal of establishing itself in an area.
> (Oxford English Dictionary, 2019)

Yet, for Indigenous peoples around the world who have been subject to its effects, colonisation has carried predominantly aggressive, disempowering, and destructive overtones.

A colonial narrative carries a specific purpose: typically, it serves the exclusive interests of the coloniser and casts aspersions on those who might challenge those interests. It holds its own superiority in the highest of regard and promotes this at many different levels of society through various mechanisms. It universally reinforces the inferiority of others, with cumulatively damaging effects on their socio-cultural cohesion.

The implementation of colonisation processes can have dual benefits for the coloniser. Firstly, the slow (or sometimes swift) disappearing of the Indigenous other. This serves to expedite colonial authority and control over sought-after lands and natural resources. Secondly, these newly acquired assets are able to be divvied up and redistributed to newly arriving communities, often at a healthy profit, creating a bankroll for further development to service future demand from would-be immigrants. These processes are often secured by parallel initiatives, such as deliberate and strategic acts of invasion, coercion, alienation, dispossession, subterfuge, and violence.

> Cultural invasion, which serves the ends of conquest and the preservation of oppression, always involves a parochial view of reality, a static perception of the world, and the imposition of one world view upon another. It implies 'superiority' of the invader and the 'inferiority' of those who are invaded, as well as the imposition of values of

the former, who possess the latter and are afraid of losing them (Freire 1986, p. 159).

The process of colonisation becomes increasingly effective when spread across successive generations with the "colonised" becoming increasingly absorbed by and implicated within the dominant order. Unwittingly, over time this contributes to one's own oppression and cultural erosion – a self-perpetuating process of erasure.

To borrow from Paolo Freire's Theory of Antidialogical Action, oppression achieves its purpose through "conquest, divide and rule, manipulation, and cultural invasion" (Freire 1986, p. 6). Gayatri Spivak's concept of the subaltern further underlines the invisibility and loss of agency that occurs in the process of colonisation, particularly for women:

> In the context of colonial production, the subaltern has no history and cannot speak, the subaltern as female is even more deeply in shadow (Spivak 1988, p. 287).

As such, "colonisation" as it is used here is understood less in terms of its definition as per the Oxford English Dictionary but is more closely aligned with Spivak and Freire's theories around subjugation and oppression.

The strength and endurance of the colonial narrative is exemplified in a great many books dedicated to the history of Christchurch city. These celebrate the citys development, distinctive architectural heritage, important civic events, key figures and organisations in its exemplary development, as well as the transition of model English families from immigrants to "pioneers" to settlers, citizens and significant property holders. The tenacity of this narrative is evident in a recent publication from 2013, two years after the earthquakes of 2011, in a book compiled by leading Christchurch newspaper, The Press, (Gorman, 2013). Its publication overview reads:

> A fascinating review of Christchurch two years after the earthquakes devastation, with analysis of the social, economic and demographic changes and implications. This extensive text by The Press' team of experienced reporters gives an up-to-the-minute and expert insight into all the factors surrounding Christchurchs recent tragic past and challenging yet promising future.

Well, not quite "all" the factors. Tribal collective, Ngāi Tahu, and mana whenua, Ngāi Tūāhuriri, have little discernible mention in all 300 or so pages of this book. In parallel to this are a multitude of colonial histories, stories and figures, and ghost-like images of edifices, the physical forms of heritage long ago removed that continue to "hover" above empty sites. In Christchurch,

Figure 5. John Robert Godley – Founder of Canterbury - 1850 – statue in central Christchurch, Cathedral Square. (Photograph: ©Whaitiri, 2020).

Figure 6. James Cook Statue, Victoria Square. (Photograph: ©Whaitiri, 2020).

we are currently negotiating our way through a doubly "imagined" city – some might say doubly erased. (Fig. 5)

Our contemporary cities are not immune to the processes of colonisation, in fact they remain the bastions of its implementation. The early cities of self-governing British colonies enshrined culturally loaded ideologies in stone, in name, in aesthetic form. These ideologies are celebrated, memorialised in statues of past "heroes" and plaques declaring the deeds of exemplary citizens, serving to perpetuate the dominant order of the past. (Fig. 6)

History privileges the ideals, actions and best interests of those who manage and control it and those who court its beneficial favour – while actively ignoring the interests of those who have been pushed beyond its gaze. Lamentably, if left unquestioned, redundant ideals and values of the past may unwittingly form the building blocks of influence for ongoing urban development processes and contemporary city-making.

Transforming praxis from exclusion to inclusion, from colonisation to decolonisation

It is important to acknowledge that the colonial history of Christchurch is fundamental in the historical and social context of this place. To be clear, it is not the colonial social history that is under scrutiny here, but more the politics of exclusion that tend to accompany it.

In the current socio-political climate as we debate who we are as citizens of a bicultural country, perhaps we should be considering further who we are as citizens of a bicultural city. As such, this paper calls into question the appropriateness of perpetuating the imagined colonial city as the status quo. It now asks:

How might Māori and other Indigenous peoples engage with colonial cities in a contemporary context?

Opportunities for Indigenous peoples to participate in the contemporary re-visioning of such a city are mediated by:

- existing built-form and spatial layouts;
- residual plans, policies and infrastructure developed to serve particular agendas;
- barriers to accessing higher level decision-making and implementation processes;
- appropriate legislation, policy and precedent to maintain ongoing equity in all processes.

Radical educationalist Paolo Freire calls the methodology of the "oppressor" "antidialogic action" (which, as mentioned previously, is characterised by conquest, manipulation, cultural invasion, and the concept of divide and rule) (Freire 1986, p. 159). The notion of "decolonisation" in our contemporary urban context could logically call for an opposing equally aggressive response to begin to redress, what some might call, the "excesses of colonisation"[14] (Williams, 2018).

Instead, in countering antidialogic action, Freire advocates alternatively for "dialogic action" which is characterised by: *cooperation, unity, organisation,* and *cultural synthesis* (Freire, 1986).

Cultural synthesis does not deny the difference between two views; indeed, it is based on these differences. It *does* deny the invasion of one *by* the other, but affirms the undeniable *support* each gives *to* the other (Freire 1986, p. 183).

Figure 7. Pikihuia i te Ao, i te Pō artwork by Lonnie Hutchinson on west facing windows of Te Omeka, Christchurch Justice and Emergency Services Precinct (Artwork ©Hutchinson, 2015. Photograph: ©Whaitiri, 2020).

In the post-earthquake recovery of Canterbury and Christchurch such questions have arisen in relation to the status of tangata whenua and mana whenua within local and regional government. Formalised multilateral statutory partnerships between central, local government and tangata whenua that evolved from a Treaty of Waitangi (New Zealand's founding document, signed 1840) foundation were fundamental for negotiating and developing agile and adaptive frameworks that could respond to tikanga[15] and catalyse better participation. Decision-making and implementation in the interests of all parties. (Fig. 8)

In the recent mana whenua-led publication Grand Narratives (Tau et al., 2016) Ngāi Tūāhuriri are located in the enduring landscape that pre-existed the laying of the city's concrete platform, as well as side by side with colonial settlers and subsequent generations. The leading chapter "Grand Narrative for Christchurch" resists defaulting to distant mythologies and is firmly placed in the socio-historical context of colonial settlement, as well as the past and future development of the city.

> From the devastation, opportunities emerged. Central government, local government, Māori and community leaders recognised the opportunity to create a new city using a partnership approach, informed and shaped by public consultation and participation. It was an opportunity to recognise, embrace and acknowledge our shared history and shared future (Associate Professor Te Maire Tau in Tau et al., 2016, p. 3).

The Grand Narratives anticipated imminent urban development through the recovery process and became a tool of analysis, mapping and layering for a reimagined bicultural city with mana whenua as a fundamental partner to civic regeneration processes.

In Christchurch, how this is all being manifest remains a work in progress. It is being negotiated at a local and regional government level in the post-earthquake recovery of the city. Fundamental to this are: mutual respect; a willingness to work together; inclusive and iterative decision-making processes; self-determination and agency – mana motuhake. The close examination of local government authority internal processes, in terms of their ability to integrate Indigenous ways of knowing, doing and being at conceptual and ideological levels is a key step. (Fig. 9)

Figure 8. Parerau detail, artwork in Victoria Square by Jen Rendall (Artwork ©Rendall, 2018. Photograph: ©Whaitiri, 2020).

Figure 9. Parerau - artwork by Jen Rendall is a garland of mahinga kai species etched into low wall that rests behind the statue of Queen Victoria, Victoria Square. (Artwork ©Rendall, 2018. Photograph: ©Whaitiri, 2020).

Decolonisation of urban spaces by Wāhine Māori

The disparity between male and female participation in local and central government decision-making in New Zealand remains marked. Christchurch celebrates social radicals such as Kate Sheppard and the Suffragette Movement, who advocated for womens rights in the late nineteenth century. As a result of their efforts, in 1893 New Zealand women won the legal right to vote in parliamentary elections, the first self-governing country in the world to do so. By 1981, almost 100 years later, only 8% of Members of Parliament, decision-makers at a national scale, were women (Ministry for Culture and Heritage, 2019). In mainstream governmental decision-making, the disparity for wāhine Māori far exceeds even this underwhelming figure.

---

14. Matua Haare Williams in kōrero at Nā Te Kore: From the Void (Ngā Aho International Indigenous Design Forum, 2018).
15. Tikanga: customary system of values and practices that have developed over time and are deeply embedded in the social context.

The Māori Women's Welfare League (established in 1951) is an organisation that acutely understands this disparity and actively advocates for the social, economic and spiritual wellbeing of Māori women and their whānau. The effects of rapid Māori urbanisation stemming from the 1930s prompted wāhine concerns regarding "housing, health, finance and racism" (Christchurch Libraries, ND). The League became an effective platform for lobbying government on issues that Māori women deemed important and became the conduit for suitable action at local, regional and national levels. The League has nurtured articulate, empathetic, experienced, and grounded wāhine who span generations and spheres of influence. With the wellbeing of Māori women and families as a fundamental kaupapa[16], the Māori Womens Welfare League is manaaki through and through, a pure expression of mana wāhine at work within urban contexts and wider society.

The League has been active for almost 70 years, which begs the question:

Why are our modern cities often bereft of physical manifestations initiated by Māori women and, in a global context, by their other indigenous counterparts?

Are women's cultural creative practices less acceptable, less worthy or less noble than other forms of civic creative expression? Are wāhine subject to exclusion both explicitly, by definitions of what is acceptable and normative in the urban public realm (and the fine arts), and tacitly, by the policies, infrastructure and procedures that propel the historical status quo? To what extent can equity be negotiated within these processes?

Ngā Whāriki Manaaki: Woven Mats of Welcome[17]
(Ngāi Tahu artists: Reihana Parata and Morehu Flutey-Henare). (Fig. 10)

In the re-emerging fabric of Christchurch there is a quiet, unassuming presence that weaves through the inner city. Following the sinuous curves of the Ōtākaro, a gentle female presence rises, brushing the surface at ground level along the basalt-paved pedestrian promenade of Te Papa Ōtākaro[18], then dips down again, concealed within the folds of Papatūānuku[19].

Ngā Whāriki Manaaki (translated as "Woven Mats of Welcome") is an integrated paving project by Reihana Parata and Morehu Flutey-Henare. It is situated in the public realm of Christchurch inner city and was facilitated by mana whenua organisation, Matapopore, in partnership with Christchurch Earthquake Recovery Authority (the Crown agency charged with catalysing the earthquake recovery of Christchurch). The mana Māori wāhine influence that underlies this serial artwork positions creative practices that draw from a traditional base longitudinally throughout the inner city.

A whāriki is a finely woven floor mat. It provides warmth and comfort, a place to sit, lie and rest for those who enter a traditional whare.[20] Typically, these are woven from natural materials, ideally a fine hollow-section sedge – paopao or kuta (*Eleocharis sphacelate*) – that provides material strength, as well as excellent insulating qualities. Traditional whāriki are often woven with patterns that recall whānau, hapū[21] and iwi[22] whakapapa,[23] stories and associations. Some values that sit behind traditional weaving practices and were embedded in these artworks from the outset are: manaakitanga,[24] whakamanuhiri[25], aroha[26], whānau, whanaungatanga,[27] rangatiratanga,[28] wairuatanga.[29] Not only are these drivers for creative process but they also potentially influence those who engage with these works and pursue their deeper meanings. Ngā Whāriki Manaaki is a public realm artwork with clear social purpose.

Integrated paving designs are a frequent element of public realm design. What is unusual in this case is the departure from conventional methods of procurement, conceptual development and implementation. Highly significant and exceptional, particularly in the context of the first colonial city of New Zealand, are the creative

---

16. Kaupapa: platform, layer, topic, policy, matter for discussion, plan, purpose, scheme, proposal, agenda, subject, programme, theme, issue, initiative.
17. For Matapopore Project Sheet refer to https://matapopore.co.nz/wp-content/uploads/2016/05/1124_CRCL_MP_Nga-Whariki-Manaaki.pdf
18. Avon River Precinct.
19. Papatūānuku: Earth, Earth mother and wife of Rangi-nui – all living things originate from them.

20. Whare: house, building, residence, dwelling, shed, hut, habitation.
21. Hapū: kinship group, clan, tribe, subtribe – section of a large kinship group and the primary political unit in traditional Māori society. It consisted of a number of *whānau* sharing descent from a common ancestor, usually being named after the ancestor, but sometimes from an important event in the groups history. A number of related hapū usually shared adjacent territories forming a looser tribal federation *(iwi)*.
22. Iwi: extended kinship group, tribe, nation, people, nationality, race – often refers to a large group of people descended from a common ancestor and associated with a distinct territory.
23. Whakapapa: genealogy, genealogical table, lineage, descent – reciting *whakapapa* was, and is, an important skill and reflected the importance of genealogies in Māori society in terms of leadership, land and fishing rights, kinship and status. It is central to all Māori institutions. There are different terms for the types of *whakapapa* and the different ways of reciting them including: *tāhū* (recite a direct line of ancestry through only the senior line); *whakamoe* (recite a genealogy including males and their spouses); *taotahi* (recite genealogy in a single line of descent); *hikohiko* (recite genealogy in a selective way by not

Figure 10. Reihana Parata & Morehu Flutey Henare attribution inscribed in basalt stone on each of the thirteen Whāriki Manaaki. (Artwork ©Parata & Flutey-Henare, 2015. Photograph: ©Whaitiri, 2020).

agents chosen to develop these works.

The official overview of the project reads:

Ngā Whāriki Manaaki – Woven Mats of Welcome

Ngā Whāriki Manaaki are a series of 13 creatively designed weaving patterns that feature within Te Papa Ōtākaro/Avon River Precinct. Collectively, the Whāriki are a core element of the Ōtākaro | Art by the River, positioned within the river promenade. Each Whāriki is an arrangement of natural stone pavers of varying shades and colours. In sequence, they reference the whakamanuhiri process of welcome for all peoples visiting Christchurch and support the guiding principle of the rebuild for Ngāi Tahu, 'Kia atawhai ki te iwi - Care for your people'.

Kia tau tonu rā ngā manaakitanga i ngā wā katoa.

May manaaki form the basis of all that we do all of the time. (Morehu Flutey-Henare and Reihana Parata)

The Whāriki are designed by expert weavers Reihana Parata (Queens Service Medal) and Morehu Flutey-Henare (Master of Applied Indigenous Knowledge), with technical support from contemporary artist Wayne Youle (Bachelor of Design).

---

following a single line of descent); *ure tārewa* (male line of descent through the first-born male in each generation).

24. Manaakitanga: hospitality, kindness, generosity, support – the process of showing respect, generosity and care for others.

25. Whakamanuhiri: Ngāi Tahu-specific term for the welcoming, entertainment and hosting a guest (a similar function to the pōwhiri for other iwi).

26. Aroha: to love, feel pity, feel concern for, feel compassion, empathise.

27. Whanaungatanga: relationship, kinship, sense of family connection – a relationship through shared experiences and working together which provides people with a sense of belonging. It develops as a result of kinship rights and obligations, which also serve to strengthen each member of the kin group. It also extends to others to whom one develops a close familial, friendship or reciprocal relationship.

28. Rangatiratanga: chieftainship, right to exercise authority, chiefly autonomy, chiefly authority, ownership, leadership of a social group, domain of the *rangatira*, noble birth, attributes of a chief.

29. Wairuatanga: spirituality.

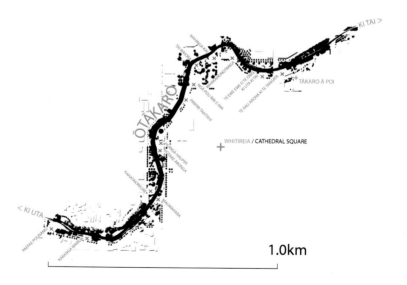

Figure 11. Map layout of Ngā Whāriki Manaaki through the inner city of Christchurch.

Each Whāriki serves a different purpose and carries a specific name and story that is related through patterning.[30] They represent key Ngāi Tahu traditions and protocols that emulate the process of whakamanuhiri for the city – how Ngāi Tūāhuriri bring in and care for visitors and residents within their rohe. Ngā Whāriki Manaaki dually embed recurring and enduring mana whenua and mana wāhine presence in the unfolding pedestrian experience of the city.

The thirteen Whāriki in order from Hospital Corner (Antigua Street roundabout at the river end) to Tākaro ā Poi (Margaret Mahy Family Playground) are:

1. **Paepae Pounamu** – Ngāi Tahu, People of the greenstone waters.
   Located on Oxford Terrace at Antigua Street, near Christchurch Hospital (Fig. 12)

2. **Karanga Wairua** – Spiritual call of welcome.
   Antigua Street, near St Michael's (Fig. 13)

3. **Maumahara** – Remembering our fallen in battle.
   Cashel Street, Bridge of Remembrance (Fig. 14)

4. **Kahataioreore** – Intergenerational relationships between tīpuna and mokopuna.
   Park of Remembrance (Fig. 15)

Figure 12. Paepae Pounamu (Artwork ©Parata & Flutey-Henare, 2015. Photograph: ©Whaitiri, 2020). The beginning of Te Papa Ōtākaro, this is the first step in the whakamanuhiri process, welcoming all peoples to the city.

Figure 13. Karanga Wairua (Artwork ©Parata & Flutey-Henare, 2015. Photograph: ©Whaitiri, 2020).

---

30. For fuller explanation of Ngā Whāriki Manaaki narratives and patterns refer to: https://www.otakaroltd.co.nz/assets/Documents/GeneralDocuments/P41650-ARP-Whariki-Mats-Walking-Booklet-FA-web.pdf.

Figure 14. Maumahara (Artwork ©Parata & Flutey-Henare, 2015. Photograph: ©Whaitiri, 2020). Whāriki laid in front of the Bridge of Remembrance.

Figure 15. Kahataioreore detail (Artwork ©Parata & Flutey-Henare, 2015. Photograph: ©Whaitiri, 2020). The Terraces (Oxford Terrace) in the background.

5. **Pūtake Aronga** – Whānau permeates everything we do.
Oxford Terrace near Worcester Boulevard (Fig. 16)

6. **Huinga Hau Pīpī** – Protocols in the welcoming ceremony.
Intersection of Oxford Terrace and Worcester Boulevard (Fig. 17)

7. **Piripiri Takitahi** – Togetherness.
Te Pae, Christchurch Convention, and Exhibition Centre (Fig. 18)

8. **Ngā Pou Riri e Iwa** – The nine tall trees that made up the Ngāi Tahu claim.
Market Place / Victoria Square (near Te Pae, southwest corner) (Fig. 19)

9. **Tai Waiora** – Water resources, wai or water to drink, wai for good health.
Market Place / Victoria Square (Papanui Bridge) (Fig. 20)

10. **Mahinga Kai** – Customary practice of gathering food and resources.
Market Place / Victoria Square (near Colombo Street bridge, north east corner) (Fig. 21)

11. **Whakahonotanga** – Strengthening the connections between tangata whenua and manuhiri.
Oxford Terrace – between Market Place / Victoria Square and Tākaro ā Poi Family Playground (Fig. 22)

Figure 17. Huinga Hau Pīpī (Artwork ©Parata & Flutey-Henare, 2015. Photograph: ©Whaitiri, 2020). ChristChurch Cathedral and Whitireia / Cathedral Square in background.

Figure 16. Pūtake Aronga (Artwork ©Parata & Flutey-Henare, 2015. Photograph: ©Whaitiri, 2020). The Canterbury Club and former site of Puari Pā on opposite riverbank in background.

Figure 18. Piripiri Takitahi (Artwork ©Parata & Flutey-Henare, 2015. Photograph: ©Whaitiri, 2020). Canterbury Provincial Council Buildings and the former site of Puari Pā, on opposite riverbank in the background, Te Pae (new Christchurch convention centre) behind.

Figure 19. Ngā Pou Riri e Iwa (Artwork ©Parata & Flutey-Henare, 2015. Photograph: ©Whaitiri, 2020), at the Armagh Street entrance to Market Place / Victoria Square looking towards Papanui Bridge and the Town Hall.

Figure 21. Mahinga Kai (Artwork ©Parata & Flutey-Henare, 2015. Photograph: ©Whaitiri, 2020). At Colombo Street entrance to Market Place / Victoria Square with Te Ahikaaroa (by carver Riki Manuel) in the background.

Figure 22. Whakahonotanga (Artwork ©Parata & Flutey-Henare, 2015. Photograph: ©Whaitiri, 2020).

Figure 20. Tai Waiora (Artwork ©Parata & Flutey-Henare, 2015. Photograph: ©Whaitiri, 2020). At the Papanui Bridge crossing to Market Place / Victoria Square, with statues of Captain Cook and Queen Victoria in background.

12. **Te Eweewe O Te Ono, Ki Uta Ki Tai – Hapū, from the mountains to the sea.**
    Along Oxford Terrace, near Tākaro ā Poi family playground (Fig. 23)

13. **Te Rau Aroha Ki Te Tangata** – Family wellbeing.
    Tākaro ā Poi / Margaret Mahy Family Playground (Fig. 24)

Figure 23. Te Eweewe o Te Ono, Ki Uta Ki Tai (Artwork ©Parata & Flutey-Henare, 2015. Photograph: ©Whaitiri, 2020) – Tākaro ā Poi family playground in background.

Figure 24. Te Rau Aroha Ki Te Tangata (Artwork ©Parata & Flutey-Henare, 2015. Photograph: ©Whaitiri, 2020).

Ngā Whāriki Manaaki give recognition to the high value of the Ōtākaro river to Ngāi Tūāhuriri and Ngāi Tahu. The paving patterns are consistent in materiality but distinct in the visual narrative each relates. The narratives expand across space and time, each depicting its own interaction with contemporary urban, cultural and historical contexts. They speak of tikanga, of culturally specific protocols of welcome and engagement. They recall a pre-urban natural environment that was healthy and abundant, that sustained local Māori well in excess of their everyday needs, providing ready access to mahinga kai – a fundamental for effective society and good intertribal relations. The Whāriki respond to adjacent colonial forms and environmental features, complementing and expanding on what is already there. They recount significant moments in time, shared histories as well as historical oversights neglected from the past civic story. They speak of the importance of family, love, kindness and caring, of relationships forged in collective experience, of intergenerational and cross-cultural interactions. They project a strong and distinctive identity that is grounded in the whenua, in whakapapa, in faith and endurance. The many and varied aspects of this artwork are all integrated into designs inspired by traditional weaving patterns and practices and applied to a limited palette of five natural stone colours in regular 80 x 80mm modules.

Reihana Parata and Morehu Flutey-Henare are beautiful and generous creators. The Aunties, as they are affectionately known, have worked together for many years. They have honed the arts of raranga[31] and whatu[32] alongside many other expert weavers. They, in turn, now pass on their knowledge to those eager to engage with the practices of their elders[33]. To work alongside them is both humbling and a privilege.

Reihana and Morehu feed their creative practice by observing and analysing examples around them – then they unravel, reconfigure, adapt and augment during the making process. They are cultural experts on a great number of levels, as well as creative innovators of weaving traditions. They were an inspired choice of creators for the first major landscape intervention by mana whenua in the post-earthquake recovery of Christchurch City.

In speaking about artefacts from past generations:

> Morehu and I, we create our own style, our own garments, even our own patterns. It's not right for us as weavers to take those traditional designs and copy them. Both Morehu and I will change designs. It is never exact (Reihana Parata, as quoted in Revington, 2015).

Reihana and Morehu are culturally grounded, articulate and compelling, but beneath their sweet demeanour, they are forthright and politically astute. Some of their formidable strength lies in the spectrum of their life experiences, their ability to communicate openly and honestly with others, to draw out individual abilities and teach without dictating, to call-out a situation for what it is, when need be, as well as convey deep empathy and care for others.

For Reihana and Morehu, the idea of bringing their work into the urban public realm, integrating it into hard landscaping was a natural progression of their creative cultural practices and ethos. They understood the implications of placing Māori cultural works in publicly accessible spaces, particularly in terms of exposure to damage – both incidental and, regrettably, willful. They set to the difficult task of how to frame these works so that they would be robust, not only physically, but also culturally and spiritually.

In manifesting these values and stories in physical form in the public realm, these works begin to influence the way that the wider citizenship of Christchurch relate, not only to the city, but more importantly, towards each other. These works will serve to elevate the application of genuine care, consideration and compassion for others, as well as the parallel histories of mana whenua as high priority for the city. While their physical medium of choice might be harakeke,[34] their spiritual medium is aroha (love) and manaaki (consideration and care for others).

Manaaki in the City

In Te Ao Māori, manaaki is a deep-seated responsibility. It extends beyond the dictionary definition of hospitality as the friendly and generous reception and entertainment of guests, visitors, or strangers (Oxford English Dictionary, 2019). Manaakitanga is an obligation to shelter and protect, to care and provide not only for those we choose to extend it to, but for anyone who might tread the path to our front door, anyone in need. Mahinga kai, the knowledge and values associated with customary food-gathering places and practices, is of central importance to Ngāi Tahu and forms the very basis of manaaki. Without ready access to good mahinga kai, manaaki is compromised significantly.

---

31. Raranga: to weave, plait (mats, baskets, etc.).
32. Whatu: finger-weaving, fibre-weaving.
33. Tīpuna: ancestors, grandparents – plural form of tipuna and the eastern dialect variation of tūpuna.

34. Harakeke: New Zealand flax, Phormium tenax - an important native plant with long, stiff, upright leaves and dull red flowers. Found on lowland swamps throughout Aotearoa/New Zealand. It has straight, upright seed pods. This is a general name for the harakeke leaf and the plant itself, but each different variety has its own name.

Manaaki is, first and foremost, the responsibility of mana whenua, the collective of people who maintain cultural authority within a specific area. To deny visitors manaaki is a huge offence, a social blunder that can bring shame on a family, on a collective, on a tribe. Considering this, we begin to understand the fundamental importance for mana whenua of the natural landscape of Christchurch before it became a city. As a vital source of food and natural resources, access to the pre-urban natural landscape dictated the level of generosity that could be extended by the hosts. Thus, mana whenua, mahinga kai and manaakitanga are inextricably bound.

Whakapapa, in its fullest sense, is also represented in the Whāriki – holistic connections to peoples around us, those who come before and after us, but also to the peoples and elements of the wider world and to the atua who reside in all around us. Our direct connections and associations with land, waters, sky, elements, flora and fauna give Māori a distinctive ecological and ethical foundation that drives urban revitalisation priorities and strategies.

Faith, belief, endurance, spirituality and traditional protocols of tikanga are bound up within these artworks. The retelling of Ngāi Tahu traditions in the public domain and the acknowledgement of our expert tāua[35] through inscription of their names and tribal affiliations in basalt stone reinforces their agency in cultural regeneration and intergenerational knowledge transmission (see Figure 10 – attribution of artists names inscribed in basalt stone). Ngā Whāriki Manaaki connect us all to the urban landscape – mana whenua and manuhiri,[36] Māori and tauiwi[37] alike.

Colonial cities are domains that have historically little regard for Māori, Indigenous, or First Nations peoples, their culture and heritage, and assimilation within the dominant societal structure has been the historical approach to the urban integration of Māori. With over eighty percent of Māori now living in urban situations (Statistics New Zealand, 2013), the vast majority of Māori society are living in a diasporic-like state, increasingly alienated from their tūrangawaewae.[38] This, paired with the over-representation of Māori in poor socio-economic indicators and statistics (including poverty, mental and physical health, homelessness, crime, abuse, suicide, and unemployment) raises as critical the issue of addressing Māori well-being in urban environments (Ministry of Health, 2018a, 2018b; Newsroom, 2019; Statistics New Zealand, 2012, 2014). The wide-ranging effects of colonisation remains a real, ongoing contemporary problem.

35. Tāua: female elder (Ngāi Tahu).
36. Manuhiri: visitor, guest.
37. Tauiwi: foreigner, European, non-Māori, colonist; person coming from afar.
38. Tūrangawaewae : domicile, standing, place where one has the right to stand - place where one has rights of residence and belonging through kinship and whakapapa.

In 2013, Te Kupenga: Māori Wellbeing survey shed light on what contributes towards Māori senses of wellbeing and found that cultural identity and connectedness were fundamental factors (Statistics New Zealand, 2014). Connection to whānau and tūrangawaewae, as well as cultural and spiritual restitution through practicing Māori faith and tikanga, through language revitalisation, and creative expressions of identity were all primary indicators that positively influenced Māori wellbeing.

An important question for local and central government to pursue is:

How might we more effectively build cultural representation into our urban centres and potentially have a positive influence on Māori wellbeing and associated socioeconomic statistics?

In today's world, women tend to remain as the central caregivers of a family unit, highly attuned to individual concerns, needs, and aspirations, often charged with negotiating family and life dynamics with the best interests of all in mind. As that central figure they have a unique perspective and, as such, the above question is one that Māori (Indigenous and First Nations) women are well positioned to respond to action. Until the aforementioned socio-economic statistics begin to equalise, it would seem that wāhine Māori, as directed by their intuitions, knowledge, and expertise would be worthwhile parties to the reconceptualisation and implementation of public realm, civic buildings, and infrastructure of our future cities.

Reihana and Morehu are disarmingly matter of fact in their explanation of their project:

Aunty Doe describes their involvement in the project by saying simply, "We were called, and we came, and were here. That's virtually it." Aunty Morehu agreed, "For us, it's just about Ngāi Tahu being in the city. That's enough for us really" (Brankin, 2016).

The Aunties do not stand alone – Ngāi Tūāhuriri and Ngāi Tahu stand beside them. They received a tono (request) from mana whenua and rose to it. As guided by mana whenua, these wāhine have laid out an innovative kaupapa for the city: one that draws from the knowledge of elders while sitting alongside and graciously acknowledging the colonial past; one that confidently declares mana whenua, Ngāi Tūāhuriri and Ngāi Tahu; one that can move us forward beyond ideological stasis towards a revisioned bicultural civic future. Ngā Whāriki Manaaki are complemented by other public realm integrated artworks by younger wāhine Ngāi Tahu contemporary artists, such as Lonnie Hutchinson, Jennifer Rendall and Piri Cowie (see Figure 7 and Figure 8).[39] Reihana and Morehu are wāhine trailblazers, female elders who have forged the way for subsequent generations to understand themselves within the public realm of the city.

As significant as this public project and others like it are, they are merely the tip of the iceberg. They are contingent on the active inclusion and participation of mana whenua, as equal partners to planning, decision making and implementation processes. Robust, honest, ongoing and, importantly, formalised relationships are key elements that drive transformational change. It relies on institutional space being carved out for mana whenua ontological, axiological and ideological roots to take hold in order to decolonise past civic preconceptions and determine equitable future outcomes.

These public realm artworks have the capacity to shift mainstream perspectives in an aesthetically appealing, engaging and non-confrontational way – reminiscent of Freire's dialogical action. They give us all a place to stand, the right to be and a way to relate, to understand ourselves and each other in an urban context with deep, multifaceted histories and futures.

Conclusion

In Western society, our appreciation of the abilities of our elders is seriously impoverished, but the works of Reihana and Morehu put that common misconception to rest. These works collectively lay the foundation for a new way of experiencing a bicultural city through mana wāhine creative expressions that privilege diversity and compassion, love and caring for others.

Reihana and Morehu bring a calm dignity and learned insight to the urban spaces of Christchurch. It stems from being wāhine Māori, wāhine Ngāi Tahu. Their maturity lends confidence, their life experience links us to their vast accumulated knowledge and to the elders of the past. They are natural teachers prepared to advocate for the principles of their tīpuna and take on significant challenges in order to advance generations to come. They impart knowledge through action, lifting us out of a static landscape of the past and placing us in a distinctly dynamic, multilayered whenua. As we walk along the river, their works take us, as a community, on a journey through protocols of engagement, invite us to acknowledge one another, invoke the words and songs of tīpuna, our ancestors. The Aunties make sure we are safe and have the things we need to lead a productive existence. They do this not only for Māori whānau, hapū

and iwi, but for all peoples who come to and come from this city. The importance of how visitors and residents alike are brought in, welcomed, cared for and nurtured within the city of Christchurch is fundamental.

To speak of manaaki as the vehicle for grounding urban decolonisation might require a massive conceptual leap for some folk, but for Reihana and Morehu it is just the way they do things.

Through Ngā Whāriki Manaaki these formidable women embed their mana and that of their people within the city of Christchurch, revealing it for all to share in.

How do the Aunties unravel and mend the colonial fabric of Christchurch?

The Aunties reweave the colonial fabric through championing and adhering to Ngā Mahi ā Te Whare Pora[40] (principles, protocols, and practices that surround the traditional weaving practices) and by celebrating and elevating Ngāi Tahutanga in the urban domain. Prioritising values such as manaakitanga automatically co-opts the ethic of consideration and provision for others – with openness, honesty, and generosity.

In recent years in Christchurch we have been confronted by events that have seriously challenged the status quo and upended ingrained preconceptions. These are events that have coerced estranged neighbours and disparate ethnicities to turn towards each other, to come together and support each other as community. As the diversity of our urban communities grow, there is an increasing need to create space and a sense of belonging for all. It is fitting that the ethic of manaaki is engraved within the enduring fabric of our city.

Reihana and Morehu demonstrate that decolonisation is not something that we subject others to, but rather, it is something that grows from within. It is a firm rejection of colonisation by a clear declaration of who we are, what and how we do things, what we believe in, what we know to be tika and pono – true and genuine. As a collective statement in the public urban realm, this is powerful stuff. Consistent with Freire's notion of dialogic action, Ngā Whāriki Manaaki are a series of affirmations and invitations, as opposed to impositions. They decolonise the ground they rest within, as well as the receptive minds that are open to engaging.

The purpose of this paper is to highlight a critical and reflective element of the regenerating city of Christchurch that meanders through its spaces with bountiful potential. It seeks to unlock and reveal aspects of these integrated and significant artworks. It encourages similar future collaborations that might shift our understanding of who we are in our shared cities.

In recent years, the longstanding epithet *Christchurch: The Garden City* is one that has been tagged as old

---

39. It is also worth noting that a Ngāi Tahu tāne (male) creative presence preceded the 2011 earthquake recovery with works associated with Te Hononga (Christchurch City Council Central Headquarters – opened 2010), a joint development by Ngāi Tahu Properties and Christchurch City Council with artists Ross Hemera and Fayne Robinson. Te Kiheru Wai ō Tahu (2014) by Lewis Gardiner (Ngāi Tahu) was part of the High Street Transitional Project and Te Ahikaaroa by Riki Manuel (Ngāti Porou) in Victoria Square.

---

40. Ngā Mahi ā Te Whare Pora: The art of weaving.

fashioned and passé, as somewhat questionable and redundant (Clarke, 2018; Truebridge, 2017). By pursuing and debating the status and autonomy of Tangata Whenua[41] and Tangata Tiriti,[42] as we are doing in contemporary cities of New Zealand, we are establishing common ground for both to have recognition. As we move forward, perhaps it is time to consider the Christchurch city's epithet afresh and embrace one that is reflective of our dual heritage, that celebrates the Treaty partnership resting over us at a broader societal level.

Taking into account the potential for the creative practices of wāhine to decolonise colonial Christchurch and reset it as a contemporary bicultural city for a multicultural community, an alternative city epithet is offered here:

Christchurch: Te Whāriki Manaaki

In closing, a final tono[43] to local government policy and decision makers, to planners, urban designers, architects and extended project teams that influence the future look, shape and feel of our cities – look to your public realm spaces and ask:

> *Is mana wāhine[44] represented in the contemporary urban fabric of the city?*
> *Do you hear our voices resonate, see our vision manifest in form, space and aesthetic experience of place?*

If it is difficult to respond positively, there is some work to do to catalyse this and do justice to mana wāhine experience and perspective. Feel free to cite *Parata & Flutey-Henare, 2015* as your precedent study, a prime exemplar of the importance of mana wāhine as an enduring influence in our urban spaces.

In November 2018, the last of the thirteen Whāriki Manaaki were installed and blessed prior to opening the inner city river corridor to the people of Christchurch. A large rōpū[46] from the project team and other contributors attended – people who may not previously have worked in a professional capacity with Māori, with mana whenua, with wāhine; people who may never have heard the word manaaki before this project, but had come to know it instinctively through their professional mahi[47] and understood the importance of this enduring message as woven into public realm urban fabric. Reihana, a wāhine

Figure 25. 'Ngā Whāriki Manaaki' blessing and hīkoi[45]. Reihana Parata (artist) accompanied by Larissa Cox-Winiata (Matapopore) lead a group of people associated with the project along the two kilometre length of the artwork - November 2018. (Photograph: ©Whaitiri, 2018)

toa in her early eighties, walked the two kilometre length of this serial artwork followed by a procession of hi-vis clad project team devotees. It was a perfect day.

Kia tau tonu rā ngā manaakitanga i ngā wā katoa.
May manaaki form the basis of all that we do all of the time.

---

41. Tangata Whenua : local people, hosts, indigenous people - people born of the whenua, i.e. of the placenta. and of the land where the peoples ancestors have lived and where their placenta are buried.
42. Tangata Tiriti : people of the Treaty (of Waitangi), the converse of Tangata Whenua.
43. Tono: application, invitation, request, claim, tender, commission (a piece of artwork).
44. Interchange the term mana wāhine with indigenous or First Nations womens influence.

---

45. Hīkoi: step, march, hike, tramp, trip, journey.
46. Rōpū: group, party of people, company, gang, association, entourage, committee, organisation, category.
47. Mahi: work, job, employment, trade (work), practice, occupation, activity, exercise, operation, function.

Bibliography

Ansley, B. (2011). *Christchurch Heritage: A Celebration of Lost Buildings & Streetscapes.* Auckland, N.Z.: Random House.

Brankin, A. (2016). Toi Iho: Bringing Soul to the Rebuild. Retrieved from https://ngaitahu.iwi.nz/our_stories/toi-ihobringing-soul-to-the-rebuild/.

Burke, J., & Burke, J. B. (1848). *Burkes Peerage: A Genealogical and Heraldic Dictionary of the Peerage and Baronetage of Great Britain of the British Empire* (10th ed.). London: Henry Coburn Publisher.

Christchurch City Council, & Boffa Miskell Limited. (2007). *Banks Peninsula Landscape Study: final report.* Christchurch, N.Z.]: Christchurch, N.Z.: Boffa Miskell.

Christchurch Libraries. (ND). Christchurch Street and Place Names. https://my.christchurchcitylibraries.com/christchurch-place-names/.

Clarke, L. (2018). *Is Christchurch still known as the Garden City?* MetroNews. https://metronews.co.nz/article/is-christchurch-still-known-as-the-garden-city.

Cookson, J. (2000). Pilgrims Progress - Image, Identity, and Myth in Christchurch. In G. Dunstall & J. E. Cookson (Eds.), *Southern Capital: Christchurch: towards a city biography, 1850-2000* (pp. 13-40). Christchurch, N.Z.: Canterbury University Press.

Cyclopedia Company Limited. (1903). *The Cyclopedia of New Zealand [Canterbury Provincial District].* Christchurch: The Cyclopedia Company Limited.

Dunstall, G., & Cookson, J. E. (2000). *Southern Capital: Christchurch: Towards a City Biography, 1850-2000.* Christchurch, N.Z.: Canterbury University Press.

Fitzgerald, J. E. (1863). *A Selection from the Writings and Speeches of John Robert Godley.* New Zealand: Press Office.

Freire, P. (1986). *Pedagogy of the Oppressed.* New York: Continuum.

Gorman, P. (2013). *A City Recovers: Christchurch two years after the quakes.* Auckland: Random House New Zealand.

Hutchings, J., & Lee, J. (2016). *Decolonisation in Aotearoa: Education, Research, and Practice.* Wellington, New Zealand: NZCER Press.

Lynch, K. (1960). *The Image of the City.* Cambridge [Mass.]: Cambridge Mass. Technology Press & Harvard University Press.

Matunga, H. P. (2000). *Urban ecology, tangata whenua, and the colonial city.* Paper presented at the Urban biodiversity and ecology as a basis for holistic planning and design: Proceedings of a workshop held at Lincoln University 28-29 October 2000., Christchurch, New Zealand: Wickliffe Press.

Ministry for Culture and Heritage. (2019, 20-Dec-2018). New Zealand women and the vote. https://nzhistory.govt.nz/politics/womens-suffrage.

Ministry of Health. (2018a). Māori Health Statistics: Health Status Indicators.

Ministry of Health. (2018b). Māori Health Statistics: Socioeconomic determinants of health - Socioeconomic indicators. Retrieved from https://www.health.govt.nz/our-work/populations/maori-health/tatau-kahukura-maori-health-statistics/nga-awe-o-te-hauora-socioeconomic-determinants-health/socioeconomic-indicators.

Newsroom. (2019). A $98m Approach to Tackling Māori Incarceration. Retrieved from https://www.newsroom.co.nz/2019/05/10/579061/new-approach-to-tackle-maori-incarceration-rates.

Oxford English Dictionary. (2019). https://en.oxforddictionaries.com/.

Priestley, B. (1990). *Christchurch: city of cities.* Christchurch, N.Z.: Bascands.

Revington, M. (2015). The Art of Weaving. *Te Karaka.*

Rice, G. (2008). *Christchurch changing: an illustrated history* (2nd ed.. ed.). Christchurch, N.Z.: Canterbury University Press.

Rice, G. (2014). *Victoria Square: cradle of Christchurch.* Christchurch, New Zealand: Canterbury University Press.

Spivak, G. C. (1988). Can the Subaltern Speak? In C. Nelson & L. Grossberg (Eds.), *Marxism and the Interpretation of Culture* (pp. pp. 271-313). Urbana, IL: University of Illinois Press.

Statistics New Zealand. (2012). NZ Official Yearbook 2012. New Zealands Prison Population. Table 2: Ethnicity. Retrieved from http://archive.stats.govt.nz/browse_for_stats/snapshots-of-nz/yearbook/society/crime/corrections.aspx.

Statistics New Zealand. (2013). Statistics map population by area and ethnicity. Retrieved from http://archive.stats.govt.nz/StatsMaps/Home/People%20and%20households/2013-census-map-ethnicity-as-a-percentage-of-total-population.aspx.

Statistics New Zealand. (2014). Te Kupenga 2013: Māori Wellbeing Survey. Retrieved from http://archive.stats.govt.nz/browse_for_stats/people_and_communities/maori/TeKupenga_HOTP13.aspx.

Strongman, T. (1984). *The Gardens of Canterbury: A History.* Wellington: AH & AW Reed.

Tau, T. M., Rice-Edwards, A., Tikao, D., England, J., Parata-Goodall, P., & Stevens, M. J. (2016). *Grand Narratives* (Matapopore Ed.). Christchurch: Canterbury Earthquake Recovery Authority.

Truebridge, N. (2017, 03 May). Christchurch Mayor says Garden City needs to clean up if it wants to keep reputation. *The Press.* Retrieved from https://www.stuff.co.nz/the-press/news/92164488/christchurch-mayor-says-garden-city-needs-to-clean-up-if-it-wants-to-keep-reputation#comments.

Twain, M. (1897). *Following the Equator (A Journey around the World).* Released online in 2006: Project Gutenberg.

Wilson, J. (1989). *Christchurch: swamp to city: a short history of the Christchurch Drainage Board, 1875-1989.* Lincoln, N.Z.: Te Waihora Press for the Christchurch Drainage Board.

Wilson, J. (2005). *City Pride, civic trust.* Christchurch, N.Z.: Christchurch Civic Trust.

Chapter 1.5: The Contemporary Indigenous Village: Decolonization Through Reoccupation and Design

Daniel J. Glenn – Apsáalooke (Crow) Nation

Daniel J. Glenn AIA, AICAE, is the principal architect of 7 Directions Architects/Planners, a Native American-owned firm based in Seattle, Washington, specializing in culturally and environmentally responsive architecture and planning. He is a member of the Ties in a Bundle Clan and child of the Greasy Mouth Clan of the Apsáalooke (Crow) Nation of Montana. Mr. Glenn, a graduate of the MIT School of Architecture and Planning and Montana State University School of Architecture, has more than 30 years of experience in architectural practice and he has taught architectural design at the University of Washington, Arizona State University, Montana State University and the Boston Architectural Center.

Prior to colonization, Turtle Island was home to thousands of Indigenous villages. Along coastlines and rivers, on the banks of lakes and streams, in the Great Plains and deserts, in the forests and across the tundra, these villages provided sanctuary, community and housing for countless generations of Indigenous people. They were designed and built in a wide variety of typologies, each reflecting the climate and natural resources of each region and the technology and culture of each tribe. With colonization, the great majority of these communities were destroyed, many systematically burned, like the longhouses of the Coastal Salish, or abandoned following forced removal, with few exceptions—including some Pueblos in the Southwest, and isolated villages in the far north.

For the past several years my firm, 7 Directions Architects/Planners, has had the opportunity and the honor to participate in the design of new housing for multiple Indigenous communities, both in rural and urban areas. Internationally, the design of housing in colonized Indigenous communities has continued as it did throughout the colonial era, with little or no input from Indigenous people. This has played an integral role in the larger colonial project of stripping away our culture and heritage. In the United States, housing in tribal communities has been directed for most of the reservation era by the Bureau of Indian Affairs and by U.S. Department of Housing and Urban Development (HUD). As a young man in the 1980's, I was involved in the design of housing projects for tribes in which the

house plans and site designs were controlled by HUD and the BIA. A 1996 assessment of tribal housing noted that federal housing policies did not, "respond adequately to the diversity of housing conditions and needs in Indian Country," leading to the recommendation that housing programs, "must also accommodate the legitimate demands for self-determination made by Native American tribes as sovereign nations" (Kingsley et al., 1996).

In 1996, Native Americans on a national commission established by the US Congress assisted in drafting the *Native American Housing Assistance and Self-Determination Act* (NAHASDA) to identify alternative strategies for the development, management, and modernization of housing for Native Americans. While the majority of housing developments have not substantially changed in design since NAHASDA, there have been efforts around the country by tribal communities to incorporate the voice of their people more directly in the design and construction of housing and to create more culturally and environmentally responsive housing. Many of these efforts, including some of my own projects, were documented in the study, *Best Practices in Tribal Housing: Case Studies 2013 by the Sustainable Native Communities Collaborative* (2013). The projects discussed below have been carried out after this study was completed.

This paper will focus on four projects carried out by 7 Directions Architects/Planners over the past five years. Through the presentation of these communities and their design, we will explore design of the contemporary Indigenous village, including challenges of reoccupying colonized lands, the integrative design process applied to bring community voice into the design, and considerations in providing for current needs and contemporary lifestyles while reflecting and honoring the traditions of each Indigenous community. All of these projects take place on lands that were reclaimed by Indigenous people after they were taken away through the colonization process. We will begin with an overview of the design and implementation of Plaza Roberto Maestas, a mixed-used urban housing community on land reclaimed through an activist occupation in the 1970s that was completed in 2016. Next, we will discuss a project which is currently under construction, the Stillaguamish Village, a mixed-use and multi-generational community for the Stillaguamish Tribe on 80 acres of reclaimed forested land in Arlington, Washington. We will then review the master plan for a Muscogee (Creek) elder's village in Okmulgee, Oklahoma, on land that once was part of the Indian Territory where the Muscogee people were forced to settle in the 1830s following their removal from their traditional homelands in the Southeastern region of the United States. Finally, we will conclude with a project in Weogufka, Alabama, on land reclaimed by a group of Creek people returning from relocated communities in Florida and Oklahoma.

Contemporary Indigenous Architecture

In the essay entitled, "A Discourse on the Nature of Indigenous Architecture," Professor Hirini Matunga defines Indigenous architecture as, "Architecture from within the people of this place and their relationship with each other; their cultural values, knowledge and principles, their land, environment, geography, and climate. It is architecture using their natural resources, materials, and construction methods and introduced materials, technologies and approaches adapted, adopted, and nuanced to their cultural and social needs. It is also architecture embedded in an ever-evolving Indigenous people and place-based aesthetic using their palette, colors, designs, patterns, geometry, sculptural forms and shapes. In other words, an architecture ultimately redolent of their narrative about their relationships with their place-now, back in time and into the future." The projects discussed below have all been designed to reflect this definition of an "Indigenous architecture."

Re-Occupation

In the fall of 1972, a group of activists began a peaceful occupation of an abandoned public school on Beacon Hill, a diverse neighborhood in Seattle, Washington. The activists were led by Roberto Maestas, a young Chicano teacher of English from New Mexico. The group was seeking a new home for their language program that served seventy Latino students (*History and Evolution*, n.d.). The occupation was one of several similar efforts around the country to gain a foothold in a society that has systematically marginalized Indigenous people and people of color. Two years earlier in Seattle, Fort Lawton, a surplus military compound, was occupied by urban Indian activists led by Bernie White Bear who were seeking the restoration of fishing rights and land in the city of Seattle. The action was a direct response to the removal of Indigenous people from the city a century earlier, in 1865, when the Seattle Board of Trustees passed Ordinance No. 5, which forced the removal of all remaining tribal members from the city (Thrush, 2007).

These two successful occupations led to creation of El Centro de la Raza at the former Beacon Hill School, and the United Indians of All Tribes Foundation at Fort Lawton. The two communities supported one another's efforts both during their occupations and afterward in building their respective organizations. Both have remained on those sites for nearly fifty years, providing invaluable social services and cultural resiliency for the city's Latino and Urban Indian communities. Roberto Maestas and Bernie White Bear were two of the four civil rights leaders from that era who became known as the Gang of Four in Seattle. The others were Larry Gosset, Jr., an African American leader, and Bob Santos, a Filipino American activist. The four leaders worked to unite Latino, Native American, African American and Asian American communities in their mutual struggles for social justice in Seattle, a city which had historically segregated each of these communities from the majority Euro-American population (Santos & Iwamoto, 2015).

Envisioning the Beloved Community

In the fall of 2009, I had the opportunity to meet with Roberto Maestas and Estela Ortega, his wife and partner in the leadership of El Centro de la Raza. The two had been together during the occupation and over the last four decades building what they call "The Beloved Community" at El Centro de La Raza, named for the philosophy espoused by Dr. Martin Luther King. The King Center, founded by Coretta Scott King, defines the concept in this way:

> Dr. King's Beloved Community is a global vision in which all people can share in the wealth of the earth. In the Beloved Community, poverty, hunger, and homelessness will not be tolerated because international standards of human decency will not allow it. Racism and all forms of discrimination, bigotry, and prejudice will be replaced by an all-inclusive spirit of sisterhood and brotherhood (The King Philosophy, n.d.).

At the time, I was the Executive Director of Environmental Works, a non-profit community design center in Seattle that had worked with El Centro for many years. We were meeting to discuss the development of a new housing community adjacent to the former Beacon Hill School building on a one-acre parcel of vacant land owned by El Centro. By this time, El Centro de la Raza had become a highly successful social services organization serving thousands of low-income people every year with a variety of services including a food bank, a bi-lingual child development center, job services, legal-aid services. While providing a central social and cultural hub for the Latino community of the region, the center also served a culturally diverse population as "The Center for People of All Races" (*Our Mission*, n.d.). Roberto and Estela envisioned a large-scale redevelopment of the site that

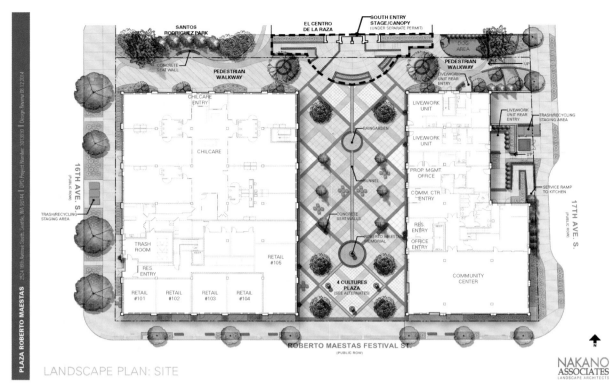

Figure 1. Site Plan of the Plaza Roberto Maestas in Seattle, Washington. Rendering courtesy of the West Studios.

would serve low-income people with affordable housing, expanded childcare services, and retail space for small-scale local businesses, all centered around a large plaza that would become a cultural center for El Centro residents and the surrounding neighborhood.

The vision that we discussed that fall became a reality in 2016, following seven years of community organizing, planning, community workshops, a successful zoning change, fund raising, design and construction. I led the design effort as the Design Architect, first with Environmental Works in the concept phase, then with my own firm 7 Directions Architects/Planners in partnership with SMR Architects in the implementation phase. The project is known as the Plaza Roberto Maestas, in honor of Roberto and his lifelong service to the community. Sadly, he did not live to see its completion, but Estela Ortega succeeded him as the Executive Director of El Centro de la Raza and successfully led the community through development of this vision. The project has become a model in the region for mixed-use, transit-oriented development that serves a diverse community and integrates culture, economy and sustainability on a large scale. The project includes 110 units of affordable housing in two six story buildings that frame a large central plaza with the historic Beacon Hill School at the terminus.

The plaza is designed to reflect the traditional plazas of Mexico, which have roots both in colonial Spanish architecture and Mesoamerican architecture of the Aztec and Mayan cultures. Plazas are the heart of the village,

the town, and the city throughout Latin America. The Latino community in the Seattle area, until now, has not had such a central gathering place. The Centilia Cultural Center, which fronts the plaza on the east side, provides an indoor central hub of activity for social and cultural events. *Centilia* is a *Nahuatl* (Uto-Aztecan) term meaning, "to join together, to become one." The project seeks to provide a place for cultural resiliency in an urban environment. It is at once a home for the Latino community of the region while also a welcoming environment for the diverse cultures of the neighborhood and the city. This is reflected in the culturally significant artwork that has been central from early in the design process. (Fig. 1)

Celebrating the Four Cultures

In the façade of the Centilia Cultural Center, there is a large, two story tile mosaic that overlooks the plaza. The design was created by the Mexican artist Gonzalo Espinosa in collaboration with 7 Directions Architects/Planners. The central figure of the mosaic is a Latina mother, breastfeeding her baby, with her fist raised high in the air. Above her are the images of members of the Gang of Four, Roberto Maestas, Larry Gosset, Jr., Bernie White Bear, and Bob Santos, who come together to support one another in their mutual struggles in Seattle while serving the four communities they represent: Latino, Native American, Asian American and African American. Beneath her are depictions of women from each of those

Figure 2. Nahuatl (Uto-Aztecan) dancers engage in a ceremony during the opening of the Plaza Roberto Maestas in 2016. Photo by Daniel Glenn.

communities raising her up and supporting her. The mural represents several aspects of the community at once. It celebrates the diverse women who are at the heart of El Centro's success and the leadership of the movement for social justice in Seattle. This piece also reflects a Lushootseed (Coastal Salish) creation story called "Lifting the Sky." This is a story about unifying in the face of adversity told to me by a Lushootseed speaker and elder named Vi Hilbert in the early 1990s. It is the story of a time in early creation when the sky had fallen so low to the ground that the people could no longer stand up, and they had to come together to lift the sky back into place. They cut down cedar trees and used them as poles to lift the sky, and all the tribes of the region with all their different languages and cultures had to unify in this effort to succeed. We used this as an allegory for the four diverse communities coming together in Seattle in the civil rights movement. (Fig. 2)

The mural is only one part of an extensive integration of culturally specific artwork in the plaza and the buildings of Plaza Roberto Maestas. We needed to determine creative ways to access funds for these works in a context in which art was not an allowable expense of the funding sources supporting the project. The base of both buildings is reinforced concrete frame with large three-foot wide columns supporting the five floors of wood frame structure above. This lack of funding was solved by a neighborhood design guideline that requires this type of concrete base to be clad in brick, which was determined to cost over $300,000. (Fig. 3)

Figure 3. Columns with inset painted tilework and mask reliefs at the base of the building. Mosaics by artists Louie Gong and Gonzalo Espinoza. Photo courtesy of 7 Directions Architects/Planners.

Figure 4. The sculpture by Casto Solano of Roberto Maestas and Lifting the Sky on the day of the commemoration of the sculpture in 2017. Photo by Daniel Glenn.

We asked the city if instead of brick, if we could incorporate mosaic tile into the base. With the redirected funding, we put out a "call for artists" and brought together a diverse team of local and international artists to develop artwork for the buildings that represent the four cultures. We led a collaborative multi-day charrette with the artists to generate the designs for the 32 columns on each building. We selected a Salish, African, Mayan and Chinese mask to represent the four cultures in a relief that is mounted to an inset at the top of each column, and incorporated into the flooring of the Centilia Cultural Center and the residential floors. The local artists included Cecilia Alvarez, a Cuban American, Louie Gong, a Nooksack and Chinese artist, Al Doggett, an African American artist, myself, from the Crow Tribe of Montana and Kimberly Deriana, a Mandan-Hidatsa architect. The tilework and many of the designs were developed by a team of Chicano, Mexican and Indigenous artist in Tucson, Arizona, led by Gonzalo Espinoza and Alex Garza. (Fig. 5)

At the entranceway to the plaza, Roberto Maestas can be seen striding forward in full figure bronze. (Fig. 4) He stands in front of a striking assemblage of seven tubular steel poles that rise upward for several feet before bending and curling in an abstracted cloud formation high above the plaza. In the summer, water vapor mists from the formation, and multi-colored translucent panels above these clouds cast a rainbow of color onto the plaza in the sunlight. The sculpture is intended to represent the "Lifting the Sky" story with the poles holding the sky aloft. The work is by a Basque artist from Spain, Casto Solano. Solano is known for his work which combines highly realistic bronze figures and architectural scale abstract sculpture. Estela Ortega was adamant that Roberto Maestas be represented in bronze, as she pointed out

Figure 5. Artists and architect team at the El Centro Gala with two of the surviving members of the Gang of Four. Left to right: architect Daniel Glenn, artist Cecilia Alvarez, architect Kimberly Deriana, artist Al Dogget, Gang of Four member Larry Gosset, Jr., artist Gonzalo Espinoza, Gang of Four member Bob Santos, El Centro Board Chair Ramon Seliz, and artist Louis Gong, 2016. Photo courtesy of 7 Directions Architects/Planners.

Figure 6. Stillaguamish tribal members present their concept plan during the "kit-of-parts" site design exercise. Photo by Daniel Glenn.

there are very few people of color represented as bronze figures in the city or nationally.

The Plaza Roberto Maestas represents a form of decolonization of the city. In its origin, its design and in its function, the project represents a small piece of the city that has been carved out to serve and celebrate displaced Indigenous people and marginalized people of color. It is an intentional community, built and managed by a non-profit organization that is led and operated by empowered people of that community. It is a rare instance in which land has been reclaimed from colonizers through occupation and built into a "beloved community" through decades of work.

Stillaguamish Village

High above the banks of the Stillaguamish River, north of the city of Arlington, Washington, a new community is being built by the Stillaguamish Tribe of Indians on eighty acres of forested land that has been reclaimed by the Tribe. The new Stillaguamish Village is part of an effort to rebuild community and culture after more than a century of displacement and the loss of their status as an independent tribe. At the time of the signing of the Treaty of Port Elliot in 1855, which marked the beginning of the reservation era in the Pacific Northwest, there were 20-25 villages along the Stillaguamish River. Like most Salish people of the region after the treaty was signed, the land of these people was taken, their villages and plank longhouses were destroyed, and they were forced onto reservations. Without being granted official tribal status, the Stillaguamish did not receive their own reservation. Tribal members were forced to disperse to

other reservations in the area. Following a fifty-year effort by Stillaguamish descendant Esther Ross, beginning in the 1920s, the tribe received federal recognition only in 1976 (Ruby & Brown, 2001). Since that time, the tribe has been working to regain lost tribal lands, beginning the effort with a small housing community built in 1986 on a site within their original territory using funds from the Department of Housing and Urban Development, which is required by treaty to provide housing to tribal communities. In 2004, the tribe relocated members from the housing site and built the Angel of the Winds Casino near a major transportation corridor north of Seattle, Washington. With the success of this economic development effort, the tribe has been working to buy back their original lands along the Stillaguamish River. And in 2014, the tribe regained Reservation Designation on these lands. In the fall of 2015, our firm, 7 Directions Architects/Planners, was hired to lead development of a master plan for a new Stillaguamish Village on an 80-acre site along the Stillaguamish River, with a design team that includes Herrera civil engineers and West Studio landscape architects. The project is a first effort to build a contemporary version of a Stillaguamish Village in their original homelands.

The first phase of the master plan is currently under construction with completion expected in 2021. The site includes an existing community center and parking area. The remainder of the site is largely forested. Working with the Stillaguamish Tribe's Housing Department, led by Stillaguamish Tribal member Chris Boser, we led a community-based design process that engaged tribal members in an envisioning process to determine uses for the new village and develop the design.

Figure 7. Elders Longhouse structure at the Stillaguamish Village. Photo by Daniel Glenn courtesy of 7 Directions Architects/Planners.

EXISTING

- **A** COMMUNITY CENTER
- ✲ EXISTING CULTURALLY MODIFIED TREE
- – – – PROPERTY LINE

PHASE ONE DEVELOPMENT

- **B** ELDER'S SUPPORTIVE HOUSING
- **C** ELDER'S GARDEN
- **D** ELDER'S COTTAGES
- **E** PAVILION
- **F** FITNESS CENTER
- **G** WELLNESS CENTER
- **H** CANOE SHED
- **I** FIRE CIRCLE
- **J** MEDICINE GARDEN
- **K** NEIGHBORHOOD PARK
- **L** SINGLE FAMILY HOMES
- **M** YOUTH TOWNHOMES
- **N** MULTI-USE TRAIL (GRAVEL)
- **O** FOREST LOOP TRAIL (WOOD-CHIP)
- **P** TRAIL-HEAD PARK

FUTURE PHASES 2 & 3

- **Q** ALL-AGES ADVENTURE NATURE PLAYGROUND
- **R** COMMUNITY GARDENS
- **S** SINGLE FAMILY HOMES
- **T** NEIGHBORHOOD PARK
- **U** SPORT COURT
- **V** TOWNHOMES
- **W** TRAIL TO RIVER
- **X** FUTURE TRAIL-HEAD PARKING

SCALE: 1" = 100'   NORTH

Overall Community Plan
STILLAGUAMISH VILLAGE

HERRERA   7 DIRECTIONS   The West Studio

Figure 8. Master Site Plan for the Stillaguamish Village in Arlington, Washington. Rendering and design by 7 Directions Architects/Planners and the West Studio.

Figure 9. Stillaguamish Village Canoe Workshop, the first completed building in the village. Photo by Daniel Glenn.

The design team facilitated a "kit-of-parts" design exercise with the community in which tribal members developed site plan alternatives using color-coded icons representing site uses and building types placed on a site map. In addition, the design team presented our research on traditional Stillaguamish villages and structures as well as examples of sustainable housing developments as case studies. Through this process, a series of design options emerged and were further developed to be presented back to the community. From these, a "consensus plan" began to emerge. (Fig. 6)

The final plan for the Stillaguamish Village centers around the existing community center. New community facilities are located around the perimeter of the large parking area which serves the community center. These include a Canoe Workshop, a Wellness Clinic, a Boys and Girls Club, a "Plank House Pavilion," and Elder's housing. A large new linear park extends from the community center area and continues down to an overlook of the Stillaguamish River. A parkway road system runs along this park and provides access to three new housing communities that are carved out of the wooded site. The first of these housing communities and all of the community facilities comprise the Phase One development that is currently under construction. The majority of the site's forested land is preserved by the master plan with the new buildings carefully sited to minimize disruption of the forest and to provide a tranquil and wooded setting for the new homes and facilities. (Fig. 8)

All of the buildings and homes for the Stillaguamish Village are designed to emulate the traditional plank longhouses that originally housed the people along the Stillaguamish River. The structures incorporate both the linear form and the simple shed or gable roofs of plank houses, and incorporate traditional materials, including cedar and timber framing. In a hybrid of ancient form and contemporary design, modern materials and technologies are incorporated to create sustainable architecture. (Fig. 7) The intent is to create a new community that is recognizably distinct as a Stillaguamish Village and celebrates the culture of the people, while providing economical, sustainable and durable buildings that respond to the climate and place. Wherever possible, trees harvested from the site are being utilized in the structures, as part of the timber frame construction of the larger buildings or incorporated into the porches of homes.

The Stillaguamish Village is another form of decolonization of Indigenous lands. The development of Stillaguamish Village is a historic step towards the reestablishment of the Stillaguamish people along the banks of the Stillaguamish River where they had lived for millennia. (Fig. 9)

Muscogee (Creek) Nation

In 1830, the United States Congress passed the Indian Removal Act, which forced Indigenous people of the Southeastern United States to relocate, including people of the Muscogee (Creek) Nation. The removal of Creek from their homelands in Alabama and its surroundings began in 1834, when they were forced westward into what was then the Indian Territory of Oklahoma. The forced marches westward led to the deaths of thousands along the way and came to be known as the Trail of Tears. The Creek settled in eastern Oklahoma and established a new government in 1866, placing their capital in the town of Okmulgee, Oklahoma. The Nation had relative independence in their new homeland until Congress passed the Curtis Act in 1998, which ended tribal governments, and the Dawes Allotment Act, which subdivided tribal owned lands into individual allotments. During this period, the Creek Nation lost more than two million acres of land to the federal government and non-Native settlers. They also lost their tribal recognition, which they did not regain until 1970. Since then, the tribe has slowly rebuilt their land and tribal rights from their base in Okmulgee. Like the Stillaguamish, the tribe has been forced to buy back their own land on the open market one piece at a time.

Muscogee Elder's Village on Reclaimed Tribal Land

In 2018, our firm, in partnership with the local firm New Fire Native Design Group, was hired by the Housing Department of the Muscogee (Creek) Nation to design a new housing community for tribal elders on a 36 acre site in their capital city of Okmulgee, Oklahoma. New Fire is led by the Oklahoma-based architect, Jason Holuby, a Muscogee Nation tribal citizen. Our firm was brought onto the team because of our expertise in housing for tribal communities. The site, purchased by the tribe for housing development, is currently farmland bordered on the south and west by non-tribal housing subdivisions. This land parcel is one of many now owned by the tribe, each bought in the process of regaining land for housing and tribal buildings.

Our design team studied the site, which is a largely open field with some stands of trees and three large ponds in the center. We began the design process by studying traditional Muscogee villages that were located in the tribe's original homelands. When the tribe was forced into Oklahoma, they did not rebuild their traditional villages in their new homeland, and as one of the Five Civilized Tribes, they were already largely assimilated into western styles of housing before their removal from the Southeast. However, the tribe has retained a strong connection to their cultural traditions, and tribal members continue to practice traditional dances and ceremonies.

The Muscogee people's traditional villages and structures reflected the culture, climate, and regional materials of their original homelands. This project is part of the larger ongoing effort by the Muscogee people to rebuild and regenerate their cultural traditions, not by replicating those traditional structures, but by reflecting and celebrating them in ways that respond to current needs, technologies, and available resources in their current homeland in Oklahoma.

Traditional Muscogee (Creek) Villages

Traditional Muscogee (Creek) villages were compact communities with homes organized into clan clusters that surrounded a central gathering space of ceremonial spaces and a Council House, which was often a circular structure. The compact villages were a sustainable way of inhabiting the land and left the balance of land for agriculture, hunting and traditional uses. The village structure strongly supported community interaction. A modern version of this village type can similarly be designed to strengthen social connections and support cultural resiliency. The Housing Department staff informed us that while they would like to honor their traditional culture in the development, due to the variety of cultural and religious traditions of modern Muscogee people, it would require a sensitive approach that can be embraced by all tribal members, including those who no longer follow tribal traditions. They also have specific, designated ceremonial sites so they indicated that they do not want to replicate any ceremonial grounds or structures on this site.

Traditional Creek Architecture

The homes, community and ceremonial structures of the Creek people utilized locally available resources and a highly sustainable form of building. The homes were typically smaller rectangular or round houses with open floor plans, gable or hip roofs. The walls were constructed of an earthen wattle and daub type structure with timber framing.

The architecture of traditional Creek culture contains significant symbolism and meaning. The cardinal directions, connection to the seasons, and to the earth and sky and to the movement of the sun, give the architecture meaning. There is the opportunity to imbue some of this meaning into development of a contemporary architecture with cultural resiliency. Another key part of culturally responsive design is the use of culturally significant patterns and colors. After discussions and presentation of other tribal precedents, the Housing Department staff embraced the idea of emulating those traditional forms and utilizing patterns in the architecture through patterned brickwork, concrete panels, tilework, flooring patterns and acoustic wall panels.

Master Plan

During a Design Workshop with the Housing Department staff, a Consensus Site Plan was quickly developed from preliminary site studies conducted by the Design Team. (Fig. 10)

The consensus plan is based primarily on the studies of traditional villages of the Muscogee Nation. The design divides the site into six smaller neighborhood clusters, each with shared open space, as well as a large central park that includes the three existing ponds. Traditionally, the villages were divided into clan clusters, each with their own ceremonial fire and gathering space. Smaller neighborhoods create a sense of community and provide passive site security by subdividing the larger community into smaller residential communities where everyone will be able to know their neighbors.

Like the traditional villages, a fire pit area is included within each cluster for gatherings and family events. The lots are laid out in order to provide views and access to open space from each unit as well as to provide solar access to the units for solar ready homes. The six clusters are located on either side of a large central park. The Elders Center and Picnic Pavilion are in the center of this park at the heart of the site. A roadway system provides two main access points to the site from the main roadway and loops around the central park, providing access to each of the six neighborhood clusters. A one-way loop road provides access to the housing units and creates a shared open space at the center of each cluster.

Elders' Cottages

Initially, the Housing Deparment's intent was to develop a multi-generational community that would include elder's housing as well as family housing. Later in the process, the Housing Department staff determined that their priority is to build housing only for their elders on this site. The floor plans were developed in a "kit-of-parts" exercise during the design workshop with input from housing department staff. The homes are designed to provide a comfortable, affordable, "cottage-style" home with an open floor plan to maximize space. The homes include front and rear covered porches, a single car carport with an enclosed storage area. The simple rectangular form, open floor plan and large overhanging roofs reflect the traditional houses of the Muscogee people. Although the climate in Oklahoma is distinct from the hot, humid environment of their original homelands, the long hot summers of Oklahoma require a similar response to the sun, calling for passive cooling with large overhanging roofs and shaded outdoor space. While the traditional villages of the Muscogee had nearly identical repeated typologies, the contemporary homes are designed with multiple variations in roof type, porch type, colors and materials to create a sense of variety and individuality with repeated floor plans. The homes are

Figure 10. Tom Harjo with the Muscogee (Creek) Nation Housing Authority discussing the preferred concept site layout during a "Kit-of-Parts" Design Workshop with Department staff. Photo by Daniel Glenn.

designed as wood frame structures with a combination of brick and lap siding for durability with culturally expressive patterns in the brick base.

Elders Center

An Elder's Center is planned for the center of the village. The design for the center is based on the traditional round Council House at the center of Muscogee villages. As a modern variant of this structure, the center is designed as a dodecagon. Like the traditional structure, it has a doorway that faces east and which leads into a central round gathering space. This space traditionally was daylit only by an oculus for smoke and light at the apex of the roof. In this interpretation, daylight is brought in from above with clerestory windows through elevating the roof of the gathering space. The gathering space is surrounded by the other programmed spaces, providing circulation for the building in an efficient use of space while keeping activity space visible to visitors to encourage interaction and community building. A southern doorway opens out to a covered walkway leading to an outdoor covered picnic/BBQ pavilion in the same form as the main building. Both the pavilion and

Figure 11. Perspective view of the Muscogee (Creek) Nation Elder Center which is at the center of the new Elders Community designed by 7 Directions Architects/Planners and New Fire Native Design Group in Okmulgee, Oklahoma. Rendering courtesy of 7 Directions Architects/Planners and New Fire Native Design Group.

the gathering space are structured with heavy timber column and beam construction. The base of the building is clad with a cast stone panel that is imprinted with a wind pattern that moves around the entire building. Above, the walls are clad in local sandstone to reflect the building tradition of the region which was used to build the tribe's first council building, a historic structure that remains in the center of the town of Okmulgee. The stone will match the stone on the tribe's contemporary Round House, which houses their courts and is the focal point of their administrative complex in Okmulgee. The intent is to create an architecture that is distinct to the tribe and recognizable to tribal members and visitors as Muscogee Creek. (Fig.11)

Akhvse Tutcenen

The Muscogee (Creek) Elders Housing Community was named *Akhvse Tutcenen* (Three Ponds) by the Tribe's cultural department in the Muscogee language. This commemorates the three ponds that have been preserved on the site and which are the heart of the new community. The tribe intends to stock the ponds for the elders to fish there with their grandchildren. The project begins construction in the summer of 2020 and will include 67 new homes for Muscogee elders.

Akhvse Tutcenen is another form of decolonization by an Indigenous people. The Muscogee (Creek) Nation is rebuilding their culture and their tribal homeland in a place far from their original home. They are building on the lands they were forced to relocate to and which they subsequently lost again in pair with the destruction

of their tribal sovereignty. The resiliency of the tribe is demonstrated in successful efforts to buy back their own land on the open market and to build new communities for their people. This project is just one of many undertaken by the tribe, but it will be the first housing community designed to reflect and celebrate their cultural heritage. (Fig.12)

Ekvn-Yefolecv: Returning to the Earth, Returning to our Homelands

Six hundred and eighty miles away from Okmulgee, Oklahoma, near the town of Weogufka, Alabama, there is a small group of Muscogee people who have undertaken a remarkable effort to return to their homeland and build a new community in their original territory, where they were forced out 185 years earlier. The group is a non-profit foundation called *Ekvn-Yefolecv*, which means Returning to the Earth, Returning to our Homelands in the *Maskoke* language (Maskoke is an alternative spelling of Muscogee). The foundation seeks to build an "Indigenous-led Ecovillage Community" on a 500-acre wooded site near the Appalachian Trail in Coosa County, a remote rural county between Birmingham and Montgomery, Alabama. According to the foundation, the area was once home to thriving Maskoke villages. In 2018 the foundation engaged our firm to develop a master plan for this ecovillage on the site. The project is a more direct effort at rebuilding a contemporary Maskoke village, with the intention of creating an "ecovillage" that reflects the traditional village, built using locally available materials, ceremonial grounds at the center and clan clusters

Figure 12. Overview of the master plan for Akhvse Tutcenen (Three Ponds) Elders Village in Okmulgee, Oklahoma. Rendering courtesy of 7 Directions Architects/Planners and New Fire Native Design Group.

surrounding traditional fires. In its statement of intent, the foundation states that, "the Maskoke community is not only reclaiming a portion of our ancestral homelands for conservation and healthy living, but we are also creating a space to practice our culture, reflective of Maskoke traditional, philosophical, and cosmological worldviews."

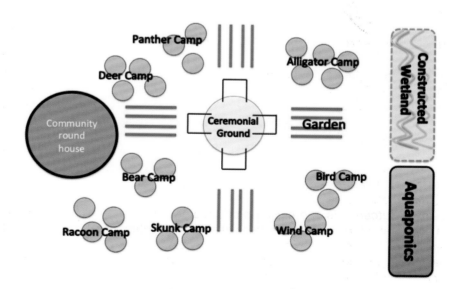

Figure 13. Conceptual Site Plan developed by the organization Ekvn-Yefolecv to guide the site planning for the project. Diagram courtesy of Ekvn-Yefolecv.

The master plan developed for the site includes a planned residential village designed to expand over time as the community grows, ceremonial grounds, and a Council House for community gatherings and education. The larger site includes an agriculture and aquafarm, which will focus on the reintroduction of native species including bison and sturgeon, and a retreat center, which will provide both an income source for the community and a place where the language, culture, and history of the Maskoke people can be disseminated to tribal members and to the larger community.

Marking a presence in their Maskoke homeland, where their language will once again be spoken and their ceremonies practiced, their teachings passing down to new generations is a bold and beautiful endeavor and one that defines the meaning of "decolonization."

Each of the projects discussed above represent distinct efforts by Indigenous communities to decolonize a small part of a colonized land through occupation and the construction of new Indigenous-led communities for Indigenous people. The Plaza Roberto Maestas is an example of a displaced community of Indigenous people establishing a new home where culture, language and art can be practiced and celebrated while providing affordable homes for a diverse community. Stillaguamish Village is providing tribal members an opportunity to return to their traditional homeland along the Stillaguamish River in a sustainable and culturally supportive environment. The Muscogee (Creek) Elders Village of *Akhvse Tutcenen* will provide a home for elders of the tribe on land retaken by the tribe for the benefit of their people. And finally, *Ekvn-Yefolecv* Ecovillage represents a return to traditional homeland and a more radical vision of a future in which Indigenous people seek to build a contemporary version of their ancient traditional villages. Through these efforts, and similar efforts by Indigenous people across Turtle Island, we are seeing concerted efforts towards the decolonization of a colonized land, one small step and one small community at a time.

Figure 14. The project is an ambitious effort in its early stages of design and planning, but it represents a powerful exemplar of "decolonization" of traditional homelands by an Indigenous people. The act of returning to the place where they were forcibly removed and reestablish Figure 13: Overview of the proposed Maskoke Ecovillage in Weogufka, Alabama. Rendering by 7 Directions Architects/Planners.

Acknowledgements

Much thanks to El Centro de la Raza, the Stillaguamish Tribe of Indians, the Muscogee (Creek) Nation, and the *Ekvn-Yefolecv* for the honor and privilege to work with your communities. Thanks to the staff of 7 Directions Architects/Planners, including Luis Borrero, Kimberly Deriana, and Laila Montenegro, and our many collaborators in the design of these communities. Thanks also to my daughters, Eleanor Pryor Glenn and Lucyanna Farwell Glenn, for assistance in editing this text.

References

Blosser, Jamie; Corum, Nathaniel; Glenn, Daniel; Kunkel, Joseph; Rosenthal, Ed ; *Best Practices in Tribal Housing: Case Studies 2013*, Prepared by the Sustainable Native Communities Collaborative for: U.S. Department of Housing and Urban Development Office of Policy Development & Research (PD&R) November 2014.

History and Evolution. (n.d.). http://www.elcentrodelaraza.org/history-evolution/.

Herbig, C., et al. *Assessment of American Indian Housing Needs and Programs: Final Report.* Washington DC: Department of Housing and Urban Development.

Matunga, Hirini. A Discourse on the Nature of Indigenous Architecture, pages 303-330, *The Handbook of Contemporary Native American Architecture*, edited by Elizabeth Grant, Kelly Greenop, Albert Refiti, and Daniel Glenn, Springer, 2018.

Native American Housing Assistance and Self-Determination Act (NAHASDA) Washington DC: Department of Housing and Urban Development.

Our Mission. (n.d.). http://www.elcentrodelaraza.org/aboutus/.

Brown, John A. et al. *Esther Ross: Stillaguamish Champion*, University of Oklahoma Press, 2001.

Santos, Bob and Iwamoto, Gary *The Gang of Four: Four Leaders, Four Communities, One Friendship,* Chin Music Press, 2015.

The King Philosophy. (n.d.) https://thekingcenter.org/king-philosophy/.

Thrush, Cole. *Native Seattle: Histories from the Crossing-Over Place.* University of Washington Press, 2007.

Figure 1. Steel columns.

Chapter 1.6: Seeking Cultural Relevancy in Diné Communities
Finding a Center Place in Modern Diné Buildings

Richard K. Begay Jr, Diné – Navajo Nation

Richard is an architect—an artist and a visionary. Richard was born in Ft. Defiance, Arizona which is in the heart of the Navajo Nation. He has practiced in Arizona since receiving his Bachelor of Architecture degree from the University of Arizona's School of Architecture. With over a decade of design leadership and mentoring, Richard has emerged as a leader in Native American design—weaving contemporary esthetics with traditional inspiration.

His design approach, rooted on culturally sited responsive design, explores the boundary between people and place stating Indigenous design naturally includes the spiritual, the human cultural aspect, and a revered connection to the natural world—where living in balance with nature exist. This intrinsic teaching places us in harmony with the natural world. He explains, "Children are taught early fundamentals of the overarching philosophy on the interconnectedness of people and place, both of which are inextricably linked."

Richard has been featured in Aboriginal Architecture— Living Architecture, a 2006 Mushkeg Productions Inc., in co-production with the National Film Board of Canada and in association with APTN. He has contributed to several publications relating to culture and design and has presented at conferences, colleges, and universities. Richard is an Associate and design leader for SPS+ Architects in Scottsdale.

WE ARE CONNECTED TO MOTHER EARTH

We are connected to mother earth. We are the five-fingered children of Diné Bikéyah—simply speaking, we are children of nahasdzáán shi ma ("mother earth"). To strengthen this sacred connection, Diné families adhere to traditional teachings of placing a child's umbilical cord beneath the soil. In doing so, the child symbolically transitions from the care of their natural mother to being nourished by their earthly mother.

Families observed traditions of the young. During the first few weeks, the umbilical cord dries and detaches naturally. Parents are obligated to bury this sacred feature beneath the soil near the child's homestead within the four sacred mountains. This bond ensures our connection to

the natural soil, the air, plants, and water as these elements nourish and heal. My cord is buried at Tselani-Cottonwood community near my paternal grandmother's land.

Figure 2. Kids in mud.

CRAFT

Growing up deep in the heart of the Navajo Nation was adventurous. From the high plateau desert with sandstone monuments, to high ponderosa growths, there were many places to explore. There was no such thing as being lost in dense foliage during a fall crisp morning or being bombarded by evening summer mosquitoes near the sheep corral. We enjoyed the day's timeclock. My cousin, brothers, and I were obsessed with constructing tools from nearby trees. At times we fabricated archaic-looking weapons made from juniper branches. In some notion, design was occurring. Who knew tactile exploration became a foundation for learning. A further example of our *juvenile creativity*: We would gather tree sap from ponderosa, pinyon, and junipers, mix it into the size of a baseball and place it at the end of a stick. We would then ignite it and to our surprise, a sparkling display of colored fire balls dropping to the ground followed. The smell of beautiful red fire drops, green to blues, and even yellow hues followed by a soft pitch sound remains a permanent memory.

Figure 3. Sheep Corral Morning.

Figure 4. Water Flow.

Figure 5. Lavendar Bloom.

Figure 6. Landscape water tank.

Figure 7. Cornfield base.

Figure 8. Sheep Paths.

Working for master rug weavers. As young children, little did we know the importance of various plants and dry tree bark were to my grandmother and aunts. My cousins and I were often instructed to gather juniper bark and oak leaves from nearby hillsides or from plateau flats up on Balakai Mesa. As simple of a task it was for us, we were oblivious to the purpose of our mission. The passages of orchestrated tasks and simple living in rural northeast Arizona would nurture a fundamental understanding of Diné way of life. Seeing the rabbitbrush shrub give way to a marigold-yellow color dye for carded wool in boiling water was basic for quite some time. Over time, the appreciation of the artistic process of rug weaving as a Craft combined with the concept of playing on earth, in earth, and with earth inspired me to seek a unique and experimental path towards design.

Retrieving materials from open trash pits, tree bark, and even from sheep corrals was a popular pursuit. Finding the best pinon tree to create our own tree house was a journey. We knew to stay away from trees that were struck by lightning and to not harvest wood from ancient structures. Salvaging plywood or palettes from grandmother's sheep corral was easy and resourceful. The plywood was perfect to place horizontally between tree branches. Our tree space was simple and functional though temporary. The gaps in the corral gave way to our thievery.

It is through these experiences of salvaging and constructing in an area limited in resources yet abundant with natural materials that has led to a path of curiosity and discovery. Seeing our uncle construct the family's dome structure in various locations was intriguing. The original cedar logs were cut nearby. In addition, the tree bark was gathered locally along with soil from the adjacent footprint. The bark was used as infill material between the horizontally stacked logs. The soil was mixed with water to a workable mortar and placed firmly into the joints. The composition was of Place.

Designing in nature should be natural and straightforward. The natural environment is by design where there exists a natural order in the universe—with rain clouds, the rocks, and the trees. Understanding there is a spiritual connection to the universe and to the six sacred mountains of Diné Bikéyah. It is essential to design structures to Place, to its origins. By doing so, structures "Will last and tell a story," (Vigil Gatewood, Pawnee/Diné). Simple and resourceful building will be the most economical and ecological way to construct—and for structures to embody a cultural authenticity of their context.

As a Native American architect, understanding of Place is foundation; and listening to our elders is a way of inheriting critical knowledge of who we are as indigenous people. As children we are taught to respect the world we live in; to understand there is interconnectedness, acknowledging a sense of mystique, and to know there is a delicate ratio among junipers, the canyons, and water as they provide a way of sustaining life.

ARCHITECTURE AND BEAUTY

The Diné-built environment is both modern and traditional. The trajectory of modernism on native lands has done little to inform self-identity yet has accelerated the way housing and even larger communities are developing. To build fast has always been a driving force due to many variables, most due to rural factors. Traditional structures are constructed by a simple methodology rather than how fast it can be constructed. Songs touch on Beauty in the sense of wholeness or interconnectedness and how buildings are part of a process of living in balance. What is considered beauty to an elder medicine person is different from another person. The medical person sees beyond the ochre color sunsets. He sees traditional structures as shelter or places of spiritually simple to construct and places of refuge.

Beyond the three-dimensional structures, there exists a symbiotic link to nature, to the cosmos, the seasons—an element of timelessness. The Diné term for this is called Hozhó ("beauty"). The organic forms found in nature not only inspire, they provide a foundational framework to regional placemaking. For example, my grandmother's corn field is located at the base of Balakai Mesa. It is located strategically as it receives flows from rainstorms coming off the tributaries. Not only is this a great example of settlement planning, it is a historical precedent as to how Diné families or clanships are organized around food sources and grazing patterns. The typology of the built environment from traditional structures to larger community buildings provides a visual contrast between a modern architectural language and the *rarity and beauty of the Diné culture.*

Figure 9. Hogan morning.

Figure 10. Landform light texture.

Figure 11. Log house.

Figure 12. Plaster window.

With such deep meaning and purpose of Hozhó relating to architecture, there are discrepancies between the modern structures and the beauty of Place. Shelter has always been the basic function of habitable dwellings. As a designer, I have thought extensively on finding solutions for better living conditions for the Diné. As with other communities, the housing conditions in Native America is considered alarming. Introduction of creative ideas is needed to further develop pathways towards realistic solutions for a place that is described as a spiritual threshold between earth and sky. Concepts of innovation should not be limited to experimentation but should include viable long-term planning and implementation.

Costly resources and inadequate funding mechanisms have disrupted the process of affordable housing. Comparing cost per square foot, there is approximately a difference of $80 to $100 per square foot within the price of a home being constructed on the Navajo Nation compared to urban living structures in Phoenix, AZ. Rural Diné become fluent with various lending opportunities as viable solutions. However, when financing issues associated with the entire construction become clearly visible, many families tend to withdraw from the concept of home ownership. The process of *buying a home* is a foreign concept and most elderly Navajos living in rural areas are not familiar to this process, especially with fixed incomes.

In addition to insufficient technical assistance, changes in leadership, and availability of land, both the family parcel and densely populated communities have become the framework for low initial investments between planning and sustainable development. As a result, community buildings and housing structures deteriorate more rapidly, resulting in costly repairs and restorations. However, many of these rehabilitation periods express a unique, tangible vernacular of modern industrial materials mixed with loose facades of varying materials. For example, a dwelling originally constructed with logs and plaster on the exterior facade may now include concrete block, wood siding, or painted plywood. In addition to this mixing palette, there are volumes of rooms complementing the original form in a random yet functional juxtaposition. A typology of form and materials articulates the landscape as a tectonic that is greatly attributed to land, culture, technology, politics, and economy.

When you travel in the heart of the Navajo Nation, people will generally build with simple methods of construction or utilize resilient strategies such as salvaging. As a designer, I find delight and inspiration in seeing a Chevy engine hood used as the gate to a palisade sheep corral.

There is beauty in prayer, in rug weaving—even with light and textures found in landforms and strata. Natural water paths and the sprinkle of pollen floating from cornstalks create a background for how structures interact and are properly sited on the landscape.

To fully comprehend the meaning of *beauty* beyond what we may understand of the Diné, it is essential to seek a better understanding of people and place along with how structures become a framework for social, ideological, and ceremonial meaning and purpose. Beauty in architecture exists.

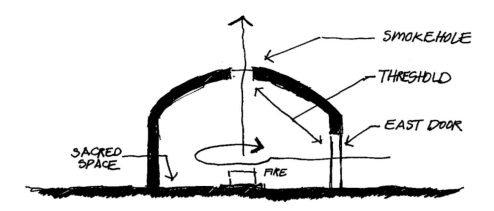

Figure 13. Hogan section diagram.

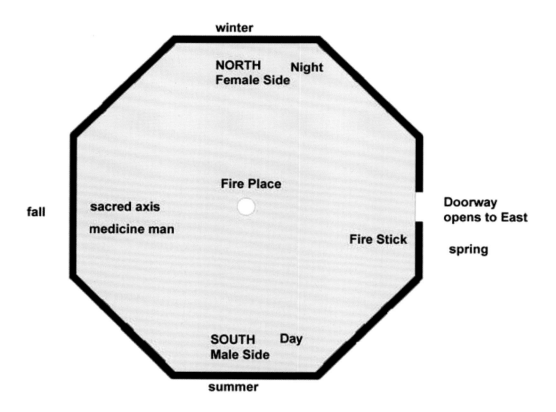

Figure 14. Hogan floor plan.

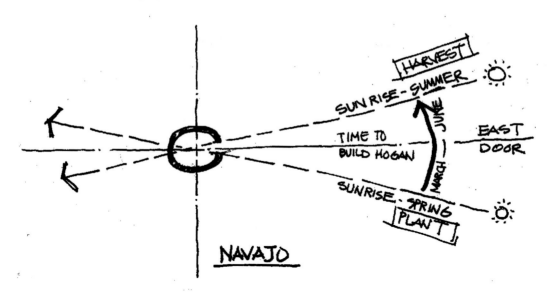

Figure 15. Hogan time to build.

THE CENTER PLACE

Diné family settlements show several homes clustered next to each other—mostly by the mother's daughter(s). In addition to these dwellings there are other structures within the homogenous landscape. They include shade arbors, sheep corrals, sweat lodges, and earth ovens. One of the most important spaces within this cultural landscape is the female Hogan, or "hooghan." This structure is the center of family, or simply the Center Place. It represents the spiritual center where all elements of nature and the Diné's way of life are expressed in their physical forms and proper apertures. The doorway faces east to align with where the sun rises. From here, thoughts arise with first light of day. This is the threshold to enter while the smoke hole is centered above the fire hearth. The top opening is functional in allowing smoke to escape yet it is the spiritual threshold connecting earth to sky. When families enter the Hogan in a clockwise protocol around the hearth, they become the link between mother earth and father sky.

The floor plan of the Hogan inherently represents special points relating to concepts of duality, cardinal directions, day and night, and lifeways. Songs and prayers are essential—they instruct how and when ceremonial structures are used, planned, and constructed. Family settlement planning involves locating a Hogan near permanent ranches. They should not be located near previous ancient ruins, flood areas, or in high wind patterns. Hogans are constructed utilizing modern materials due availability and ease of construction techniques. Traditional Hogans are less visible since their tectonic construction relies on scarce cedar logs.

INDIGENEITY

Change is needed. Housing entities such as the local Tribally Designated Housing Entity (TDHE) or collaborations with higher education institutions are accelerating the path for housing opportunities. However the push for creative ideas is limited to the status quo, whether leadership or funding. The financial model should also be a steady precedent along with exploring new sustainable materials in addition to researching common materials such as wood, earth and perhaps the use of straw bales. Exploring adaptive reuse and implementing recyclable materials is advantageous as it minimizes carbon footprint impact and can be visually pleasing when used as a building material.

Figure 16. Hogan afternoon.

Figure 17. Daugther and Aunt in Cornfield.

Progress towards Indigeneity. In southern Utah, there are several homes being designed and constructed with simple palette of materials such as wood, metal, and earth. The University of Utah's DesignBuildBluff is a community outreach design-build program aimed at creating pathways for sustainable healthy living for southern Utah Diné families. The program involves placing student teams near a family's homestead within the chapter community to design and construct a habitable dwelling. Students adapt to rural areas by spending several months on site. Diné families, as the beneficiaries, offer temporary residency and opportunities to share traditional teachings and history. By strengthening these types of successful partnerships and moving past what could be labeled as a trophy opportunity, goals are achievable. The benefit is simple, to improve the way of life by providing safe, affordable homes that are visually appealing, resource efficient and easy to maintain.

Exploring the use of Straw bale as a building material is another alternative. Use of wheat straw bales as a load bearing material has several advantages relative to cost. It is grown and harvested through Navajo Agricultural Products Industry near the Four Corners, therefore is readily available as a regional material. It inherently has high thermal resistance resulting in lower heating and cooling cost and is easily constructed using mildly skilled personnel. From a cultural context, straw bales would be suitable. As a by-product of wheat, it is comparable

to corn stalks. Corn is considered sacred. It has many traditional uses and is symbolic in the Diné's way of life and stories. It is used in several delicacies such as alkan ("cake") during the Kinalda or coming of age ceremony for young girls. Harvesting of the corn and gathering of the pollen is the first part of a closed loop process. The by-product is the remaining stalk. The stalk is collected and placed nearby in a tree or in a barn. It will be food for livestock during the winter. The closed loop process follows traditional teachings of limiting food waste. Like building with traditional materials that are not overly processed, corn stalks are encouraged to return to the earth. Therefore adapting wheat straw bales, as a building material, may seem prudent.

Navajo structures, whether constructed of lumber, logs, or straw bales, are quite fascinating in appearance since they represent a sense of place between cultural traditions and a relationship to the land.

As indigenous designers and architects, it is our responsibility to contribute "gifts"bestowed among us by bridging an authentic way of planning from seven generations prior to the next seven generations.

Figure 18. Logs.

MODERN AND TRADITION

Interpretation of the Center Place - an exploration of incorporating traditional Diné culture in larger facilities.

Senator John Pinto Library, Diné College Shiprock Campus, Shiprock, New Mexico USA

Architect: DLR Group Year 2008.

Designers: Richard K. Begay Jr and Karl Derrah

Senator John Pinto Library, located in Shiprock, New Mexico near the Four Corners, is a tribal college facility deeply rooted with traditional Diné concepts in its well-considered design. It is a modern, unique building with secular well-lit spaces and a Hogan-inspired room that seeks to restore the link between traditions of storytelling and importance of education and language.

Tribal colleges, such as Diné College, have excelled in pursuing and gaining accreditation by blending tradition with modern concepts of whole teaching and learning. The college's mission has always been to provide educational opportunities for the Diné, especially the youth. Its strength has centered on critical education with self-determination by integrating economic, social, and political concepts with Diné history and language.

Then Diné College President Ferlin Clark. "A new library at our Shiprock campus is vital towards increasing educational opportunities for students within the northwest region of New Mexico." The library was not only to become a facility to expand the current needs of the campus, it was stated to be one of the more unique, highly visible structures to incorporate Diné values in its architectural design.

The Consultation Process.

To transcend the ordinary and be truly unique, a thorough understanding of the phrase hózhóogo naasháa doo ("in beauty I walk") must be embraced. It is a phrase which conveys the internalizing principles/philosophy of Diné Knowledge towards Sa'ah Naagháí Bik'eh Hózhóón; translated as living in balance with nature to a state of Hozhó ("beauty"), where harmony exist between self, nature, and natural order of the universe.

It was important that a harmonious design process informed a framework for planning the new library, where authentic Diné values of Sa'ah Naagháí Bik'eh Hózhóón were embraced and exercised. Prior to completing the design phase, each team member participated in an abbreviated "beauty way" ritual to ensure protection and that proper planning of the facility was exercised in context. It was held in a traditional Hogan north of the Campus near the San Juan, River. Words such as harmony and beauty embodied the concept of Hozhó. "From here on, there will be blessings," narrates an

Figure 20. Steel columns.

Figure 21. Library west.

authentic point of Diné philosophy and its impact on planning and design structures.

The team, both architects and builder, sat in protocol inside the traditional Hogan. The healer's paraphernalia was placed appropriately on the west cardinal opposite the east doorway. The healer himself sat north of his place-setting ensuring the ceremonial act was conducted according to songs and prayers.

Enriched with Diné wisdom, the team developed planning and design goals that would guide decisions throughout the design and construction process. Goals such as welcoming spirit, cultural relevance, and conversational character poised not only as genuine touchstones for planning, but for how the structure, over time, would remain relevant.

Building as "elder passing down knowledge"

The existing master plan for Shiprock campus reflects a similar approach to the central campus located in Tsaile, AZ—where the concepts of Diné philosophy informs the organization of campus site plan. Using the circle as a structural form, buildings such as the library are prearranged according to concepts of Sa'ah Naagháí Bik'eh Hózhóón, which is the educational philosophy of the college. The concept of Sa'ah Naagháí Bik'eh Hózhóón is learning through:

> (Nitsáhákees) East – Beginning of day, thinking commences.
> (Nahat'á) South – Planning and learning, conducting life skills.
> (Iiná) West – Living, empowering the mind.
> (Siihasin) North – Assurance, fulfillment, knowledge, and wisdom.

Arrival to the campus is from the east leading to a parking lot and a roundabout. Entry into the campus follows the cyclical, clockwise movement of sun reinforcing ideological values associated with each cardinal direction.

With purpose, the library was sited north of the existing classroom building. It is here the library, with its soft curved forms, will coexist with the strongly constructed hard forms of the classroom building—both acting as wisdom elders for students and community. The library is positioned northerly, held to Siihasin or towards the direction of wisdom and knowledge.

Near the library's entry, hardscape, and landscape plantings are organized by the building's curve forms and honor traditional plant field patterns. Early cornfields were planted with distinctive patterns, each with meaning and holistic purpose. One pattern, a clockwise spiral, was used to represent harmony. Gentle circular landscape forms represent these traditional "corn fields" to honor the past and provides a welcoming spirit to the library.

The building responds to the holistic world view of Diné teachings by integrating traditional forms such as the Hogan. A central gathering space otherwise known as the Storytelling Room is shaped similarly to a traditional Hogan. It is uniquely clad in blue, translucent panels—evoking the color of ceremonial smoke rising from fire in daylight—and likewise transcends to the color of the sky above. The room's doorway faces east to allow sunlight to penetrate the interior between the months of August and May through a vertical slot in the building's east wall. The width of the slot is spatially dimensioned to where the sun rises on each third week in August and May, thereby enriching the educational space throughout the school's calendar year with blessings associated with eastern morning light: Ha'a'aah.

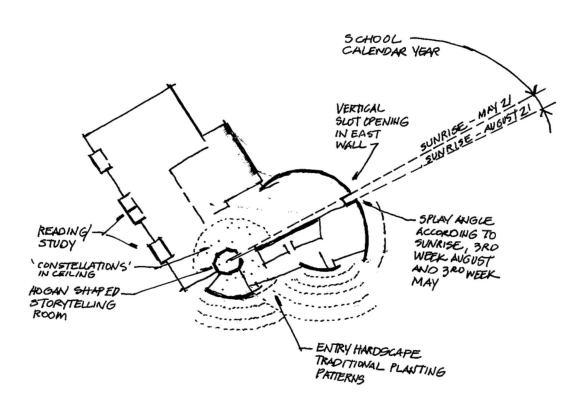

Figure 22. Floor plan diagram.

Figure 23. Blue cladding.

Figure 24. Stars.

Figure 25. Scale.

Beyond the Hogan's blue cladding, steel columns anchor the sacred Center Place in a rare abstract: to symbolically tell the emergence story of the Diné. The columns represent long reed grass stems. It is told through Dine' Bahane ("story of the Navajo") the emergence from previous worlds to the current world was on a reed grass stem. The steel columns, each cut to various lengths, cater to a natural organic appeal yet they are critical and expressive of an earth-sky relationship.

So' Bah Hane' (Story of the Stars)

Outside the Storytelling Room, light fixtures are purposely arranged in star constellation patterns to further reinforce Diné teaching of the importance towards the seasons and concepts of family. The constellations Nahookos Bika'ii (Big Dipper) and Nahookos Bi'aadii, (Cassiopeia) represent the father and mother of the family, or protectors of the family. Both constellations revolve around central fire hearth, Nahookos Bikq ("north star") and are significant at early spring and autumn evenings when they are visible in the northeastern sky. By integrating Stories into form, the building seeks to represent an authentic way of incorporating songs and prayers, history, stories—for children and community.

Seeking cultural relevancy in Diné communities is truly a socially driven practice. It starts with listening to those who will inherit the building. It is the idea of seeking special tactile moments and determining how to manifest a culture's life-long journey into a built structure of materials and light. It is a journey of awareness and discovery. For us, the design of Senator John Pinto Library is a modern architectural artifact that preserves culture in abstract and, exquisitely, ensure its "appropriateness to Place"—whereas the building itself recedes and the spatial experience is both compelling and celebrated.

Truly, we have touched on seeking a modern Center Place.

Chapter 2.0: Not Dead Yet

Timmah Ball – Ballardong Noongar

Timmah Ball is a writer and urban researcher of Ballardong Noongar descent. Timmah holds a Masters of Urban Planning and a Bachelor of Creative Arts, both from the University of Melbourne. She has written for The Griffith Review, Right Now, Meanjin, Overland, Westerly, Art Guide Australia, Assemble Papers, The Big Issue, The Lifted Brow, the Victorian Writer magazine and won the Westerly Patricia Hackett Prize for writing.

The architect enters the room
Wearing a black velvet blazer
Crisp white shirt, skinny leg jeans
A caricature – oozing "starchitect" cool
He's won the tender
To design an Aboriginal health centre
He's saving our lives
One commission at a time
He promises community engagement
Indigenous design through collaborative consultation
Hand in hand
We'll Reconcile
Treaty unsigned
Another scrap in the pile

The meeting starts
MacBook Airs charged, iPhone on silent
His portable projector
Boldly animates the wall
With technical drawings, gum leaves, and kangaroo paw
His young assistant smiles with eyes that beguile
Their knees uncomfortably close
And a suffocating power clenches the room
His presentation ends with a photo
A black hand holding a white hand
Cos' it's all okay

Nothing ever happened here they say

Mobs gently start to share their stories
But the loudest voices are white
The complexity of colonisation erased
Although a white council officer knowledgeably explains
That the design should reflect the river
White voices drown out community who sit silently by the end
I guess they speak better than we ever can

The "starchitect" leaves smugly
Muttering how he likes to explore Australia's deep cultural dimension
Another project to boast about
Bringing cred and status to his illustrious career
The health centers vital
But no one can guarantee
There'll be free services
For those in need

Back in the office
I sit at my desk
On the thirty-fifth floor, my window
Lingers on the William Barak building
An Aboriginal leader
Designed by a white man
Gazes down Swanston Street
Moving through the city
Other identities thrive
On the periphery;
Street art by Lisa Kennedy
On an old postbox in Bourke Street
A torn Gary Foley poster

Clinging to the railway's underpass

Fierce, fighting, alive
Denied a spot in the public eye
And I wonder if
A living black face
Could ever exist
On a 31-storey building

Cos' whose land is it anyway?
A bunch of white academics from RMIT proclaim
Another urban planning conference on the way
Colonial property rights will be erased
Alternative living, squats, and co-housing
Yarning circles and lemon myrtle flavors
The new themes of our progressive left-wing white saviours

Anti-eviction and anti-gentrification
We need to re-organise our neo-liberal property relations
Squats for the rich and a high interest mortgage for the poor
Just before they decolonise us all

Chapter 2.1: Blak Box

Kevin O'Brien – Kaurareg and Meriam

Kevin O'Brien is a descendent of the Kaurareg and Meriam people of north-eastern Australia. Kevin founded Kevin O'Brien Architects in 2006 and joined BVN Architecture as a principal in 2018. Kevin is based in Brisbane and was Professor of Creative Practice at the University of Sydney from 2016-2019. Kevin's work is based on the idea of "Finding Country" previously exhibited as an official collateral event of the 2012 Venice Architecture Biennale. "Finding Country" as an ongoing project attempts to address the questions of urban invasion and territorial claims; questions that Kevin has extended through four spheres of action: profession, academia, creative practice and community service. Kevin's current focus is in understanding the inherent scientific capital that enabled Aboriginal people to exist in harmony with Country for over 50,000 years.

BLAK BOX

The following explanation of the Blak Box project is written from my perspective as a practising architect engaged to complete a commission with cultural and technical requirements.

BACKGROUND

In June 2017, I was invited by Urban Theatre Projects (UTP) in Bankstown to design a pavilion that would enable a deep listening experience. The purpose of the experience was to connect the visitor to concepts of Indigeneity through sound and form. It was also to consider a construction methodology that would ensure it could be assembled and dissembled with ease throughout Australia with minimum labour and cost.

CONTINUITY

The central challenge of the project was to create a room for sound. Research led me to the central courtyard of the Holyoake Cottage in Hawthorn by Michael Markham of FIELD Consultants (winner of the Victorian Architecture Medal in 2000). This courtyard, formed by unequal glass panels and doors, define an asymmetrical round in plan.

Under foot is timber decking and above is a waterhole to the sky. Here, under the shade of a tree a place for sound exists as a setting for conversation.

Commonly misunderstood as a homage to the Roy Grounds House (winner of the Victorian Architecture Medal in 1954), the actual origin of the courtyard can be found in a room on the second level of the Villa Snellman in the outskirts of Stockholm by Eric Gunnar Asplund circa 1917. This unusually formed room complete with timber panelling, a fire place and a window was understood to be the perfect room for conversation due to the multiple decentralised focal points removing reverberation.

This asymmetrical round was not blindly copied into the plan of Blak Box. Where Villa Snellman had fire, and Holyoake Cottage a water hole, Blak Box was bound to the ground.

COUNTRY

When Indigenous people in Australia speak of country it is understood in a special way. This is not limited to spiritual and sustainable relationships but in the context of this project it shall suffice to characterise this connection as one of belonging. The intent of Blak Box is to travel throughout many Countries on this continent. I could not think of a better way to remind the visitor of the Country they stand on other than by exposing the ground and offering a direct physical connection.

Furthermore, the original design proposal included the burning of the ground prior to the erection of the structure to extend an olfactory condition and remind the visitor of the traditional use of fire.

REPRESENTATION

In plan, the asymmetrical round is in a square. Unlike the Holyoake Cottage the faceting of the polycarbonate panels is calibrated to full panel widths. Unlike Villa Snellman, it has only one opening. Unlike either it has the natural ground underfoot. What is shared, however, is the presentation of a setting for sound.

Figure 1. Blak Box interior. Image by Barton Taylor, used with permission.

The presence of opposing conditions has always held my attention and the opportunity to continue this exploration was offered in two ways. Firstly, the daytime solid appearance of the structure is rendered translucent through the watery effect of the polycarbonate panels at night. And secondly, the reduction of form is such that the regularity of the external square is contradicted by the irregularity of the internal round. Both ways permitted the use of light as a further contribution to the experience.

The architecture of the Blak Box endeavours to locate an idea of Indigeneity as an interdependent condition with global connections. It stands in direct opposition to the anthropological pursuits that historically isolate and classify Indigeneity as being separate from the modern world, thus affecting a false sense of purity in the past prior to contact. It follows that attempts to re-present Indigeneity as a matter of shape is patently flawed.

Blak Box presents the end point of a process concerned with the articulation of a cultural setting and the resolution of technical conditions.

PERMANENCE

Blak Box utilises a lightweight aluminium frame bolted together and clad with screw fixed polycarbonate panels. The roof is made of interlocking insulated panels. It takes a team of four up to five days to erect and install. The reconstruction of the structure is its permanent condition, rather than the structure as permanent construction. This means the relevance of the project is in the appetite for commissioning new sound and light compositions for each location.

To date, two installations have occurred. The first of three annual instalments at Barangaroo was in June 2018. The sound piece was titled "HumEchoChorus"

and combined soundscapes and oral histories of the Barangaroo harbour headland. The second installation was in January and February this year at Blacktown as part of the Sydney Festival. The sound piece was titled 'Four Winds' and combined haunting stories of the Darug people and their experience with the intergenerational effects of colonisation. From the 1st-17th of November this year, Blak Box will return to Barangaroo with a new sound piece and accompanying light show titled *Momentum*. The theme of this new piece is that the past has not passed and uses the 1983 music video for David Bowie's "Let's Dance" as a starting point.

AGENCY

In 2001, the Jewish Museum was opened in Berlin. The design was led by Daniel Libeskind, an architect of Jewish heritage. In 2004, the National Museum of the American Indian was opened in Washington, D.C. The design was led by Douglas Cardinal, an architect of First Nation heritage. In 2016, the Smithsonian National Museum of African American History and Culture was opened in Washington, D.C. The design was led by David Adjaye, an architect of African heritage. These examples share an idea in common, that of agency.

For projects with significant cultural credentials at stake, it follows that agency and therefore agents of that culture, should be included from beginning to end. The preceding examples demonstrate a position where the elevation of culture informs every part of the process and project. I look forward to the day Australia pursues cultural projects with a similar maturity. As a practicing architect I naturally argue for the involvement and design leadership of architects of Indigenous heritage with similar ambitions and capability.

Figure 2. Blak Box at night. Image by Barton Taylor, used with permission.

UTP's business is culture. It creates storytelling works from western Sydney and takes them to the world. In commissioning Blak Box as a storytelling project for Indigenous peoples, UTP understood that a cultural project of this nature required Indigenous people from beginning to end. On the client side, Liza-Mare Syron, on the sound composition Daniel Browning, on lighting Karen Norris, and myself as architect. UTP extended a genuine respect for my Indigenous heritage, how it informed my world view together with recognition of my ability as an architect.

Blak Box may not carry the gravitas of a permanent cultural monument, but it does have a keen sense of culture as a living condition invested in agency.

Figure 3. Black Box approach at Barangaroo, Sydney. Image by Barton Taylor, used with permission.

Chapter 2.2: The Whare Māori and Digital Ontological Praxis

Reuben Friend – Ngāti Maniapoto

Reuben Friend is an artist and curator of Māori (Ngāti Maniapoto) and European-New Zealand heritage. His current work as the Director of Pātaka Art+Museum in Porirua, Wellington since 2015 provides strong opportunities to work with leading Indigenous artists from Australia, North America and the Pacific Rim. Previous to this he was the Senior Advisor for Treaty Relations at the Wellington City Council where he helped to develop the Waka Eke Noa Effectiveness for Māori Strategy. From 2009 to 2013 he worked at City Gallery Wellington as the Curator of Māori and Pacific Art, curating numerous exhibitions with leading Aotearoa New Zealand, Australian and Pacific artists.

In(Digi)nous Aotearoa: Virtual Histories, Augmented Futures

Virtual histories are a genre of fiction writing that apply a "what if" scenario to history to suggest how the world might look today had events of the past played out differently. For example, what would the world be like today if Christopher Columbus had not discovered the Americas? Or, what if Abel Tasman had not discovered Aotearoa New Zealand? Of course neither Columbus nor Tasman were responsible for discovering either of these lands, and it is these types of virtual histories that are perpetrated as truthful historical accounts which indigenous artists often seek to address in their art.

Digital mediums hold huge potential to address and critique these types of incorrect historical misconceptions, with modern day digital technologies being both mobile and instantly accessible online. For Māori artists, however, the use of digital mediums to house and transmit information raises ethical questions around kaitiakitanga (guardianship) of sacred knowledge and the appropriateness of making cultural material accessible online. In 2017, Pātaka Art Gallery and Museum in Porirua, Wellington, brought together a group of Māori digital artists whose artworks addressed these types of virtual histories. The themes that emerged from this project centred around a question of how customary structures derived from the marae atea (ceremonial courtyard) and whare whakairo (carved meeting house) might inform a Māori digital ontology – culturally specific

ways of considering how Māori knowledge might be stored, labelled and accessed online in accordance with Māori values and worldviews.

The exhibition was titled *InDIGInous Aotearoa: Virtual Histories, Augmented Futures* and it was exhibited at Urban Shaman Aboriginal Art Gallery in Winnipeg, Canada in 2017. In developing this project, a conceptual *whare* was established in the name of *Te Uira*, the Māori personification of lightning. This grounding provided the conceptual framework to house and accommodate conversations about Māori art and knowledge in the digital age. This philosophical basis was conceptualised by artist Kereama Taepa whose virtual *waharoa* (gateway) occupied the central area of the exhibition space. Wearing a headset, viewers saw a greenstone gateway levitating in the centre of the gallery, acting as an entrance and also as a *mauri* stone.[1]

At the entrance of the gallery, fashion, and textile artist Suzanne Tamaki's AR-enhanced photographs of Māori women took centre stage as both the *mauri stone* and *karanga* (welcome call). Through the use of a smart phone app, the photographs became coded semiotic forms, concealing AR digital replicas of Māori *taonga* (treasured objects) housed in Te Papa's collection. These coded digital images could only be accessed through the *InDIGInous Aotearoa* app, suggesting a possible avenue for Indigenous communities to manage access to, and security of, cultural material in the digital age.[2]

Reweti Arapere and Johnson Witehira created digital poupou (carved pillars), printed and AR-enchanced representations of carved ancestral figures, arranged in the gallery in accordance with the customary structures of a *whare whakairo*. Completing the exhibition were Rachel Rakena and Rangituhia Hollis, whose works could be viewed as virtual *marae atea* spaces through animated environments projection-mapped onto objects

---

1. It is customary to place a *mauri* stone at the base of a new house before it is dedicated and opened to the public as a symbol of the *mana* (prestige) and *mauri* (energy) of the people who occupy the house.
2. For more on the InDIGInous Aotearoa app created by Planbeta go to https://www.planbeta.co.nz/indiginous-info.

Figure 1. Kereama Taepa's virtual waharoa, or gateway, can also be viewed on a VR headset and monitor hanging in the middle of the room. In the background Rangituhia Hollis's *Oko Ake* (2016) projection shows imagined worlds and animated environments from the artist's childhood. Photo courtesy of Urban Shaman Gallery, 2017.

or explored through digital environments.

The following is an abridged version of the exhibition catalogue that accompanied the exhibition.

Virtual Histories

Dr Johnson Witehira's 2016 videogame, *Half Blood*, wastes no time in throwing the book at virtual histories surrounding the settlement of Aotearoa New Zealand. Built on a simple 2-D scrolling platform game format, *Half Blood* places gamers in the role of an early nineteenth century European missionary in Aotearoa New Zealand who is attempting to convert the local Māori communities to Christianity. Armed only with "the good word," gamers are tasked with repeatedly throwing bibles at various Māori characters until they are "civilised" and adorned in Western attire. Ostensibly presented as a comical depiction of the process of colonisation, *Half Blood* makes serious reference to the role that Western academic and religious writing has played in the erasure of customary Māori knowledge and cultural practices. (Fig. 2)

The title of the game, *Half Blood*, refers to the idea of losing blood, or life points, within a game.[3] Witehira invokes this term as a response to his personal position as an artist and academic of both Māori and European colonial settler heritage. In seeking to reconcile this "half-blood" duality, Witehira proposes video games as an alternative site to work through difficult histories, outside of formal academic and fine art forums.

To facilitate this discourse further, Witehira has developed a second version of the game in which the avatar is an early Polynesian navigator who has recently arrived in Aotearoa New Zealand. Players of this game set out to kill the now extinct Northland seal colonies of Aotearoa New Zealand. Here Witehira seeks to address virtual histories on both sides of his family tree, with this iteration of the game being an attempt to confront stereotypes of Māori as "ecological warriors" who are supposedly in tune with nature and the environment. In

---

3. Tamati-Quennell, Megan. *Wheako whakarara. Side by side.* Auckland; Objectspace (2016) p.2 http://archive.objectspace.org.nz/.

Figure 2. Dr Johnson Witehira's 2016 videogame *Half Blood* in *InDIGInous Aotearoa: Virtual Histories, Augmented Futures,* Urban Shaman Aboriginal Art Gallery, Winnipeg, Canada, 2017. Photo courtesy of Urban Shaman.

Figure 3. Kereama Taepa's 2008 videogame *Space Invasion* in *InDIGInous Aotearoa: Virtual Histories, Augmented Futures,* Urban Shaman Aboriginal Art Gallery, Winnipeg, Canada, 2017. Photo courtesy of Urban Shaman.

doing so, *Half Blood* presents some difficult ethical and moral decisions for both the developer and players of the game. By reducing complex cultural histories down to a simple linear gaming narrative there is a risk of disconnection between the intent of the artist and the level of cultural understanding possessed by the viewer.

As a proposition, *Half Blood* provokes questions about cultural safety and cultural competency in the digital age, and for the indigenous artist and digital developer it raises questions around how best to reconcile the appropriate mode of representation for indigenous characters and narratives within gaming environments.

Māori sculptor, printmaker, and game developer Kereama Taepa was confronted with the need to develop a personal ethos around this issue in 2008 when he released the first iteration of his *Space Invasion* video game. The video game took the original characters from the famous 1980s arcade game and reshaped them into symbols of British monarchy and government. As the game progresses, these figures slowly descend on to a small Māori whare (house) that players of the game can control at the bottom of the screen. (Fig. 3)

The game was intended to reference the process of colonisation, the loss of Māori sovereignty, cultural material in Aotearoa New Zealand, and this mode of representation has found similar success with North American First Nations artists such as Nicholas Galanin (*Space Invaders*, 2013), Steven Paul Judd, and Elizabeth LaPensée (*Invaders*, 2015). However, LaPensée argues that the technical limitations of these types of gaming platforms present difficulties for indigenous artists and developers who are seeking to address more complex cultural narratives.[4]

So how might indigenous digital developers create gaming platforms and interactive digital environments that are capable of conveying complex cultural narratives in a manner that is also respectful of cultural worldviews and sensibilities?

Taepa has sought to reconcile this question by developing a philosophical basis for his digital art practice that is premised on customary Māori belief systems. His conceptual framing draws on Māori art historian Jonathan Mane-Wheoki's 1999 essay for the *Hiko! New Energies in Māori Art* exhibition at the Robert McDougall Art Annex in Christchurch. In this essay, Mane-Wheoki declares that Te Ao Hiko (The Age of Electricity) has officially arrived with the advent of the roro-hiko (the computer, or more literally translated "electric-brain").[5]

---

4. LePensée, Elizabeth. "Games as Enduring Pressence", in *Indigenous Art: New Media and the Digitall; Public Art Culture Ideas* v37 n54, ed. Igloliorte, Heather, Julie Nagam, and Carla Taunton. Toronto: York University, (2016) pp.189-183
5. Mane-Wheoki, Jonathan. *Hiko ! New Energies in Māori Art.* Christchurch; Christchurch Art Gallery (1999) p.2 www. christchurchartgallery.org.nz.

Figure 4. Kereama Taepa's VR headset hangs in front of his 3-D printed whakapi sculptures in *InDIGInous Aotearoa: Virtual Histories, Augmented Futures,* Urban Shaman Aboriginal Art Gallery, Winnipeg, Canada, 2017. Photo courtesy of Urban Shaman.

Taepa argues that the idea of an "electric-brain" was not a new concept for Māori. He locates a customary basis for this assertion via the eponymous Māori ancestor Te Uira who is said to exist as the personification of lightening. Given that the human brain processes information via electric signals, Taepa argues that all manufactured objects, both real and virtual, are created as a result of electronic processes. For this reason he believes that there should be no difference in the cultural value or tikanga (cultural protocol) of taonga created in physical or virtual space. Rather, Taepa posits it is our relationship with the manufacturing processes of these objects that needs to be reconsidered. (Fig. 4)

For Taepa, the ability to sculpt in virtual reality environments, where he is able to overcome the laws of physics and gravity, enables him to carve taonga Māori in a way that would be impossible in physical space. Taepa then 3-D prints these objects, a process he refers to as whakapī – meaning to "make like a bee" – a term which he uses to communicate a Māori understanding of 3-D printing as an additive manufacturing process. This differentiates 3-D printing from the reductive process of customary Māori wood carving called whakairo – meaning to "make like a maggot".

Augmented Futures

Augmented reality is another digital platform that is finding success with many Māori artists and digital developers who are seeking to engage with more complex histories and narratives within their storytelling. As a medium for artistic exploration, augmented reality allows for real-time interactions between objects in the physical world and interactive online digital content, enabling indigenous artists and developers to communicate layered stories and experiences onsite at places of interest to indigenous communities.

Figure 5. One of Suzanne Tamaki's AR-enhanced images placed on a plinth triggered a digital replica of a mauri stone on the phone. Ironically, this taonga is a forgery that was sold to the Dominion Museum but was of such high quality that the museum has chosen to retain it in the collection of the Museum of New Zealand Te Papa Tongarewa. Photo courtesy of Urban Shaman Gallery, 2017.

Māori photographic artist and fashion designer Suzanne Tamaki has been collaborating with Māori digital developer Joff Rae Kopu and his team at the Immersive Space Programme to develop an augmented reality application especially for Māori artists. The project seeks to suggest how indigenous communities might assert ownership over intellectual and cultural material in the digital age. The project has a specific intent in providing Māori access to taonga held in museums and private collections around the world.

Tamaki has named this project *Augmented Reality Taonga (ART)*. *ART* uses pixel recognition technology to create trigger points within Tamaki's photographic works which, when viewed through a smart phone, generate virtual digital replicas of Māori taonga sourced from the Museum of New Zealand Te Papa Tongarewa. Each of the 3-D generated objects featured in the application appear to be Māori carvings made in the nineteenth century when steel tools introduced by European traders led to new innovations in whakairo Māori. (Fig. 5)

These objects are however merely examples of high quality forgeries that were fraudulently sold to museums and collectors in Aotearoa New Zealand. Tamaki and Rae have sought to reclaim these forgeries by 3-D scanning them and turning them into digital code. These scanned objects now exist in cyber space where they can be displayed as Māori replicas of European replicas of Māori taonga. In this way Tamaki takes ownership of these high-end forgeries and presents them as "virtual taonga."

Using the same application, Māori mark-maker and street artist Reweti Arapere has employed a layer of augmented reality to his sculptures and drawings as a means of engaging with new generations of young Māori. Arapere believes that this new generation, having been raised as "digital natives" from birth, expect to be able to drill down into deeper layers of information about real world objects via online content. The layers of augmented reality in Arapere's artwork activate Māori language text that appears to emerge from the mouth of each of his graffiti-style sculptures and drawings – a relatively simple gesture that plays an important role in normalising Māori language in everyday interactions. (Fig. 6)

For new generations of indigenous people, digital experiences are an integral part of their identity and to a large degree their sense of personal worth can be attributed to the types of online interactions they engage in. As a teacher and an advocate for at-risk-youth, Arapere has seen strong possibilities in digital media as a tool to reconnect young Māori people with their ancestral language and customs. As Arapere states, "there is no sustainability if we don't focus on our rangatahi (young people)."[6]

6. Reweti Arapere, artist interview recorded by the author on 25 October 2017.

Figure 6. *Whānui Atua* (2017) ink on card by Reweti Arapere in *InDIGInous Aotearoa: Virtual Histories, Augmented Futures* exhibition. Photo courtesy of Urban Shaman Gallery, 2017.

Mapping Virtual Space

While video games, 3-D printing, virtual reality and augmented reality artworks continue to present exciting possibilities for how Māori and indigenous artists internationally might engage with digital media in the future, certainly the most common form of digital Māori art practice at this moment in time is large scale, immersive projection installations featuring animated or filmic moving image environments. The most notable of these being Lisa Reihana's blockbuster exhibition *In Pursuit of Venus [infected]* shown at the Auckland Art Gallery in 2015, and *Emissaries* shown at the Venice Biennale in 2017.

The 2001 exhibition *Techno Māori: Māori Art in the Digital Age* held at Pātaka Art+Museum and City Gallery Wellington surveyed the work of Reihana and several other prominent Māori artists to explore how digital media might operate within a Māori paradigm.[7] One of the younger artists in the exhibition was Rachael Rakena. Rakena's works in the exhibition featured a series of digitally manipulated photographs showing

swimmers diving into a pool of digital text. Rakena titled the series *rere-hiko* – meaning flowing-electricity or electrical current – as a means of responding to the sense of impending dislocation from personal interactions and physical connectedness that online interactions had introduced. As she notes in her artist statement in the then-innovative CD-ROM exhibition catalogue,

> I have continued to use images of swimmers immersed in water with no references to land to explore the idea of shifting identities; of the freedom that might exist in an undefined space with no place to stand, no tūranga [place to stand], and maybe no responsibilities. This has been mixed with emails, a relatively new forum for kōrero (dialogue) amongst the iwi (nation).[8]

At the time these new forms of communication and other emerging possibilities of cyber space were alien territory for many Māori artists and activists who had exerted a lot of time and energy locating themselves firmly within the political and cultural environment of Aotearoa New Zealand. As Rakena goes on to state:

---

7. Mills, Maree. "Pou Rewa, the Liquid Post, Māori Go Digital?" in *Indigenous Art: New Media and the Digitall; Public Art Culture Ideas* v37 n54, ed. Igloliorte, Heather, Julie Nagam, and Carla Taunton. Toronto: York University, (2016) p.17.

8. Rachael Rakena. "Rachael Rakena, Artist Statement", in *Techno Māori: Māori Art in the Digital Age*, Wellington; City Gallery Wellington, Pātaka Art + Museum (2001) CD-ROM.

Figure 7. Images of children running through water are projected onto ceramic blocks placed onto a glass-like black table-top in *Everything between you and me* (2017) by Rachel Rakena and Hana Rakena on display in *InDIGInous Aotearoa: Virtual Histories, Augmented Futures.* Photo courtesy of Urban Shaman Gallery, 2017.

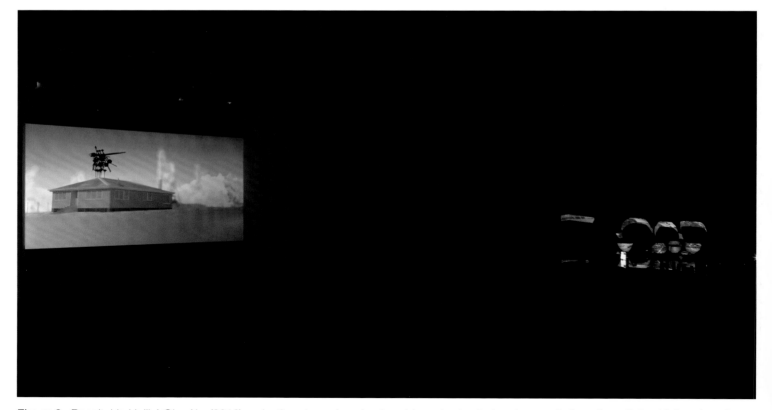

Figure 8. Rangituhia Hollis' *Oko Ake* (2016) projection shows imagined worlds and animated environments from the artist's childhood, and on the left is *Everything between you and me* (2017) by Rachel Rakena and Hana Rakena on display in *InDIGInous Aotearoa: Virtual Histories, Augmented Futures.* Photo courtesy of Urban Shaman Gallery, 2017.

One of our key points of reference in identity is the whenua [land], our tūrangawaewae [ancestral lands]. By taking this reference away I am exploring new places that we might identify with and relate to or from.[9]

As technology has advanced over the past two decades, Rakena has sought out increasingly innovative means of exploring these virtual spaces and ideas around disconnection. Utilising 3-D projection mapping technologies, Rakena has been able to manifest virtual spaces into physical realities. Her projection installation, *Everything Between You and Me* (2017), on display in *InDigiNous Aotearoa*, was made in collaboration with her sister Hana Rakena. In this work Hana and Rachael's children are seen projection mapped onto Hana's hand sculpted ceramic vessels. The children appear to run across the surface of the vessels, splashing and playing in a pool of black water. (Fig. 7)

The artworks continue Rakena's sustained investigation into water as a metaphor for both connection and dislocation. As Pātaka Exhibitions Officer and Māori moving image artist Bridget Reweti notes in her essay in this catalogue, Rakena locates a customary foundation for this concept in the Tongan idea of vā (or wā and wāhi in Māori), meaning a space between two distinct points. For many Oceanic cultures, water can represent the vā ("space") between two island nations, but water also provides the means of connection – a duality that resonates with contemporary ideas of connection and disconnection inherit to online interactions.

This interest in exploring the recent past and the unknown future through digitally constructed environments is shared by Māori digital animation artist Rangituhia Hollis. Hollis' largest work to date, *Oko* Ake (2016), was created entirely with animation software used in the film industry. The work consists of a three channel projection installation and an immersive soundscape that looks at the interconnectedness of the contemporary world, an idea which Hollis explores within the context of his local environment.[10]

Beginning with an ominous old black Ford Cortina cruising through the night, Hollis makes specific references to the in-between spaces that he experienced as a child, travelling between the small rural Māori communities of his whānau (family) in Waipiro Bay and Hawkes Bay on the East Coast of the North Island of Aotearoa New Zealand. From there the scene shifts to an urban city environment, specifically the home where the artist lived during his years of study at Auckland University's Elam School of Fine Art. The subsequent

scenes and cityscapes slowly fly the viewer through a digital elevation of Auckland's Queens Street, in the central city, where insect-like robots hurriedly scurry up and down apartment blocks and office buildings. Floating up and down the exterior wall of one of the buildings is a giant golden graffiti-like sculpture that spells out the word *Hawaiki* – the ancestral homeland of Māori prior to the settlement of Aotearoa New Zealand. (Fig. 8)

The environments in Hollis' work present dual rural and urban perspectives on the Māori concept of tūrangawaewae (place and belonging), something that is similarly explored in Rachael Rakena's works. These artists use this mode of presentation to process their thoughts around ideas of connection and disconnection, concepts that are vitally important in an increasingly impersonal digital age.

All of the technologies and artworks featured in *Aotearoa* suggest possible avenues for indigenous futures, enabling indigenous communities to assert control over intellectual and cultural material. But perhaps most importantly, they operate to culturally and geographically ground the artists and their communities as indigenous peoples in the digital age. This, as Mane-Wheoki has said, is a process of "acculturating and indigenising the new technology for creative and expressive purposes."[11]

9. Ibid.
10. Bruce E Phillips, *Rangituhia Hollis, Oho Ake* . Auckland; Te Tuhi (2016) p.1 www.tetuhi.org.nz.
11. Mané-Wheoki, "The Resurgence of Maori Art."

Chapter 2.3: Rangi's Turn

Elisapeta Hinemoa Heta – Ngātiwai, Wāikato Tainui, Samoa

Elisapeta Heta is an engaged and politically active artist and graduate of architecture. Brought up in West-Auckland / Tāmaki Makaurau, she was entrenched in the realities of urban Māori and second-generation diaspora Pacific Island families. She is now a Senior Associate at Jasmax, where she co-founded the Waka Maia collective, which works within design teams to embed a Māori world view into design outcomes, to facilitate political and cultural conversations, and to support in the upskilling of the office and its' understanding of Te Ao Māori (the Māori world).

Elisapeta is interested in how space and place can have a positive impact on the lives of the communities in which they function, and takes every opportunity to mentor, support and run outreach programmes for Māori and Pacific Island youth. She has had significant involvement with many collectives, including Architecture+Women NZ and Ngā Aho – the national network of Māori design professionals. In 2016 she was co-opted to the Board of the New Zealand Institute of Architects to help implement Te Kawenata o Rata (a covenant) between Ngā Aho and the NZIA, recognising Te Tiriti o Waitangi.

Preamble

This story came about during the *Indigenous Placemakers Residency* on Menacing Island (Toronto Islands in Lake Ontario) in the lands of the Missassaugas of the Credit First Nationals People, of Toronto. (Toronto, Canada). The residency enabled many of us to consider what "placemaking" might mean considering many of our Indigenous world views would suggest that we are made by place, which then enables us to make places/spaces; that we are given agency because of place, we are not giving place agency, or in extreme cases taking agency away (like in the case of oil pipelines going through waterways). Therefore, often a tension ridden dynamic arises between multiple and conflicting world views of Indigeneity and modern-day colonialism, capitalism and individualistic human-centred thinking. During the residency, I chose to take the time to write prose, and poetry that would attempt to articulate this tension. Drawing from personal experience, second hand and

witnessed accounts, I sought to blend past, present and future, seen and unseen. The narrative below is an example of a contemporary tension whereby some non-Indigenous practitioners, having learnt some basic Māori language and cultural skills, see themselves as culturally competent. However, some wield this perceived cultural competence in a way which makes clear they lack a deeper understanding of the political landscape and cultural nuances that sit at the heart of Māori knowledge and understanding. It shows how a little bit of knowledge can be used to actually diminish and demean Indigenous people given that colonisation has severed many of us from our language, culture and confidence to stand as cultural experts. Yet the narrative offers hope asserting that we have the ability to weave our emotional journey back to place and language, despite disconnection and trauma, in the hopes of discovering traces of healing.

Ngā mihi
Elisapeta

Rangimarie looked around the room, shaken.

"Steady yourself, girl."

She held back the dam of trembling waters in her body, cross that she might be visibly unsettled. Normally, her face could rest steady and almost defensive. But today –

"They can't know you"re scared."

Or scarred, she realised.

The man in front of her, stood. Speaking in that "I learnt enough te reo to feel culturally superior" way. He was so good at drawing out. Dangling his sentences from the heke when he needed to. Above everyone, morally, physically. Towering.

Tee-nah kow-tow kar-tow-ah

His h e a v y annunciation ripped through her ribs.
She felt her shoulders sigh: "How dare he speak for me?
        … I wouldn't know what to say
    anyway."

Tears prickled at the back of her throat.
Though Rangi never met her Nanny, this was a familiar ground. An overwhelming feeling that her Nanny would have looked on, heartbroken.

The nostalgic longing for a guiding hand dug its way back out of the earth and hung from Rangi's chest. As if she was wearing generations of shame around her neck. She clasped her taonga in her right hand.
Is this manaia for protection, or is it a noose?

It seemed like nothing more than the never-ending reminder of what she could not do.

(softly)
Kāo, baby.
Breathe.
Breathe.

> *koh Marcus tar-ku in-gow-a*
> *koh n-gah-ti parkehar a-haw*
> *me-heh artu ki te arh-tu-a,*
> *teenaa, kow-eh[1]*

She was sure she could feel thunder crackle in the air. As if the atoms were cringing.
Her hair stood on end. Wiri. Wiri.

> *Te pou*
> *Te pou*
> *Te tokotoko i whenuku*
> *Te tokotoko i whērangi*

She bit her lip; positive it was bleeding.
That it was bleeding in her language.
That it would bleed her out into a drain in the earth and that maybe she could slip away to the sea?
And that no one would notice.
"What was Marcus mumbling now?"

> *re-ray re-ray-haw pie-maaar-re-ray*
> *hay me-he key tay fa-ray nay*
> *tee-na kow-eh*

Sssssnap! The ihi hissed around her ears.
"Did he just introduce himself before acknowledging anyone else?
The gods?
The Atua?"

Crrrrrack! The humidity in the room sparked;
sweat, in the centre of her
lower spine

> cough, cough.

Marcus looked around the room, pausing for effect.
The pou took no notice. Slept.

> *hay me-he key tay haw kai-n-gah*
> *Tee-na kow-taw*

She could feel pulsating up her legs.
Is this what "waewae tapu" meant?
Was "tapu" creeping into her body through her legs because of the lava flowing out of Marcus's mouth?
A rumbling, rupturing ripped in every vein.

… and she wanted to cry her saltwater tears

> *Hay me-he key ar parpar tuuar nookoo,*
> *Tee-na ko-weh eh tay fi – re*

SLAM! A door out of site, shut so loudly that everyone in the whare jumped.
Even the pou woke, winced and the tukutuku now looked slightly off axis.

Marcus stopped.

> *Aue! Ha ha ha.*
> *He teenoh "breezy" nai-ar-nei, nehh?*

The taumata shuffled, sniffled, waited.

Kōtiro

Rangi's head whipped around. No one sat behind her, but she could hear –

E, kōtiro.
Do not be afraid
Calm your heart

> *Uh. Um. Ahem.*
> What was that?
> Why is Rang-gee speaking?
> Marcus, at this point, turned to stare at Rangi,
> as if to tell her to be quiet,
> but she wasn't speaking so who –

Rangi felt her ears pop to the beat of her heart.
"Is Marcus shuffling in his spot?" Rangi thought: "Why is he looking at me?"
She looked behind her again
"He … he never looks flustered. But he's gone all red and I –

Calm your heart

And remember

– who is talking to… me?"

A light chuckle
As the wind,
As the walls, she
was gently laughing

A pīwaiwaka flew into the whare and landed at the feet of the pou tuarongo.
Hine-nui-te-pō watched.

… kōtiro

Rangi's head was spinning.
She could see little dots in the corners of her eyes, sprinkling through the room.
She clutched to the heart shaped leaf in her pocket that she grabbed as she walked onto the ātea, today.

āe, he rongoā
my girl, you are safe
breathe.

A fantail!

"Oh no."

Rangi knew that Marcus had read something, somewhere, once upon a time about fantails being tohu – a sign – but he didn't know what of.
He was interrupted midway through reading that story, he told Rangi that lunch break, cornering her, the only Māori girl in the office, because "he the needed to take his son's to ripper rugby, and then the kids to the mall and –" Rangi lost interest by then…
But Marcus, he was "sure he understood the idea, because he got that spiritual stuff … ya know?"

Rangi remembered feeling as if she pushed a smile as far to the front of her face as she could every time she heard Marcus tell the story about fantails being a "tohu".

He liked the way "a sign" felt.
It made him feel good.

He carried on with his mihi.

Ar-piti hoe-no tar-tie hoe-no

Twitch

Tay hu n-gah mar-tay key tay hu-n-gah mar-tay

Pīwaiwaka looked right at Marcus.
Rangi watched, curious what the tohu saw…

Ar-piti hoe-no –

"Im sorry" mouthed Rangi, instinctively to Pīwaiwaka.

She wanted the manu, the whare, and the whenua to know, she had tried to find her way home
She had tried to prepare.
But where do you start, alone in Te Pō?
Exactly there,
Darling,
In your potential

Her colleagues had told her they wrote the agenda, for today, and they knew that tikanga meant that Marcus should speak.
And they knew that meant she had to sing a song
and they said that means she sits at the back because "women didn't speak in the olden days, and they only wanted the 'pow-firi' to last 10 or so minutes."
So of course, Rangi the Māori girl who couldn't argue, did what they "knew."

Even though her dreams the night before, had tipped her up-side down. And parking up in the carpark today, and looking at the ātea, nothing felt distant anymore. She couldn't place her finger on why but. Something felt
She felt –

Tar-tie hoe-no tay hu-n-gar oar-rah key tay hu-n-gar oar-rah

Tangihia tangihia,
Kōtiro hoki mai tōu roimata
You know this place,
your skin
feels it

Whare creaked as Tawhirimatea blew hau into its cobwebs.
Rangi could feel the wind on her back. Pushing, nudging, trying to encourage her wairua out from under the dirt.

K ō t i r o !
Whakarongo
Tītiro

At this point her colleague Rachel, loudly opened her waiata booklet, clearing her throat for Te Aroha.
The lights in Rangi's eyes strobed brighter.
Tāwhiri blew.

Kaua e whakamā
The voice said, firmer now
But shaking too, as if
It was also

... crying

Rangimarie realised her face was wet.
All at once:
Piwaiwaka flew straight at Marcus's face, causing him to duck and stumble.
The wind blew Rangimarie to her feet.

Wailing began
Aue te mamae
E hine...

Thud.
Marcus, was pushed to sit by hands not there.
Rachel stunned.
Both of their faces contoured like the whakairo, tilted and mouths open.

Rangimarie wailed softly, unable to hold back the ocean in her chest.
Her heart ache cracked to the surface, unbound by constrained frames of time.

Marcus managed to splutter
Ran-gee what –

"This man does not speak for me" her voice sounded old.

The taumata softly smiled

Kia ora

Tenā Koe, Bub

They sat upright and listened.

"My name is Te Rangimarie o te Whenua,
and I think...
I'm sure that...
This...
s my marae...
I have not been to this whare since my Matua died when I was two.
He named me.
His name was Pīwaiwaka.
He was cheeky, and beautiful but was lost to me, as was this place, until today."

The pou all watched

The tukutuku straightened

Pī returned to the ngahere,
His job done.

"I know I had lost my way, but no one else will speak for me again."

Glossary

ātea	or Marae ātea is courtyard – the open area in front of the *wharenui*
atua	God, gods, deity, ancestor with continuing influence
hau	wind, breeze, breath
heke	Expressed rafters in the ceiling. All parts of the "wharenui" or carved house have anthropomorphic relativity to that of the ancestor it represents. As such the rafters are part of the rib cage.
Hine-nui-te-pō	the goddess of "Te Pō (the underworld), she receives the souls of the dead into the underworld
ihi	essential force, excitement, thrill, power, charm, personal magnetism – psychic force as opposed to spiritual power (*mana*). Sometimes describes as an electric energy
kāo	"no"
kia ora	hello, thank you, an informal hello, an acknowledgement or statement of recognition of what someone has said or done, in approval
kōtiro	girl
manaia	stylised figure used in carvings
manu	bird
Māori	indigenous New Zealander, indigenous person of Aotearoa New Zealand; normal, usual, natural, common, ordinary
marae	courtyard – the open area in front of the *wharenui*, where formal greetings and discussions take place. Often also used to include the complex of buildings around the *marae*
matua	father, chief
mihi	an informal speech of acknowledgement, introductions and thanks
ngahere	forest, bush
pīwaiwaka	see also (shortened) Pī; fantail, *Rhipidura fuliginosa* – a small, friendly, insect-eating bird of the bush and domestic gardens which has a distinctive tail resembling a spread fan; important in the story of how humans became mortal, they can bring warnings of death, or messages from beyond the physical realm
pou	post, upright, support, pole, pillar, goalpost, sustenance; support, supporter, stalwart, mentor, symbol of support, metaphoric post – someone, a group, tribe, gathering or something that strongly supports a cause or is a territorial symbol, such as a mountain or landmark, representing that support
pou tuarongo	back wall post of a meeting house – supported the ridge pole in the back wall of a meeting house. The back wall of the house is representative of the realm of the dead, the intangible, or the past
powhiri / pohiri	see also the misspelled ""pow-firi""; welcome ceremony
taonga	precious item of significant meaning and importance
tapu	be sacred, prohibited, restricted, set apart, forbidden, under *atua* protection
taumata	distinguished orators, speakers" bench
Tāwhiri-mātea	see also (shortened) Tawhiri: god of the winds, clouds, rain, hail, snow and storms
Te Aroha	the name of a very commonly sung waiata (song) at pōwhiri
te reo	literally means "the language", colloquially used to mean the Māori language.
Te Pō	the dark, a state of being, one of the stages/times of the night and in the creation of the world
tikanga	correct procedure, custom, habit, lore, method, manner, rule, way, code, meaning, plan, practice, convention, protocol – the customary system of values and practices that have developed over time and are deeply embedded in the social context
tēnā koe	a formal hello, to one person
titiro	look, inspect, examine, observe, survey, view
tohu	sign, mark, symbol, emblem, token, qualification, cue, symptom, proof, directions, company, landmark, distinguishing feature, signature

tukutuku	ornamental lattice-work - used particularly between carvings around the walls of meeting house
waewae tapu	newcomer, rare visitor - a person who has not been to a particular *marae* or place before; literally translates to scared (tapu) legs/feet (waewae)
waiata	song, chant
wairua	spirit, soul – spirit of a person which exists beyond death
whakairo	carving, carvings
whakarongo	listen
whare	house, shortened term for wharenui (big house) or whare whakairo (carved house) the main structure on a marae
wiri	to tremble, shiver, shudder, shake, quiver.

Further explaination

"Te pou. Te pou. Te tokotoko i whenuku. Te tokotoko i whērangi..."   "*The supports, The sustenance. The provision/protection from Papatuanuku. Provision/ protection from Ranginui (above)...*"

This is the beginning of the lyrics to the moteatea (chant), well known

in the tribe of Ngāpuhi

"āe, he rongoā"   "yes, (it is) medicine"

"Tangihia tangihia, kōtiro hoki mai tōu roimata"   "girl, let out your tears! Mourn, grieve"

"Kaua e whakamā"   "do not be ashamed"

"Aue te mamae. E hine"   "Oh girl, oh the pain…"

The far-right column of text is Marcus's point of view. This is largely to illustrate him verbally delivering a "mihi" or a speech of acknowledgement within the welcome ceremony but has been written in the way te reo Māori (the Māori language) is phonetically heavily mis-pronounced by non-Māori, with heavy New Zealand accents. Losing the beauty, meaning, nuance and poetics of the language and its place within a sacred exchange.

Chapter 2.4: Niimii'idiwigamig – Anishinaabe Roundhouse a place of connection

Eladia Smoke – Anishinaabekwe from Obishikokaang

KaaSheGaaBaaWeak/Eladia Smoke is Anishinaabekwe from Obishikokaang/Lac Seul First Nation, with family roots in Alderville First Nation, Winnipeg, and Toronto. Eladia has worked in architecture since 2002, and founded Smoke Architecture as principal architect in 2014. She is a Master Lecturer at Laurentian's McEwen School of Architecture. Her career includes principal architect with Architecture 49, Thunder Bay, and architect with Prairie Architects, Winnipeg. Eladia has served on the RAIC's Indigenous Task Force since its inception, 2015. Eladia was on the Unceded international team of Indigenous designers and architects; led by Douglas Cardinal, that represented Canada at the 2018 Venice Biennale.

Introduction

The Anishinaabe roundhouse is a pre-contact building typology in current use in our nations. It is a public building type, hosting activities that impact the larger community. It is in use "wherever Anishinaabeg gather" (Johnson, 2018), so its range covers several provinces and states across northeast USA and Canada. Its architectural significance revolves around its symbolism, materiality, and spatial expression, which expresses in microcosm the macrocosmic belief systems and cultural practices of Anishinaabeg.

The roundhouse is found within Anishinaabe territories, centered on the Great Lakes region, northeast woodlands and subarctic regions (Benton-Banai, p.99). Anishinaabe is a general term that means "from whence was lowered," (Benton-Banai, p.3) and expresses a larger cultural group that includes several groups, including Ojibway (Ojibwe | Chippewa), Potawotami, Odawa, Missisauga, Algonquin, and Saulteux.

The Elders consulted here, and others, say our teachings are ideally shared in Anishinaabemowin (Ojibway language). To describe the roundhouse academically, in English, may prompt a wider audience to support Anishinaabeg in extending and strengthening these teachings, including those about roundhouse and its role in sustaining life.

Information Sources and Limitations

In 2018, Henvey Inlet First Nation commissioned Smoke Architecture Inc. to provide architectural services to design a roundhouse. To support this professional work, I conducted an investigation of the roundhouse in the oral tradition, through conversations with Anishinaabe Elders, PaShawOneeBinace | Ralph Johnson and Colin Mousseau, with supporting information from other Elders and knowledge carriers. As Dr. Lawrence Gross describes, the activity of gathering information about one's own culture is a lifelong activity (Gross, p.2-3).

The ongoing process of designing a roundhouse with Henvey Inlet has shown there may be several valid answers to the same question; architecture reinforces cultural ideation and may take multiple forms in its specificity. We are exploring a spiral glulam roof structure, and a central clerestory aligned with the summer solstice sunrise, June 21st, Indigenous People's Day in Canada. The roof slope extends outward toward posts rising from the land to form gateways at paths up to the building, and to acknowledge this place grows out of land-based teachings. For a community in transition, a dynamic form may resonate, compared to the balanced, symmetrical, more static form of most roundhouses.

There are several roundhouse sites referenced, mainly in present-day Ontario; known roundhouses are also located in Minnesota and Michigan. Writing on the roundhouse building type is limited, so research presented here is in the exploratory style. There is one paragraph mentioning a "Drum Dance Lodge," which appears similar to the roundhouse, in Nabokov & Easton's *Native American Architecture*. Nabokov states that this type arose "in the late nineteenth century," where "the Drum Dance began replacing the Midewewin rituals" (Nabokov 71). Midewiwin is the formal religion of Anishinaabeg (Gross, 210). Regarding the range of this building type, Nabokov says "examples of such many-sided dance lodges are found across the Great Plains." Nabokov also suggests a development of this building type, where roofed halls replaced open arenas to host the Grass Dance (Nabokov, 71).

This does not completely match descriptions from Elders, who say the roundhouse is a building type that was in use by Anishinaabeg prior to European contact; also, Mide ritual has not been replaced (Johnson, 2019). Whereas the only Anishinaabe referenced by Nabokov is Basil Johnston, the sources used here focus on Anishinaabeg authors, Elders, and knowledge carriers.

Written discussion about roundhouses is rare for several reasons. Anishinaabe knowledge transmission has been primarily through oral means, using storytelling with an experiential focus (Gross p.162-65, 172-75). Genocidal and colonial restrictions impact Indigenous knowledge transmission. Indigenous ceremony was illegal in Canada between 1880-1951, so our knowledge carriers and Elders have been justifiably reticent to share knowledge concerning ceremonial practices except with trusted individuals (Johnson 2018). In Canada between 1880-1961, status Indians who earned a degree were subject to compulsory enfranchisement, that is, forced to relinquish their government-recognized status as Indians if they chose to pursue higher education.

Smallpox epidemics reduced North America's pre-contact human population by an estimated 95%. Forced relocations of communities caused upheaval and compromised land-based cultural underpinnings (LaDuke, 12). Residential schools in Canada (boarding schools in the USA), forbade children to speak their language, curtailing oral intergenerational transmission of knowledge. Death rates in these "schools" were very high and abuses of all types were endemic, causing intergenerational trauma. Continuing this pattern into the present day, Indigenous children in Canada represent 52% of children in foster care, but only represent 7.7% of the child population under 14 years of age; in some regions, 90% of children in care are Indigenous (Philpott, 2017).

Within the scope of this article, it was not feasible to visit multiple roundhouses in person, therefore analysis relies on photographic examples, speaking with Elders and community members, and through the exploratory medium of design. While the roundhouse is a ceremonial space, ceremonial details are not provided here and are more appropriately shared through time spent with Elders (Waindubence, 2018). Anishinaabe epistemology relies on the dynamism of this personal interaction (Gross, p.170-172), whereas the written word is static, less ideal for the transmission of certain types of knowledge.

Ceremonial and Public Uses

The roundhouse facilitates a realm of activity that effects the community as a whole. Activities include formal meetings; to "deal with community issues, they'd come together around the drum." It is also a space used for learning, such as training programs, learning how to process animals taken in a hunt, or healing programs, "especially when you're dealing with social issues that affect the community, you'll go inside the roundhouse to address those." Activities are mediated: "There was always a person watching it—people couldn't just go

in there; they'd check with the Elder to make sure the activities were appropriate" (Johnson, 2019).

Activities may include naming ceremonies, shaking tent, healing ceremonies, when people are asking to know their clan, and annual celebrations. In inclement weather, powwow may be held there as well (Johnson, 2019). These ceremonies have meanings that relate to a spatial understanding that is reinforced by the lodge itself (Petahtegoose, 2018).

The roundhouse is also often used as a staging area for the sweat lodge ceremony. Colin Mousseau said the sweat lodge should be directly north of the roundhouse. There are cultural teachings associated with the cardinal directions, and location and orientation are significant. Ralph Johnson's roundhouse on his property at one time provided change rooms to a sweat lodge nearby. This use arrived through a dream, where "there were two bears who were outlining a path from that building to the sweat lodge."

Wayne McQuabbie, Chief of Henvey Inlet, and his wife, Wanda McQuabbie, also envision the roundhouse as a place to perform funerals, but Ralph Johnson is not familiar with funerals as a common use for roundhouses.

In each of these roundhouses, knowledge transmission, ceremony, and meetings that concern larger community implications occur, and an Elder representative approves activities and takes care of the space.

Connections

The spatial configuration of the roundhouse is an expression of interconnection. Winona LaDuke explains that architecture reinforces and manifests the paradigms of Indigenous culture, where "rituals are frequently based on the reaffirmation of the relationship of humans to the Creation," and are "continuously reinforced in Midewiwin lodges …" (LaDuke, p.12).

The roundhouse reinforces kinship "with the land and all the things that are animate on the land" (LaDuke, 1999 p.2). The Anishinaabe concept of animism elucidates the significance of gestures imbedded in the roundhouse typology. Dr. Lawrence Gross writes, "To think of things as being dead or inert is not the way the Anishinaabeg think." Dr. Gross's spiritual mentor, Tom Shingobe, taught that "the whole world is spiritualized. What this means is that there is nothing that is inanimate. All things are alive and acting alive" (Gross, p.102).

Ralph Johnson says that the project of Anishinaabeg on this continent was to develop a state of constant wonder through the realization and reinforcement of interconnection with the rest of life (Johnson 2018). The name for this lifelong project is mino-bimaadiziwin, to restore and sustain life, a phrase literally translated as "the good life" (Gross 210-213). As architect Douglas Cardinal writes, "The measure of a man is seen through the prospering life that surrounds him" (Cardinal 54).

Building elements reinforce and re-weave these connections as a teaching tool. In the case of the roundhouse, there is a connection to the earth, sky, and the four cardinal directions. This is sometimes referred to as seven directions: up, down, east, south, west, north, and center (Gross, p.43-44).

Circular Footprint, Orientation, Doorways

The overall footprint of the building is a segmented circle. Ralph Johnson describes the "original design," built with stacked horizontally laid logs "like a log cabin," with each side overlapping so the ends lock together. The number of sides varies, often eight or twelve depending on the circumference. The circle is a metaphor for cycles that govern the rhythms of the natural world. Movement of people during ceremony is circular and follows the direction of the sun (Benton-Banai, p.16).

Windows aren't typically located in the walls; however, Ralph Johnson recalls that in Waynejikoming, there were four windows toward the four cardinal directions. He does not recall them ever being opened and he can't explain why they were included at that roundhouse. Colin Mousseau also confirms there are no windows in the walls, rather light and ventilation is typically through the central clerestory.

The principle entrance is east, toward the rising sun and away from prevailing winds. The space between central columns aligns with the cardinal directions. Colin Mousseau describes four central columns, as seen in the Watersmeet roundhouse. Ralph Johnson says there are often more than four columns, and they form interior gateways reinforcing this directional emphasis. He recalls:

> In Seine River, there are twelve posts in the middle, and that's quite a large roundhouse. Nigigoonsiminikaaning is the smallest roundhouse I know of and they have 8 posts, because it's like a doorway for each direction (Johnson, 2019).

Ralph Johnson remembers the roundhouse in Lac la Croix has two doorways, the primary door in the east, and one in the west that is sometimes opened for cross ventilation. In the Meno Ya Win hospital roundhouse, there are four doorways, one toward each cardinal direction, the primary one toward the east. Wanda McQuabbie initially indicated the door for the Henvey Inlet roundhouse should be in the south, then after consideration indicated that it can be in the east as recommended by Colin Mousseau. Ralph, thinking about his own roundhouse that has doors that aren't in the east direction, surmises that this might have an individual significance:

> In mine it doesn't open to the east, it opens to the northeast and the southwest. There are different teachings as well; when she's saying south door; you have to explore more where that's coming from. They also have a contrary lodge that has a west door. There's a "beginning of time lodge" that has a southeast doorway, and they talk about why the doorways are facing that direction (Johnson 2019).

Teachings surrounding traditional funerals include two doors, one for the body to enter, and another for it to leave. Ralph remembers when funerals were held in homes where there was only one door, the body would be passed through a window. For those in the physical world, using one door is more appropriate, for instance the roundhouse at Rat Portage has a single door. Even in roundhouses that have two doors, such as Serpent River, only one is used regularly. Ralph Johnson remembers that "even as kids, we'd be told that we don't just run through the house through both doors, because we'd come in one door and leave out of the same door" (Johnson, 2019).

As discussed above, the reason for the atypical door position in Ralph Johnson's roundhouse came from a dream. This comfort with different answers to the same question is an aspect of Anishinaabe epistemology, where "the things we experience are put here by the Creator for us to experience uniquely on an individual basis" (Gross 173). Therefore the direction of entrances is mediated by situational forces that may vary from the traditional design.

The "original design" of a roundhouse, as Ralph Johnson expresses it, is a single non-partitioned, multi-function space. However, many contemporary roundhouses have defined rooms and complex programs, such as Thunderbird House, Serpent River, and Shawanaga.

Even where there is significant deviation from the original typology, the resulting space is still a roundhouse. For instance, the roundhouse inside of Meno Ya Win Hospital is embedded within a modern health care facility. The roundhouse outside of Art Petahtegoose's home is not in fact round but is an open-air rectangular roofed area that is primarily used for teaching. At Shawanaga, additions to the roundhouse have created an extended building that includes several related functions.

Connection to Earth & Sky, Central Posts, Drum, Motion

In the vertical direction, there is a connection to earth and sky. In Anishinaabemowin (Ojibway language), the word for earth is aki, meaning land. The spirit name for the earth, Shkagamik-Kwe, means "fresh earth" (Pegahmagabow, 2018). Ralph Johnson says:

> Waynejikoming doesn't have a floor in their main dance area, because you're on the earth. Because they also do other ceremonies in there, like shaking tent. People insist that it must touch the earth. Lac Croix also has earth as their floor in their main dancing area.

Concerning the Meno Ya Win hospital roundhouse, Ralph recalls:

> It's got a hole in the middle of the floor, so there's a panel and there's earth you can pull up, so if there's any need for in ceremony to touch the earth you can open or move that panel to the side.

The drum is also set in the center of the roundhouse. Henvey Inlet Chief Wayne McQuabbie had a dream in which he cared for a "big drum"—this is a style of drum that sits on the ground. The drum is a living thing and has a drum carrier who cares for it. The beat of the drum represents the beating heart of Shkagamik-Kwe, and the drum aligns us to this rhythm (Smoke 2016).

Connection to sky is through a ring of operable clerestory windows. positioned above the central columns which support a higher portion of roof. The sky is the realm of birds, celestial bodies, the stars and constellations, sun, and moon, and there are teachings and stories of how each of these supports life. In this central area, there may be a small fire, and a smudging ceremony usually introduces other events. The rising of smoke carries the thoughts, prayers, and intentions of persons who are gathered to our ancestors in the spirit realm (Johnson, 2018, 2019), and to Gichi-Manidoo, the great mystery or great spirit (Benton Banai, p.2). Henvey Inlet also has ceremonies that require darkness, so these openings need opaque coverings. In each case, the functions of the building are reinforced and facilitated by the design of this central connection to sky.

Materiality, Modern Amenities

Historical roundhouses were made entirely of wood, with no metal components, whereas contemporary roundhouses may have modern amenities. Material choice will bring the spirit, presence, and support of that material into the object being made, contributing to its life over time (Smoke 2015, Labelle 2016). Colin Mousseau said there should be a cedar tree planted beside the main door when the roundhouse has its birthing ceremony. This tree watches over the building and grows with it.

The material for the Henvey Inlet roundhouse is wood from land cleared for a new wind farm energy project, which will also provide funding to support building this roundhouse. Ralph Johnson comments,

> Before contact, they didn't use any metal in the construction… in Waynejikoming, the Elders there insisted on no metal used in the construction. Others I've seen, they use metal beams and they're a lot bigger.

Ralph Johnson recalls there were heaters and electric lighting at the Wayneji, Nigigoonsiminikaaning, and Seine River roundhouses, but elsewhere, such as Lac La Croix and Rat Portage, a wood stove is the only source of heat.

Meno Ya Win hospital, Shawanaga, and Thunderbird House roundhouses are fully modern buildings.

While materiality is a significant and deliberate choice, it is also one made with a particular community in mind, and with advice from Elders who guide the design of the building and who will continue to care for it.

Responsiveness, Resilience

The roundhouse reinforces and manifests cultural teachings in its role as a public building, where decisions impacting the larger community take place. While there is a primary building form, each roundhouse reflects the experiential epistemology of Anishinaabeg; this primary form is mediated through dreams, perspectives from Elders who guide the design and care of the building, and the context and priorities in different communities.

The roundhouse reinforces and sustains connections that are integral to the flourishing of life. There is a connection between earth and sky with the heartbeat of the drum at the center. The entrance and central columns acknowledge the four cardinal directions, bringing them together with earth, sky, and center. These seven directions inspire and reinforce a greater resonance between human activity and the movement and cycles of life.

Within, activity is under the care of an Elder associated with the building. These activities affect the community as a whole. The roundhouse is so requisite to community life that Ralph Johnson says, "I think there should be one in every town." While the type is originally a single, undifferentiated space, there are examples of roundhouses that have separate rooms for different activities and uses, showing a situational adaptation to suit specific requirements. The roundhouse arises from a deep affinity with the land, and as resilient and adaptive as the land is, so is the form that connects us with it.

The beat of the drum in Anishinaabe cultural teachings represents the beating heart of Shkagamik-Kwe. Beating the drum and hearing the drum aligns the player and hearer to this rhythm, harmonizing the individual with the greater cycles of life. The drum is the heart of the roundhouse.

Bibliography

Benton-Banai, Edward. *The Mishomis Book: the voice of the Ojibway.* University of Minnesota Press and Indian Country Communications Inc., 2010.

Cardinal, Douglas, with George Melnyck, editor. *Of the Spirit*. NeWest Press. 1977.

Gross, Lawrence. Anishinaabe Ways of Knowing and Being. Ashgate 2014.

Johnson, Ralph | PaShawOneeBinace. Interviews by Eladia Smoke, 2018 May 25 and 2019 Jan 18.

Labelle, Marcel. "Jimaan | Birchbark Canoe Design-Build," ARCH 2515 EL/FL Design Studio 3: Landscape 1. Build session and lectures, Laurentian University McEwen School of Architecture, Sudbury, Ontario, Oct-Nov, 2016-2017.

LaDuke, Winona. "Recovering the Sacred: the power of naming and claiming." Haymarket Books, 2016.

Mousseau, Colin. Interview by Eladia Smoke, 2018 Oct 17.

Nabokov, Peter, and Robert Easton. "Native American Architecture." Oxford University Press, 1989.

Pegahmagabow, Julie. "Anishinaabemowin Immersion Learning for Youth and Adults." Aktikameksheng, 2018 Oct 11.

Petahtegoose, Art. "Wigiwam Design-Build," ARCH 2515 EL/FL Design Studio 3: Landscape 1. Build session and lecture, Laurentian University McEwen School of Architecture, Sudbury, Ontario, 2018 Sep 12.

Philpott, Jane. "Minister Philpott speaks at the Assembly of First Nations Special Chiefs Assembly." Speech, Ottawa, Ontario, 2017 Dec 6. Government of Canada: Indigenous Services Canada. https://www.canada.ca/en/indigenous-services-can-da/news/2017/12/speech_for_jane_philpottministerofindigenousservicesattheassembl.html.

Smoke, Dan and Mary Lou. "REL2236A Indigenous Spirituality." *Drum birthing ceremony*. Brescia University College, London: ON, 2015 June 10.

Waindubence, Gordon. Interview by Eladia Smoke, 2018 Aug 16.

Chapter 2.5: kitche migawap âcimowin – Tipi Tectonics: Building as a Medicine

Krystel Clark – Montreal Lake Cree Nation in the Boreal Forest region of Saskatchewan

Introduction

My Spirit name is osk-îskwêw[1] which was translated by my grandmother as "a young woman, young at heart," and it means that I will always be defined as osk-îskwêw even in my old age. I am inspired with designing with nature. Specifically, how a design can revitalize an individual's well-being. I explore the iconic Cree dwelling: kitche migawap[2] to evaluate Indigenous design principles. The deduction of the research is to propose alternate building practices as a strategy to implement Cree cultural significance into building construction and create spaces for occupants who want to feel connected to their traditional identity and promote health. The exploration of the Cree Tipi's construction and structure is investigated to reveal pre-colonial concepts that can be implemented into a building by interweaving traditional knowledge with technical applications. The documentation will be guided by Cree oral histories ("stories") from my Indigenous heritage, originating from Montreal Lake Cree Nation in the Boreal Forest region of Saskatchewan and additionally from academic sources.

kitche migawap: Traditional Tipi

Tipis were not only a home, but a culminate representation of Cree culture. Today we understand the Tipi to have come from many different first nations, usually conical in form with straight wooden poles to support a cover made with animal skins and an opening to draw out smoke from the fire.[3] The photograph titled *Buffalo Tipi 1878* demonstrates a traditional Tipi dwelling and cooking Tipi structure used for smoking meat.[4]

This Native conical dwelling is best known by the Sioux Nation as Tipi or teepee.[5] Typically defined as the home for nomadic people.[6] The term nomadic to describe the lifestyle of Indigenous nations. To grasp the Tipi lifestyle the term nomadic will be re-defined. Nomadic[7] implies that Indigenous people had no place of their own but merely moved from one place to another.

To explain, the movement patterns of Indigenous people and their homes is defined by Laurel,[8] my sister, and a student from the Indigenous relations program at the Laurentian University in Sudbury, Ontario, can be demonstrated in the map illustrating the Cree dialect[9] area across Canada, illustrates the *Cree Dialect of Canada 2001*. The Cree dialect language map corresponds with the *Boreal Forest Map of Canada 2011,* which demonstrates the Cree regional boundary.

Tribes hunting and gathering grounds or territory were distinguished by environmental markers. For example, an Elder from Batchewana stated an area, typically, extended to the fields of wild rice or a body of water as a landscape landmark and beyond that point would be another "tribe" area.[10] The Cree Tipi region is identified through this process. Therefore, The Boreal Forest is the traditional territory of the Cree Nation and they traveled the great expanse of their home. The entire area was their home and therefore they were not nomadic people. It is

---

1. Dr. Earle Waugh Dir Center for Health, Miyo Wahkohtowin Community Education Authority (MWCEA), and University of Alberta, "Nehiyaw Masinahikan, Online Cree Dictionary," Interllimedia Technologies Inc.
2. Elder Mary Lee, *Cree Nehiyawk Teaching,* 2016.
3. Adolf Hungrywolf, *Tipi: Traditional Native American Shelter (*Summertown, TN: Book Publishing Company. 2006) 6.
4. Robin Pepin, Indigenous Cree Knowledge Holder in discussion with the author, December 2018.

5. Adolf Hungrywolf, p. 6.
6. Ibid., p. 65.
7. Nomad described by Dictionary.com, 1. a member or tribe that has no permanent abode but moves about from place to place usually seasonally and often following a traditional route or circuit according to the state of the pasturage or food supply. 2. Any wanderer; itinerant.
8. Laurel, Indigenous Student, in discussion with the author, December 2018.
9. Dialect described by Arden Ogg, *Indigenous Mapping Workshop 2017: Supporting Cree as a 21st Century Language,* Cree language… [is not] one language or even one family of dialects. it is…a continuum of languages. The different between dialect and language well is how well speakers can understand each other.
10. Unknown, Batchewana Story, in design studio discussion with the author, January 2017.

important to reevaluate terminology as a way to reclaim Indigenous stereotypes and represent ourselves.

Cultural Tectonics: The Cover, Poles, Earth, and Fire

The entire process of making and erecting a traditional Tipi embodies cultural significance since the act of making a Tipi is shared with the community. The woman erected, constructed and designed the Tipis. The cultural significant of the Tipi resonates with the woman, her surroundings, and the significance roles woman held prior to colonization. The Tipi convey the narrative of gender roles regarding the Tipi which I will define as cultural tectonics: The cover, poles, earth, and fire. In the Cree language the central fire is iskwuptew,[11] woman is iskwew, and more than one woman is iskwewuk. Woman were named after the fire, which is powerful since it honors the sacredness of that fire.[12] An old woman in Cree is notegweu or notaygeu meaning, "when an old lady covers herself with a shawl."[13] A Tipi cover is like an old woman with a shawl and it embraces the teachings and the values of community that the women hold. An old woman always has room for more children and great grandchildren to come into her circle, and this is the meaning for the Tipi cover. When the is Tipi erected properly the poles are covered and the Tipi stands with dignity, just as a woman who covers her legs with a skirt which represents the circle of life. It is a symbol to embrace life and visually looks like a woman standing with her arms out saying, thank you to everything.

The Tipi ceremony is the same as picking sweetgrass.[14] The sweetgrass is picked, then braided with the intentions to gift the bundle. A prayer is said during the process of picking and braiding the sweetgrass. The sweetgrass is then burned and the prayers are released and help the receiver. It is the same with a Tipi being constructed for the first time. The Tipi must face east because it represents the beginning of creation. Prior to making a Tipi, tobacco is offered to Mother Earth by sitting humbly on the ground and acknowledging everything used from Mother Earth since everything we are borrowing from her is needed to make a Tipi.[15] The Tipi is the spirit and body of a woman. The woman represents family, community, and values that bring balance into our lives. When a Tipi is constructed it involves a ceremony to respect the value of the woman's teachings.

Tipi Tectonics: The Cover, Poles, Earth, and Fire

Tipi tectonics will establish a framework to better understand the differences between Western and Indigenous design concepts. My process of exploring the Tipi included consistent dialogue with a knowledge holder, my Cree mother. The colors demonstrate the flow of the fires smoke by outlining how the air flows through the Tipi. I placed my mother's sketches within the work. She would draw an image to demonstrate different parts of a Tipi would have been constructed and used. I redrew the image beside hers to gain an understanding, and she would usually correct me, so that narrative is in the artwork. (Fig. 1)

The Tipi revealed a tectonic language of how Indigenous construction and methods can be implemented into today's infrastructure. In the twenty-first century typical construction conveys the tectonic language of resistance, or "to repel" by creating airtight building envelopes that resist wind, water, insects, and thermal bridging. The systems are created to control spaces by adjusting the interior environment with advanced technological systems to create an artificial well-tempered environment. In contrast, the Cree Tipi tectonics language can be described as nisitohtamonâhk, as, "field of meaning," which means literally, "the land and territory of understanding."[16] I use the term to define Tipi tectonics since the environment is fundamental to the function of the Tipi. In other words, the Tipi embodies and adapts to its surrounding environment to function.

This phenomenon is reoccurring with the Tipi for example, the exterior wind moves or "flows," from the base of the Tipi up the liner and escapes through the roof opening. The modern window, if it is operable can be opened to allow wind into the building. Typically, a building's air intake is recycled within a confined space and can only let in fresh air through windows. The Tipi opening, and wooden pole structure reveals the path of water after a rainfall. The smoke flap is manually closed by the outer poles and the rain flows down the cover, however some of the rain enters the opening at the top of the Tipi. The rain droplets run down the inner side of the structural poles. Two short sticks are placed parallel against the inner pole with sinew to create a gap between the liner and structural poles, this allowing a path for the water to flow.[17] The liner stays dry and the water has a path directly to the earth. This underlining theme I used describe the occurrence is *Sâpociwan* "it flows through": sapo- "through"; -ciwan, a verb stem that denotes flowing.[18] This theme is constant with the wind movement

11. Elder Mary Lee, 2016.
12. Ibid.
13. Ibid.
14. Ibid.
15. Ibid.

16. Neal McLeod, *100 Days of Cree* (Canada: University of Regina Press, 2016), 230.
17. Reginald and Gladys Lauren. *The Indian Tipi It's History, Construction, and Use* (New York: The University of Oklahoma Press, 1957) 66, diagram b and 69.
18. Neal McLeod, 60.

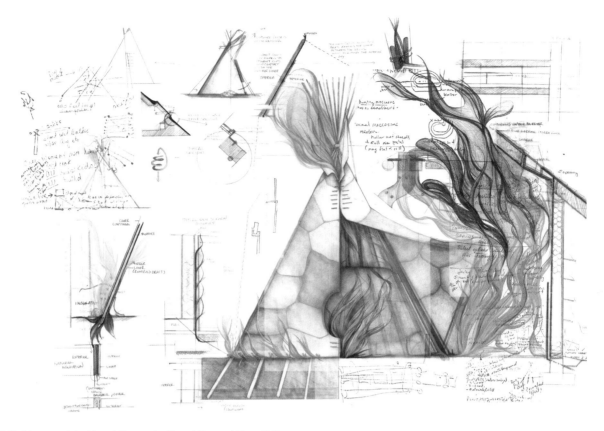

Figure 1. nisitohtamonahk: Hand Drawn in Graphite and Pencil Crayon.

and the fire's warmth. I develop this method to emphasize the Tipi tectonic expression. (Fig. 2)

The corresponding twenty first typical construction skylight detail, however, reveals the narrative of repelling the rainwater. The skylight opening is tightly sealed with metal flashing to resist any water from compromising the barrier.[19] The fire in the Tipi is made inside a small hole under the smoke hole and closer to the front.[20] The warm air rising inside the Tipi draws in cold air from outside, from beneath the cover, up the lining, creating a draft for the fires smoke to "flow" up through the smoke hole.[21] The smoke, fire, and heat fill the space and warms the occupants. In the woodstove detail the heat transfer is contained within its structure. The fire is lit within the woodstove and tightly sealed allowing the heat to build up and warm the surrounding air. The **corresponding construction detail illustrates a** woodstove with a pipe that extends through the wall assembly to intake outdoor air into its system. The smoke is directed up the shaft and exits through the roof assembly and demonstrates a controlled heating system. (Fig. 3)

The process of implementing Indigenous design concepts and cultural significance to a twenty first building construction must start in a meaningful way. The Tipi teachings start the âcimowin[22] and methodology to design. The Cree Tipi uses fifteen poles to make the structure and each pole holds a teaching. The Tipi does not have to face east all the time.[23] The first three poles are tied together to form a tripod and fortify the structure are named obedience, respect and humility. The first pole is obedience and means to accept guidance and wisdom by listening to traditional stories, our parents, grandparents, and Elders. The second pole is to respect by honoring Elders, strangers, and all of life. The third pole is humility and it is to be humbled in our understanding our relationship with creation. Notice the poles are in a reciprocal frame[24] network and support

19. Francis D.K. Ching, *Building Construction Illustrated Fifth Edition* (John Wiley & Sons, 2014) Sections 8.36-8.37.
20. Reginald and Gladys Lauren, 108.
21. Ibid., 64.

22. âcimowin defined by Cree Dictionary.com as, story.
23. Elder Mary Lee, 2006.
24. Reciprocal Frame described Olga Popovic Larsen as "structures consisting of linear flat or inclined elements which support each other and are arranged in a way to form a closed circuit or unit. The assembly formed in such a way is a stable geometrical configuration and forms a spatial structural system, most commonly used for roof structures, where the members share the load and transfer it down to a ring beam, columns

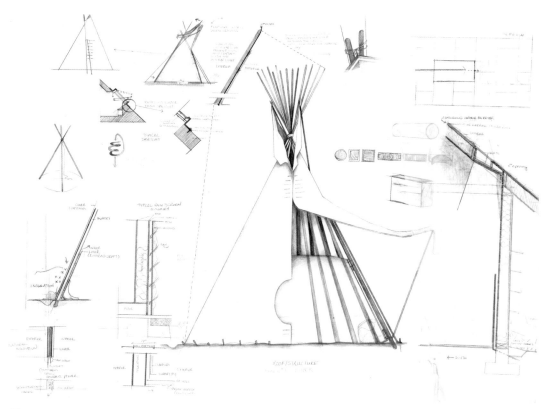

Figure 2. Ventilation Diagram Hand Drawn in Graphite and Pencil Crayon.

Figure 3. Heat Transfer Diagram Hand Drawn in Graphite and Pencil Crayon.

one another to stand. The teaching is in order to make a family you need three: two parents and the child to make that balance.[25] The tops of the poles have many teachings and each one points in a different direction. The poles represent our need in the strength and support of our families, communities and our acceptance that everyone's journey point is different, and each pole has a its own teaching. The poles are the foundation to good design and structurally displays how each participant shares the load in the design process.

Bibliography

Boychuk, Rick. "War for the Woods: Boreal Forest Agreement." *Canadian Geographic* 2011. https://www.canadiangeographic.ca/article/war-woods-boreal-forest-agreement.

Ching, Francis D.K. *Building Construction Illustrated Fifth Edition.* John Wiley & Sons, 2014.

Dr. Earle Waugh Dir Center for Health, Miyo Wahkohtowin Community Education Authority (MWCEA), and University of Alberta. "Nehiyaw Masinahikan, Online Cree Dictionary." Interllimedia Technologies Inc. http://www.creedictionary.com/about.php.

Elder Mary Lee. *Cree Nehiyawk Teaching.* Invert Media Inc, 2006.

Hungrywolf, Adolf. *Tipi: Traditional Native American Shelter.* Summertown, TN: Book Publishing Company, 2006.

Larsen, Olga Popovic. "Reciprocal Frame (RF) Structures: Real and Exploratory." Springer Link, 2014. https://link.springer.com/article/10.1007/s00004-014-0181-0.

McLeod, Neal. *100 Days of Cree.* Canada: University of Regina Press, 2016.

Ogg, Arden. "Indigenous Mapping Workshop 2017: Supporting Cree as a 21st Century Language." 2017. https://creeliteracy.org/2017/11/06/indigenous-mapping-workshop-2017-supporting-cree-as-a-21st-century-language/.

Pepin, Robin. Indigenous Cree Knowledge Holder in discussion with the author, December 2018.

Reginald and Gladys Lauren. *The Indian Tipi It's History, Construction, and Use.* New York: The University of Oklahoma Press, 1957.

Roberts, Laurel. Indigenous Student in discussion with the author, December 2018.

Unknown, Batchewana Story in discussion with the author, January 2017.

---

or supporting walls, in *Reciprocal Frame (RF) Structures: Real and Exploratory*, Springer Link, 2014. https://link.springer.com/article/10.1007/s00004-014-0181-0.
25. Elder Mary Lee, 2006.

Chapter 2.6: The Indigenous Peoples Space: Architecture as Narrative

Eladia Smoke – Anishinaabekwe from Obishikokaang, David Fortin – Métis Nation of Ontario and Wanda Dalla Costa – Saddle Lake First Nation

KaaSheGaaBaaWeak/Eladia Smoke is Anishinaabekwe from Obishikokaang/Lac Seul First Nation, with family roots in Alderville First Nation, Winnipeg, and Toronto. Eladia has worked in architecture since 2002, and founded Smoke Architecture as principal architect in 2014. She is a Master Lecturer at Laurentian's McEwen School of Architecture. Her career includes principal architect with Architecture 49, Thunder Bay, and architect with Prairie Architects, Winnipeg. Eladia has served on the RAIC's Indigenous Task Force since its inception, 2015. Eladia was is on the Unceded international team of Indigenous designers and architects; led by Douglas Cardinal, the team represented Canada at the 2018 Venice Biennale.

Dr David Fortin is a member of the Métis Nation of Ontario and the RAIC Indigenous Task Force that seeks 'ways to foster and promote indigenous design in Canada'. He was co-curator of UNCEDED: Voices of the Land, a team of Indigenous architects under the leadership of Douglas Cardinal, that represented Canada at the 2018 Venice Biennale in Italy. Since January 2018, David has worked with the National Research Council of Canada to coordinate community input for housing in remote northern locations for an upcoming Technical Standards publication. In 2019, David T Fortin Architect Inc., in joint venture with Smoke Architecture and Wanda Dalla Costa Architect, worked for the Assembly of First Nations to provide an Indigenous vision for the new Indigenous People's Space in Ottawa. David is the Associate Director of the Maamwizing Indigenous Research Institute and the current Director of the McEwen School of Architecture.

Wanda Dalla Costa, AIA, LEED A.P. holds a joint position at Arizona State University between The Design School as Institute Professor, and the School of Construction as Associate Professor. She is a member of the Saddle Lake First Nation and has spent nearly 20 years working with Indigenous communities in North America. Her current work focuses on re-operationalizing Indigenous ways of knowing, being and connecting in contemporary architecture education and practice. Her interests include co-design methodologies, Indigenous place-keeping and climatic resiliency based in regional architectures.

Dalla Costa was the first, First Nation woman to become an architect in Canada, and was part of the team of Indigenous architects that represented Canada at the 2018 Venice Biennale. Dalla Costa's coursework at ASU includes Indigenous Planning, Architecture and Construction and a multidisciplinary Indigenous Construction Studio, where architecture, construction and planning students work directly with tribal communities. Her company, Redquill Architecture is based in Phoenix, Arizona.

Background // Enji-zhitoong maanda

On Indigenous People's Day 2017, Prime Minister Justin Trudeau announced that the former U.S. Embassy in Ottawa would be re-purposed as a space for Indigenous Peoples. The Indigenous Peoples Space will encompass the 100 Wellington Street building, 119 Sparks Street (currently a CIBC bank), and a future infill to connect the two existing buildings. This site is on the traditional, unceded territories of the Algonquin Nation.

The Assembly of First Nations (AFN), in collaboration with Inuit Tapiriit Kanatami and the Métis National Council, has partnered with our team to develop a model that will inspire the long-term vision for the Indigenous Peoples Space. The future building will effectively represent First Nations, Inuit and Métis Nation peoples' cultures and histories in such a way that Indigenous governments, institutions and organizations can conduct Nation to Nation business and further our self-determination.

Indigenous People's Day gii-aawang 2017, gii-dbaajma Prime Minister Justin Trudeau wi U.S. Embassy ko gaa-aawang, Ottawa etek, bkaan wii-zhi-nakaazang, Maanpii Kiing Wenzkaajik wii-nakaazwaat. Wi 100 Wellington Street wiigwaam 119 Sparks Street (CIBC zhoonyaa- gamik megwaa yaawang) gewe, kina Indigenous Peoples Space da-aawan, aabtaweyiing gewe zhiwida-zhichgaade gegoo wii-aan'koosing nanda niish wiigwaaman. Algonquin Nation da-kiimwaa aawan tek sa maanda; gaawii gii-bgidna-ziinaawaa maanda da- kiimwaa.

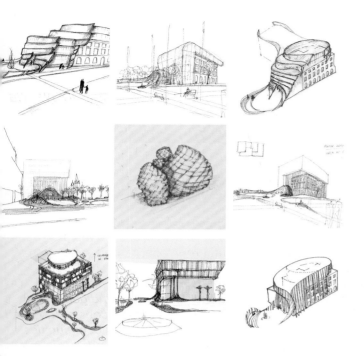

Figure 1. Preliminary sketches represent a collaborative and iterative process.

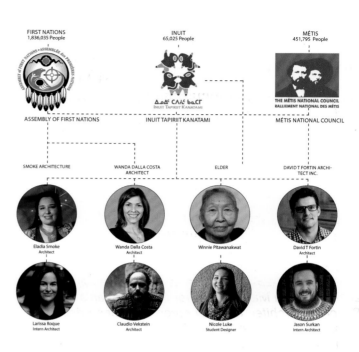

Figure 2. A diverse team of designers undertook conceptual design for the Indigenous People's Space, commissioned by Assembly of First Nations in association with Inuit Tapiriit Kanatami and Métis National Council.

Assembly of First Nations (AFN), Inuit Tapiriit Kanatami gewe, miinwaa Métis National Council, gii- wiijbizoondwak wii-wiijnakiimgowaang zhitoowaang gegoo waa- naadmaagemgak niigaan naabing wii- waabndaming e-zhi-mnwaabjichgaadegba maanda Indigenous Peoples Space. First Nations, Inuit, Métis Nation gewe debendaagzijik ezhi-bmaadziwaat, zhaazhi gewe gaa-bi-zhiwebziwaat, da-zhinoomaadim maanpii pii wiizhchigaadek maanda, wii-naadmaagemgak gonda Maanpii Kiing Wenzkaajik bemaaknigejik, institutions miinwaa organizations gewe wii-bminzha'mawaat maanda gina gegoo bemiikming Nation to Nation zhi-nakiing, wii-maajiishkaawaat gewe maanda naagdawendizying. Idaa-gchinendaami gegiinwaa dbaajmayek enendmek e-zhichengba niigaan naabing.

Mzinbiiymaang waa-zhitoowaang, gbizdaagoom miinwaa gwiijnakiimgoom wii-noondwindwaa miinwaa wii- mnaaj'indwaa gonda Maanpii Kiing Wenzkaajik eyaajik maanpii. Mii maanda e-niigaani-mkwendmaang.

Diverse Team // Waajiiwejik Maanda Nakiitming

Our team has Métis, Anishinaabe, Plains Cree, and Inuit representatives, with voices from youths to Elders. Our team is deliberately diverse and carefully structured for a collaborative design process. The process is just as important as the final project; this is how we build a rich understanding of place, embody Indigenous heritage, and welcome visitors from the local community and abroad. It is important to place our Elder, Winnie at a prominent position in the design process.

Ni'aak maanpii wiijiiwewak Métis, Anishinaabe, Plains Cree, miinwaa Inuit, eshkniigjik gewe miinwaa Getzijik. Nooch wiya dgobi maanda sa maamwizing miinwaa na'ii nda-zhi-nakiimi, kina wiya wii-noondwin enendang dbaaknigeng waa-zhinaagok maanda ezhtoong. Naasaap piichi-ndawendaagot weweni wii-zhi-nakiing maamwizing, gaawii go wi ezhchigaadek maamdaa eta wii-mkwendming; mii wi ezhi-gwekwendming mooshkin wii-nsastaming zhiwi sa etek gegoo, ezhi- zhinoomaageng gewe Maanpii Kiing Wenzkaajik kina gaa- bi-aan'kenmaageyaat, miinwaa ezhi-mno-daapnindwaa giwi nooch ngoji wenjbaajik baandgejik maanpii.

Our Vision // Ge-Zhiwebkiba

As Indigenous architects, we recognize the potential narrative of this historic site, and its challenges. This is a vision of Indigenous values, honouring our Elders and the Algonquin Peoples. We design by listening and working collaboratively toward an expression that celebrates Indigenous presence. This is our first priority.

Maanda architects Maanpii Kiing Wenzkaajik aawyaang, waabndaanaa ge-naajmangba maanpii sa maanda wii-zhichgaadek, miinwaa waa-zhi-znagak. Na'ii makwendaanaa da-zhiwebkiba, da-mnaadenjgaadek maanpii Maanpii Kiing Wenzkaajik gechi-piitendmawaat, mnaadenmindwaa Getzijik miinwaa Algonquin-ak.

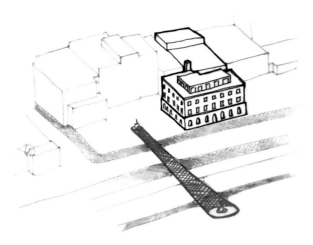

Figure 3. A nation-to-nation axis is drawn between Canada's Centennial Flame and the Indigenous People's Immemorial Flame.

Nation to Nation Axis

The Algonquin Gathering Circle is directly opposite Parliament. The Sacred Fire on axis with the Centennial Flame honors the nation-to-nation connection between Indigenous peoples and Canada.

Myaa gaama'iing Parliament temgat wi Algonquin Gathering Circle. Centennial Flame zhi-dbishkoo temgat wi Gchitwaa-Shkode, wii-zhinoomaageng enaangoondwaat Maanpii Kiing Wenzkaajik miinwaa Canada, naasaap piichgaabwiwaat.

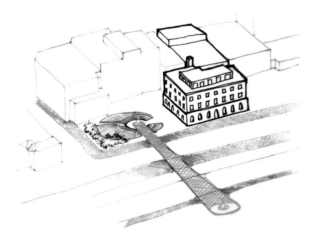

Figure 4. Connection to Mother Earth is expressed through an outdoor garden of year round activity.

The Land – Maanda Ki

Our Elders teach that we are close to Mother Earth. An Indigenous garden and celebration space invites visitors into a sacred space of year-round programmed activity.

Gda-penmandwaanaa gminaadenmaanaa gewe Shkakmigkwe, zhi-kinoomaagewak Getzijik. Na'ii maanpii da-tenoon, gtigaanens Maanpii Kiing Wenzkaajik en'kaazwaat gtigaadenik, miinwaa waa-dnakmigak bebaayaajik da-bi-biindgeyaapa gegoo sa maanpii nakmigak; nooch gegoo da-nakmigat maanpii gbe-bboong miinwaa gbe-niibin.

Wigwam Inner Structure + East Entry – Biinjiyiing Wiigwaam + Waabnong Dzhi-biindgeng

The Birchbark | Wiigiwaas panels of pre-contact Algonquin architecture inspire transparent glass panels to lightly envelope the Beaux-Arts facade of 100 Wellington Street, a European typology on unceded Algonquin land. The east entry honors a sunrise of new beginnings.

Wiigwaasan ko gaa-zhi-nakaazwaat Algonquin-ak gii-zhigeyaat jibwaa-dgoshnowaat wyaabshkiiwejik, mii gaa-mkwendmaang gii-naaknigeyaanh waasechganaabkoon wii-toong zaagji'iing wii-giitaasing zhiwi, wi sa wiigwaam gaa-zhichgaadeg wyaabshkiiwejik gii-bi-bminzha'waawaat Maanpii Kiing Wenzkaanjin. Mii go naa dbishkoo toong maanda wiigwaam mkakoong wii-zhinoomaageng. Da-giizhootemgat zhiwi biinjiyiing. Gaawii geyaabi wyaabshkiiwejik da-bminzha'waa-siiwaan Maanpii Kiing Wenzkaanjin. Waabnong dzhi-biindgeng, mii mnaadenjgaadek maanda kina wii-mno-aanji-maajtaang.

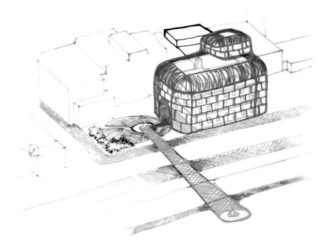

Figure 5. The pre-contact precedent of wigwam inspires a paneled vitrine that respect fully displays the heritage building and improves its envelope.

Wigwam Outer Structure – Zaagjiyiing Wiigwaam

As in the Algonquin wiigiwaam's bentwood supports, a second layer holds the glass shingles against the inner structure and provides insulation for the heritage building.

Dbishkoo shkaatgoonsan gii-zhoobaagnaawaat Algonquin-ak wiigwaam gii-zhitoowaat, zhaazhwaach ndi-zhnaagtoonaa wi naakmachgan waa-mnjimnigemgak pii niwi waasechganaabkoon zhiwi toong zaagjiyiing zhiwi wiigwaaming.

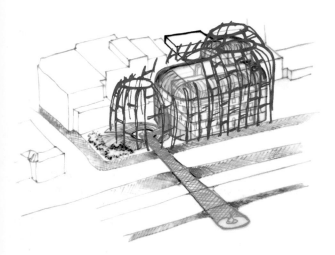

Figure 6. The wigwam inspires an outer framework reminiscent of bentwood structure.

Honoring the Gift – Mnaajtoong Maan'goong

It is an honor to be gifted a blanket. In marriage ceremonies, this gesture represents the uniting of two unique individuals. We wrap the existing building together with outdoor space, connecting our visitors in an embrace.

Gchi'ii wi miin'goong waaboowaan. Naabwijik maanda miin'gaazwak wii-zhinoomaageng ezhi-bezhgowaat gonda niish bemaadzijik. Mii dash maanda mekwendming naasaap zhitoong maanda wiigwaam wi gewe zhiwi kojiing waa-tek.

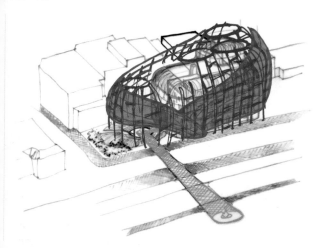

Figure 7. A blanket embraces the gift and visitors alike in sacred space.

The Regalia – Dbishkoo kwe gchitwaawkonyet zhi-zzegaachgaade maanda wiigwaam

We honor this gift by wrapping it in a regalia of decorations reminiscent perhaps of snowshoes, feathers, jingles, drying frames, gems. Each piece is designed by an Indigenous community so that our diverse peoples are all present. It changes over the years, resilient, beautiful, old gifts returned, new gifts applied, a unified but diversely inflected voice.

Wii-mnaadendmaang maanda maan'goowaang, nooch gegoo nda-zhi-zzegaatoonaa; na'ii ndan'kaaznaa nooch gegoo da-mkwenjgaadegba – aagmak gnamaa, miigwanak gewe, zhenwensan, naaksijganan toong gegoo baasming, miinwaa siniinsan nooch ezhi-mnwaandegin. Bebkaan Nishnaabe-kiing ngoji wenjbaajik zhitoonaawaan nanda nooch gegoo e-zzegaachgengin. Aanjchigaadenoon nanda aapiichin – gaa-miin'goong e-zoongkin, genaajwangin, neyaap miigwem, gshka'ii maan'goong dash chigaade – wii-zhinoomaageng nooch nsweyaan'gizwaat Maanpii Kiin Wenzkaajik, maamwi shwii go giigdawaat.

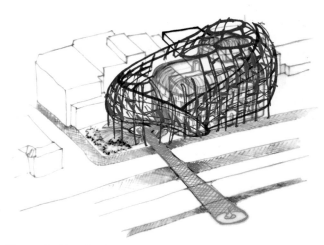

Figure 8. Regalia dances in a constant state of change as communities across the continent offer crafted gifts applied to the blanket framework, given back again in continual rotation.

Sacred fire + Welcome Park – Gchitwaa-shkode + Welcome Park

Walk along the Nation-to-Nation axis into this space of welcome, wrapped in regalia, around the sacred fire, to the East entry. Sit and look back to Parliament. Diverse cultural performances gather around the sacred fire each season.

Bi-biindgek maanpii, dbishkoo giizhooshewyek da-nendaagot. Giitaawsek gchitwaa-shkodeng, waabnong shkwaandeming dash ga-ni-zhaam. Nmadbik; Parliament gnawaabndamak. Nooch gegoo ezhi-mmaanjiinjik da-yaawak giitaayiing gchitwaa-shkodeng niibing, dgwaagik, bboong, mnookmik gewe.

Figure 9. Outdoor seasonal activities welcome visitors to this garden under a shared blanket, along an axis that connects our two fires.

Community Kitchen – Jiibaakwegamik Kina Wiya Debendang

Our narrative continues as visitors enter the building with Elders on one side and children on the other; all generations are welcomed and at home here.

Wii-ni-aabdaajmayaang: Biindgeyaat bebaa-yaajik, getzijik mbaneyiing yaawak, binoojiinyik dash gewii oodi npaajiyiing. Kina go wiya zhanda daa-biindge miinwaa endaat yaaji da-nendam.

Spatial Storyline from Wellington Street to Sparks Street – Enaabiising Naajmowin Wellington Biinish Sparks

The history and narratives of our nations are shared with augmented reality along a public path that connects Parliament to Sparks; this colonnade may be opened or closed; windows look onto an exhibition space for dancing, drumming, singing, art.

Miikaans Parliament da-nji-maajiimat; Sparks da-ko-namat. Na'ii zhiwi miikaansing da-zhinoomaadim, gaa-bi-zhiwebak, enaajmaying gewe. Daa-nsaaknigaade maage go daa-gbaakwigaade maanda colonnade; waasechganan gewe te-noon gegoo maanpii nakmigak wii-waabmindwaa naamjik, e-dewegejik, negmajik gewe, miinwaa mzinbii'ganak mzinniik miinwaa wi dnawa nooch gegoo zhinoomaading.

Figure 10. Spatial storytelling: moving along a journey of prediscovery, visitors are immersed in an augmented reality from Wellington to Sparks Street.

Offices Connected by Atrium – wii-waasetek kina endzhi-nakiiyaat

The inherent hierarchy of the historical building is fluidly reconnected with light; a glowing core builds kinship between earth and sky. The meeting and private spaces that encircle this core and look over Parliament inspire our representatives to speak for our nations

Mno-waasete kina zhanda bebkaan bmisgaak wii-waabndaming kina wiya naasaap piitendaagzit. Biindgeyaate bebkaan kina wiya yaat, waabndiwak dash kina zhanda en'kiijik. Parliament debaabminaagot. Waabndmawaat wi, da-mkwendaanaawaa zhanda en'kiijik ge-zhi-gnoodmawaawaapa wiiji-Nishnaabewaan.

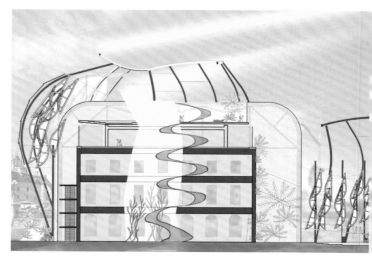

Figure 11. Reconnecting the earth and sky through the historical building.

Gathering of Nations Circle – Gathering of Nations Circle

At the place of connection to sky, a circular meeting space allows representatives to meet in a space that honors protocols such as pipe ceremonies. Views over Parliament connect to the outdoors with layers of roof garden.

Zhanda ge-dzhi-n'kweshkdaadwaat bemaadzijik, waawyeyaa wii-gshkitoowaat weweni wii-naagdoowaat ezhchigeng pwaagan zgaswaanin gchi-nakmigzing. Pakwaaning waawaaskoneyin gtigaadenoon; Parliament debaabminaagot.

Rooftop Garden and Cafe – Pakwaaning Gtigaanens Miinwaa Cafe

At celebrations and events, the outdoor roof garden and cafe look directly over Parliament, while the building wrap extends gently above to provide privacy and a comfortable environment with shade and shelter.

Nooch gegoo nakmigak, Parliament da-debaabndaanaawaa eyaajik zhiwi gtigaanensing wi pakwaaning etek, bekish dash da-aagooshnook wii-bwaa-waabmigwaat kina wiyan, miinwaa da-kajgaa, da-dbinwaa gewe.

Figure 12. Gathering of Nations Circle is a space for protocols such as pipe ceremony or smudge before meetings, looking out over the parliamentary precinct.

Regalia // Dbishkoo Kwe Gchitwaawkonyet Zhi-zzegaachgaade Maanda Wiigwaam

This wrap honors the gift and makes it our own. The ribs might be those of our mother, the decorations her skirt. All our nations are present here, each decoration gifted and returned in an ongoing cycle

Mnaadenjgaade maanda wiigwaam gaa-miin'goong, gda-daapnanaa dash maanda giinwi wii-dbendmang. Niwin pigegning ezhnaagkin, mii dbishkoo gashnaa eyaangin, wi ezhi-zzegaachgeng, mii dbishkoo wdoo-skirt. Nooch ngoji wenjiijik gonda sa Maanpii Kiin Wenzkaajik daa-zhitoonaawaa gegoo maanpii wiigwaaming waa-zzegaachgeng wii-tenik wiinwaa bimaadziwniwaang wenzkaanik wii-tenik maanpii Ottawa. Maamnik da-ke-teni wi maagweyaat, mii dash neyaap da-miindwaa, bekaanak dash miinwaa gnamaa daa-miigwenaawaa. Memeshkdoonming maagweng, mii maanda wiigwaam ezhi-zzegaachgaadek.

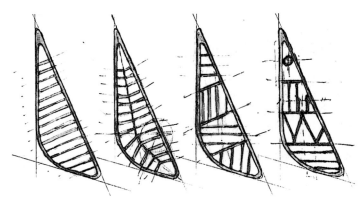

Figure 13. Displaying Indigenous material culture inspired by regalia, gifts crafted in our communities are in constant rotation, mounted on the blanket framework facade.

Chapter 3.0: K'alii'aks

luugigyoo patrick stewart – Killerwhale House of Daxaan of the Nisga'a Village of Gingolx

luugigyoo patrick stewart is a member of the Nisga'a Nation in northwestern B.C. from the community of Gingolx, a member of the Killerwhale House of Daxaan. He is an architect, artist, activist, writer, poet and advocate for Indigenous homeless in Canada.

K'ALII'AKS

Lisimshl wahl k'alii'aks tguna.

wil baxhl aks

silkwhl axkw, silkwsaxs

lukw, geehlt

axdii wil saabaxt,

ksagalgolhl ihlee'e.

Lisims.

THE RIVER

The river is the Nass,

the running water.

Night and day,

moving restlessly,

never ending,

like blood flowing.

The life of a Nation.

Chapter 3.1: Warburdar Bununu: rebuilding as renewal
Our Voices II conference talk: a reflection piece, University of Sydney 5th July 2019

Jason De Santolo – Garrwa and Barunggam

Dr Jason De Santolo is a researcher & creative producer. His tribal affiliations are Garrwa and Barunggam. He is associate professor of Indigenous Research in the School of Design at University of Technology Sydney and an adjunct associate professor in the Institute for Sustainable Futures. He previously worked as a Senior Researcher in Jumbunna Institute for Indigenous Education and Research where he led New Media and the Indigenous Research Synergies strategy. Jason co-edited Decolonizing Research: Indigenous storywork as methodology (2019) with Jo-Ann Archibald and Jenny Lee-Morgan (Zed Books). His latest documentary Warburdar Bununu/Water Shield (2019) explores water contamination in his homelands and Borroloola, Northern Territory.

Abstract

Warburdar Bununu is a notion that we can care for & maintain relationships with water through our ancient cultural land-based practices of sustainability. In particular the concept of bununu or shielding focuses on song as a profound practice for transforming the way we rebuild Indigenous societies amidst the ongoing assault of colonisation. As a documentary film Warburdar Bununu joins the lineage of *Two Laws* (1981) filmmaking that comes from my tribal homelands in the Gulf of Carpentaria in the Northern Territory and the township of Borroloola.

As a strategic Indigenous story work response to water contamination, Warburdar Bununu emerges from a doctoral journey that activated "song line" renewal within a Garrwa and Yanuwa research paradigm of transformation (De Santolo, 2018). As a moment of Indigenous design activism Warburdar Bununu offers an inspiring glimpse into emotional resonance and the potential of decolonising film research practices. In this short reflection I share insights into the film design elements of the project as climate justice activism & in particular the assertion that "Culture is stronger than contamination."

Introduction

Song lines before Treaty. Trees before Treaty. Land before Treaty. Water Before Treaty. Country before Treaty.

Gadrian Hoosan (Garrwa and Yanyuwa community leader).

Address to the Climate Strike rally of 80,000 people on Gadigal lands, Sydney City Sept 20, 2019.

Warburdar Bununu is a notion that we can care for & maintain relationships with water through our ancient cultural land-based practices of sustainability. In particular the concept of bununu or shielding focuses on song as a profound practice for transforming the way we rebuild Indigenous societies amidst the ongoing assault of colonisation. As a documentary film Warburdar Bununu joins the lineage of *Two Laws* (1981) filmmaking that comes from my tribal homelands in the Gulf of Carpentaria in the Northern Territory and the township of Borroloola.

As a strategic Indigenous storywork response to water contamination, Warburdar Bununu emerges from a doctoral journey that activated "song line" renewal within a Garrwa and Yanyuwa research paradigm of transformation (De Santolo, 2018). As a moment of Indigenous design activism Warburdar Bununu offers an inspiring glimpse into emotional resonance and the potential of decolonising film research practices. In this short reflection I share insights into the film design elements of the project as climate justice activism & in particular the assertion that, "Culture is stronger than contamination."

Figure 1. Scott McDinny, Warburdar Bununu film shoot, Sandridge Outstation 2018.

Culture is stronger than contamination

I just got a gig in School of Design at UTS and lead the Indigenous Research Synergies strategy here – it is a re-imaginary for some of the Indigenous research, activism and story work that we do in the self-determination and education space. I recently published Decolonizing Research, Indigenous Story work as Methodology (Zed books) with my cherished international relations, the esteemed Prof's Jo-Ann Archibald and Jenny Lee Morgan. It marks a new point in the movement to protect homelands and languages and our cultures through the transformative way of Indigenous story work (Archibald, 2008). This is now informing my filmmaking and I am really proud of this films impact for our communities' struggle for clean drinking water. Warburdar Bununu is really a strategic alignment with our old ways of storying our Country as Homelands through our own cultural lens. The most prominent being *Two Laws* (1981), which was coproduced with our Elders and united the four tribes of the region into one voice against mining. *Two Laws* is celebrated as evoking a paradigm shift in documentary making (Ginsburg, 2008).

With this lineage behind us we were sick of seeing all these NGO style videos about our movements and leadership and wanted to share strength and wisdom of our ancestors and youth working together. The main character in Warburdar Bununu is Scotty McDinny, my nephew. He is one of our tribal youth leaders and a cultural leader for Seed Indigenous youth climate justice network in Australia. In the film he asserts a strong fundamental message in response to the water contamination of our rivers and bores: "Culture is stronger than contamination." How does this statement make you feel in a moment of absolute climate and social crisis, does it resonate with an experience or an anxiety? There

is an emotional landscape behind Warburdar Bununu. It is an echo of deep cultural concepts and because of this the film design ecology is guided by our own story protocols, laws and trajectories of liberation across key Indigenous rights campaigns. Culture is stronger than contamination is deeply tied to the notion that our song lines are powerful living manifestations of authority and knowledge and therefore hold greater value than Western rights conceptualisations in things like treaty making. In a way it speaks to an ancient intent behind our homeland movement. To rebuild a self-determining society, we must adhere to cultural ways as practices of renewal, where the foundations of meaning making are framed around ways, we relate to life sustaining elements, such as water.

We are not solely driven by economics of developmental institutional power or other Western notions of the renewable. Authority over Country does not reside in Western sources, it comes from our songs, dances, stories, arts and continued practices of hunting, being and occupation of our lands (Raheja, 2010) (Bradley, 2012) (Koch, 2013) (Hoosan, 2014). Our communities may be at the frontline of the extractive industries, but they have the absolute strength, privilege and responsibility of maintaining ancient practices of renewal that have been handed down for a thousand generations and beyond. The main reason for this assertion is simple, the origins of our work to rebuild our homelands is driven by much deeper emotional connections and older philosophies of belonging and being on Country.

Emotional resonance

There were two important sensory elements to be mindful of in the film design activism space of Warburdar Bununu. One is deeply personal – emotional resonance, how do we understand storying well-being in relation in in our current environmental climate crisis? The other concerns the inter-relational dimensions of film/video. How do we relate, respond and activate film design impact solutions that challenge unfairness, bigotry, racism, patriarchy, and a broader hegemony? Emotional resonance is intuition, it is that gut feeling when you know something is not quite right, it is energetic and organic. Emotional resonance can be inspired by a sun shower in a park and the communion of shared connection (De Santolo, 2019). Emotional resonance evokes deeper connections with the elemental things in life, and through deeper awareness the inter-relational dimensions of life sustaining systems. Our inner curiosity drives this journey. Of importance are the relationships with the basic elements of water, light, fire and earth, air. They are foundational ways of understanding connection to living ecosystems and ancient Indigenous knowledge systems and practices of renewal. As Uncle Max Dulumunmun Harrison shares with us: "See the land ... the beauty: hear the land ... the story. Feel the land ... the spirit."

Indigenous theories, methodologies and praxis are brimming with the emotion and energy that connects people to land over thousands and thousands of years. In this way Indigenous peoples have understood cycles and rhythms of nature, from the deep biological and ecological knowledge systems held in our song lines, to the clapstick as first mobile phone (Harrison, 2019). These propositions inform and are exquisitely embedded into our practices, song, dance, art, design – embodied and now disrupted but not destroyed by colonisation. By engaging emotionally in this space, we can connect intrinsically with meaning making in dynamic shared knowledge spaces. In this context there is vast potential in tracing new ways of communicating and enacting ancient Indigenous practices. It helps ground multiple standpoints, perspectives, worldviews and perspectives in Country, whether its city scape or bush homeland.

Revitalising traditional fire systems is one of these powerful dynamic spaces that benefit the land, all beings and all people (Gothe 2018, Steffensen 2019). Bridging knowledge principles are a beautiful key to working towards climate justice that can be adaptable, Country based and community empowered. Victor Steffensen articulates this in his significant leadership in revitalising traditional fire practices across the continent and now overseas through the emergence of Firesticks as a national grass roots movement. Victor calls the action that drives this transformation "praction," a term emerged in conversation with his Elders (Steffensen, 2019).

Can methodologies like "praction" reorientate our understanding of practice-led research and design thinking? Can it allow us to decolonise and challenge meaning making propositions and historical trajectories that are carefully crafted narratives sourced in state discourses of control? Through the magic of design, we are definitely able to offer insight into new ways of seeing and meaning making in the world but how do we take this further in the relational ecology of Country. We need to take decolonising design further as a project that emerges from Country and homelands, as design justice, as Indigenous design activism.

It that way, Warburdar Bununu offers a moment where new ways of iterating and interpreting film impact so that meaning can be mutually responsive to intersectional dimensions of colonial domination and the decolonial project (O'Brien, 2018) (Constanza-Chock, 2018) (Newcomb, 2008). With so many of us now living off our homelands there is urban dimension, a reality that most of us live in cities now. Kevin O'Brien helps us frame this as an imagined city context: "And the ceremonies and rituals and social settings that need to occur with it, then become the things that generate the new form of an imagined city." (O'Brien, 2018). The generosity of Indigenous story work offers us a simple way to regenerate new understandings of ceremony, ritual and ancient knowledge practices though meaning making experiences that are embedded and relate with liberational aspirations and new framings of Indigenous self-determination.

Indigenous story research & film design activism

Warburdar Bununu was created using elements of Yarnbar Jarngkurr, talk story.

Yarnbar Jarngkurr is a foundational story work research approach that emerges from action and a doctoral study on Garrwa and Yanyuwa homelands. As a decolonising research methodology Yarnbar Jarngkurr strategically aligns with Garrwa principles, laws and ancient practices of autonomous sustainability and has vast potential within relational collaboration and international rights driven contexts (De Santolo, 2018). Story research involves important processes for respecting existing localised Indigenous research principles and video protocols. The interactive and reflexive process has shifted my own creative research practice and also informed the development of story and knowledge sharing principles and protocols unique to Garrwa and Yanyuwa's lived experience.

Embedded within Yarnbar Jarngkurr is a story research methodology with three key interrelated foundational principles: Darrbarrwarra, Karja Murku and Ngirakar Bununu (De Santolo 2018, p.56). In particular, I focus on Ngirikar Bununu here and the trajectory of this Garrwa notion that our cultural practices are powerful, energetic and can shield/protect our homelands. Ongoing threats to the region are becoming overwhelming as multinational interest in gas, uranium, and other extractives heightens. Reconnecting with the beauty and power of these ancient discourses is one of the exciting outcomes of this story research process as it has helped to shape principles and protocols for the sharing of these stories through Indigenous video practice. I engage the term, story research process, from Jo-Ann Archibald as it emphasises story as a core aspect of the research process and highlights the scholarly vision of Indigenous Storywork (Archibald, 2008). Paradoxically, the sharing of these songs has powerful shielding capabilities for sacred sites and homelands. Engaging with story work has been personally enriching for my own and my family's well-being. As an energetic interaction the act of rebuilding as renewal it also holds deep emotional resonance to my homelands. Warburdar Bununu attempts to convey a message of compassion and hope in a political context of extreme colonial oppression for colonisation is in a constant process of design. Colonisation is not just the violent act of stealing lands, killing people, and destroying ecosystems. Colonisation is storied to divide people, to taint place through hatred and greed, to destroy love for the world and us by othering all that is diverse. Colonisation continues to push our languages towards extinction and neoliberal forces target our homelands and song line sacred sites for extraction. In more recent times colonisation is mining, in speaking back to the empire colonisation is revealed as being in an era of contamination.

For Garrwa Elders shielding is also about communicating sustainable autonomy as an overt challenge to extractive industries in the Northern Territory - where exploration licenses cover 80% of the entire landmass (Hoosan, 2014) (Kerins, 2017). The lifting of the fracking moratorium by the NT Labour gunner Govt was a deep blow to all the voters who trusted the promise that they would not frack the NT. Colonisation is a story that is constantly asserted by design in order to maintain the status quo and the domination of Indigenous peoples, the original and only true custodians of this continent. So how do we all free ourselves from this false paradigm, how can we transform our lived realities? How can we truly engage with practice led research, design thinking and making and tackle these large complex problems if we do not free ourselves from the very foundations of the colonised society we live in? The rebuilding as renewal story work paradigm offers some hope as it is informed by decolonising strategies that can enhance revitalisation of languages and transform our research and creative practices. In a way this work begins renewing the story worlds of our ancestors as a critical cultural survival strategy.

Storying an era of contamination

"Old and young united we are stronger. But we need jobs on Country for young fellas like my nephew here, publicly funded by all Governments. With this people power, I know we can make this just transition real for all people. That's why we are all here!" (Gadrian Hoosan, *Climate Strike rally*, 2019).

Warburdar Bununu is one of those beautifully held collaborations and film design activism has influenced its ongoing impact. It has helped us to story our experiences of contamination as colonisation of our sacred relationship to water and in doing so has connected our experiences with the broader climate justice movement. Indigenous story research also has potential here to open up hearts and minds to ancient systems of knowledge and practices as climate justice solutions.

The Indigenous research paradigm allows this expansive space to maintain focus on the reassertion of self-determination, revitalisation of language and culture, and the transformation of ways we educate and story our lived realities. In particular Indigenous story work emerges as a unifying theory in the decolonising methodologies movement, aligning Indigenous theories of transformation with assertive self-determination strategies (Smith, 1999), (Behrendt, 2019). Despite the innovation of creative methodologies across disciplines and diverse communities of practice there is a deeper imperative to interrogate existing research design practices (spatial, visual, material). In doing so I hope we can glimpse into Indigenous ways of knowing, being, doing and in that

way feel the deeper elements of consequence, for design is always manifesting in a relational world, design holds vast potential to maintain and sustain us within our own storied existence. It can help us to see colonisation and locate it within our own lived reality. It can help us to reorientate our creative, research, design practices in dynamic ways so as to feel connected to Indigenous paradigms and movements (Cayete, 2015).

On Sept 20, 2019 Indigenous Speakers lead the Climate Strike on Gadigal lands in Sydney. This student led Global Climate Strike called out to workers and all peoples to join them. More than four million people across the world and 163 countries joined in the action. This was the biggest day of action for Climate Justice in World History and it is growing. On the day 80,000 strong rallied on Gadigal lands in Sydney. Significantly the first five invited speakers were Indigenous from this continent and across the Pacific. The speakers connected Indigenous struggles to protect lands, waters and ways of life that are deeply under threat from mining, fracking, government inaction and the climate crisis.

Scotty joined our local family Elders Aunty Rhonda Grovenor Dixon & her daughter Nadeena Dixon on stage for the welcome to Gadigal country in the Domain. Most of the Indigenous speakers wore Warburdar Bununu t-shirts because the meaning behind it deeply connected us in this shared experience of the climate crisis in our homelands and on stage. Aunty Rhonda shared an emotional moment after the rally saying how proud she was to welcome and speak in the Domain to thousands of supportive youth. It had reminded her of the legendary Elder statesman of the movement Chicka Dixon "the Fox," her father and his moments speaking in the Domain. She said it was an emotional moment also because, "we came together once again in the right way, the cultural way, as protectors of the lands, for clean rivers and healthy community."

It was a truly proud moment to hear one of our leaders Gadrian Hoosan speak with such passion and connect our family and tribal experiences through respect and determination to stand strong in the winds of change. His delivery encapsulates a lot of the intent of Warburdar Bununu, it offers a generosity of spirit and hope alongside clear critiques of govt inaction, songlines are without a doubt more important than what may become a falsely inspired treaty making process in Australia.

To stand with all young people of the world, Indigenous peoples, students and workers, unions, all striking for the climate and Mother Earth. Our song lines show us all the way forward, they hold the key to protecting Country. Culture is stronger than contamination. Why would we want to Treaty with a government that wants to destroy our Country? A Government that lifted the moratorium on Fracking, a govt that tortures our young people. Water is Life. Together united we will win, and we will survive (Gadrian Hoosan, *Climate Strike rally. 2019.*)

The families and Scotty in connecting with Uncle Max were rebuilding and re-orientating our stories of resistance into actions of renewal. In solidarity we were standing with student strikers, families, unions, workers, activists and Indigenous peoples across the continent and Pasifika, through the Pacific Climate Warriors. It felt meaningful amidst the continued struggle against fracking and mining and all the many injustices experienced here in Australia and across the world.

Conclusion

At one level Warburdar Bununu sits in a lineage of authority over Country to which we continue to story our lived experience of colonisation over different contexts. Today it is storying an era of contamination. Indigenous film design activism is playing an important role here for the family and clan. It is revealing entanglements that are both positive and negative. Through deep, respectful relational collaboration we can rebuilding our society through story research paradigms that manifest a sustainable way forward for our future generations, as families, clans, tribes and nations. The work continues and grows in significance, I am so excited to be in this space. We are navigating through complex social and political influences, but we must be careful to hold integrity and fluidity and not became essentialist in how we story our future pathways of liberation (Borrows, 2019). Warburdar Bununu is necessarily fluid and organic, it holds its own ethics and teachings for our own people, it holds story as law and therefore resonates beyond time and space. Warburdar Bununu is deeply aligned to the broader Indigenous rights movements and resurgences across the world. We are proud to have screened it and shown solidarity with our international Maori relations at the significant occupation site Ihumatao in Aotearoa NZ. It also speaks to the climate justice movement and it cannot be whitewashed in a way that others may think.

So how do we further activate Indigenous story research in design as an innovative proposal for exploring the meaning making synergies between Indigenous story work and research design practices — spatial, visual, material. This decolonial project gathering is powerful for ultimately, we seek life in this important moment, yet we cannot move forward alone. We share the same breath in this moment of climate and social crisis. Only together can we truly honour the power of shared ancestral visions and practices of renewal. There is hope in this shared knowledge space, where story world potential activates transformative Black Indigenous transitions and the rebuilding aspirations for autonomous self-determining Indigenous societies.

Bibliography

Archibald, J.A. *Indigenous Storywork: Educating the Heart, Mind, Body and Spirit*. UBC Press, Vancouver (2008).

Behrendt, L. "Indigenous storytelling, Decolonizing institutions and assertive self-determination – implications for legal practice," in J. Archibald, J. Lee-Morgan, & J. De Santolo (Eds.) *Decolonising Research, Indigenous Storywork as Decolonizing Research Methodology,* pp. 175-186, London, Zed books (2019).

Bradley, J. *Singing saltwater country: journey to the song lines of Carpentaria.* Allen & Unwin, Sydney (2012).

Borrows, J. *Law's Indigenous Ethics.* University of Toronto Press, Toronto (2019).

Cayete, G. (2015). *Indigenous knowledge and Western science: Dr Gregory Cajete Talk,* BANFF Centre, viewed 16 June 2017 at: https://www.youtube.com/watch?v=nFeNlOglbzw

Constanza-Chock, S. Design Justice: towards an intersectional feminist framework for design theory and practice, Design Research Society 2018. Catalyst, University of Limerick.

De Santolo J. "Shielding Indigenous worlds from extraction & the transformative potential of collaborative research*,"* in: D. Fam, L. Neuhauser & P. Gibbs (Eds.) *Transdisciplinary Theory, Practice & Education: The Art of Collaborative Research and Collective Learning,* pp. 175-186, London, Springer (2018).

Koch, G. "We have the song, so we have the land: song and ceremony as proof of ownership in Aboriginal and Torres Strait Islander land claims," AIATSIS Research Discussion Paper No. 33, Canberra (2013).

Ginsburg, F. *Breaking the law with Two Laws: reflections on a paradigm shift.* Kanymarda Yuwa/Two Laws – Special DVD Dossier, Studies in Documentary Film 2: 2, pp. 169-174 (2008).

Greenaway, J. "Embracing cultural sensitivities that celebrate First Nations perspectives," in R. Kiddle, L. Stewart & K.O'Brien (Eds.), *Our Voices, indigeneity and architecture.* California, United States, ORO Editions, Our Voices Publishing Collective, pp.155-163 (2018).

Harrison, D, M. Introduction, Design family & Country BrownBag Workshop, March 14, Indigenous Design Synergies, Design Innovation Research Centre, UTS (2019).

Hoosan, G. "Gadrian Hoosan: the land is the most important thing for indigenous people," *The Guardian*, viewed 10 October 2016 https://www.theguardian.com/commentisfree/2014/oct/10/gadrianhoosan-the-land-is-the-most-important-thing-for-indigenous-people.

Kerins, S. "Open Cut: Life on an Australian Frontier," *Arena Magazine*, Issue 150 (2017).

Newcomb, S. *Pagans in the Promised Land: Decoding the Doctrine of Christian Discovery*. Golden, CO. Fulcrum Publishing (2008).

O'Brien, K. (2018). In conversation with Kevin O'Brien, Indigenous urbanism, accessed Oct 1, 2019 https://indigenousurbanism.simplecast.com/episodes/in-conversation-with-kevin-obrien.

Pihama, L. "Kaupapa Maori Theory, Transforming theory in Aotearoa," *Te Kotahi Reader*. University of Waikato, Hamilton: pp.5-16 (2015).

Raheja, M. *Reservation Reelism: Redfacing, Visual Sovereignty, and Representations of Native Americans in Film*. University of Nebraska Press, Lincoln (2010).

Smith, L. *Decolonizing Methodologies*. London, Zed books (1999).

Van Leeuwen, T. *Speech, music, sound*. Palgrave Macmillan, United Kingdom (1999).

Van Leeuwen, T. "Multimodality" in J. Simpson, (ed). *The Routlege Handbook of Applied Linguistics*. Routlege, Milton Park, Abington: pp. 668-682 (2011).

Wilson, S. *Research is Ceremony, Indigenous research methods*. Fernwood Publishing, Nova Scotia (2008).

Chapter 3.2: Designing with Country
Rethreading Aboriginal Culture into the Design Fabric of Sydney's Built and Natural Environment through Language, Place and Memory

Dillon Kombumerri – Yugembir and Danièle Hromek – Budawang, Yuin

Dillon Kombumerri is a Yugembir Goori of the Gold Coast, Queensland and grew up on North Stradbroke Island (Minjerriba). He is a strategic design thinker and social conciliator with a passion for projects that seek to improve the health, well-being and prosperity of Indigenous communities. With over 25 years of experience in architectural practice he brings his own unique Indigenous perspective to re-imagining the built environment. During this time, Dillon has also been teaching and lecturing globally in many forums to shine a light on the hidden value of Indigenous knowledge and how it can positively influence private and public agencies to deliver better outcomes for the built and natural environment.

Dr Danièle Hromek is a Budawang woman of the Yuin nation. She is a spatial designer, speculative designer, public artist, and researcher. Her practice works in the intersection of architecture, interiors, urban design, performance design and fine arts. Her work often considers the urban Aboriginal condition, the Indigenous experience of Country and contemporary Indigenous identities. Danièle's research contributes an understanding of the Indigenous experience and comprehension of space, and investigates how Aboriginal people occupy, use, narrate, sense, dream and contest their spaces. It rethinks the values that inform Aboriginal understandings of space through Indigenous spatial knowledge and cultural practice, in doing so considers the sustainability of Indigenous cultures from a spatial perspective.

This collaborative writing was achieved through a series of yarns between Dillon and Danièle. Yarning is a culturally appropriate method of conversation and sharing knowledges.

This writing was possible with thanks to Deb Verhoeven from the Faculty of Arts and Social Sciences at the University of Technology Sydney.

We acknowledge the Traditional Custodians of Country throughout Australia and abroad, and their continuing connection to culture, community, land, sea and sky. We pay our respects to Elders past, present, and future. We acknowledge the First Peoples of the Sydney area, who have strived to retain and reclaim their cultures, languages, identities, and connections to Country despite colonisation. We recognise the valuable contribution made by Aboriginal Sydney to community, narratives, spaces, and places.

Introduction

According to their narratives and histories, Aboriginal people have always lived in the place now called Sydney. As custodians of the land they have loved and cared for it since time immemorial, and the land has likewise cared for them, providing sustenance, nurturing, and home.

Time was not known or recorded in the same way as it is now; however, an event occurred in the year identified by the Gregorian calendar system as 1788 that changed things indelibly for the First Peoples. In one version of the story,[1] one day, 11 enormous white birds floated into

---

1. The story conveyed here is related to one shared by Dwayne Naja Bannon-Harrison (Yuin/Gunai man with Watchabolic and Yorta-Yorta kinship connections), originally told by Uncle Warren Foster (a Djiringanj Elder from Wallaga Lake), about Captain Cook's journey north up the east coast of Australia past Yuin Country, published with permission in Hromek's doctoral thesis (2019). There is a linked story from Gweagal Country around Botany Bay; Cora Gooseberry (daughter of Moorooboora, of the Murubora tribe) told colonist George French Angas of her father's reaction to the arrival of the First Fleet. Angas (1789) reported, "On the approach of the vessels, the natives [sic], who had never seen a ship before, imagining them to be huge sea-monsters,

he harbour. These birds were known from the Dreaming as vicious terrifying creatures who used to scoop people up in their beaks, chew them up and spit them out. The Gadigal people on the shore pointed their spears at the enormous birds, shouting, *Wara wara! Wara wara!* ["Be gone, go far away!"].[2] However, the birds stayed, and in fact have never left. In effect those enormous white birds did scoop up the First Peoples, chewing them up and spitting them out.

Obviously in this story the enormous birds were the First Fleet ships, carrying Governor Arthur Phillip and the British to the shores of Sydney. Remarkably, Aboriginal people survived in the city became known as Sydney, continuing their culture, stories, knowledges and families. They maintained strong connections with their lands and the resources offered by Country, sharing them with new inhabitants. As Sydney grew into a city and spread west, north and south towards the mountains, rivers and harbours, the original inhabitants were joined by displaced Aboriginal people from elsewhere in New South Wales and across Australia to live, work, find relatives, and create new relationships. Together they now form the extensive diverse community which forms *Aboriginal Sydney*.

The land Sydney sits upon is home to a number of Aboriginal groups with differing names and languages. As their names originated from an oral tradition with multiple dialects, and colonisers have not always well understood Aboriginal ways of forming words, there are many ways of saying and spelling them. Included within these are Darug (Dharug, Daruk, Dharook, Oharruk), Eora (Iyora, Lyora, Iora), Dharawal (Darawal, D'harawal, Tharawal, Turuwal, Turrubul), Gundungurra (Gandangarra), Deerubbin (Dyarubbin, Dooraban), Ku-ring-gai (Guringai, Kurig-gai, Kuringgai).[3] We acknowledge that Sydney is a contested space, both physically and politically. We also acknowledge that in Aboriginal knowledge systems and worldviews there are many ways of knowing, many truths and diverse perspectives. Likewise, there are many truths

about places containing diversity in the knowledges, stories, histories and understandings of that place, and First Peoples' spaces had and still have overlaps, interstitial spaces, merged areas, fluidity and nebulosity. All are respected in this writing.

Country, which holds space and knowledges, does so in part through memory, including individual memory, collective memory and the memory of Country itself. In particular, in urban environments such as Sydney that have been changed so dramatically through colonial forces, memory is central. One means of relating memory directly back to the land is through the naming of places. First place names originate with First languages and sites of importance. Like place names, many Indigenous peoples' ways of mapping – for instance, walking Country, performing on Country or narrating Country – are a way of connecting to Country and are integral to designing with Country. While Aboriginal culture and heritage has to date been largely missing from the planning context, recent changes in governmental policies requires the sustainable management of built and cultural heritage including Aboriginal cultural heritage. Designing relationally and collaboratively with Country is integral to the future of placemaking, design and architecture in Sydney as a means for capturing a wider narrative of history and place.

Invisible Sydney

It is a common experience for First Peoples to feel invisible in public spaces. The seeming absence of Indigenous peoples from the colonial landscape extends to historical accounts, colonial narratives and literature, as well as legislative decision-making processes and policy, including the planning and design disciplines. This supposed lack of an Indigenous presence in urban contexts occurred partially because Aboriginal people were driven out of emerging townships, partially because they were then written out by authors (Stanner, 1968) and planners, and then, in part through government policy such as the model of assimilation developed by Adolphus Peter Elkin in collaboration with the Commonwealth government (Elkin cited in Gray, 2007). This resulted in forced assimilation into colonial spaces. Settler colonialism, as is experienced in Australia,

> Wants Indigenous land, not Indigenous peoples, so Indigenous peoples are cleared out of the way of colonial expansion, first via genocide and destruction, and later through incorporation and assimilation. The settler colonial discourse turns Indigenous peoples into savages, unhuman, and eventually, ghosts (Tuck & McKenzie, 2015).[4]

were so terrified that they ran into the bush, and did not stop to look back until they reached a place now called Liverpool, distant about twenty miles, where they hid themselves in trees!" cited in K. V. Smith, 2006). This story is substantiated by a report printed in London by an anonymous officer (Unknown, 1789), who wrote, "The natives [sic] alarmed, ran along the beach in seeming great terror, and made much confused noise; they seemed very frightened, so much that they took their canoes out of the water upon their backs and ran off with them into the country, together with their fishing tackle and children."

2. Uncle Greg Simms (Gadigal, Dharug, Gundungurra, Yuin Elder) confirmed the meaning of these words, and the understanding within the above story.

3. These various spellings are collated from numerous sources including Troy (1994), Green (2010), Karskens (2009), Attenbrow (2010) as well as directly from Elders including Uncle Greg Simms 2015, 2016, 2018) and Aunty Fran Bodkin (2016, 2017, 2018).

4. Eve Tuck is Unangax and an enrolled member of the Aleut

This erasure of Aboriginal peoples from the spaces of Sydney, both literal and written, has continued into contemporary discourse, creating the misconception that urban Aboriginal people are inauthentic, have lost their culture or are newcomers to the urban environment (Ireland, 2013). On the contrary, Sydney has always had, has, and will always have an Aboriginal presence.

The Australian Bureau of Statistics (2018) confirms that contrary to common perception, Indigenous people predominantly live in populous urban areas with about 81% living in cities and regional areas and more than one third living in major cities. There are more than 70,000 Indigenous peoples living in the Greater Sydney area. Aboriginal people who live in a "traditional" tribal context have historically been mislabelled as "real Aborigines [sic]," which establishes the marginalisation of urban Aboriginal peoples who are by default "out of place" (Langton, 1981).[5] This misperception "tacitly affirms the essentialist position that authentic Aboriginality is always prior or distant: away in the past or away on the frontier" (Byrne, 2003). Greenop and Memmott also discuss contemporary urban Aboriginal culture as being "unreadable" to many non-Indigenous people who might see only a "culture of poverty" or "welfare dependence". A common misreading that occurs is a culture so altered from "proper" Aboriginal culture (by this they mean from the remote interior of the continent, or from a remote archaeological past) that it is therefore "no culture" (Greenop & Memmott, 2006). And yet in western value systems,

> Much of what it means to be a subject and citizen is embodied in cities. Cities insulate us from natural processes; they are the places where the delineation of public and private space is most marked, the division of labour most developed and the impersonal relations of the market most concentrated. The idea that civilisation obtains its most mature expression where population densities are highest is a profoundly European one (Morgan, 2006).

This inequity of values and rights towards urban Indigenous peoples that western society places in relation to cities has enduring impacts on Indigenous populations because it effectively makes them placeless in a metropolitan context. Outcomes associated with placelessness are suicide, high levels of incarceration, ill health, lowered life expectancy, loss of identity and intergenerational insecurity (Havemann, 2005).

Nonetheless, and despite living in changing and different spatial paradigms, Aboriginal peoples continue to find ways to connect to Country, continuing storytelling practices, finding refuge in each other, inhabiting the in-between interstitial spaces as well as creating new ways to move through the urban landscape. Narratives and cultural practices from the Aboriginal Sydney community ensure their voices continue to exist, and more recently, be heard. Despite this, architecture and design has yet to draw level in ensuring Indigenous voices are noticeable in the design of public spaces and urban places.

Present Absences of Country in Memory

Country holds memory both tangibly and intangibly. Marcia Langton (2002) describes this in relation to how Aboriginal people see the landscape as follows:

> The way that *Bama* [Aboriginal people] perceive landscapes is thus rather like the way that someone with a reasonable astronomical knowledge in Western culture perceives the night sky resplendent with twinkling stars. As one looks at the stars, there is the simultaneous sense of perceiving something that is present, the view itself sensed visually at that time, and of perceiving things that are past, the stars whose deaths many thousands of light years ago are perceived as the twinkling radiances in the black depths of space. And again, at the same time, there is the knowledge behind these perceptions, that we can only know these things because of our understandings of time as past-present-future. The future is implicated in our understanding of the past and the present ... Space and temporality are intertwined ... It is in this metaphysical construction that place is marked, inscribed with *Story*, given meaning, and guiding human movement in the process.

Irrespective of changes that occur to the material aspect of Country, those memories remain in place albeit imperceptibly. The changes to the land in Sydney through the processes of colonisation have been immeasurable palpably and perceptibly. Uncle Greg Simms[6] (cited in Hromek, 2018) discusses these changes in relation to Aboriginal peoples' relationships to land and Ancestors and how those memories are held in Country, saying,

> It is still our spirit Country; our spirit still lies there. No matter that they build city on it, it is still a place we can always go back and heal ... it is all changed but it is still Country. You still get healing from that place. Just go back take off your shoes, walk around on the land to regenerate the soul. Call out the spirits of your Ancestors. That is what

Community of St. Paul Island, Alaska.
5. Marcia Langton is a descendant of the Yiman and Bidjara nations of Queensland.

6. Uncle Greg Simms descends from the Gundungurra (water dragon lizard people) of the Blue Mountains, the Gadigal (whale people) of the Dharug nation around Sydney, and the beach plover people of the Budawang people from the South Coast.

the Old People taught us. We have got to go home to talk to the Old People, talk to the spirits of our Ancestors.

It is here, in the memory of Country, that space and time become intertwined inextricably. Time is known and measured through cosmological and seasonal cycles,[7] as well as through patterns of the mundane, and of mobility. Time is relational space. Time is understood through the everyday lived experience of the changes of Country, the movement around and mapping of Country through travel, and countless generations of knowledge sharing. Seasons are not fixed and do not adhere to western calendars or numerical ways of knowing time. Western calendars or numerical ways of knowing time are, in effect, a construct of our society rather than actuality. By this we mean, Wednesday is only Wednesday because we all agree as a society to acknowledge it as such. Indigenous ways of marking time relate to Country and events happening on Country; a particular flower blooming may indicate the travelling of whales which designates the coming of a new season, for instance. It is this knowing of time in relation to Country which, to us, seems based in reality. It is Country that tells First Peoples when the time is right. It is the messages of Country which First Peoples – and all those with whom we share Country, including animals, plants, waters, rocks, winds, rains, and other people – must learn to read intimately and respond to appropriately. Therefore, temporality is fluid, based on phenomenological experiences of events occurring and recurring in place, here and now, oriented to an awareness of flow, relationships and atmosphere. The material and tangible changes to Country note time, while the imperceptible and intangible expressions of time are marked in story, knowledges and memory (Bawaka Country, Wright, Suchet-Pearson, Lloyd, Burarrwanga, Ganambarr, Ganambarr-Stubbs, Ganambarr, & Maymuru, 2015; Hromek, 2018; Langton, 2002; Larsen & Johnson, 2012;

L. T. Smith, 2012)[8] [9] [10].

Bawaka Country et al. (2015) discuss memory, or "present absences," of Country in relation to mining on their lands thus:

> In Yolngu Country, there is bauxite mining. Yolngu campaigned against the mining, but it proceeded regardless. Now, many trees and some Country have been removed. Those trees aren't there anymore but Yolgnu still sing them, Yolgnu still keep them alive remembering them. Like a young person who took their own life, or an ant crushed thoughtlessly under a human foot, their gurrutu [the complex networks of kinship that link individuals and groups to each other] still holds them. These are the present absences of gurrutu, of Bawaka's co-becoming.

In Sydney around the shorelines, there were shell middens; they still exist in some places. These middens are evidence of a long history of relationship between people and place, of generations of kin visiting the same site, sharing food and stories, holding ceremony with folk from afar, or simply routine existence. The shells were highly prized by the colonists to make lime for use in constructions, so while the middens themselves may no longer exist in the same way, shells from middens can be seen in the cement aggregate of colonial architecture. Those beautiful shell monuments, reported to be up to 12 metres high in places, their materiality and objective, while no longer existing tangibly, are rememberable, along with those who created them. Not only are they still visible in colonial architecture, but the intangible elements relating to the people and culture who created them are likewise existing in memory, narrative, and cultural practice as present absences. Memories of Country held in Country are supported by our languages, which inherently contain knowledges about the land, its care and ourselves. The visibility of storylines such as these are relatively invisible in architecture and require agency to encourage thinking and considerations in this way.

First Languages are the Vibrations of Country

First Peoples' creation stories tell us we originated from our lands, that our histories and connections to Country are very ancient, "From the absolute beginning of the world. Our landscapes can be recreated in places that are

---

7. For instance, Shannon Foster (D'harawal Saltwater Knowledge Keeper) explains the six seasons of Sydney in a contemporary context (2015a), naming them as Burran (time of the kangaroo, hot and dry weather, January to March), Marrai'gang (time of the spotted tail quoll, wet becoming cool, April to June), Burrugin (time of the echidna, short days that are cold and frosty, June and July), Wiritjiribin (time of the lyrebird, cold and windy days, July and August), Ngoonungi (time of the flying fox, cool weather becoming warmer, September and October), and Parra'dowee (time of the short finned eels, warm stormy weather, November and December). These seasons are described in more detail in the book *D'harawal Seasons and Climatic Cycles* by D'harawal Elder Aunty Fran Bodkin (2008).

---

8. Bawaka is an Indigenous homeland on the water of Port Bradshaw in Arnhem Land off the Gulf of Carpentaria in the north of Australia. Research is conducted in collaboration with Indigenous and non-Indigenous people, with Bawaka Country as lead author.
9. Jay T. Johnson is Native American from the Delaware and Cherokee peoples.
10. Linda Tuhiwai Smith is a Māori academic who affiliates to the Ngāti Awa and Ngāti Porou iwi.

so far altered that it can bring back memory" (Freeman, 2016b).[11] Aunty Julie Freeman continues: "Our stories are accurate histories of this place. We were here when it was ice. We have stories about the first blooms on eucalypts. We were here when other things were forming along with ourselves and our thinking, but we share this world with every other scape – sky, sea and land – and every other living creature that inhabits all of those things" (Freeman, 2016b). Developing alongside us, in that deep time of history, were our languages. Arlene McInherny[12] (recorded by Browning, 2019)[13] describes Indigenous languages as being "the vibrations of the land." She says:

> Whatever is living in [an] area is having a conversation with each other, so they have a similar vibration in the sound of their words … if you were to sit and watch carefully by the river, you can see that Country is talking to other things in the Country … The fish are moving with the dolphins and the river is moving with them as well. Our relationship with the ocean … us as water, we have a lot of water in our being … we are part of the water cycle, everything is part of the water cycle. If there are threats on the waterways ultimately, we are threatening us. If you speak the vibrations of the land, then you bring the fertility of whatever you are speaking, so you sing it up.

Furthering this notion, Aunty Julie says that "[l]anguage is like the wind … a living entity … Languages reflect their own world views, they reflect their own landscapes and their own beliefs" (Freeman, 2016a). She describes languages as being unique to Country and landscapes as they express the most intimate things that nobody other than those who have evolved with that Country can know (Freeman, 2016b).

Languages hold the memory and truth of Country, often referring to geographic events that occurred thousands of years before (Pascoe, 2007).[14] Languages are the repository of our history, they contain our identity, our unique worldview, culture and social values, and they are our legacy to the rest of humanity (Crystal, 2012). Uncle Bruce Pascoe (2007) writes that the "ancient

stability of all Aboriginal languages is proof of their existence over millennia, and their intimate linguistic connections to a specific landscape is proof that they have remained in that place since the language was developed."

Embedded into languages are our duty of care towards Country. In Dharug language from the Sydney region the word used to mean "welcome" is warami.[15] While it is used to welcome, according to Aunty Jacinta Tobin[16] (2012), the actual meaning is "I see that you have come from far away." Likewise the phrase used as a greeting in Dhurga from the South Coast of New South Wales, walawaani njindiwaan, actually means "I hope you've had a safe journey here," and/or, "I hope you have a safe journey home" (Boyenga, 2015).[17] While these words do not translate precisely into how they are now used, these small insights into greetings in First Languages recognise that as First Peoples we acknowledge not only our own responsibilities to place, but others' also as we see their origins as being from – and having obligations to return to – another place. It acknowledges ones' position and our culture of care for Country. Likewise, protocols are embedded in language; dídjurígur from Dharug, now used to mean thank you, translates to "I've had enough, over to you"[18] (Locke cited in Hromek, 2019). It speaks to the unspoken learned protocol for sharing, particularly in the sense of giving and receiving food. Similarly, in Bundjalung, bugulwan is a means of wishing someone well or expressing gratitude or affection. That these are the closest words to mean "thank you" in English is of particular note in terms of understanding culture and sharing practices in a society. The languages of the east coast rarely have words of salutations or small talk, as Aboriginal people had no use for them (Browning, 2016), which speaks to the abundance of Country.

All entities in Country, human and more-than-human (the wind, a beetle, a buru [kangaroo],[19] a waratah flower – highly valued for burial ceremonies), hold knowledges and Law, and all things have their way of communicating. All things create and send messages and meaning in their own languages. Furthermore, deceased Ancestors never depart from the landscape; the land is full of ancestral

---

11. Aunty Julie Freeman is a Traditional Owner of the Wreck Bay Aboriginal Community on the South Coast of New South Wales. Her mother is of the Gurawarl (Wonga pigeon) clan from Botany Bay (Kamay), and her father was a Wandandiandi man of the Yuin nation.
12. Arlene McInherny is a Biripi woman who speaks Biripi, a dialect of Gathang language.
13. Daniel Browning is a descendant of the Bundjalung people whose traditional land is on the far north coast of New South Wales. Through his mother, he is a descendant of the Kullilli people of south-western Queensland and the Traditional Owners of the Gold Coast hinterland.
14. Uncle Bruce Pascoe is of Bunurong, Yuin and Punniler panner heritage.

15. Spelled in a number of ways including worímí, as noted earlier, warami has a linguistic relationship to the word that was recorded to be heard from the people on the shore when the First Fleet came in: wara wara, "go far away."
16. Aunty Jacinta Tobin, a Borborngal (kangaroo) and Canamadagal (possum) people of the Dharug nation, works to reawaken the Dharug language.
17. Kerry Boyenga is a Dhurga speaker from the South Coast of New South Wales.
18. Michelle Locke, a Boorooberongal (kangaroo people) woman of the Dharug nation, provided this translation.
19. Buru means kangaroo in Dharug as taught to Hromek by Uncle Greg Simms.

spiritual presences who can be heard expressing their spirit presence. Ancestors must likewise be spoken (or sung out) to in the appropriate language; an act of caring for Country, others and oneself (Bawaka Country, Wright, Suchet-Pearson, Lloyd, Burarrwanga, Ganambarr, Ganambarr-Stubbs, Ganambarr, & Maymuru, 2015; Burarrwanga et al., 2014; Langton, 2002).[20] Humans are part of Country, yet we are not the most important part of Country; we are a single entity that comes together with others to make up the whole of Country. Not all messages sent by Country and other entities of Country are for humans; it is not the role of humans to know all about Country. However, it is our role to listen and hear the messages that Country and non-humans coexisting in Country are sending – not only with our eyes and ears, but with our whole body and being.

Language is an indicator of our psychology, a way of thinking within a culture. Noam Chomsky (2009) indicates that "languages are the best mirror of the human mind." He claims that language is innate. By this he means that our brains have a pre-existing mechanism that allows for language to be processed, and this mechanism is activated by our environment. As First Peoples, our innate connection to language is through Country. We make these connections consciously by walking Country, yet on other levels Country communicates with us. Subconsciously, through our Dreams, we can find connections and answers sent to us from Ancestors and by Country.

Stories of Creation in Naming of Places

Indigenous peoples have creation stories, not colonisation stories. Stories about how we came to be in or from a specific place. Our relationships to land contain our knowledges, ways of being, and origins. Furthermore, Indigenous peoples are known by their places, or indeed place names (Tuck & McKenzie, 2015; Tuck & Yang, 2012). Therefore, not only are we intrinsically tied to our lands, we are known by them and named by them. In now-Sydney, the Gadigal[21] are thought to be named after the place to which they belonged; gulgadya is the name for the grass tree or *xanthorrhoea* (regrettably not widely found in the Sydney area any longer) and -gal means "people" (Troy, 2019).[22]

The protocols of language, one of which is to speak the language of the land you are on, can be of help to designers and planners specifically in relation to the

renaming of places. Uncle Stan Grant Senior[23] says that language does not belong to people, rather it belongs to the land. He indicates it is disrespectful to the land to go to another's Country and not speak the language of that land, a protocol not observed by non-Indigenous peoples (Grant cited in Tan, 2016). First Peoples had experiences of visitors well before the British arrived (for instance, the Dutch, and in the far north of the continent, the Makassans), all of whom left. It was therefore reasonable, especially considering their care relationships and protocols relating to language and care of Country, to expect the British would likewise depart. Regrettably, the arrival of the British was brutal for First Languages to the extent that now language in Australia is dominated by English. English has caused the extinction of many First Languages and threatened others. British colonists instigated this when First Peoples were not allowed to speak their languages as speaking language was seen as primitive in need of civilisation; by controlling language they controlled culture. However, English is not the language of this land, and does not adhere to the protocols of language, including in relation to how places are named.

The naming of places is an important reflection of a nation's cultural and linguistic heritage (Rayburn, 1997). Historian Sam Furphy (2002) describes a place name as "not only a signifier for the *space* to which it refers, but also the stories, emotions, histories and people which are associated with that space. Names enable people to communicate about these more abstract notions as much as they represent a distinct geographical space." However, naming places also remains an effective colonial tool used by surveyors and cartographers to extinguish existing habitation of land. Place names and maps are symbols of knowledge, power and colonial possession. European names signify knowledge and ownership, and in doing so they effectively suppress Indigenous knowledges and custodianship. When the colonists arrived, while they replaced many original names with colonial names, they also recorded some Aboriginal names of some places, though not always correctly or in a way that respected the diversity of the peoples responsible for and using those places. Despite retaining these Aboriginal names, however, they were not necessarily recognising Indigenous history or inhabitation of a place; rather, they were appropriating language to suit their purpose, and possess it for themselves. The knowledge associated with a name is stored in the collective memory of those who use it; thus in appropriating an Aboriginal name without also embracing the culture, history and language, the colonisers did not necessarily carry the associated meanings with the name

20. Laklak Burarrwanga, Banbapuy Ganambarr, Djawundil Maymuru, Merrkiyawuy Ganambarr-Stubbs, Ritjilili Ganambarr are all Yolŋu people, from Bawaka in North East Arnhem Land.
21. Gadigal is also spelled Cadigal and Caddiegal.
22. Jakelin Troy is a Ngarigu woman whose Country is the Snowy Mountains.

23. Uncle Stan Grant Senior is an Elder of the Wiradjuri people of inland New South Wales.

(Furphy, 2002). Conversely, colonial place names likewise mark the truth of colonial history, and while in some cases these names are offensive, the question is whether removing that name also removes the opportunity for truth telling regarding horrific events that occurred in that place.

In contrast with the colonial practice, whereby places are named after an individual person or a place far away (often in the mother country), Aboriginal ways of naming generally focuses on the Country, and on geographic or topographic features, plants or trees, or animals that are specific to that place, rather than the names of the language or nation group territories. Most Aboriginal place names are words from the vernacular, the language of that particular tract of Country that originated from that place. Some sites had (and have) multiple names, determined by the diverse groups that used and cared for them. Therefore, the boundaries around sites might also be nebulous and moveable. Recent attempts to find names with Aboriginal origins for places have not always respected language protocols and some sites have been named after revered Ancestors and Elders. While in Aboriginal culture it is important to honour Elders, the issue remains if doing so through place names is an objective and appropriate way of naming according to protocols, or a construct of colonialist tendencies.

One of the challenges of rediscovering original names is that many Aboriginal place names were subsequently moved away from their true location by non-Aboriginal people. For instance, Jelleindore is three and a half kilometres from the waterhole it is named after, Billagoola is eight kilometres to the south and Katoomba 15 kilometres to the north-west of their original locations (J. Smith, 2009). Additionally, there is often a significant gap in colonial written recordings of language and original pronunciation and they propose new spellings to reflect the most probable articulation for some names (Troy & Walsh, 2009). This means that the historical void is left open for interpretation or assumptive processes.

Uncle Bruce Pascoe says place names show how deeply and intimately our Old People knew the land. He says by learning the name, you learn your Country (Pascoe recorded by Milton & Abbott, 2019). Discussing the meaning of the name of the Jinoor (Genoa River), which means foot, Uncle Bruce points out that it has a more profound meaning than just a body part; it evokes the ceremonial pathway that connects the coast to the mountains. These expressive words that describe places mean something to people and Country and reclaiming them through renaming is a means of showing respect.

Culture is a Map of the Landscape

All cultures engage in some means of representing space or mapping, and "[m]apping, like language, is a cultural process that reflects the ontological and epistemological structures of that culture" (Pearce & Louis, 2008).[24] Aboriginal ways of mapping land may be performative or gestural, representing the lived experience of a place. Some maps can be understood as a kind of mental map, a storying of movement across ground. Some maps are ceremonial or sung, such as in a song line in which routine movements across the land creates a mapping of the landscape, while knowing the stories and songs enables travel. Other means of mapping include physical imprinting on the terrain or plant materials, petroglyphic embedding into rock, or inscriptions on paper. Aboriginal mapping is a process of tangibly and intangibly inscribing into the land in which "[o]ur mappings accentuate the lived experience of spaces, and thus our maps are phenomenologically spatialised" (Hromek, 2018). Marcia Langton (2002) further describes the memorial and sensorial means in which Aboriginal mapping occurs:

> Representations of people, spirits, and landscapes are symbols in a rich variety of rites, from the merely petitionary to the profoundly cosmological. The cultural map through which the landscape is re-inscribed with the cultural memories, regulations, and logic of the Elders is marked and memorialised through social experience.

Western geospatial technologies such as digital maps, satellite images, geographic information systems and global positioning systems have shown to be essential for protecting cultural sovereignty, which it does by conveying Indigenous cultural knowledge to people from outside the community. Indigenous knowledge is inherently spatialised, as it is related to recurring processes, site specific knowledges and is embedded into the landscape through the names and stories of places which contain the meanings, relationship, and interconnectivity of a place (Pearce & Louis, 2008). As Indigenous cultural knowledge is spatialised and placed, spatial representations such as maps are effective means and tools of presenting such knowledge and associated landscapes.

While contemporary Aboriginal means of mapping includes new technologies, our ancient techniques encompassed walking Country in which maps were made by foot. Movement across the land, as an act of caring for Country, inherently creates a lived experience of places. Through our travels we learn about Country, how to care for important sites, cultural lore, and wayfinding through storytelling. The values First Peoples place on the land extends from wide-ranging meaning and monumentalisation of landscapes, to intimate knowledge of specific sites. In Sydney, many of the roads follow original Aboriginal tracks, with the major roads originating from regularly utilised trails and the smaller pathways

---

24. Renee Pualani Louis is a Hawaiian woman.

becoming side streets. According to Jakelin Troy (cited in Daniel, 2018), the way Sydney is now laid out mirrors the use of boundaries and connecting thoroughfares that Aboriginal people used. We walk in the footsteps and live in the spaces of those who were here before and of course are still here.

Shannon Foster (2015b) describes the methods in which pathways are maintained by the D'haramuoy, the Keeper of the Flame. The D'haramuoy is, "a specially appointed member of a Clan designated to learn and hold the Dreaming knowledge that is fire: when to burn, what to burn and the purposes behind it – of which there are many." Creating and maintaining a walking path is one application of this firestick farming and land management knowledge, and Sydney is planned around ancient walking tracks that were inscribed into the bush using these ancient skills. Foster (2015b) continues,

> When the Europeans landed on the sandy shores of our sparkling harbour, not only did they comment on the highly manicured appearance of the landscape, but they naturally decided to explore the well-trodden paths of the local Aboriginal people who had been maintaining these walking paths with the use of fire for thousands of years. One of the first paths wandered down by white men led directly west to Parramatta and is now known as George Street. Not far from there, a path led to a fresh water supply and is now known as Pitt Street. There was a path running south connecting Sydney's two main waterways War-ran (Sydney Cove) and Gamay (Botany Bay) … the University of Sydney is perched on the ancient path that ran south west and is now known as City Road/King Street Newtown. The list goes on and the same can be said for other main roads such as Oxford Street and Warringah Road.

Pathways and tracks are inherently performative, "the cognitive connections, the social interactions, and the relationships that they bring into existence, are themselves marked by trails and movements and actions along them. For this reason they are deeply intertwined with songs, stories and narratives" (Turnbull, 2007). Culture is a map across the landscape in which not only are the individual places important but the routes between them. In this way we understand the cohesive narrative of the whole of the landscape as a map.

Designing Collaboratively in Relationality with Country

Like walking Country as a means of mapping, contemporary Indigenous designers and architects use indicators of Country as a means of design. For instance, the songs and dance of a place, in which the story of that place is told, may likewise be an indication for a design for that place. Pascoe (2014) details the ways First Peoples designed in collaboration with Country, as colonists described beautifully manicured landscapes, clever aquaculture systems, agricultural cultivation and innovative structures that responded to local environments and landscape settings. The devastating impacts of colonisation, with its disruptions to Aboriginal landscapes, peoples and cultural practices has created an amnesia of history. However, Country has memory and dormant memories can be re-stitched back together, re-dreamed back to life. Working in harmony with the land, Aboriginal architecture and design incorporates a total expression of cultural values in relation to the local ecology and the places people live and practice culture. These methods of design consider not only those who came before us, but those many generations into the future, as well as the more-than-humans with which we share Country.

The colonialist construct of architecture remains more or less unchanged since colonists first arrived at now-Sydney's shores. The disciplines of architecture and planning have not changed; the colonial processes that enabled the unfettered invasion and destruction of Indigenous peoples' lands and lives. Yet First Peoples designing in collaboration with Country challenges and contradicts the western obsession of humans being the most important consideration in design. For First Peoples we do not consider ourselves to be at the centre of everything or separate from Country – including the design process. Considering humans hierarchically at the top of architecture or planning puts at risk landscape and nature, where they are reduced to second order priorities. By elevating nature, or even more importantly, Country as the highest priority with all other entities that share Country included on the same level as humans – future sustainability is inherently incorporated, as Country nurtures and cares for all in return.

We propose centring Country intrinsically changes the processes of design and doing so is necessary for not only the future of designing in a sustainable way, but also our own future and that of the planet. Centring Country in design requires First Peoples, as part of Country, to be there at the beginning of the process all the way through to the completion of the project. Centring Country needs those First Peoples whose essences originated with that Country to be the readers and translators of Country, in order Country is respectfully included in the engagement process. This is a fundamental shift in the practices of architecture, design and planning in which First Voices are heard throughout a project and Country is centred in the project.

There is therefore a space in policies, planning, conversations and even design drawings in which Aboriginal peoples and their ways of knowing the world can inhabit and grow into, ensuring that going forward their voices are known and forthright in this space. The missing voice of First Peoples talks to questions of ethical responsibility. There should be a mutually beneficial transaction when the design industry works

Figure 1. Hierarchical design, redrawn by authors acknowledging the work of Steffen Lehmann (2010).

Figure 2. Relational design with Country, redrawn by authors acknowledging the work of Steffen Lehmann (2010).

with Aboriginal communities. Architecture must become the middle ground which can benefit all participants.

Conclusion

Aboriginal voices and knowledges are largely missing in relation to design, placemaking and architecture in now-Sydney. The legal and spatial fiction of *terra nullius* became justification for colonial territorial acquisition and voiding First Peoples of their lands, commencing with the lands that came to be known as Sydney. This was undoubtedly enabled in part due to the perceived erasure of Aboriginal peoples from the city landscape. It is also partially due to the requirement of colonisation for "space-conquering economic growth" as a key feature of modernity, in which the "place-based, sustainable, state-free social order [of Indigenous peoples], have been chronic obstacles to modernisation to be overcome by whatever means" (Havemann, 2005). Despite the perceived absence, Aboriginal peoples have always lived in now-Sydney, they still do, and always will. First Peoples' ways of knowing the world and being in spaces have ensured our knowledges about those spaces have remained in languages and places. Resistance to colonial processes came in overt ways, but it also came in hidden and covert ways, through narratives and memory for future generations to now access through means such as story and movement.

In this chapter we have considered the ways in which language, place and memory relate to design and architecture from an Indigenous perspective. We reflected on how understanding these elements of Country can change the design process to start to centre Country instead of people. This is a first step in the process of designing in collaboration with and relationality to Country. Understanding Country as the library of all knowledge, the holder of perpetual memory, and the ultimate guide to place is the beginning of designing with Country. They are the foundations of a new way of understanding the design process in which as a whole the industry needs to look inwardly to reconfigure the colonial practices it still enables and embodies. Using Indigenous methods of connecting to Country and ways of knowing the world, it is possible to challenge the existing paradigms that govern the disciplines of architecture, design and planning. Like Midnight Oil sang: "The time has come to say fair's fair. To pay the rent, to pay our share" (*Midnight Oil*, 1987).

Reference List

Attenbrow, V. *Sydney's Aboriginal past: Investigating the archaeological and historical records*. Sydney: UNSW Press (2010).

Australian Bureau of Statistics. (2018). 3238.0.55.001 – Estimates of Aboriginal and Torres Strait Islander Australians, June 2016. Retrieved from http://www.abs.gov.au/ausstats/abs@.nsf/mf/3238.0.55.001

Bawaka Country, Wright, S., Suchet-Pearson, S., Lloyd, K., Burarrwanga, L., Ganambarr, R., Maymuru, D. "Working with and learning from Country: decentring human author-ity." *Cultural Geographies, 22*(2), pp. 269-283 (2015).

Bawaka Country, Wright, S., Suchet-Pearson, S., Lloyd, K., Burarrwanga, L., Ganambarr, R., . . . Sweeney, J. "Co-becoming Bawaka: Towards a relational understanding of place/space." *Progress in Human Geography, 40*(4), 1-20. doi:10.1177/0309132515589437 (2015).

Bodkin, F. *D'harawal: Seasons and climatic cycles*. Sydney: F Bodkin & L Robertson (2008).

Bodkin, F. "Yarn with Aunty Frances Bodkin" in D. Hromek (Ed.), *D'harawal Country* (p. Bidiagal/D'harawal). Mount Annan Botanic Gardens, NSW (2016).

Bodkin, F. [Personal communication with Aunty Frances Bodkin on D'harawal Lands] (2017, 5 December).

Bodkin, F. "Yarn with Aunty Frances Bodkin" in D. Hromek (Ed.), *D'harawal Country* (p. Bidiagal/D'harawal). Mount Annan Botanic Gardens, NSW (2018).

Boyenga, K. Learn a Dhurga greeting [video]. Sydney: Australian Broadcasting Corporation and Education Services Australia Ltd (2015).

Browning, D. "Word Up: Evelyn Araluen." *Awaye* [video]. Sydney: Australian Broadcasting Corporation (2016).

Browning, D. "Word Up: Arlene McInherny." *Awaye*. Sydney: Australian Broadcasting Corporation (2019).

Burarrwanga, L., Ganambarr, B., Maymuru, D., Lloyd, K., Ganambarr-Stubbs, M., Ganambarr, R., . . . Wright, S. (2014). Welcome to my Country: seeing the true beauty of life in Bawaka. September 15. Retrieved from https://theconversation.com/welcome-to-my-country-seeing-the-true-beauty-of-life-in-bawaka-31378

Byrne, D. R. "Nervous Landscapes: Race and space in Australia." *Journal of Social Archaeology, 3*(2), pp. 169–193 (2003)..

Chomsky, N. *Cartesian linguistics : a chapter in the history of rationalist thought* (3rd ed.). Cambridge: Cambridge University Press (2009).

Crystal, D. *English as a Global Language*. Cambridge: Cambridge University Press (2012).

Daniel, S. (2018). "Walking in their tracks": How Sydney's Aboriginal paths shaped the city. *Curious Sydney*. 17 May. Retrieved from http://www.abc.net.au/news/2018-05-17/curious-sydney-aboriginal-pathways/9676076

Foster, S. (2015a, 3 June 2015). The 6 Seasons of Sydney. Retrieved from http://sydney.edu.au/news/science/397.html?newsstoryid=15064

Foster, S. (2015b). The Aboriginal science behind Sydney's nightmare traffic. Retrieved from http://sydney.edu.au/news/science/397.html?newsstoryid=15394

Freeman, J. "Objects are connections to traditions: Aunty Julie Freeman on landscape and language" in E. Pike (Ed.), *Jonathan Jones: barrangal dyara (skin and bones)*. Botany NSW: Kaldor Public Art Projects (2016a).

Freeman, J. (2016b). Spot Fire 1 – Reading country – Aunty Julie Freeman. Retrieved from https://vimeo.com/170559810

Furphy, S. "British Surveyors and Aboriginal Place Names: New South Wales and Port Phillip, 1828-1851" in T. Banivanua Mar & J. Evans (Eds.), *Writing Colonial Histories: Comparative Perspectives*. Carlton VIC: University of Melbourne, Department of History (2002).

Gray, G. *A Cautious Silence: The politics of Australian anthropology*. Canberra: Aboriginal Studies Press (2007).

Green, R. "Reclamation process for Dharug in Sydney using song" in J. Hobson, K. Lowe, S. Poetsch, & M. Walsh (Eds.), *Re-awakening languages*. Sydney: Sydney University Press (2010).

Greenop, K., & Memmott, P. "Contemporary Urban Aboriginal Place Values in Brisbane." Paper presented at the 8th Australasian Urban History/Planning History Conference, Massey University, New Zealand (2006).

Havemann, P. "Denial, modernity and exclusion: Indigenous placelessness in Australia." *Macquarie Law Journal, 5*: pp.57-80 (2005).

Hromek, D. "Always Is: Aboriginal Spatial Experiences of Land and Country" in R. Kiddle, P. Stewart, & K. O'Brien (Eds.), *Our Voices: Indigeneity and Architecture* (pp. 218-237). California, United States: ORO Editions (2018).

Hromek, D. *The (Re)Indigenisation of Space: Weaving narratives of resistance to embed Nura [Country] in design*. (PhD). University of Technology Sydney, (2019).

Ireland, J. "The case of Agnes Jones." *History Australia, 10*(3), pp.236-251 (2013).

Karskens, G. *The Colony: A history of early Sydney*. Crows Nest, NSW: Allen & Unwin (2009).

Langton, M. "Urbanizing Aborigines the social scientists' great deception." *Social Alternatives, 2 no. 2*: pp.16-22 (1981).

Langton, M. "The Edge of the Sacred, the Edge of Death: Sensual Inscriptions" in B. David & M. Wilson (Eds.), *Inscribed Landscapes: Marking and making place* (pp. 253-269). Hawaii, HI: University of Hawaii Press (2002).

Larsen, S. C., & Johnson, J. T. "In Between Worlds: Place, experience, and research in Indigenous geography." *Journal of Cultural Geography, 29*(February): pp.1-13 (2012).

Midnight Oil. "Beds Are Burning." On *Diesel and Dust* [song]. Sydney: Columbia (1987).

Milton, V., & Abbott, S. To learn your country, start by learning its Aboriginal names [video]: Australian Broadcasting Company (2019).

Morgan, G. *Unsettled Places: Aboriginal people and urbanisation in New South Wales*. Kent Town, SA: Wakefield Press (2006).

Pascoe, B. *Convincing Ground: Learning to fall in love with your country.* Acton, ACT: Aboriginal Studies Press (2007).

Pascoe, B. *Dark Emu: Black seeds agriculture or accident?* Broome, WA: Magabala Books (2014).

Pearce, M. W., & Louis, R. P. Mapping Indigenous Depth of Place. *American Indian Culture and Research Journal, 32*(3), pp.107-126 (2008).

Rayburn, A. *Dictionary of Canadian Place Names.* Toronto ON: Oxford University Press (1997).

Simms, G. "Yarn with Uncle Greg Simms" in D. Hromek (Ed.), *Darug Country* (p. Gadigal/Darug/Gundungurra/Yuin). Sydney (2015).

Simms, G. "Yarn with Uncle Greg Simms" in D. Hromek (Ed.), *Darug Country* (p. Gadigal/Darug/Gundungurra/Yuin). Sydney (2016).

Simms, G. "Yarn with Uncle Greg Simms" in D. Hromek (Ed.), *Darug Country* (p. Gadigal/Darug/Gundungurra/Yuin). Sydney (2018).

Smith, J. "New insights into Gundungurra place naming" in H. Koch & L. Hercus (Eds.), *Aboriginal Placenames: Naming and re-naming the Australian landscape:* ANU ePress and Aboriginal History Incorporated (2009).

Smith, K. V. "Moorooboora's Daughter." *National Library of Australia News, (June)*: pp.19-21 (2006).

Smith, L. T. *Decolonizing Methodologies: Research and Indigenous Peoples* (2nd ed.). London: Zed Books (2012).

Stanner, W. E. H. *After the Dreaming: Black and white Australians--an anthropologist's view.* Sydney: ABC (1968).

Tan, M. (2016). "Yamandhu marang? Language does not belong to people, it belongs to country." *The Guardian.* Retrieved from https://www.theguardian.com/culture/2016/sep/01/yamandhu-marang-language-does-not-belong-to-people-it-belongs-to-country

Tobin, J. Say hello in Dharug [video]. Sydney: Australian Broadcasting Corporation and Education Services Australia Ltd (2012).

Troy, J. *The Sydney language.* Canberra: Australian Institute of Aboriginal and Torres Strait Islander Studies (1994).

Troy, J. (2019). Trees are at the heart of our country – we should learn their Indigenous names. *The Guardian.* Retrieved from https://www.theguardian.com/commentisfree/2019/apr/01/trees-are-at-the-heart-of-our-country-we-should-learn-their-indigenous-names

Troy, J., & Walsh, M. (2009). "Reinstating Aboriginal placenames around Port Jackson and Botany Bay" in H. Koch & L. Hercus (Eds.), *Aboriginal Placenames: Naming and re-naming the Australian landscape.* Canberra: ANU ePress and Aboriginal History Incorporated (2009).

Tuck, E., & McKenzie, M. *Place in Research: Theory, methodology, and methods.* New York: Routledge (2015).

Tuck, E., & Yang, K. W. "Decolonization is Not a Metaphor." *Decolonization: Indigeneity, Education & Society, 1*(1): p.1-40 (2012).

Turnbull, D. Maps Narratives and Trails: Performativity, Hodology and Distributed Knowledges in Complex Adaptive Systems – an Approach to Emergent Mapping. *Geographical Research, June 45*(2): pp.140–149 (2007).

Unknown. An authentic and interesting narrative of the late expedition to Botany Bay, as performed by Commodore Phillips, and The Fleet of the seven transport ships under his command … with particular descriptions of Jackson's Bay and Lowd Lowe's Island. In: W Bailey (1789).

Chapter 3.3: Contested Ground – Weaving Stories of Spatial Resilience, Resistance, Relationality, and Reclamation

Danièle Hromek – Budawang Yuin nation

Dr Danièle Hromek is a Budawang woman of the Yuin nation. She is a spatial designer, speculative designer, public artist and researcher, her practice works in the intersection of architecture, interiors, urban design, performance design and fine arts. Her work often considers the urban Aboriginal condition, the Indigenous experience of Country and contemporary Indigenous identities. Danièle's research contributes an understanding of the Indigenous experience and comprehension of space, and investigates how Aboriginal people occupy, use, narrate, sense, dream and contest their spaces. It rethinks the values that inform Aboriginal understandings of space through Indigenous spatial knowledge and cultural practice, in doing so considers the sustainability of Indigenous cultures from a spatial perspective. This chapter originates from her PhD, completed at the University of Technology Sydney.

Introduction

One of the motivations behind my research is specifically relating to my grandmother feeling invisible in colonised spaces, over time I have sought to investigate and understand how a vibrant, bubbly, chatty lady could ever be perceived thus. This is not an irregular experience for many First Peoples, especially when it seems our spaces held by Country have been covered by concrete, glass and asphalt. This apparent absence of First Peoples in spaces is no accident; Aboriginal peoples have been driven out of urban centres, not only from early town spaces, but more recently from inner-city suburbs, to become fringe dwellers; in what is often referred to as 'the Great Australian Silence' (Stanner, 1968), they have been written out of city life by authors, academics and civic planners; and forcibly assimilated into 'settler' spaces by cruel welfare policies. This erasure continues in contemporary discourse with the misrepresentation that Aboriginal people living in urban spaces are inauthentic, have lost their cultures, or are newcomers to the urban environment, irrespective of their constant contribution to civic life (Ireland, 2013).

It is difficult not to link this invisibility with being part of the Hidden Generations – those who became 'ghosted',

forgotten, lost and ignored somewhere between escaping unsafe policy and spatial restrictions, and avoiding becoming part of the Stolen Generations. Aunty Fran Bodkin[1] calls the Hidden Generations the Dudbaya'ora – the Hidden Ones.[2] Her son, Gawaian Bodkin-Andrews,[3] says the Hidden Generations are those whose Bloodlines sit in the often-ignored ether between the missions and the Stolen Generations (G Bodkin-Andrews 2018, pers. comm., 8 August). Sometimes hiddenness was accomplished literally by hiding – there are stories in my family of children being sent running into the bush to hide when unrecognised cars approached their homes. Some people opted for placelessness, leaving their traditional lands to live somewhere they were unknown. Some hid right in the middle of white society by claiming to be of another heritage. And some hid their Aboriginal identities from their children, so they grew up not knowing who they were. In fact, my Ancestors used all these tactics to keep our family intact. It is difficult to calculate how many families located in and around the areas of first colonial impact became hidden, because there are those who remain concealed. It seems likely to be more substantial than thought considering the alternatives of being herded onto missions or reserves, restricted to the fringes of urban centres, or the risk of having children removed; becoming invisible was the safest of a bunch of poor options.

At the same time, and paradoxically, in the eyes of the dominant white culture, Aboriginal peoples are hyper-visible, specifically in relation to non-Indigenous spatial expectations in terms of how spaces 'should' be used or inhabited. Spatial hypervisibility is based on the perception of difference; it causes the scrutinisation of otherness and leads to the misinterpretation of nonconformity to the predominant spatial paradigm, or in this case, the imported laws of the land. Consequently, the white gaze causes discomfort for First Peoples using

---

1. Aunty Fran Bodkin is a descendant of the D'harawal people of the Bidigal clan from the George's River/Woronora catchment area
2. Dudbaya'ora means "Hidden Ones" in D'harawal.
3. Gawaian Bodkin-Andrews is a member of the Bidigal clan within the D'harawal nation.

urban spaces. Paul Havemann discusses the extreme visibility of Aboriginal peoples thus:

> The imperatives of modernity are space-conquering economic growth and its attendant processes of statist order building. Indigenous peoples, with their place-based, sustainable, state-free social order, have been chronic obstacles to modernisation to be overcome by whatever means – typically by violence concealed behind liberal legalities (2005, p. 57).

He goes on to discuss the enduring effects of colonisation, or 'placelessness', for First Peoples, including suicides, high levels of incarceration, ill health, lowered life expectancies, loss of identity and intergenerational insecurity (Havemann, 2005). Greenop and Memmott (2006) also discuss Aboriginal culture located in urban spaces as being 'unreadable' to many non-Indigenous people who see only a 'culture of poverty' or 'welfare dependence' or a culture so changed from 'proper' Aboriginal culture (by which they mean from the remote interior of the continent, or from a distant archaeological past) that it is therefore 'no culture'. Yet in western value systems:

> Much of what it means to be a subject and citizen is embodied in cities. Cities insulate us from natural processes; they are the places where the delineation of public and private space is most marked, the division of labour most developed and the impersonal relations of the market most concentrated. The idea that civilisation obtains its most mature expression where population densities are highest is a profoundly European one (Morgan, 2006 p. 155).

The inequity of principles and privileges that the dominant spatial paradigm places on First Peoples in relation to cities has enduring impacts as it effectively makes First Peoples in an urban context placeless. Regardless, while in colonial spaces we may seem, both, invisible and hyper-visible, unrepresented and uncomfortable, we have nevertheless continued to experience and know Country within the metropolitan landscape.

The reaction of my family to these contradictory spatial expectations of invisibility and hypervisibility was to leave their traditional lands. They had other reasons to leave as well: reserve managers started to become problematic along with other events such as massacres of kin and colonial policy that began to impact their lives. They sailed a steamboat from Currowan on the Clyde River near Batemans Bay in Yuin Country on the New South Wales South Coast to Eungai near Nambucca Heads near the border of Gumbaynggirr and Dungutti Countries on the middle of the northern coast. This happened in my third great grandparents' time, around 1885. It was a remarkable voyage in many ways, not least because at least two families, including children and Elders, travelled

800 kilometres on a small boat. It was on that boat trip that they started to become hidden; in making that impossible decision to leave their traditional lands, they moved towards safety but to somewhat obscurity as well. Unquestionably my family was indelibly affected by this impossible decision; however, it would be remiss of me to accept this as the final truth. The gift of my heritage means I have the right to contest and reconstruct the perceptions and actualities of our stories and spaces. It is my privilege to carry the narratives and cultural practices shared by my family and wider kin networks, and with that privilege comes the responsibility of resilience, resistance, relationality and reclamation.

Aunty Fran describes how the bushland is woven, with stories woven into it. She says plants cannot live alone, they need the earth and the anchorage it provides. There is a wonderful diversity of plants, and likewise a diversity of Aboriginal peoples, with their roots woven together, communicating with each other (Yarn with F Bodkin 2018 on 22 June). Metaphorically, like the bush, this chapter contains stories shared by women from family, kin and wider networks, which are woven together, interconnecting collectively from their ancestral roots. This chapter responds to Indigenous peoples' experiences of trauma, dispossession and the onslaught of colonisation through a series of situated narratives. It includes narratives of how Aboriginal communities have resiliently maintained their love for kin, family, community, Country, and their relationships with land, Ancestors, culture, knowledges and stories. The stories describe how Aboriginal peoples – specifically women – occupy, use, narrate, sense and contest their spaces, from institutional to domestic. These woven narratives claim the ground; lives intertwine literally and figuratively to bind back to the earth, place and Country. Cultural/spatial practice/research methods of connecting expression and words through doing are adopted, explored and 'named up'[4] (Bessarab 2018, pers. comm., 17 May)[5] in this chapter. These are quieted voices being heard, invisible people being seen. In this way, our spaces are not only reclaimed, they are also constructed anew.

Naming Up Methods

Through the sharing of stories, I also share the methods developed, practised and used in the process. While I do not claim to be the creator of these approaches – I

---

4. While attending a workshop about yarning facilitated by Dawn Bessarab (2018, pers. comm., 17 May), she described how she "named up" yarning as an Indigenous research method. She chose the phrase "named up" because while it is something Aboriginal people have always done; she is the first to write about it as an academic method.
5. Dawn Bessarab is of Bardi (West Kimberley) and Indjarbandi (Pilbara) descent.

believe they are collective iterative ideas and methods used by generations of Aboriginal peoples before me – I am naming them up and relating them to spatial practice.

Resilience: Making-Yarning Process

A Method of using Dialogue to Lead Practice

Some years ago, a very dear friend of mine passed away from cancer. Around the same time my beloved grandfather passed on, as did an uncle and a mentor from my youth. It was a distressing time, impacting my life significantly to the extent I myself fell ill not long after. During the period my friend was unwell, I wanted to spend as much time with her as I could manage. However, as I observed her health deteriorating and was distraught by other events occurring around her, I experienced compounded traumas. I was also living far from family at that time, so did not have access to my usual support networks. Yet I had one mechanism for coping which in many ways carried me through the experience: making.[6]

In one of our customary family women's gatherings – that included my grandmother Gloria Nipperess,[7] my mother Robyn Hromek,[8] my aunty Lynne Lovett[9], my cousin Jenny Gillis,[10] my sister Siân Hromek,[11] and my cousin Caitlyn Murch[12] – we yarned about making. We mutually agreed that making was a means we used to manage demanding situations, and in some ways it was therapeutic. Unconsciously we turn to making to find psychological comfort from environmental and other stresses that surround us. Siân described how when she is making, she goes to another level, almost like meditation. She said, "You feel a mix of calm and excited about what you're making. You're almost sort of not even there. Sometimes I look back at what I've made and go, wow, did I make that?" (Yarn with S Hromek, 2018 on 27 January). Jenny likewise described that when her sister Joanne died and she could not concentrate on other work, she needed something in her hands just to keep moving, something to clear her mind (Yarn with J Gillis, 2018 on 27 January). Making is one of the ways we adapt to circumstances, perhaps by keeping our hands and

minds busy, but also, because frequently at the same time as we make, we yarn.

Yarning is a means of communication inherited from the previous generations who perfected this method of cultural sharing. Walker et al.[13][14][15] discuss the importance of yarning as a family saying, "Family yarning captures the family and personal connections and relationships that exist … in regards to land, spirituality, and kinship … Family yarning is part of the process of connecting and social positioning that occurs as participants discover their relationality to one another" (2014, p. 1222). In their research about yarning, Dawn Bessarab and Bridget Ng'andu identified four types of yarning, including therapeutic yarning. They describe therapeutic yarning not as counselling, rather an opportunity for those involved to listen and provide support. When stories are given voice, they are confirmed or reinterpreted. Consequently, "the meaning-making emerging in the yarn can empower and support the participant to re-think their understanding of their experience in new and different ways" (2010, p. 41). As the yarn evolves, stories from those involved become woven together, enabling the patterns of life and connectivity to reveal and resolve themselves. Beth Cuthand[16] furthers this idea in relation to storytelling:

> We come from a tradition of storytelling, and as storytellers we have a responsibility to be honest, to transmit our understanding of the world to other people … In this process, there is something more than information being transmitted: there's energy, there's strength being transmitted from the storyteller to the listener (1989, p. 54)

In the energetic exchange that happens in the process of sharing stories, or what Jo-anne Archibald[17] calls "story energy" (2008, p. 85), strength is restored between speaker and listener, both the relationship between them and as individuals. As narratives – and within them, cultural knowledges, histories, and teachings – are shared, one's place in the world and how we interact with events is better known and understood.

Like yarning, making is part of our inheritance, a gift from our Ancestors to keep us connected. It also provides a means to teach culture and cultural practices to our young ones, who are included in the process of making yarning. Caitlyn, at our family yarns, brings her children with her to be part of that continuation of sharing and

---

6. In this context, making is the process of doing, forming or producing. For the women in our family, making includes crafting, such as knitting, sewing or crochet, as well weaving and cooking. For me as a spatial designer, making might also include drawing, modelling, fabricating, composing.

7. Gloria Nipperess is a Budawang woman of the Yuin nation, and an Elder of my family.

8. Robyn Hromek is a Budawang woman of the Yuin nation.

9. Lynne Lovett is a Budawang woman of the Yuin nation.

10. Jenny Gillis is a Budawang woman of the Yuin nation.

11. Siân Hromek is a Budawang woman of the Yuin nation.

12. Caitlyn Murch is a Budawang woman of the Yuin nation.

---

13. Melissa Walker is a Palawa (Tasmanian Aboriginal) woman.

14. Bronwyn Fredericks is a Murri woman from Southeastern Queensland.

15. Kyly Mills is a Kamilaroi woman.

16. Beth Cuthand is Cree and grew up in Saskatchewan and Alberta.

17. Jo-anne Archibald, also known as Q'um Q'um Xiiem, is from the Stó:lô First Nation in British Columbia.

earning; it is a normal part of our sharing and learning process. Continuing a tradition of making while yarning connects back to times of strength and is an act of reaffirming and renewing the link between the past and those to come.

The practice of making while yarning has been passed through my family via generations of women, who developed this means of creating resilience. Making through yarning teaches strength and endurance by shared meaning-making and collective actions. While in my family it is not only females who yarn up to make, it is often associated with women's business. Everyone in attendance at the aforementioned women's gathering described their experiences of learning how to make, being taught by and learning from mothers, grandmothers, aunties, cousins, and each other while sharing stories and dialogue. Caitlyn described the weekends when we would go to Nanna's [our great-grandmother, Alma Darby[18]] and all the aunties would bring their crafts and sit around talking about whatever they were working on (Yarn with C Murch, 2018 on 27 January). This familial habit of coming together to make and yarn during times of ease establishes a device for managing or maintaining resilience during times of hardship.

A common definition of resilience is positive adaptation despite adversity (Luthar, 2006). Cultural resilience is the capacity of a distinct community or cultural system to absorb disturbance and reorganise while undergoing change in order to retain the key elements of structure and identity that preserve its distinctness (Healey, 2006). What seem like minute acts of resilience, namely making while yarning, may not appear sufficient to deflect the enormous impacts of colonisation and cultural suppression; however, they need to be understood in the context of the strength of stories being (re)told and of kin being together.

Cultural resilience, according to Heather Builth, is maintained in individual families irrespective of, or perhaps because of, cultural change. She says, "Despite the huge losses in population as a result of the recent occupation of this land by non-Indigenous nationalities, there has been a failure to quell an existing cultural knowledge or separate people from it" (2009, p.25). Irrespective of the determined efforts to control relationships and prohibit the speaking of languages, as well as incarceration, dispossession or placelessness, cultural knowledge lives on in families. "[T]heir inherited intangible cultural heritage remains with them, and the nature of it means that it will not easily be forgotten. As long as it remains a part of these people's history it will connect them to their often alienated [C]ountry"

(p. 25). Resilience as a means to enduring changing environments has been gifted to us while we learned to manage change over countless generations. Our ancient means of embodying resilience, "is a blessing as it is without doubt that our ancestral DNA prepared us unknowingly for what was to come with the onslaught of colonisation" (Lee 2017, p.214).[19] To view cultural change as cultural loss disrespects the large, but also the small, acts of cultural resilience by our Ancestors.

Spaces, held by Country, likewise sustain resilience. Aunty Fran Bodkin describes the site of a massacre as being, "the most peaceful place, calm, beautiful and welcoming" (Bodkin, 2016). The Appin Massacre occurred in 1816 in D'harawal Country. Ordered by Governor Lachlan Macquarie, soldiers pursued D'harawal women and children off the cliff at Broughton Pass. The true number of people murdered in the massacre is unknown, with at least 14 confirmed. (Irish, 2017; Karskens, 2009) Despite the atrocity that occurred in this place, Aunty Fran says the site protects itself and returned to what it always was, a traditional birthing place. This remarkable spatial resilience exists despite. Despite colonised space. Despite trauma of the land. Regardless of conflicts in identity and stresses associated with acculturation, the resilience of the land and a resolve to maintain relationships with Country provides fortitude to our own resilience. Through the resilience stored in Country, and offered to us in the making process, we can retrieve resilient knowledge and behaviour.

Minute acts of personal resilience through making while yarning captures thoughts and conversations into the made object or physical entity. In the process of making tangible cultural heritage through yarning, intangible cultural heritage is captured. When one is Dreaming up an object, yarning makes a perceptible difference to the entity in its form, its materiality and its intentions. Thus, yarning, in conjunction with the activity of making, forms part of the method, foundation and materialisation of the resultant physical entity. The yarned-up object becomes shaped by the cultural, spatial, socio-political, and speculative discourse that occurs during the process of making. The enclosed words create enduring remembrances of the people and events spoken about, but also restoration that occurs through expression. A cycle of making and yarning, yarning and making – a method of minute acts of resilience – is therefore encased in a process of curative action.

Resistance: Mapping Through Walking Practice

A Method of Caring for Country via Movement

---

8. Alma Evelyn Brown (nee Darby) has heritage from the Budawang people of the Yuin nation.

19. Vanessa Lee is from the Yupungathi (Cape York Peninsula) and Meriam (Torres Strait Islands) Nations.

As a result of and despite their simultaneous invisibility and hypervisibility, Aboriginal women have experienced and continue to experience violence in colonial spaces, institutions, and at home (Behrendt 1993; Dudgeon 2017; Watson 2017).[20] [21] [22] Not only do Indigenous women have colonial forces they must contend with, they also have to contend with patriarchal systems and class structures, which force them to the bottom via the strategies of classism, sexism, and racism. Describing her as "the most beautiful lady," my grandmother Gloria Nipperess tells a story of the only time she saw her grandmother, Margaret Ann Brown,[23] cranky. It was when my grandmother was around eight years of age and her mother, Alma Darby, was seven months pregnant. My grandmother says it was the first time Margaret had visited her daughter in their home in Rutherford in the Hunter Region of New South Wales. Margaret witnessed her son-in-law "punch up" his wife, then followed him upstairs clutching a hairbrush to confront him, and said, "Joe Darby, if you punch my daughter again, I will hit you with this!" My grandmother says Margaret was "a skinny little thing, about six stone," and if he had backhanded her, she would have been knocked to the ground. Distressingly as a result of his violence the baby was lost, yet due to Margaret's fierce defiance he did not hit his wife again (Yarn with G Nipperess, 2018 on 27 January). Later in life, my great-grandmother showed similar defiance of her husband; many in my family speak of her actions towards him with pride as she put him in his place.[24]

Women's resistance to colonisation, racism, sexism, and classism comes in many forms, from marching the streets, to ensuring the wellbeing of loved ones, to sharing narratives. As Indigenous women are often primary caretakers for our young ones, and find innovative ways of responding to adversity, all forms of resistance by them are key to continuing culture. Resistance in this context is defined as refusing to comply or accept something, fighting against something (or someone) that is attacking, or the ability to not be affected by something, specifically adversity. I believe the defiant attitude exhibited twice by my twice great-grandmother filtered down through the generations, and even grew, so what started as resistance has also become resilience.

Telling this story about her grandmother, mother and father was a form of inadvertent[25] resistance on the part of my grandmother; storytellers and stories themselves "become mediums for Indigenous peoples to both analogise colonial violence and resist it in real ways" (Sium & Ritskes, 2013, p. V).[26] While in this story my great-grandfather is only an allegory for colonial violence, his violence was absolutely patriarchal and racial,[27] and clearly it was also physical. Yet by sharing these stories of violence, my grandmother employs "acts of creative rebellion" (Sium & Ritskes, 2013), and in speaking them she is not only engaging in truth telling, but providing space for healing to occur. Truth telling about injustices experienced in the past is important for First Peoples as a means of coming to terms with conflict and upheaval. Truth telling our true history is key to ensuring a cohesive shared future. Telling the truth, in this instance, directly answers the impetus my grandmother herself gave to me; she feels invisible because colonisation caused it to be so, from the very first instance of the untruth of terra nullius, an empty land void of people, to a father not acknowledging his daughter's heritage. Truth telling is therefore resistance.

Despite these compounding types of violence, despite living in a very different spatial paradigm, despite finding themselves in a colonised landscape, Aboriginal peoples continue to connect to Country. As Sarah Prout and Richard Howitt state:

> Indigenous populations have not lived in a cultural vacuum and their contemporary spatialities cannot therefore satisfactorily be explained away as the result of a nomadic predisposition to 'wander'. Rather, contemporary Indigenous spatial practices are iteratively informed by a complex set of geographical, historical, demographic,

20. Larissa Behrendt is a Eualeyai/Kamillaroi woman.
21. Pat Dudgeon is from the Bardi people of the Kimberley area in Western Australia.
22. Irene Watson belongs to the Tanganekald and Meintangk Boandik First Nations Peoples, of the Coorong and the southeast of South Australia.
23. Margaret Ann Brown is a Budawang woman of the Yuin nation.
24. My great-grandmother's considered actions to empower herself in an unbalanced and abusive relationship were spoken of at length by Gloria Nipperess, Robyn Hromek, Lynne Lovett and Jenny Gillis at the women's yarn mentioned previously, and at many other times through my life.

25. I use the word "inadvertent" advisedly; I spoke at length with my grandmother about telling this story in order she would know the context within which it was being used, and why I wanted to include it. I asked her if it would make her anxious to know this story could be read by anyone, and she said, "Well, it's the truth," and she felt it was important it be told. While my grandmother may not see this as an act of resistance, I do, as truth telling can be confronting not only for those hearing the truth, but those telling it. In this way, I feel, my grandmother is the epitome of resistance.
26. Aman Sium sees himself as being simultaneously – and equally – Tigrinya, Indigenous, Eritrean and African.
27. My great-grandfather used to call my grandmother, his own daughter, in derogatory terms for Aboriginal women, for instance, "black gin." The reason he was violent towards my great-grandmother in this instance was because it was her Black mother who was there to support her during her pregnancy, not his white mother.

socio-cultural, and economic considerations … These include relationships to family and [C]ountry, life-stage and degree of engagement with mainstream social and economic institutions (2009, p. 398).

One means for connecting to Country has been our persistent movement around the land, a means through which we have challenged colonial perceptions. Aboriginal peoples have found refuge in the interstitial and in-between spaces and developed tactics to subvert the spaces of the restricted landscape. We have found new means of mobility, and created new ways to move through the landscape. In this manner our invisibility has been useful, as indeed has our inherited and cultural movement around Country.

While spending time with Elders and Knowledge Holders both on Country and talking about Country, many have described their means of connecting to Country. A common theme has been to walk Country, with many specifically stipulating being barefoot. My grandmother, a renowned walker until well into her eighties, speaks of inherently knowing which direction to move due to her ability to read Country and to retain clear navigational memories (Yarn with G Nipperess, 2018 on 27 January). Uncle Greg Simms[28] describes taking off his shoes and walking Country as a means of finding healing and communicating with the spirits of Ancestors (Yarn with G Simms 2015 on 28 October). Ambelin Kwaymullina[29] expresses the 'work' of movement that generations of Aboriginal women have undertaken in terms of their continuing connections:

> [F]or generations of Indigenous women, there was no 'work' that was not part of living and a part of renewing the life in others. When women moved through the [C]ountry gathering food, we walked the trails that the Ancestors had walked and we sang the songs that told the stories of those Ancestors, the stories of [C]ountry. We took only certain foods, at certain times, in certain quantities. Our journeys – far from the random, nomadic wanderings of the European imagination – were ones of purpose, of teaching, of celebration and of caring for [C]ountry. Our "work" was a task that sustained and renewed ourselves, our connections to each other and the connections between women and [C]ountry. The whole is more than its parts and the whole is in all its parts. This is what it was, and is, to live holistically in a holistic reality (2017, p. 101).

Aunty Joan Tranter[30] said whenever she gets scattered in her thoughts (specifically related to the urban environment) she finds some grass in a park or sand at the beach and spends time reconnecting with Country. Aunty Joan says synthetics such as concrete, asphalt, carpet and even shoes can block interactions with Country, which is detrimental to our wellbeing (Tranter cited in Hromek, Hromek & Hromek, 2015). While urban centres, with their straight lines, paved streets, manicured parks, foreign materiality, glass, asphalt and concrete create the sense for many that Country is distant, this is not so. Country exists in city spaces. Certainly, it might be harder to 'hear' or sense, however, Country still holds us all in urbanised spaces.

For me as a maker, connecting to Country occurs through moving over Country while (re)telling the stories embedded into the land, inextricably weaving landscapes into made objects. For makers who are also collectors, the objects we make are derived from materials of Country (and some not-of-Country[31]). Walking as a method enables practices of care to occur; a form of cultural care of Country through knowing, seeing, communicating with Country and collecting materials provided by Country for cultural and performative practice. But also, literally collecting undesirable foreign elements not-of-Country.

In the movement process a storying or mapping occurs, connected directly to place and practice. Ingrid Seyer-Ochi says, "Our sense of place is shaped through our experiences directly with it, our understanding of history it embodies, and our interactions across its changing social and structural landscape" (2006, p. 170). She calls the ways in which people make sense of the built and historic layers, the natural landscape and the lives made possible by this landscape, *lived landscapes*. Expanding on this, for First Peoples, these are lived *relational* landscapes. Mapping Country through walking creates a map of the lived experience of places, in a way, a true knowledge of place. Mapping lived experience enables a knowing of places through the senses, which interact with our emotions; it is an embodied learning of the relational narratives of that place through space and time. Navigating using Country as a means for movement embeds encountered stories into made objects. The route 'drawn' into the landscape links, and at times follows, the narratives of places; this is meaningful movement that not only retells stories but writes them anew.

Walking Country, as we have always done, is a means

---

28. Uncle Greg Simms descends from the Gundungurra (water dragon lizard people) of the Blue Mountains and the Gadigal (whale people) of the Dharug nation, as well the Budawang (beach plover people) of the Yuin nation.
29. Ambelin Kwaymullina belongs to the Palkyu people from the Pilbara in the north-west of Western Australia.

---

30. Aunty Joan Tranter belongs to Wakka Wakka Country, and also Kamilaroi Country, which is her mother's Country.
31. While the collecting process is often associated with materials of Country, it also can include materials not-of-Country, that is, not native to that location. Many have been discarded or dislocated from other Countrys, or even other countries, and thus belong elsewhere.

of reclaiming space and resisting colonial and other forms of violence. Spending time on Country with Elders and Knowledge Holders enables urbanity to be seen through a different lens, a 'Country lens'. Irrespective of whether they are in the countryside or an urban landscape, Elders and Knowledge Holders, from animated excitement to complete silence, share the knowledges of places, using a different filter to see and know the expressions of Country. In doing so, they negate the supposed voids of terra nullius, they resist the perception of invisibility and the truth is told, because they are with and caring for Country.

Relationality: Storying Making Knowledge

A Method of Sharing Knowledge through Narrative

Aunty Fran Bodkin tells a story of how she learned from her mother about the relationality of everything. In her story, her mother provocatively asks young Fran to make a series of observations. These observations continued through her life, inevitably amalgamating for Aunty Fran a realisation of how everything in Country is related to and reliant upon everything else. The story starts at Tempe Station near the Cooks River in Sydney, where they stood on the bridge looking into the water. Aunty Fran says:

> So, I looked in the water and in those days Cooks River had a beautiful white sandy bottom. On the bottom the water didn't look that deep, but at the bottom were sharks laying on that white sand, just gently flapping their side fins. She [her mother] said, 'What do you see?' I said, 'Oh look at the sharks. Mum, they're sunbathing!' I'll always remember that. She got this awful flipping look on her face. Have a closer look, what are they doing? Then I saw suckerfish dropping off from the side and swimming upstream up Wolli Creek. 'Oh Mum, the sharks are having babies. They're swimming up the stream.' She said, 'Do they look like sharks?' 'No, Mum, they look like fish.' She said, 'I want you to remember that.' So, I did. And I never forgot it. That was the first time she gave me one of those puzzles (Yarn with F Bodkin, 2018 on 22 June).

While Aunty Fran was repeatedly removed by welfare from her parents as a child, she always ran away and found her way home. Whenever young Fran returned her mother would do a period of intensive teaching. One time she ran home, her mother took her to the Georges River Bridge in Liverpool:

> Just down from the bridge is a weir, we were standing near the weir and she said, 'What is happening?' Now it was the most wonderful thing I had ever seen. The entire weir was covered in huge eels all spilling out of the weir and falling into the water. And there were so many eels it looked as if you could walk across the water on their backs. It was beautiful. She asked, 'What's happening?' and I said, 'Oh,

Mum, look at the eels, isn't that amazing!' She asked, 'Where are they going?' 'Down the river.' 'Where does the river go?' 'Botany Bay, which is the same place that the Cooks River goes.' 'Where would they go from there?' 'Out into the sea.' 'Good girl. Remember that.' And then after that Mum died (Yarn with F Bodkin, 2018 on 22 June).

Aunty Fran's Mum passed away when Aunty Fran was a young teenager. However, her ways of teaching and the provocations she left enabled her narrative to continue to be learned. Some years later, Aunty Fran went to university to take environmental studies. One of the subjects was marine studies, which included an excursion to Heron Island off Queensland, where there is a research station. The sharks had been trained to come in at sunrise and sunset for feeding:

> You could swim amongst them and study them in between the feeds and they didn't hurt you or anything. I got to talking to one of the other scientists and who was studying the sharks. I told him what Mum had done, and he said, I know where the eels go! So, we stole the university boat (okay, we didn't steal it, we took it!) out to the Coral Sea and at that time of year all the eels had come down out of the rivers and up to the Coral Sea where they spawned and died. And waiting to eat dead and dying eels were the sharks. I thought, there's the key (Yarn with F Bodkin, 2018 on 22 June).

After returning home to Sydney, Aunty Fran investigated the final part of the cycle:

> When the sharks came back down south into the rivers, I waited and followed the suckerfish up to the headwaters. They spawned and died. And waiting to eat them were the eels. And then I had this wonderful thing, a circle (Yarn with F Bodkin, 2018 on 22 June).

Aunty Fran's story continues to a realisation that when even the smallest part of this circle was taken away, every other part is affected. And by considering the whole, all the minute parts are also relationally considered as they not only make up the whole, but rely on each other in order to be the whole.

Relationality in this context means the state or condition of being relational, informing ways of knowing, being and doing. Aileen Moreton-Robinson[32] and Maggie Walter[33] discuss this in terms of Indigenous women's epistemologies, which are, "informed by relationality; we

---

32. Aileen Moreton-Robinson is a Geonpul woman from Minjerribah (Stradbroke Island), Quandamooka First Nation (Moreton Bay) in Queensland.
33. Maggie Walter is a member of the Palawa Briggs/Johnson Tasmanian Aboriginal family descended from the Pairrebenne people of Tebrakunna Country, North East Tasmania.

are related to others by descent, ancestors, [C]ountry, place and shared experiences. Flowing from a world that is organic, alive and inhabited by ancestral beings who guide and shape life, ... one cannot know everything, ... everything cannot be known and ... there are knowledges beyond human understanding" (2009, pp. 6-7). Likewise, Shawn Wilson[34] states that knowledge is relational and shared with all of creation. He says knowledge is shared "with the animals, with the plants, with the earth" (2001, pp. 176-177). Wilson places the responsibility of accountability directly with our familial relationships, whereby we are answering to all our relations. Thus, "relatedness is embedded in our worldview" (Martin-Booran Mirraboopa 2008, p. 75)[35] and "all things exist in relatedness" (p. 81).

Likewise, stories[36] are relational in that they reveal relationships, renew them and return them to the place to which they belong. Robin Wall Kimmerer[37] says about stories told by First Peoples:

> We are told that stories are living beings, they grow, they develop, they remember, they change not in their essence, but sometimes in their dress. They are shared and shaped by the land and the culture and the teller, so that one story may be told widely and differently. Sometimes only a fragment is shared, showing just one face of a many faceted story, depending on its purpose (2013, p. 386).

Stories are a means of divulging, analysing and understanding events, keeping hold of knowledges and living space for resistance. In relation to women, Laurel Richardson says, "Women talking about their experience, narrativising their lives, telling individual and collective stories [becomes] understood as women theorising their lives" (1994, p. 927).

My grandmother is a storyteller – she even has nicknames acknowledging her storytelling capabilities. I did not inherit this gift (that went to my cousin); however, I am a listener. I have listened to narratives told around me my whole life – in fact I am told by my aunty Lynne Lovett that as a young child I demanded stories be told (though as I was an early riser, this was unfortunate for her sleep). While I may not have the talent for telling stories, I have a responsibility in the storying process as a listener. A storyteller is accountable to the story to honour its core teachings or details; each narrative has storylines, actions, characters, contexts, morals and/or themes. However, the teller also has a responsibility to ensure the story is engaging for those listening so that the lessons of the story can be captured by the listener. This may require adding their own voice to the story, making it current or updating some elements. Unlike western ways of storing knowledge, which must be written to be kept (and it could be argued, believed or trusted), for First Peoples, our knowledges are stored in stories, which are most often passed along orally. This provides the opportunity for the story to exist in many versions and be told in many voices, all of which are true and correct. The listener, for their part, must be attentive to the story, hear with openness and attend to the reasons the story is being told. Once the story has been shared, the listener then has the responsibility – if appropriate – to pass it on, and in doing so correctly honours (references) the original teller of the story. As Uncle Max Dulumunmun Harrison[38] says, we "must give it away to hold it" (McKnight 2015, p. 282).[39] The teller's final responsibility to the story is to ensure that they themself learn through the process of (re)telling it. In this way the narrative process is cyclical and reciprocal.

Places hold stories because stories are located and draw all entities of Country into relatedness. Anthony McKnight says one of the purposes of stories is "to initiate a reciprocal respectful relationship in taking care of Country, including the spirit of Country into what we do in our daily lives in the capacity of who we are" (2015, p. 287). He describes how Country also shares stories with "unseen and seen energies to activate sight and learning" (p. 287), which triggers reciprocal stories of connection so that learning can occur in a respectful relationship.

Sharing stories is sharing knowledge; it is learning about one's place and space in the world; it is energetic exchanges, it is changing perceptions and understanding and, ultimately, it is taking action. From a maker's perspective, sharing knowledge in stories can be a means of making. While the stories told during making become embedded in the object made, they also become a means for guiding, analysing or theorising about the process of

34. Shawn Wilson is Opaskwayak Cree from northern Manitoba, Canada.

35. Karen Martin-Booran Mirraboopa is a Noonuccal woman from North Stradbroke Island (southeast Queensland) with Bidjara ancestry (central Queensland).

36. In using the word "story," I acknowledge songs, dance, music, and other forms of expression as narratives. For instance, in *Earth song as story work: reclaiming Indigenous knowledges,* Frances Wyld and Bronwyn Fredericks say, "For us, songs are like stories. They are the things that we have from the time we are physically born until the time we pass into the spirit world. Indigenous people often exchanged songs at gatherings when people met to trade goods or undertake business. We believe that the songs of the earth are shared when we are open to the sweetness and the sorrow that songs can bring, along with other emotions, stories and learnings. We recognise that the earth has a song that Indigenous people listen to as story and, in return, we 'sing the world'" (2015, p. 2).

37. Robin Wall Kimmerer is an enrolled member of the citizen Potawatomi Nation.

38. Uncle Max Dulumunmun Harrison is an Elder and Lawman of the Yuin people from the South Coast of New South Wales.

39. Anthony McKnight is an Awabakal, Gumaroi, and Yuin man.

making. Stories reveal the relationships between maker and object, materials and Country, place and knowledge, all of which are rooted in the made entity. Seemingly insignificant aspects of a making process are understood further through the relationships revealed by the stories in and about a made object, thus illuminating their true significance. The learnings from the knowledges held in the stories as well as the learnings about making are therefore accessed through the process of making and storying. In this way, ways of knowing, being and doing for a maker are informed relationally through story.

Reclamation: Responsive Cultural Practice

A Method of Practice following the Signals of Country

In her book *Let the Land Speak*, Jackie French tells a story about the time six Djuuwin[40] women, whose ages ranged from young to elderly, came to lunch on her property in the Araluen Valley in the New South Wales Southern Tablelands. Araluen is located between Braidwood[41] and Moruya in the Budawang lands of Yuin Country. Jane Brown,[42] one of my Yuin apical Ancestors,[43] was born close by in Braidwood, about 60 kilometres from the coast. Early in her life she travelled to the coast and was married in Moruya. Her son, Thomas Golden Brown,[44] was born on the Clyde River just north of Moruya, and it was nearby in Batemans Bay that Jane

passed away. Thomas' son, Patrick Brown,[45] was born in Araluen. Patrick married Elizabeth Marshall[46] on the coast in Broulee, and it was Patrick and Elizabeth who made the impossible decision to journey north on the boat away from their traditional Country. French did not name the women who came for lunch, saying only that they came from a community 'down river'. The Araluen Valley was the Country of my five times great-grandmother and of many other Ancestors before and since. In her own words, French says about the visit of these women:

> These women had never been here before, but they knew my land, could tell me where the fig trees and kurrajongs were, and why. They told me to watch for the clematis in spring, to see how it would form a highway to show the young girls where to go to gather the young inner stringybark that makes waterproof fishing line and string and many other woven products.
> Five hundred or five thousand years ago, or even more, trees that gave food, medicine or other useful materials like sticky saps for bird traps or seeds for making torches were planted where they were needed, near places where ceremonies would be held, by camping sites, or as a signpost at the base of the ridge that this was the easiest way to get from the valley up to the tableland above. Everywhere we went that day, those women knew what we'd see before we came to it because their ancestors had planted the ancestors of those trees (2013, pp. 40-41).

Generations of Aboriginal women, in this case Yuin women, made a series of linked farms that were unrecognisable to invaders and so their significance was unacknowledged. Often created over hundreds of years and thousands of generations, these farms had plants deliberately sown in significant locations with seeds collected and harvested by women. Areas near good water sources, regular campsites or places of significance were turned into 'living larders' or 'mobile agriculture', ensuring a range of foods were available at different times of the year, safeguarding sustenance in years of extremes. These living larders needed to be planted only once to feed generations of families, because new seedlings took the place of older trees. Living larders undoubtedly changed the land, but they did so without disrupting the soils or ecosystems (French, 2013). They were planted sensitively, diversely and deliberately, assuring the land could manage sustainably. Plantings by women would take into consideration not only what they needed there immediately, but what their descendants might need many generations into the future.

In a similar way, Aunty Fran Bodkin says that in the

---

40. Djuuwin is another way of spelling Yuin, as are Djuwin, Juwin, and Yuwin.
41. Europeans arrived in the Braidwood area around the 1820s, and the town itself was surveyed in 1839. The town is named after Thomas Braidwood Wilson (1792-1843), a surgeon in the Royal Navy who undertook many voyages to Australia. He was originally granted land in Van Diemen's Land (Tasmania) as a reward for his exploration of and discoveries in what is now Western Australia. In 1826 he transferred this grant to New South Wales; Braidwood is located on the site of his grant. European settlement along the coast south of Wollongong commenced in 1827, when surveyors were sent to map the area. H S Badgery and Henry Burnell arrived in the Araluen Valley in the same year. Robert Hoddle followed the Deua/Moruya River to its mouth in 1828. He said of this land, "It is very barren ... at least nine tenths of it will be suitable for no purpose whatsoever." Thomas Florance surveyed the coast from Batemans Bay to Broulee and Moruya, adopting Aboriginal names for Broulee, Tomakin, Candlagan Creek and Moruya (Magee 2006).
42. Jane Brown is a Yuin woman.
43. An apical ancestor is a common ancestor from whom a lineage or clan may trace their descent. Jane Brown, recorded as being born in what came to be known as Braidwood in 1817, is listed in the Register of Native Title Claims for the South Coast People v Attorney General of New South Wales. She was born around the time Europeans arrived in that part of the South Coast, and therefore, grew up knowing them and seeing the changes occurring around her.
44. Thomas Golden Brown is a Yuin man.

45. Patrick Brown is a Yuin man.
46. Elizabeth Marshall is a Yuin woman.

Sydney area, maduri,[47] or canoes, were constructed out of three types of eucalyptus trees. While these varied according to area, Aunty Fran recalls stringybark, iron bark and rough bark tree plantings. You can still find these three trees growing near each other, planted thus to ensure the materials for constructing a maduri were easily accessible – not for those who planted them, but for many generations in the future (Yarn with F Bodkin, 2016 on 28 October).

My sister Siân also tells a story from Bundjalung Country on the far northern coast of New South Wales, where we grew up and where Siân still lives. The Bundjalung women weave with native hibiscus, specifically the inner fibres of the bark, which they use to make twine for dilly bags, fishing lines, mats and nets for fishing or hunting. The outer bark can be made into strong rope and the wood is easy to manipulate. The flowers, young stems, leaves and roots are edible, while the bark and roots can be made into a tea to treat colds and congestion. You can still find groves of native hibiscus trees growing together near water sources, and it is hard not to wonder if they were planted by women as living larders not only for food and medicine sources, but also for making. Groves of hibiscus are still being activated by Aboriginal peoples; they are used differently now, but they are still significant spaces (Yarn with S Hromek, 2018 on 14 December). As children growing up in Bundjalung Country, my sister and I learned what could be eaten and not, where to find drinking water, and how to be respectful of creatures that might be of danger to us. When we later moved to the suburbs, our neighbours thought we were wild kids; in hindsight, we were in actuality 'Country kids' who knew how to keep ourselves safe because we were taught to read and know the land and therefore had freedom in the knowledge of being safe with the land.

Country, which we know to be sentient, sends messages and signals to all entities inhabiting the land. Burarrwanga et al.[48] remind us that Country, and everything in Country, "has and tells a story. Everything communicates, through its own language and its own Law" (2014). Bawaka Country et al.[49] write:

Let's listen. Do you hear the wind in the trees? The water on the beach? The splash of the fish? That is the wind,

the trees, the water, the sand, the fish communicating. They have their own language, their own Law. Sometimes they are sending a message to humans. Sometimes they are sending a message to each other. Humans are not the centre of the universe, you see. Humans are only one part of it. Humans are part of Country along with the mullet, the tides, the moon, the songs and stories, along with the spirits, the plants and animals, the feelings and dreams (2015, p. 273).

Listening as a way of life is described by Miriam Rose Ungunmerr-Bauman[50] in her discussions about dadirri. Ungunmerr-Bauman says dadirri is something like contemplation, silent awareness or deep listening. Learning by watching and listening, waiting and then acting. An important part of dadirri is quiet stillness and waiting, about which she says:

Our Aboriginal culture has taught us to be still and to wait. We do not try to hurry things up. We let them follow their natural course – like the seasons. We watch the moon in each of its phases. We wait for the rain to fill our rivers and water the thirsty earth … We watch the bush foods and wait for them to ripen before we gather them. We wait for our young people as they grow, stage by stage, through their initiation ceremonies. When a relation dies, we wait a long time with the sorrow. We own our grief and allow it to heal slowly (2002).

Returning to Yuin Country, Anthony McKnight states, "The Yuin reality of culture can exist without the spoken/written (English) language as the real communication of Yuin culture is done in silence … Country/Yuin culture does not need English to exist; it can 'read' memory, emotion and the behaviour of the body and spirit" (2015, p. 279). McKnight says this approach is the silent voice and powerful energy that guides the experience of self-examination so that connections occur in respectful relationship with Country.

Country communicates with all entities of Country, not just humans, and it is our responsibility to silently, patiently listen for those messages and respond. Since Country is the origin of knowledge and the ultimate Knowledge Holder, the signals or messages that Country sends us may be considered specifically in cultural and performative practice as a responsive means for making. Waiting for and listening to the messages of Country, reading, hearing, knowing Country – and being known, heard, and seen in return – provides a method for making, and can form or shape what is made. The change in the form of the made object comes from awareness of Country, from responding to that which comes through

---

47. In D'harawal, maduri is a flat-bottomed canoe mainly used by women when fishing in bays and inlets.
48. Laklak Burarrwanga, Banbapuy Ganambarr, Djawundil Maymuru, Merrkiyawuy Ganambarr-Stubbs, Ritjilili Ganambarr are all Yolŋu people, from Bawaka in northeastern Arnhem Land.
49. Bawaka is an Indigenous homeland on the water of Port Bradshaw in Arnhem Land off the Gulf of Carpentaria in the north of Australia. Research is conducted in collaboration with Indigenous and non-Indigenous people, with Bawaka Country as lead author in many of their writings.

---

50. Miriam Rose Ungunmerr-Bauman is an Elder from Nauiyu (Daly River) from the of the Ngan'gityemerri language group.

the transmissions of Country.

Country has the capacity to inform and teach us about the potentiality of its spaces; Country can tell us what its spaces 'should' be like. As weavers, we learn to read the land through a maker's filter, by which I mean, the women of my family who reclaim cultural practices such as weaving have also reclaimed the ability to 'see' Country as different types of living larders or mobile agriculture; they are a series of spaces of collecting and making, irrespective of whether these spaces are in the countryside or cityscape. Siân calls them the "templates for a weaving space" (Yarn with S Hromek, 2018 on 14 December). By this she means the spaces in which there is potential for weaving to occur easily because everything that is needed is there, and not only materials but also nourishment and safety. In seeing Country thus, we (re)imagine spaces of Country where women have gathered, yarned, dined and made together for generations. We (re)tell and tell anew stories of those sites; in doing so, we (re)activate them by revisiting them and continue cultural practices there. Irene Watson describes how our laws provided for gendered spaces, "places where the Law of women was revered and provided safety for women of the community" (2007, p. 102). Likewise, Marcia Langton[51] discusses gendered spaces, saying, "Places are imbued with the gender of the Old People, the deceased ancestor's unceasing existence, as one of their essential attributes. Places are thus 'genderised' and gender emplaced. There are places where only women may go, and places where only men may go" (2002, p. 262-263). These gendered spaces still exist in the landscape as spaces of safety, action and consciousness. Our collective memories are stored there, creating spaces of remembrance and narrative. Being responsive to the stories and messages of Country gives us the opportunity to reclaim cultural practices and connect with knowledges necessarily hidden by Ancestors in order to keep them safe. Country as our master teacher and holder of knowledges is our means of (re)connecting. These micro means of (re)creating spaces of making, whether they be urban or rural, are our means of (re)claiming them as women's spaces and contesting them as Indigenous spaces.

Conclusion

Instead of considering how First Peoples have managed to adapt to the ravages of colonisation, cultural genocide, restrictive policy and rapid changes to the land, colonisers have tended to judge Indigenous peoples in terms of their perceived deficits while continuing to make exclusionary decisions. Attempts by First Peoples to reclaim land, history and knowledge have been met with colonial views of the past, and an imposed invaders' judicial system. Despite living in changing and different spatial paradigms of colonisation and capitalism, Aboriginal peoples continue to find ways to connect to Country, to continue storytelling practices, to find refuge in each other, to inhabit the interstitial spaces and to create new ways to move through the urban landscape. We also continue to connect to Country through our practices, which likewise connect us to culture.

Uncle Greg Simms has often said it is the women in our communities who are the strongest, and I doubt there are many in our family who would disagree. This chapter (narrative, story, journey) includes stories of my family, from one of the first women of our family (Jane Brown) to encounter colonial forces through to the women of today who are still fiercely holding their ground. It includes the stories of the two sisters, Elizabeth and Catherine Marshall,[52] who made the impossible decision to leave their traditional lands through to my sister and I now reclaiming our cultural heritage and practices. In actuality there have been a series of impossible decisions made by the women of our family, and what is evident is that while these decisions came from a space of resilience, resistance, relationships and reclamation, they were invariably made for love. And so, it is a story of love keeping family together as relations, community, and kin. It is a story of how love – and yarning and hard work – reconnected us with our Country.

It has been important through the process of this writing to follow the narratives backwards and return with them to now, to have the true story at hand, so that I can go back to my grandmother and say, "This is why you feel invisible in colonial spaces." It has been important to all of us as a family to tell our stories, especially those accounts that were previously kept hidden.[53] As a part of a wider familial journey, this process has given a return of pride and, for some, acceptance. It is extremely special to hear my grandmother speaking of her grandmother with such dignity and self-worth. Hearing her stories builds the identity of all of us and gives us grounding to connect to Country and wider kin networks. While we may have once been hidden, invisible, silenced peoples, through stories, practices, culture and Country, we have now come back into the light.

---

51. Marcia Langton is a descendant of the Yiman and Bidjara nations of Queensland.

52. Catherine Marshall is a Yuin woman.
53. Most of which are not shared here but are kept safely with those who hold them.

Reference List

Archibald, J-A 2008. *Indigenous Storywork: Educating the Heart, Mind, Body, and Spirit.* Stó:lô, UBC Press, Vancouver, BC.

Bawaka Country, Wright, S, Suchet-Pearson, S, Lloyd, K, Burarrwanga, L, Ganambarr, R, Ganambarr-Stubbs, M, Ganambarr, B & Maymuru, D 2015b. "Working with and learning from Country: decentring human author-ity". Yolŋu (Burarrwanga, Ganambarr, Ganambarr-Stubbs, Ganambarr, Maymuru), *Cultural Geographies*, vol. 22, no. 2, pp. 269–283.

Behrendt, L (1993) "Aboriginal women and the white lies of the feminist movement: Implications for Aboriginal women in rights discourse." Eualeyai/Kamillaroi, *Australian Feminist Law Journal*, vol. 1, pp. 27-44.

Bessarab, D 2018, "Personal communication with Dawn Bessarab on Gadigal Lands at Yarning Workshop," Bardi/Indjarbandi, *personal communication*, 17 May, Sydney NSW.

Bessarab, D & Ng'andu, B 2010, "Yarning About Yarning as a Legitimate Method in Indigenous Research," *International Journal of Critical Indigenous Studies*, vol. 3, no. 1, pp. 37-50.

Bodkin, F 2016, "Yarn with Aunty Frances Bodkin," in D. Hromek (ed.), *D'harawal Country, Mount Annan Botanic Gardens*, NSW, p. Bidiagal/D'harawal, 28 October.

Bodkin, F 2017, "Personal communication with Aunty Frances Bodkin on D'harawal Lands," Bidiagal/D'harawal, *personal communication*, 5 December, Sydney NSW.

Bodkin, F 2018, "Yarn with Aunty Frances Bodkin," Bidiagal/D'harawal, on *D'harawal Country, Mount Annan Botanic Gardens*, NSW, interviewed by D Hromek, 22 June.

Bodkin-Andrews, G 2018, "Personal communication with Gawaian Bodkin-Andrews on Gadigal Lands," Bidiagal/D'harawal, *personal communication*, 8 August, Sydney NSW.

Builth, H 2009, "Intangible Heritage of Indigenous Australians: a Victorian example," *Historic Environment*, vol. 22, no. 3, pp. 24-31.

Burarrwanga, L, Ganambarr, B, Maymuru, D, Lloyd, K, Ganambarr-Stubbs, M, Ganambarr, R, Suchet-Pearson, S & Wright, S 2014, Welcome to my Country: seeing the true beauty of life in Bawaka, Yolŋu (Burarrwanga, Ganambarr, Maymuru, Ganambarr-Stubbs, Ganambarr), The Conversation, Australia, viewed 11 May 2017, https://theconversation.com/welcome-to-my-Country-seeing-the-true-beauty-of-life-in-bawaka-31378.

Burarrwanga, L, Maymuru, D, Ganambarr, R, Ganambarr, B, Wright, S, Suchet-Pearson, S & Lloyd, K 2008, *Weaving Lives Together at Bawaka, North East Arnhem Land*, University of Newcastle, Newcastle, NSW.

Cuthand, B 1989, *Voices in the Waterfall*, Cree, Lazara Press, Vancouver, BC.

Dudgeon, P 2017, "Mothers of Sin: Indigenous Women's Perceptions of their Identity and Gender," Bardi, in P Dudgeon, J Herbert, J Milroy & D Oxenham (eds), *Us Women, Our Ways, Our World*, Magabala Books, Broome, WA.

French, J 2013, *Let the Land Speak*, HarperCollins Publishers, Sydney.

Gillis, J 2018, "Yarn with Jenny Gillis," Budawang/Yuin, on Awabakal Country, Newcastle, NSW, interviewed by D Hromek, 27 January.

Greenop, K & Memmott, P 2006, "Contemporary Urban Aboriginal Place Values in Brisbane," 8th Australasian Urban History/Planning History Conference, eds C. Miller & M. Roche, Massey University, Massey University, New Zealand, pp. 157-70.

Havemann, P 2005, "Denial, modernity and exclusion: Indigenous placelessness in Australia", *Macquarie Law Journal*, vol. 5, pp. 57-80.

Healey, S 2006, "Cultural Resilience, Identity and the Restructuring of Political Power in Bolivia," paper presented to the 11th Biennial Conference of the International Association for the Study of Common Property, Bali Indonesia, 19 - 23 June 2006.

Hromek, D, Hromek, S & Hromek, M 2015, Covered By Concrete, Budawang/Yuin, spatial map installation including video, aromas and audio, Underbelly Arts Festival, Sydney, <https://www.youtube.com/watch?v=cr3yugBBXfU&t=614s>.

Hromek, S 2018, "Yarn with Siân Hromek," Budawang/Yuin, on Awabakal Country, Newcastle, NSW, interviewed by D Hromek, 27 January.

Hromek, S 2018, "Yarn with Siân Hromek," Budawang/Yuin, on Bundjalung Country, Byron Bay, NSW, interviewed by D Hromek, 14 December.

Ireland, J 2013, "The case of Agnes Jones," *History Australia*, vol. 10, no. 3, pp. 236-251.

Irish, P 2017, *Hidden in Plain View: The Aboriginal people of coastal Sydney*, NewSouth Publishing, Sydney.

Karskens, G 2009, "The Colony: A history of early Sydney," Allen & Unwin, Crows Nest, NSW.

Kimmerer, R W 2013, *Braiding Sweetgrass: Indigenous wisdom, scientific knowledge and the teachings of plants,* Potawatomi, Milkweed Editions, Minneapolis, MN.

Kwaymullina, A 2017, "The Creators of the Future: Women, Law and telling stories in Country," Palkyu, in P Dudgeon, J Herbert, J Milroy & D Oxenham (eds), *Us Women, Our Ways, Our World*, Magabala Books, Broome, WA.

Langton, M 2002, "The Edge of the Sacred, the Edge of Death: Sensual Inscriptions," Yiman and Bidjara, in B David & M Wilson (eds), *Inscribed Landscapes: Marking and making place,* University of Hawaii Press, Hawaii, HI, pp. 253-269.

Lee, V 2017, "As Black Women Do: Aboriginal and Torres Strait Islander Women's Resilience," Yupungathi and Meriam, in P Dudgeon, J Herbert, J Milroy & D Oxenham (eds), *Us Women, Our Ways, Our World*, Magabala Books, Broome, WA.

Luthar, S S 2006, "Resilience in development: A synthesis of research across five decade," in D. Cicchetti & D.J. Cohen (eds), *Developmental Psychopathology: Risk, Disorder, and Adaptation,* Wiley, New York, pp. 740-95.

Magee, S 2006, *Moruya A Short History,* Moruya and District Historical Society Inc, Moruya, NSW.

Martin-Booran Mirraboopa, K 2008, *Please Knock Before You Enter: Aboriginal regulation of outsiders and the implications for researchers,* Noonuccal and Bidjara, Post Pressed Brisbane, Teneriffe, QLD.

McKnight, A 2015, "Mingadhuga Mingayung: Respecting Country through Mother Mountain's stories to share her cultural voice in Western academic structures," Awabakal, Gumaroi, and Yuin, *Educational Philosophy and Theory,* vol. 47, no. 3, pp. 276-90.

Moreton-Robinson, A & Walter, M 2009, "Indigenous Methodologies in Social Research," Geonpul/Minjerribah/Quandamooka (Moreton-Robinson), Palawa/Pairrebenne (Walter), in A Bryman (ed.), *Social Research Methods,* Oxford University Press, South Melbourne, VIC.

Morgan, G 2006, *Unsettled Places: Aboriginal people and urbanisation in New South Wales,* Wakefield Press, Kent Town, SA.

Murch, C 2018, "Yarn with Caitlyn Murch," on Awabakal Country, Newcastle, NSW, interviewed by D Hromek, 27 January.

Nipperess, G 2018, "Yarn with Gloria Nipperess," in D. Hromek (ed.), Awabakal Country, Newcastle, NSW, p. Budawang/Yuin, 27 January.

Prout, S & Howitt, R 2009, "Frontier Imaginings and Subversive Indigenous Spatialities," *Journal of Rural Studies,* vol. 25, no. 4, pp. 396-403.

Richardson, L 1994, "Writing: A method of inquiry," in N.K. Denzin & Y.S. Lincoln (eds), *Handbook of Qualitative Research,* Sage Publications, Thousand Oaks, pp. 923-48.

Seyer-Ochi, I 2006, "Lived Landscapes of the Fillmore," in G. Spindler & L. Hammond (eds), *Innovations in Educational Ethnography: Theory, Methods, and Results,* Lawrence Erlbaum, Mahwah, NJ.

Simms, G 2015, "Yarn with Uncle Greg Simms," Gadigal/Darug/Gundungurra/Yuin, on Darug Country, Sydney, interviewed by D Hromek, 28 October.

Sium, A & Ritskes, E (2013). "Speaking truth to power: Indigenous storytelling as an act of living resistance," Tigrinya, Indigenous, Eritrean and African (Sium), *Decolonization: Indigeneity, Education & Society*, vol. 2, no. 1, pp. I-X.

Stanner, W E H 1968, *After the Dreaming: Black and white Australians – an anthropologist's view*, ABC, Sydney.

Ungunmerr-Bauman, M-R 2002, "Against racism," Ngan'gityemerri/Nauiyu, *Compass*, vol. 37, no. 3.

Walker, M, Fredericks, B, Mills, K & Anderson, D 2014, "'Yarning' as a Method for Community-Based Health Research With Indigenous Women: The Indigenous Women's Wellness Research Program," *Health Care for Women International*, vol. 35, no. 10, pp. 1216-1226.

Watson, I 2007, "Aboriginal Women's Laws and Lives: How Might We keep Growing The Law?," Tanganekald and Meintangk Boandik, *Australian Feminist Law Journal,* vol. 26, no. 1, pp. 95-107.

Watson, I 2017, "Standing Our Ground and Telling the One True Story," Tanganekald and Meintangk Boandik, in P Dudgeon, J Herbert, J Milroy & D Oxenham (eds), *Us Women, Our Ways, Our World,* Magabala Books, Broome, WA.

Wilson, S 2001, "What is an Indigenous Research Methodology," Opaskwayak Cree, *Canadian Journal of Native Education,* vol. 25, no. 2, pp. 175-179.

Wyld, F & Fredericks, B L 2015, "Earth song as storywork: Reclaiming Indigenous knowledges," *Journal of Australian Indigenous Issues,* vol. 18, no. 2, pp. 2-12.

Chapter 3.4: Covered by Concrete – Uncovering latent Aboriginal narratives concealed in urban contexts

Michael Hromek, Siân Hromek and Danièle Hromek – Budawang, Yuin nation

Descended of the Yuin People, Budawang Tribe, Michael is a researcher and Professional Tutor at the University of Technology, Sydney's Jumbunna Institute for Indigenous Education and Research. He has a range of specialisations in the broad area of design, theory and architecture. These include the nature of design and its role towards society, contemporary Indigenous identity and how this might be formalised through the built environment and the relationships between theory and practice in planning, society and the city. Michael is currently completing a PhD at the UTS and teaches in the Bachelor of Design in Architecture covering architectural design and history and theory subjects. His thesis focuses on the idea of the urban Indigenous community in Redfern and its urban spatial values.

Born on Bundjalung Country in the Northern Rivers of NSW Sian is a Budawang Yuin Saltwater woman. A curiosity and desire to understand and work with Country has driven her study and work to explore how we may use traditional land management techniques in a contemporary context.

Studies in Conservation Land Management, Horticulture and Landscape Architecture has led to Sian participating in the cultural burning revival that is taking place on the east coast through working with the Firesticks Alliance as well as sitting on the board of directors. Other current activities include establishing a bush foods orchard and business and working in bush regeneration and land management. Sian also works a researcher and designer.

Since 2019, Siân has been a Director on the board of the Firesticks Alliance Indigenous Corporation (ICN-8778), which helps Traditional Custodians reinvigorate and reapply cultural burning practices to repair and strengthen Country and community. The Firesticks Alliance partners with communities, the private sector, governments and not for profits.

Dr Danièle Hromek is a Budawang woman of the Yuin nation. She is a spatial designer and artist, fusing design elements with installations and sculptural form. Her work derives from her cultural and experiential heritage, often considering the urban Aboriginal condition, the Indigenous experience of Country, and contemporary Indigenous identities. Danièle is a researcher and educator considering how to Indigenise the built environment by creating spaces to substantially affect Indigenous rights and culture within an institution. Danièle's research contributes an understanding of the Indigenous experience and comprehension of space, and investigates how Aboriginal people occupy, use, narrate, sense, dream and contest their spaces. It rethinks the values that inform Aboriginal understandings of space through Indigenous spatial knowledge and cultural practice, in doing so considers the sustainability of Indigenous cultures from a spatial perspective.

Introduction

Can space be reclaimed? Once a space has been changed, from one configuration to another, is it still the same? What remains of the former? What of its topography, its flora and fauna, its stories? And what of its *genius loci,* or "spirit of place?" (Norberg-Schulz, 1980).

These questions were asked through a spatial mapping project called *Covered by Concrete* that sought to uncover the latent Aboriginal history, spirit, and stories of Cockatoo Island in Sydney Harbour. This chapter will explore the process and themes of the project with an aim to position it in the broader context of establishing and embedding Indigenous design, spatial principles and knowledges into the built environment.

Wardaalimala[1] [Thinking / Method / Research]

In 2015, the Underbelly Arts Festival was on Cockatoo Island and challenged artists to produce works that engaged with the festival's audience and the island itself. We, the artists, Danièle [mama[2]], Siân [murnunggan[3]], and Michael [mayaaga[4]] Hromek are three siblings from the

---

1. Wardaalimala refers to the act of seeking in Dhurga.
2. Mama refers to an older sister in Dhurga.
3. Murnunggan refers to a younger sister in Dhurga.
4. Mayaaga refers to a younger brother in Dhurga.

Budawang people of the Yuin nation, were interested in exploring the hidden Aboriginal stories of the site.

As a beginning point, we drew upon existing methods, teachings and understandings of remembering, interpreting and presenting Aboriginal space. Two primary examples were referenced; the works by academic historian Bill Gammage and architect Kevin O'Brien from the Kaurareg and Meriam peoples.

Bill Gammage's book, *The Biggest Estate on Earth: How Aborigines Made Australia* (2012), reveals the management of Country that existed before colonisation. For us, the book acted as a lens through which Cockatoo Island could be understood. Gammage stipulates that in 1788 there was no wilderness but rather a landscape that reflected sophisticated successful and sensitive farming regime integrated across the Australian landmass, achieved through the use of fire as a tool of fuel reduction and grass promotion. It was a form of cultural land management practice that was carefully employed to ensure certain plants and animals flourished to increase access and ensure resources were abundant.

Gammage substantiated his theory through an evidence-based approach to analysing historical documents, paintings and accounts from early invaders about the Country they were experiencing and the First Peoples they came into contact with. For us, this became a clear methodology of reading Country and formulating a picture of what Country looked like before it was changed by colonial forces.

The second primary influence for the project was the work by Kevin O'Brien, in particular his work titled, *Sep Yama: Finding Country* (2012), an exhibition staged as an independent and official collateral event of the 13th Venice Architecture Biennale. In this work, O'Brien considers the Aboriginal notion of Country, claiming:

> Every part of Australia of this country has a memory. Australian cities continue to expand blindly both out and up – no one looks down, into the ground, into country. An expertise of expansion has been amassed and architects are not part of it … Architecture is a potent mechanism that can allow us to find country. It is not a technique as much a way of thinking. Acknowledgement of this relationship and its impact on memory is what must be accepted here. This simple project embraces the very notion from where I sit (O'Brien, 2007).

In this project, O'Brien asked the students to imagine their own understanding of Country by examining pre-colonial, colonial and contemporary Aboriginal understandings of Country. It questioned how cities, "historically enter states of decline, frequently associated with some form of catastrophe. Others end in a whimper. It is not unreasonable to imagine an opportunity for the recovery of Country through decline" (O'Brien & Markham, 2009). What eventuated was a mosaic of built fabric interpreted by individual students who were challenged to analyse and value the city in the post construction method. The outcome produced was a visually interesting spatial mapping that engaged with local Aboriginal knowledge. What also emerged was a model of development which was more sympathetic and in harmony with the local surroundings. This offered us an insight into O'Brien's notion of Country – which is a symbiotic condition between Aboriginal people and the environment (natural or built). Out of this symbiosis comes a spirituality that binds us to our respective Country (O'Brien, 2019). It gave us insight into how Country can be conceived, interpreted and valued; and as such was utilised as a framework for Covered by Concrete.

With these two precedents in hand, information was gathered from a variety of sources, in particular, documentation from the various authorities and stakeholders of the island including the Sydney Harbour Foreshore Authority (SHFA) and Sydney Harbour Federation Trust (SHFT). These documents offered a valuable insight into the Island's recorded and pre-recorded history. Specifically, that the island was once known as *Wa-rea-mah* (Fletcher, 2011; Sydney Harbour Federation Trust 2010, 2014). This name was found in a list of place names compiled by Governor Arthur Phillip in 1791.

The Sydney basin has changed a lot since people first settled in the area. During the height of the last ice age between 26,000 and 20,000 years ago huge sheets of ice locked up vast amounts of water reducing sea level by up to 120 metres in Sydney Harbour. During this time Aboriginal people occupied coastal environments which have since been covered by the sea and sediments. The coastline was located around 20 kilometres east of its current location and Sydney Harbour was a steep gorge, surrounded by high cliffs that had been carved out by a glacier from a previous Ice Age. As the icecaps and glaciers melted between 18,000 and 6,000 years ago the rise in sea level drowned the coastal plains and river valleys to form the estuaries and deep harbours we see today (Logan, 2007; Office of Environment and Heritage, 2016; Reid, Nunn, and Sharpe 2014).

As with many important locations, the local Aboriginal peoples shared the island. Wareamah is situated at the meeting point of two rivers, the Parramatta and Lane Cove rivers. It is also located at the intersection of several of Aboriginal groups, including the Gadigal, Gorualgal, Cammeraigal, Wangal, Wallumattagal, Birrabirragal, and although they shared a language, they had separate identities and recognised the fluid land boundaries between the groups. In Dharug language, Wareamah is believed to mean "women's land," suggesting that the island was a place for women's business (Sydney Harbour Federation Trust, 2011). The documents described the island as being accessible from the north and south sides of the harbour making it a great place for people to meet up and get together. It was covered in local vegetation growing on top of the sandstone

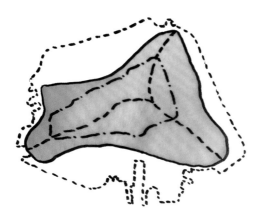

Figure 1. Wareamah showing pre-colonial and contemporary footprint. The solid line demonstrates the original shape of the island, the small dotted line shows its footprint today, and the large dotted line its ridgeline. Drawing by Michael Hromek 2015.

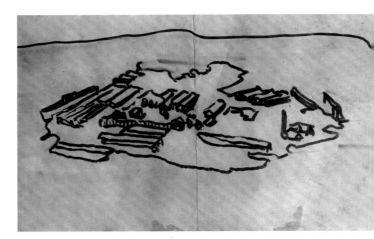

Figure 2. Artist's impression of Cockatoo Island (Wareamah) after drastic land reclamation was undertaken during the peak of its ship production during World War I and II. Drawing by Michael Hromek 2015.

rock. It was likely used for fishing and collection of food resources such as shellfish, and as a meeting place for the various local peoples who lived along the harbour foreshore including trade or ceremony (Sydney Harbour Federation Trust, 2010).

With the arrival of colonisers, the island's identity was transformed, and its use changed dramatically. The land was cleared in preparation for building and quarried for its good quality sandstone. As the sandstone was quarried and used in buildings for the colony, the refuse was thrown into the sea resulting in the island expanding from 12.9 hectares to 17.9 hectares (Fletcher, 2011; Sydney Harbour Federation Trust, 2010). The original natural shape of the island was slowly adjusted over the following two centuries as it became industrialised. (Fig. 1 and 2) Maps were therefore also important to our investigations. We sought historical and contemporary maps that demonstrated the changing shape and profile of the island.

In conjunction to written reports, early colonial paintings of Cockatoo Island before it was altered were analysed. Subsequent paintings showed sparse trees, a few small houses and a very large grassy hill. More contemporary documents such as photos for World War I were also investigated.

In our analysis we reviewed the signage on the island, which revealed a lack of information available to visitors regarding the Aboriginal connection with this site. We were concerned that the Aboriginal stories of use, inhabitation, and occupation of the island were hidden in these sources, silenced under the strata and urbanity of the site. Albert Memmi aptly describes this, saying as the coloniser "endeavours to falsify history, he rewrites laws, he would extinguish memories - anything to succeed in transforming his usurpation into legitimacy" (1965, p. 52). This silencing through not being included ensures an unbalanced and incomplete story of a place. To rebalance this "colonial amnesia" (Gandhi, 1998), we spoke with

Elders and Knowledge Holders related to the island; their stories were included in a number of ways across the project, including in a series of signs that aimed to correc the lack of information available on the island about the First Peoples' relationships with that place. (Fig. 3-4)

Djinjama[5] [Making / Process / Construction]

Concurrently with the archival research we undertook site visits where we drew sketches, took photographs, and picked a location where our spatial mapping project would be located. Existing industrial buildings provided a haunting yet spacious location for the festival. (Fig. 5) One of our hopes was to represent the Country of the island before it was destroyed. There was little evidence to help us determine plant species or animals, or the uses that people had for the island, we tried a different method for ascertaining the nature of this island's country.

We explored ways to recognise the island's past, its use, shape, profile and inhabitants. We wanted to bring some of what was taken away back to the island. To achieve this Siân visited the relatively untouched or regenerated headlands nearby and gathered native grasses, bushes, trees nuts, leaves etc. that are indigenous to this Country and therefore, we felt, indications of what the native flora of the island might have been on Wareamah. Material was collected and brought onto the island for later use.

Very early on we decided we wanted to work with the medium of concrete both as a comment regarding the overuse of concrete on the island and the built environment more generally, and also in order to subvert

---

5. Djinjama refers to making, producing or building something in Dhurga.

Figure 3. Welcome signage on Cockatoo Island. Photographed by Danièle Hromek, 2015.

Figure 4. Welcome signage on Cockatoo Island. Photographed by Danièle Hromek, 2015.

Figure 5. Industrial space of Cockatoo Island. Photograph by Danièle Hromek, 2015.

Figure 6. Bump in. Photograph by Danièle Hromek, 2015.

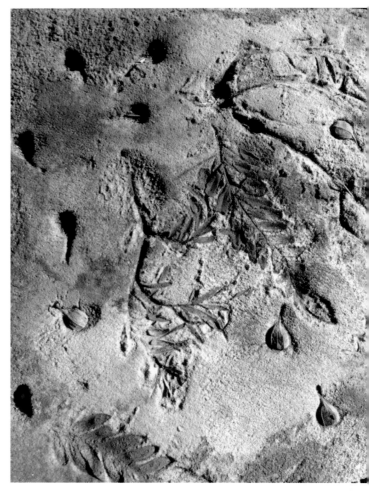

Figure 7. Burnt out flora from nearby reserves helped reconstruct a pre-colonial Wareamah. Photograph by Michael Hromek, 2015.

the colonial impacts by using a material of colonisation to demonstrate the Country of the site. We achieved this by imprinting into the concrete, using Indigenous land management techniques on the concrete, to embed it with our culture. Concrete is a material quite familiar to us, from our childhood when writing our names in wet concrete, but also in later education and employment where made concrete models for architecture and spatial design explorations.

Once we determined our location – a large engine hall from the disused industrial building on the island – we had a good understanding of how big the spatial mapping should be to adequately reflect the scale of our space, and we quickly realised we will be pouring approximately 50 concrete cubes equating a tonne of concrete. (Fig. 6) Working on site, we decided to imprint the collected vegetation into the concrete in a similar way we did when we were young when we came across wet concrete. In our method of distribution, we tried to follow some logic in terms of where certain flora species might be located

on the island. For example, gumtrees on the ridge tops of the island and more water-based plants, such as reeds, wattles, and ferns, closest to the edges. In this way we allowed Country to dominate the concrete, the coloniser, and be uplifted in priority and visibility.

A few days after pouring and imprinting the concrete, we moved some – in effect a patchwork – of the concrete blocks to the designated burning area on the island in order to burn out the materials imprinted into it. Aboriginal people have been using fire to look after Country for millennia. A slow cool burn can open up the Country and help to keep it healthy. Mosaic-burning techniques ensure that a variety of habitats and vegetation ages are developed providing food, shelter and space for animals to move about easily. It is used to keep pathways open and easily accessible. Our burning of the concrete created an interesting etching or smudging affect where the ash from the burnt flora was darker in the imprint, creating a varied surface in terms of light and dark elements. (Fig. 7-9)

Figure 8. Concrete blocks with flora imprints and burning. Photograph by Danièle Hromek, 2015.

Figure 9. Concrete blocks with flora imprints and burning. Photograph by Danièle Hromek, 2015.

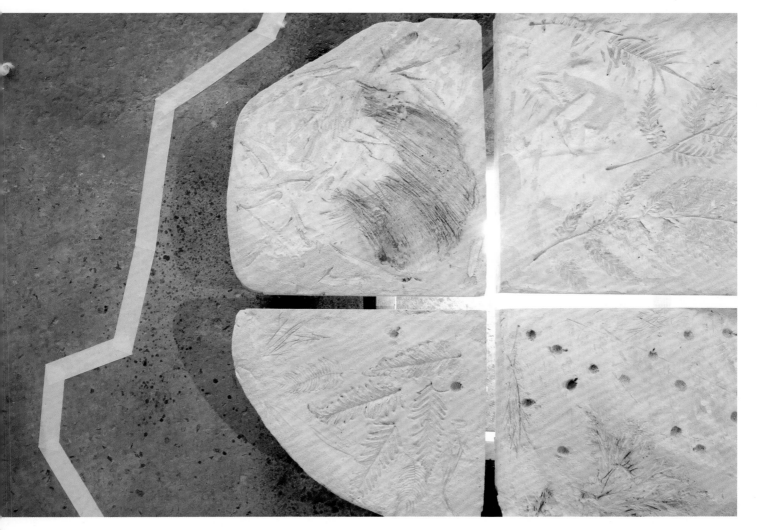

Figure 10. Outline of the current island's shape around the pre-invasion shape. Photograph by Danièle Hromek, 2015.

Figure 11. Our updated signage. Photograph by Danièle Hromek, 2015.

Figure 12. Covered by Concrete with people watching the film of Elders and Knowledge Holders in the background. Photograph by Danièle Hromek, 2015.

Figure 13. Festival visitors inspecting the project in the final night of exhibition. Photograph by Michael Hromek, 2015.

Figure 14. Covered by Concrete. Photograph by Danièle Hromek, 2015.

The concrete blocks, cast in the pre-invasion shape of the island, were arranged on a wooden frame and we installed lighting underneath to imply the stories that were streaming through the grid created by the concrete blocks. A representation of the island's current footprint was communicated via yellow tape, as if a police crime scene was cordoned off for the island. (Fig. 10)

Important to the project was the "correction" of the island's signage, which as it was, disappointingly contained only a few lines about First Peoples' inhabitation of the island. The updated signage included our findings through the research we undertook, both in the archives, and with our Elders and other community members. We also included films of Elders and Knowledge Holders discussing their experience of Country and the colonial impacts on the land. (Fig. 11)

Finally, a phenomenological or sensorial element was achieved through spraying eucalyptus gum oil around the model so when people would approach, they received a strong waft and scent of eucalyptus. Through a set of speakers hidden under the work crackled the sound of fire. (Fig. 12-14)

When the Festival ended, we were approached by the Island authority with a proposal to permanently install the work on the island. The mapping is highly contextual so to remove it from the site would diminish its meaning and significance. Furthermore, as a site-specific work which aimed to rebalance the stories of the island, it is pertinent and important that the work remains on site.

Bundjala[6] [Reflecting / Analysis / Values]

This project was a multi-layered approach in an attempt to understand and represent (and re-present) a place through a spatial intervention. The acknowledgement and engagement of the multiple layers of information about place (for instance, vegetation, topography, climate, use, culture, stories, etc.) are important to respectfully and thoroughly reflecting a place.

During our time on the island and through our research, we found that an Aboriginal Tent Embassy had been established on Wareamah in November 2000. The

_____

6. Bundjala refers to thinking or remembering in Dhurga language.

177

future ownership of the island was uncertain at the time, so they staked a claim under the Native Title Act. The group's leader, Isabel Coe, said:

> This would have been a very sacred site. It is where the rivers join and is in the middle of where the sun rises and sets over the harbour. It is part of the Milky Way Dreamtime stories. Under Aboriginal law we have already claimed it by placing the spear of the oldest lawman in NSW, Uncle Ted Gubbo Thomas in the ground (Sydney Harbour Federation Trust 2014, p. 53).

The Commonwealth Government launched legal action to have the activists removed, considering them to be trespassing and that the site was unsafe. The group stayed on the island for four months and after a series of court cases and appeals, the Supreme Court of NSW ruled against the people declaring that continuous occupation was unlikely due to the lack of fresh water. In our view, this is a narrow perspective of how Aboriginal peoples inhabit sites, not least as the peoples around Sydney Harbour were observed to be expert boats people, in particular the women, who fished from their nawis, or bark canoes, as they skilfully navigated the harbour waters. In addition, it raises the question about cyclical movement as a matter of permanence, as opposed to permanent occupation of one place without consideration of cycles (such as seasons, but also celestial cycles, or movements of animals or sea life) as a determinant of movement. As a result of the Government's actions, the Tent Embassy was forced to close, and the people were removed from the island. Nonetheless, traces of their time on the island still exist through murals and other artworks, an important remnant of resistance to colonial intervention.

Other forms of resistance explored through the project include subversion of materials or techniques introduced through colonisation, for instance, using concrete to bring awareness to the overuse of this material. Similarly, mapping has been used as a colonial construct to control First Peoples and their spaces. However Aboriginal peoples also map, for example, via moving through or walking Country; through the process of movement a knowing of the landscape occurs that creates a phenomenological sensorial mapping of Country. Our work, while it used western means of mapping, also challenged the idea of a map as a flat paper- or screen-based implement of holding the land in place. By representing the map as a spatial three-dimensional object with stories embedded, we asked visitors to reconsider maps as more than a means of navigation.

Important to the project was also reclamation; reclaiming identity of a place, but also people related to that place. By revealing and addressing some of the stories of that place – both Aboriginal and colonial – the "true history" can start to likewise be revealed and addressed. Including First Peoples' perspectives through film and written word ensured their voices were heard in the project, and made it even more specific to site, as a longer history was included.

The process of investigating, developing and delivery of the artwork left us with a sense and deeper understanding that there is a memory and story of Aboriginal Ancestors embedded into the fabric of the very earth we inhabit. Through this process we felt the layers of colonisation were peeled back to reveal a glimpse of Country, inhabited, and cared for by its people. Through the revival of cultural burning land management practices in recent years people are starting to heal Country and in turn healing ourselves in the process. Using the right fire on the right Country at the right time with the right people is in itself a practice of decolonisation.

Conclusion

We sought to uncover the spirit of the place and unveil the story of this place, and furthermore to share it with others exploring the island today. Memorialising culture through design in the urban landscape – specifically First Peoples' cultures – is key to truth telling as it changes perceptions of Indigenous peoples as being from a distant past, from a long way away. It is important to redress questions of identity for First Peoples and for Country in an urban context, especially within the largest Aboriginal community in Australia, that being Sydney. Elders and Knowledge Holders who contributed towards this project informed us explicitly that Country exists in urbanity, the spirits of Ancestors still walk and care for the city landscape. Despite being covered by concrete, Country exists in the city, narratives and memory is still accessible, and while these may be harder to sense, it is still key to culture and for care of Country. Knowing these narratives is a fundamental step in decolonising the city as it offers a view not only to the past, but to the future for First Peoples, in relation to our connections to the land and knowledges, but also to each other.

Reference List

Fletcher, P. (2011). Cockatoo Island. *Sydney Journal,* (December).

Gammage, B. (2012). *The Biggest Estate on Earth: How Aborigines made Australia.* Crows Nest, NSW: Allen & Unwin.

Gandhi, L. (1998). *Postcolonial theory.* St Leonards, NSW: Allen and Unwin.

Jeremy, J. (2005). *Cockatoo Island: Sydney's historic dockyard.* Sydney: UNSW Press.

Kerr, J. (1984). *Cockatoo Island: Penal and institutional remains.* Sydney: National Trust of Australia.

Logan, G. M. (2007). *Cockatoo Island Dockyard – Conservation Management Plan – Volume I.* Retrieved from http://www.cockatooisland.gov.au/system/files/pages/1d843de2-ed47-4ed0-bccc-4160a05ed533/files/cmp-cockatooisland-dockyard4.pdf.

Memmi, A. (1965). *The Colonizer and the Colonized.* Boston, MA: Beacon Press.

Norberg-Schulz, C. (1980). *Genius loci: Towards a phenomenology of architecture.* New York: Rizzoli.

O'Brien, K. (2007). Sanctuary Place: Sep Yama / Finding Country 5 Ways. *Architectural Review, 103.* (November).

O'Brien, K. (2012). Sep Yama: Finding Country. http://www.findingcountry.com.au/.

O'Brien, K., & Markham, M. (2009). Finding Country, Creative Work (Web-based Exhibition).

Office of Environment and Heritage. (2016). Sydney Basin - landform. https://www.environment.nsw.gov.au/bioregions/SydneyBasin-Landform.htm.

Reid, N., Nunn, P. D., & Sharpe, M. (2014). *Indigenous Australian Stories and Sea-Level Change.* Paper presented at the Proceedings of the 18th Conference of the Foundation for Endangered Languages.

Sydney Harbour Federation Trust. (2010). *Sydney Harbour Federation Trust Management Plan – Cockatoo Island.* Retrieved from http://www.cockatooisland.gov.au/system/files/pages/1d843de2-ed47-4ed0-bccc-4160a05ed533/files/management-plan-cockatoo-island-part-1.pdf.

Sydney Harbour Federation Trust (2011). Harbour Trust - Cockatoo Island, Sydney Harbour.   Retrieved from http://www.harbourtrust.gov.au/.

Sydney Harbour Federation Trust. (2014). *Re-energising History - Education kit.* http://www.cockatooisland.gov.au/system/files/pages/1191798f-d7ac-4c02-b254-93dda9fb48ad/files/educationkitfeb2014.pdf.

Chapter 3.5: Urban Manaakitanga as Counter-Colonial Mahi

Amanda Yates – Ngāti Rangiwewehi, Ngāti Whakaue, Te Aitanga-a-Māhaki, Rongowhakaata

Amanda works with Councils, iwi and communities exploring place-based, Indigenous-led strategies and actions for urban transformation in an era of socio-ecological emergency. Yates is Director of He Puna Wai-Papa-Ora | Emergent Ecologies Lab, an urban mauri ora (wellbeing) research and activation lab. She is Co-Programme Leader and Principal Investigator of the Urban Wellbeing Research Programme in New Zealand's National Science Challenge Building Better Homes, Towns and Cities: the Mauri Ora research platform explores decolonising urban mauri ora (all of life wellbeing) frameworks and tools that can help to catalyse urban system change, including in energy, transport and housing systems. She is an Associate Professor in AUT's School of Future Environments and Head of the Architecture School.

Introduction

Tāmaki Makaurau Auckland has a rich urban lineage that extends back to pre-colonial times. Tāmaki's volcanic tūpuna maunga (ancestral mountains) were nodes for a distributed urbanism that extended across the isthmus. Now, at this time of climate and biodiversity emergency (IPCC 2018, 2019) and social crises that register on Māori particularly harshly – in housing availability, in chronic health conditions for example – we urgently need to transform how we do urbanism. At this time, we need an urbanism that privileges the care and wellbeing of human, but also critically, of more-than-human entities. Might indigenous urban practices of manaakitanga (generosity, kindness, respect) enable a decolonising of urban space with widespread positive effects for human and non-human, whānau (families) and whenua (the earth/land)?

What does decolonisation mean in this urban context? Decolonisation is understood here as an ongoing socio-cultural-political process, requiring concerted action for change. Linda Tuhiwai Smith notes that decolonising practices address "the history, colonial processes, ideologies and institutional practices that structure the relations of power between indigenous people and settler society" (Smith, 2016). Given the diverse registers of structural deprivation urban Māori face such as health

and wealth inequalities and in terms of being able to access healthy homes, it is clear that the urban is not a richly sustaining space for Māori. How might the socio-cultural-infrastructural relations of cities be structured otherwise, to enable – rather than disable – Indigenous peoples and the cultural landscapes that we whakapapa (relate) to and that sustain us?

I focus here on urban food and agricultural practices, as particular spatializations of the relations of power between Indigenous and colonial cultures. I ask whether these might be potential decolonising tools? Might a practice of urban manaakitanga, understood as generosity and solicitous care to humans and more-than-humans, disrupt and begin to transform urban policy and practice?

Indigenous Urbanism

Any discussion of urban decolonisation within Tāmaki Makaurau Auckland must refer to Tāmaki's urban history and the geography of Tāmaki's volcanic field. The isthmus of Tamaki links lands north and south, and oceans east and west, connected by a volcanic field that dots across the isthmus. Some 29 volcanic cones were once inhabited by Māori. Collectively this urban agglomeration may have housed some 22,500 people (Bulmer, 2002). The smallest population was likely to have been on the island Motukorea (around 255 people) while the largest population was on Maungakiekie (in the order of 2,550 people) (Bulmer, 2002). These mauna (mountain) settlements exemplify an Indigenous urbanism strongly defined by and responsive to geology. Indeed landform not only defined urban clusters but provided negative geo-architectural space as terraces and depressions were dug to form building platforms, food stores, earth-ovens, fireplaces.

Urban gardens were protected by stone-walled enclosures to moderate temperature and protect settlements from wind. Sited on and around the maunga, these gardens grew food for consumption and storage in the hill-top pā (fortified settlements). Archaeologist Susan Bulmer notes that the cones were able to be permanent settlements because of this close-coupled urban agriculture (2002). This urban cluster probably reached its maximum size and complexity in the early 18th century: "the urban centre was a development of a new level of socio-political complexity, based on wealth derived from traditional agriculture, a strategic position in transport and communication between districts, and the proximity of a group of prosperous towns" (Bulmer 2002, p.24).

Urbanism as Colonial Project

Tāmaki was an urban centre then long before agents of the British Crown arrived from the 1800s onwards. Yet settler urbanism constructed the colonial project in timber, bricks and mortar, in roads and subsequently in the sprawls of suburbia where each separate "nuclear" family staked out its boundaries in picket fences. Māori urban ethics based on the eco-social qualities of whānaungatanga, mauritanga, kaitiakitanga (practices for relationality, life-wellbeing, life-care respectively), were not embued in the urban fabric. Rather industrial modernity constructed a colonial urban culture, a sprawling sub-urbanism defined by individual, rather than collective, ownership and aspiration.

Many Māori communities in Aotearoa now have commonalities with other colonised Indigenous groups in terms of a spectrum of disenfranchisement. The costs of colonisation are high, counted in rates of ill-health, discriminatory and disproportionate incarcerations, suicides and various injustices related to food poverty, energy and housing. There is an urban precariat whose capacity for resilience is reduced by adversity clusters of housing, energy and/or food insecurity linked together with wage insecurity. Those existing in such highly marginalised positions within capitalist-modernist systems are increasingly, in some locales and when work is available, exposed to zero-hours contracts and ultra-low wages within a temporary or gig economy model. Projections of near-future digital-automation disruption to work (particularly for already marginal jobs) suggest further potential insecurities.

These visible registers of urban inequity index a more subtle, ideational colonising built into urban structures, infrastructures, policies, and governance in Aotearoa. The urban is able to enact and sustain cultural norms and structural injustices through a spatialisation of power relations to which Smith refers. For example, Aotearoa urban planning conventions are based on the right to individual ownership of land – a concept foreign to pre-colonial Māori. Further, the single-family house has been the default norm, despite Maori whānau and hapū convention where extended kin-groups lived together in clusters. My emphasis here is on how colonisation continues to propagate through an urbanism shaped by dominant Euro-American cultural narratives, urban economies and systems: this is the urban as a cultural artefact of an industrial-modernist economy.

Colonial processes, ideologies and institutional practices manifest also in urban food cultures in Aotearoa. Here a colonial-industrial food model is normative. This model is spatialised in a range of ways, through globalised foodsheds distributed via supermarkets that contain a high proportion of highly processed obesogenic foods; through loss-leader pricing strategies that enable high-sugar products like Coca-Cola to be cheaper than water; and through urban food "deserts" or 'swamps," disproportionately located in lower socio-economic areas (Exeter et al., 2017) (Pearce, 2007), where high-energy, low-nutrient foods are the norm and little fresh locally grown produce is available.

In the carbon culture of contemporary cities foods are sourced from all over the world, with your local supermarket offering nectarines from America, mangoes and avocados from Mexico, and South American bananas, all in the dead of winter. Contemporary industrial agriculture is entirely dependent on oil for growing and for international distribution and thus creates a massive carbon footprint: This is a globalised and globalising system built on an externalising of costs (for example environmental and animal health) that enable a "cheap" often highly processed product (Stull, 2017). Such industrial food is often radically different from the whole food ingredients used in those locally specific food cultures developed over generations. Environmental scientist and food researcher Jessica Hutchings describes this industrial food system as a neo-colonial foodscape (Hutchings, 2016).

The obesogenic nature of this neo-colonial food culture is well documented as is the associated burden of diabetes, heart disease, cancer (Gregory & Jensen, 2017). This is a global phenomenon in which energy-dense, nutrient poor industrial food is one driver of what the World Health Organisation (WHO) calls a "globesity epidemic." As health researchers note the food supply in wealthy countries, and increasingly now low-middle income countries, has shifted to high volumes of energy-dense, nutrient-poor, ultra-processed foods. Research shows that Aotearoa also has a high availability and consumption of processed food (Luiten, Steenhuis, Eyles, Ni & Waterlander, 2016).

Further, an obesogenic neo-colonial food culture has a steep economic gradient that is spatialised in the "food desert" phenomenon, where fresh produce is difficult to access while fast and processed foods are prevalent in lower-income neighbourhoods (Smoyer-Tomic, Spence & Amrhein, 2006). Populations living in food deserts are exposed to an obesogenic form of food poverty from a diet low in micro-nutrients (vitamins, minerals, fibre) but packed with macro-nutrients (fat, sugar, salt). While this food presents at the point of purchase as "cheap" it is in fact highly expensive when cost externalities like biodiversity loss associated with industrial agriculture and cost of globalised public health epidemics like obesity and diabetes are factored in (Carolan, 2018). Food insecurity – a lack of access to healthy and culturally appropriate food – is an inherent outcome of this colonial-industrial macro-nutrient based food system.

Significant numbers of Māori suffer from food insecurity (McKerchar et al., 2014; Stevenson, 2013) and Māori and Pasifika are disproportionately affected (Ministry of Health, 2003; University of Otago and Ministry of Health, 2011; Utter, Izumi, Denny, Fleming, & Clark, 2018). Food insecurity is associated with a wider range of negative outcomes in wellbeing. It correlates with poorer mental health and physical wellbeing (Jones, 2017) and in adolescents is connected with obesity, increased suicide risk, school truancy, and less healthy eating perceptions and behaviours (Utter et al., 2018).

Māra Kai and Manaakitanga as Counter-Colonial Tactic

In New Zealand the urban context has acted largely as a space of erasure of Indigenous cultures and food cultures. For many Pākehā (and Māori for that matter), "Māoriness" is trapped in the confines of rurality and tradition. Urban contexts by contrast are understood as sites of modernity and globalisation. Yet, in Tāmaki these "modern" urban contexts grew up around and are overlaid upon previously vital urban Māori communities. How to return to Tamaki's pre-colonial Indigenous urbanism? How to return to Māori approaches to urban landscapes as cultural sites of ecological connection, of care? Might a concept of urban manaakitanga enable a shift in neo-colonial urban food cultures, and by extension in colonial urban structures more broadly?

A strategic return to the agroecological practices of pre-contact Indigenous urbanism of Tāmaki could begin to shift urban power relationships for Māori as access to food and its means of production is changed. The local walled and hill-side gardens and the seasonal foraging in the local forests and ocean enabled a local food culture within a vital and venerated urban-ecological landscape. A contemporary counter-colonial foodscape tactic would aim to enable food security – reliable access to healthy and culturally appropriate food – and food sovereignty – as the right to access and define healthy, culturally appropriate and ecologically sustainable foods (Nyeleni Forum for Food Sovereignty (NFFS), 2007).

Critically food security is about choice and agency in how food is produced and consumed. This is the essence of food sovereignty – where food culture aligns with cultural practices and frameworks in a way that supports local socio-cultural-ecological resilience. For Māori, as with other Indigenous groups, food security is an expanded concept that is integral within key cultural concepts and practices including those of:

> mana (authority), manaakitanga (reciprocity of kindness, respect and humanity), and mahinga kai (traditional food gathering places and practices). Mahinga kai encompasses relationships between environment and

health, and reinforces whakapapa (genealogical ties), cultural identity and resilience. … Traditionally, the ability to provide ample kai (food) was a fundamental measure of wealth, representing economic and social power, and hence bestowing mana. The serving of traditional kai at marae (meeting places) events was an expression of manaakitanga (McKerchar et al., 2014).

Manaakitanga is an interfacing of the socio-political and relational with the ecological. It is inherently concerned with growing a collective, rather than individuated, endeavour.

> [Manaakitanga] is the maintenance of whakapapa relationships of reciprocity. This is enacted through the sharing of food that contributes to the social cohesion amongst whānau, hapū and iwi. This in turn means that growing kai is something you don't do just for yourself but is something that is undertaken for a wider purpose and to be shared with the collective (Hutchings, Smith & Harmsworth 2018, p.98).

So what might a counter-colonial urban food culture look like? How might the growing of kai, enable local food agency and resilience? Whenua Warrior Kelly Francis has planted hundreds of māra kai in Tāmaki, and beyond, with the aim of enabling food sovereignty ("For the Love of the Land with Whenua Warrior," 2019). Francis has also been working at the Griffiths Gardens in central Tāmaki leading a maramataka (Maori lunar calendar) workshop bringing mātauranga Māori into the heart of Tāmaki. Community pātaka or pantries have sprung up around the country recently and Francis has devised a plan to plant Palette Gardens next to pātaka with the intention that the gardens tautoko (support) locals to grow their own food and gain some food sovereignty.

The Ōtuataua Stonefields Historic Reserve, the ancient stone fields of Ihumātao Mangere, are one of the last remaining stonefield landscapes of Tāmaki. This unique cultural heritage landscape is a reminder of the Indigenous agroecology that fed Tāmaki's maunga-based urbanism. Here Māori gardeners used stone to create warm micro-climates within which to grow the crops they had brought with them from the Pacific. There is now a new flourishing of local gardening being led by the Save Our Unique Landscape (SOUL) campaign as it resists the development of a Special Housing Area adjacent to the stone fields (SOUL, n.d.). Here gardens, and associated ecological gardening and composting workshops, are both a protest activity and a decolonising practice as they sustain an ongoing engagement with and investment in the whenua.

Ecologically oriented gardening protocols, such as Hua Parakore, aim to emphasise local sustainable gardening approaches. Uniquely Hua Parakore is a kaupapa Māori organic gardening verification system and framework that emphasises healthy soil as a first principle. Writing on this kaupapa Hutchings, Smith and Harmsworth note that it is in many ways "an expression of the wider concept of Indigenous food sovereignty" (Hutchings, Smith & Harmsworth, 2018, p. 95). Transformatively, the Hua Parakore enables and structures an approach to food landscapes that is not instrumental and extractive, but rather concerned with the "interconnectedness of natural and human elements (denoted in the term tangata whenua)" and oriented by a deep concern and respect for the whenua (Hutchings, Smith & Harmsworth, 2018, p.93).

Conclusion

Agricultural activism of the kind seen at Ihumātao, and in the work of the Whenua Warriors, is a powerful urban decolonising practice. Each seedling planted, each harvest, each whānau fed, is a disruption in the fabric of urban colonial infrastructures and spaces. These Indigenous urban agricultural interventions recall Tāmaki's earlier māra kai. Protocols like Hua Parakore are system-change tools that further enable and communicate shifts, and indeed returns, in cultural practices and food systems.

Approaching urban transformation by way of a political emphasis on decolonisation brings attention to current industrialist-modern frameworks that separate – urban and rural, local, and global, "nature" and culture. Thinking the urban through manaakitanga and urban food enables a strategic counter-colonial process, enacted through urban food cultures, processes and infrastructures. Here positive outcomes for whānau and whenua are emphasised within an urban cultural foodscape. In an era of crises – in climate, in biodiversity, in human wellbeing – such local, ecologically-connected, Indigenous food cultures powerfully enact urban system change.

References

Bulmer, S. "City without a State? Urbanisation in Pre-European Taamaki-Makau-Rau" (Auckland, New Zealand). Paper presented at the SAREC conference, Mombasa, Kenya, 2002. Retrieved from https://www.arkeologi.uu.se/digitalAssets/483/c_483244-l_3-k_bulmerall2.pdf

Carolan, M. (2018). The Real Cost of Cheap Food. London: Routledge.

95 BFM. (2 July 2019). For The Love of the Land with Whenua Warrior, Retrieved from https://95bfm.com/bcast/for-the-love-of-the-land-w-whenua-warrior-july-2-2019

Graham, R., Hodgetts, D., Stolte, O., & Chamberlain, K. (2018). "Food insecurity in urban New Zealand. The case of the Kopa family." Journal of Poverty, 22:5, 379-397, DOI: 10.1080/10875549.2017.1419533

Gregory, C.A., Coleman-Jensen, A. (2017). Food Insecurity, Chronic Disease, and Health Among Working-Age Adults. Economic Research Report 235 (U.S. Department of Agriculture, Economic Research Service, July 2017).

Hutchings, J (2016). "Bringing Maori food politics to the table: Decolonising food knowledge." In Hutchings, J., Lee-Morgan, J. Decolonisation in Aotearoa: Education, Research and Practice. Wellington: NZCER Press.

Hutchings, J., Tipene, P, Carney, G, Greensill, A, Skelton, P, & Baker, M. (2012). "Hua Parakore: Indigenous Food Sovereignty Initiative and Hallmark of Excellence for Food and Product Production." Mai, vol1, issue 2.

Hutchings, J., Smith, J & Harmsworth, G. (2018). "Elevating the Mana of Soil through the Hua Parakore Framework." Mai, vol7, issue 1.

IPCC. (2018). Global warming of 1.5°C: An IPCC Special Report on the impacts of global warming of 1.5°C above pre-industrial levels and related global greenhouse gas emission pathways, in the context of strengthening the global response to the threat of climate change, sustainable development, and efforts to eradicate poverty. https://www.ipcc.ch/sr15/.

IPCC. (2019). Climate Change and Land: an IPCC special report on climate change, desertification, land degradation, sustainable land management, food security, and greenhouse gas fluxes in terrestrial ecosystems. https://www.ipcc.ch/report/srccl/.

Jones, A. (2017). "Food Insecurity and Mental Health Status: A Global Analysis of 149 Countries." American Journal of Preventive Medicine. 53, (2). P.264-273. https://doi.org/10.1016/j.amepre.2017.04.008.

Bowers, S., et al. (2014). Enhancing Mäori food security using traditional kai. Global Health Promotion. doi:10.1177/1757975914543573.

Ministry of Health. 2003. NZ food NZ children: key results of the 2002 national children's nutrition survey. Wellington: Ministry of Health.

Nyeleni 2007. Forum for Food Sovereignty. (2007). Declaration of Nyéléni. Retrieved from https://nyeleni.org/spip.php?article290.

Bartie, P. et al., (2007a). Neighborhood deprivation and access to fast-food retailing: a national study. Am J Prev Med 32(5):375–382. doi:10.1016/j.amepre.2007.01. 009.

Smoyer-Tomic KE, Spence J, Amrhein C. (2006). Food deserts in the prairies? Supermarket accessibility and neighbourhood need in Edmonton, Canada. Prof Geogr. 58:307–326. doi: 10.1111/j.1467-9272.2006.00570.

SOUL, Save Our Unique Landscape. Ihumātao. Retrieved from https://www.protectihumatao.com.

Stevenson, S. (2013). Edible impact — Food security policy: A review of literature and synthesis of key recommendations for Toi Te Ora — Public Health Service. Whakatäne, New Zealand: Bay of Plenty District Health Board.

Stull, D.D. "Cows, Pigs, Corporations and Anthropologists," Journal of Business Anthropology, 6, 1 (Spring 2017): p.25.

Exeter, D.J., et al. (2017). "Food Swamps by area socioeconomic deprivations in New Zealand: a national study.International." Journal of Public Health (2017) 62:869–877. Retrieved from DOI 10.1007/s00038-017-0983-4.

University of Otago and Ministry of Health. (2011). A Focus on Nutrition: key findings of the 2008/09 New Zealand adult nutrition survey. Wellington: Ministry of Health.

Utter, J., Izumi, B.T., Denny, S., Fleming, T & Clark, T. (2018). "Rising Food Security Concerns Among New Zealand Adolescents and Association with Health and Wellbeing." Kōtuitui: New Zealand Journal of Social Sciences Online, 13(1): 29-38, DOI: 10.1080/1177083X.2017.1398175.

Chapter 4.0: Lineage

Kristi Leora Gansworth – Kitigan Zibi Anishinaabeg

Kristi Leora Gansworth is a citizen of Kitigan Zibi Anishinaabeg who lives and works in Toronto. She is working on a PhD in Geography at York University and focusing on water governance. Her poetry and writing are an ongoing engagement with her existence as Anishinaabekwe and she is currently at work on a full length collection of poems.

To be of the spirit. I lived in all the times
young earth, eager soil, regal origins, this island
of frond, and red clay
and ice, and fresh water, all the beings
in between—the feathers, the furs,
the scales, the wings, and crawling
legs that sweep through dirt and mud. Jubilant
grass, uncertainty in sand dunes, I lived
through the emergence of same. The evolution
of heartbeats belongs to a planet, and to the rest of them
echoes developed: a murderous crash
of starved drills, borne metal
driven into platelets
of her red flesh, the wonders of this earth
in our bodies, the flesh of those
who stand with her. I live through the days
they decorate her, prayers, crowns
of colored ribbon, dried
flowers, and ferns, and tears. Apologies. I live
between the shadows, the crashing

violations, the mournful debris of civilizations
interrupted. Mine is a journey disrupted,
which is not a journey
extinguished. I hear and join calls
to stop the bidding
of machines, I think of ejection
from darkness, the internalization of same
an arced emergence, spiraling
into breath, with care, with kindness, I look to
the calm and the trust,
the dream that began this all.

Chapter 4.1: An Architecture of Twenty-Five Projects

Michael Mossman – Kuku Yalanji

Michael Mossman is a Cairns Murri and descendant of Kuku Yalanji country. He is currently teaching and researching at the University of Sydney School of Architecture, Design and Planning, where his interest is to situate architecture in a broader Indigenous scholarship environment. As a doctoral candidate, his thesis focuses on the conversation: 'Emancipating Architecture after Invasion'. A topic designed to investigate socio-political discourse and theoretical strategies relating to 'third space consciousness', an interstitial coalescing zone of Indigenous worldviews and Western viewpoints. Through a de-colonizing Indigenous methodological framework, his thesis aims to promote engagement methods that celebrate worldview differences in ways of being, knowing and doing, to enable collaborative, innovative discourse and design.

Introduction

nyundu nganda maga nyinan. ngayu kuku yalanji, pentecost, british, irish, french. I pay my respect to the Country where you may be reading this chapter and to elders past, present, and emerging. Linda Tuhiwai Smith's revered book Decolonising Methodologies: Research and Indigenous Peoples (1999) is a thought-provoking example of Indigenous scholarship. In it, her prose negotiates the contested and contextualised terrains of Indigeneity and associated research practices. As one of the earlier examples of Indigenous voices invested in occupying and disrupting the colonial spaces of academia, Smith's book has been a key point of reference throughout my academic career. A key chapter of her book reveals the *twenty-five projects* which thematically frames a way to think about Indigenous ways of being, knowing and doing. It is both a methodology and a wayfinding device that breaks down the mystique of Indigenous community engagement and generate topics and themes for a project on many differing levels. It is our responsibility, as Indigenous designed environment practitioners and scholars, to claim, determine and affirm methodological academic frameworks that continue to control conditions of engagement.

This chapter explores the *twenty-five projects* in relation to a university-level architectural studio, the Burri

Gummin affordable housing exercise. The primary goal was to explore aspects of Indigeneity and its connections to cultures of difference in relation to architecture. By studying and using the *twenty-five projects* as a scaffolding device, thoughts and actions can be activated in architectural scholarship to empower a project narrative and unique personal stories. Attention was paid to the contextualised setting of the studio project and the participatory nature of the learning. I am uncertain of the extent Smith's (1999) projects have been applied in architectural educational settings, however in an Indigenous engagement context, it provides an innovative framework of study within community and academic scholarship. What I do know is that the testimonies I make are grounded in the events and experiences of my life, the influences that have informed my current situations, the lessons learnt from carrying out the studio exercise.

Revealing The Twenty-Five Projects

The first time I read the *twenty-five projects* chapter was in 2016. At the time, I considered my own experiences and reflected on how its themes were important to my*self* being. I was given Smith's book seventeen years after its first publication to explore as part of my doctorate candidature. It quickly became a touchstone of interest in the way its themes methodically described aspects of my own personal and professional experiences of being Indigenous and engaging with Indigenous communities. I thought that Smith's *projects* could be shared with a non-Indigenous cohort in the future. Contextually, I work within a university environment that promotes the notion of "unlearning". This idea of change-making reveals a structural shift in thinking not uncommon throughout the global academic environment. My activation of this "unlearning" notion has been to critique existing norms, acknowledge and respect ontologies, epistemologies and axiology's of difference, especially that of uniquely Australian Indigenous worldviews.

As an esteemed work in decolonising the academy and its research practices, I saw Smith's (1999) book as an essential application to an architectural educational environment. How could the *projects* be applied to architectural education? The ideal situation for this studio was to utilise Smith's (1999) *twenty-five projects* to enable student stories to flow and find differences and commonalities with narratives of an Indigenous community. An iterative process occurred throughout the semester long studio whereby the *projects* were revisited and consistently applied to the project task. Smith's (1999) prose was the first time many of the non-Indigenous students had been exposed to Indigenous decolonising scholarship. Telling all our stories using the voice of self is a representation of the diversities of truth to privilege discourse topics and in turn creates dialogue and conversations. (Smith, 1999) It has highs and lows, is not so much a formula for success but a philosophy of design and process. Our relationships with architecture revolves around the language and ethos of *being* and *knowledge systems* that only story telling from the *self*-imbues integrity and authenticity (Coates, 2012). Student buy-in was critical to the overall outcome of the studio and projects provided an ideal entry point to facilitate conversations on the intersection's architecture and Indigenous methodologies. While some of the *projects* are accessible and commonly used terms that are prominent in everyday discourse, others are more obscure and require more thought and imagination. Ultimately all *projects* promote agency and aspirational qualities designed to reach out and facilitate exchange.

What are The Twenty-Five Projects?

The limitations of this chapter requires that certain *projects* are defined in detail. This is based on the context of the case study student work. As an overview, Smith's (1999) *twenty-five projects* are listed as follows: claiming, testimonies, story-telling, celebrating survival, remembering, indigenising, intervening, revitalising, connecting, reading, writing, representing, engendering, envisioning, reframing, restoring, returning, democratising, networking, naming, protecting, creating, negotiating, discovering, and sharing. The *projects* "teach both the non-Indigenous audience and the new generations of Indigenous peoples an official account of their collective story" (Smith, 1999). The collective is important to understand as we are all in this together, each with our stories that make up a whole. As a result of this collective, all students were tasked with an exercise to facilitate dialogue in the form of illustration to express knowledge and interpretations of their own cultural narratives. The *twenty-five projects* act as thematic markers for students to critically explore the worlds between self and the studio exercise context. These *projects* enabled a consideration of ways to promote agency in the multiplicity of approaches for research, teaching, professional practice, and community-specific ways of being, knowing and doing.

The ability of Indigenous communities to retain cultural narratives and share through dialogue is a testament to the struggles faced in within a colonising state such as Australia. In my experiences in with Aboriginal communities such as Yarrabah, there has been a willingness to exchange and the themes that present are often a reflection of the *twenty-five projects* (Smith, 1999). What I think is required is a capacity for others to reciprocate these personal narratives through cross-cultural dialogue by means of understanding self. We celebrate the survival of our culture and connections to Country and encourage other to reflect upon and join in on what this means for our designed environments. The twenty-five projects offer a wayfinding device for others to explore their narratives. My own experiences of Indigeneity and presence within academia is highlighted by the themes of the twenty-five projects, therefore solidifying my own sense of belonging within the traditional norms of non-Indigenous academic environment. The presence of Indigenous scholarship in disciplines relating to how environments are designed is slowly rising with books such as Our Voices (Kiddle, R., Stewart, L., and O'Brien, K., 2018). Including the prose of non-designer such as Smith (1999) provides additional experiences of Indigeneity in academia outside architecture that can be applied within.

Architectural Studio Project

The educational experience from 2018 shares the story of a University of Sydney School of Architecture Design and Planning second year architectural studio engagement with the Yarrabah Aboriginal community, near Cairns in Far North Queensland. The aim of the studio, named *Burri Gummin* ("One Fire"), was to design housing to alleviate issues of overcrowding, homelessness and mental illness. Designed in collaboration with the Yarrabah community and University of Sydney colleague, Anna Ewald Rice, the studio facilitated a space to test ideas and reflect on their outcomes to learn from, build on and apply in future iterations. The studio was set within the framework of the broader unit of study titled "Let Every Voice Be Heard" and coordinated by Michael Muir, a University of Sydney Lecturer in Architecture.

Historically, Yarrabah was a colonial construct established on the territory of the Gungganyji tribe, the traditional owners of the immediate tropical land and sea environment. The methods of traditional custodianship and engagement with Country were and still are a prominent aspect of the local cultures. (Denigan, 2008) Complex trajectories of intersecting histories and experiences have been documented over time as its purpose as an Anglican mission formed part of a broader colonial narrative to destabilise original territorial connections for tribal groups across Australia. The Yarrabah mission was home to at least 40 tribal groups dislocation from traditional lands and forced to live within a "protected" space. The colonising condition of the built environment was imposed on Country, and its relations to local traditional Indigenous values and identities were and remain relatively disconnected.

By matching historical narratives with the *projects*, stories can be deconstructed and reconstructed through thematic interrogation and critical self-reflection. Architectural education requires rigorous attention to forms of remembering contexts, joyous, painful and everything between and the contradictions that conjure within *self*. Being on Country in Yarrabah is exhilarating, grounded and fills me with pride, all the while knowing that the past and present is one hand instilled with pain and obstacles. Yet on the other the presents challenges, aspirations, hard work and hope. The main thing for students to understand is that the community is like others, endeavouring to instil strategies and programs that will benefit future generations.

Methodological Background

The studio presented opportunities to tutor non-Indigenous students from different backgrounds and reiterate its position as a creative and reflective space. By using the *projects*, it offered chances to foster their many cultural narratives to inform a multitude of spaces of engagement between their stories and the community. While the *projects* have arisen out of social science methodologies and was influenced by research engagement with oppressed groups, its application to broader Indigenous narratives is pertinent to activating agency and impact for community engagement. (Smith, 1999) I saw the *projects* exercise as an opportunity for non-Indigenous students to relate to the many facets of community ways through a reflection of *self*. Architecture is representative of diverse cultures and communities, with worldviews of complex, contested and contradictive ways and traditions. As the studio commenced, the *twenty-five projects* methodology was tested to explore, apply and reflect upon Indigenous issues. Clearly, the architectural discipline is severely under-represented by indigenous architects and academics. However, opportunities are emerging to indigenise the space through engagement with non-Indigenous participant advocates. Indigenising the discipline means looking to the traditions and narratives of our First Nations cultures and communities and acknowledging the systems developed over thousands of generations. A reciprocation of this dialogue means a counter-exercise by non-Indigenous peers, investigating stories of self and identifying differences and commonalities. Perhaps their own stories are beset with stories of oppression and challenges? The objectives of the reciprocation are to enhance the qualities of engaging with communities and cultures of difference within mainstream societies to promote new narratives and discourse.

Concept Mapping as Emancipatory Tool

Methodologically, the storymapping exercise was promoted with the idea of using the *twenty-five projects* to provide starting points. The outcome was to situate students in positions to critically inquire, critique and reflect on one's engagement in an Indigenous decolonising space. While the actual studio was in its second iteration after an initial exercise in 2016, I have carried out this storymapping exercise in other contexts during my time in academic and professional practice to understand the cultural narratives of participants. Each time, the outcome of the exercise reveal personal and cultural differences and commonalities that can inform future directions of the task at hand. This allocation of time to culturally reflect on critical aspects of oneself, both positive and negative, were related and interwoven into the overall studio exercise narrative and its deliverables. What does become apparent is a more informed relational position of the complexities and contradictions of one's own culture with the community that is the site of the studio exercise. A bridge links cultures through a personal illustrative engagement with a reflection of *self* and critique of cultures associated with *self*.

The studio utilised the illustrative method of concept mapping to draw out personal journeys and relate back to Smith's *projects*. Concept mapping in this context can introduce a qualitative method to frame a research project, analyse themes and present interconnections in a study (Daley, 2004) In response to a cartographic act of research, possibilities emerge to theorise and action the outcome of critical investigations (Tuck, 2013). Importantly, the concept mapping aims to deconstruct and reconstruct the elements of a worldview, allowing a non-linear approach to the act of narrative sharing. (Yunkaporta, 2009) From a decolonising research framework, the alternative thoughts and standpoints of Indigenous populations within the settler-colonising paradigm pose potential mapping processes across multi-dimensional spaces of engagement. Relating the notions of Indigeneity to a westernised idea of cartographic understanding is a dialogical encounter relative to the many contexts of the research topic.

Studio Exercise Process

The message from the Yarrabah community has been clear for many years: "housing is in crisis". The beginning of semester two in 2018 saw the implementation of a second-year studio architectural studio that engaged with the issue of housing in Yarrabah. The search for ways to democratise the student experience through participatory action resulted in the personal storymapping processes. Pedagogically, the position fosters a political element encouraging open and active inquiry into social conditions which enhances the human condition (Levin & Greenwood, 2001). Henceforth, in-depth exploration of your own *self* provides an impetus to engender culture as a driver of one's designed environment. The outcomes of this process resulted in an appreciation of dialogue and its qualities of creating positions in-between the multitude of worldviews that exist within any given space. It must be recognised that the student cohort illustrated thoughts and reflections of self with immersive qualities and intimate details. One example included a student who illustrated in-depth family histories such the brutalities of cultural genocide, an example of historical events that resonates with the experiences of many Aboriginal communities across Australia. All had stories of migration and settlement, and most importantly considered and proffered storymaps with connections with Smith's (1999) *twenty-five projects*.

Studio Concept Mapping Exercise Explored

In an educational setting such as an architectural studio, understanding the narratives of a contextualised setting is often carried out remotely by desktop investigations. In most cases, a site visit to a community is seen as a logistical barrier that can inhibit engagement processes with a community. The first two iterations of the personal storymaps were produced prior to a visit on Country with the community. This reflected the processes of engaging with a community story through desktop investigations, which is a common method of exploring a contextualised architectural setting.

Massey (2005) stated that implicit engagements with conceptualisations of space results in an ordering of the world and the positioning of ourselves in relation to others, both human and non-human entities. Therefore, the intersections of the *projects* with Gungganyji Country site experiences were an important characteristic of the studio in constructing this positioning of self through the storymaps. This then led to the third iteration of the storymap produced after the site visit to accompany the final submission. With the exception of one student having visited the community previously, engagement through staged and incidental encounters with community members was a new experience for the students. It was noted that the maps did indeed evolve as a result of the experiences of being in the community with the impact of such encounters resulting in immersive responses.

There are relatively few opportunities that exist in architectural education environment to learn and apply skillsets relating to Indigenous Australian communities or issues. *Finding Country* by Kevin O'Brien is one example of architectural education, that is based on scholarship and actively pursues an agenda of historical and current Indigenous issues. Real world experiences for university students is impactful and an opportunity to educate in the community engagement space has transformative qualities. Engaging with Smith's (1999) *twenty-five projects* is a simple yet effective method of generating conversations in multiple ways, finding intersections

and appreciation of research practice with Indigenous communities. My task as an educator is to facilitate this engagement through the activation of innovative and creative methods within an emancipatory methodological framework. While the exploratory Indigenous lens of the *twenty-five projects* offered the substantial reflective device for the architecture students, developing capabilities to identify key themes is a challenging skillset to learn. As narratives and histories have a focus, a purpose and a legitimate claim of assertiveness (Smith, 1999), the exercise provides the means to express these assertions to the project task. Furthermore, the promotion of the *projects* through the course of the semester was a useful starting point for an exercise to investigate the intersections of the contextualised community with architectural education processes.

Dialogue, Engagement and Smith's Projects

As an architectural studio delegation, we were for fortunate to be hosted by the Yarrabah community to explore their space and engage in dialogue with local key stakeholders and places of importance. What started as a studio looking at housing soon became something more than just shelter. The discussion with community involved the representatives of local council, a nearby existing home that was occupied, a new house nearing completion, a house that was unoccupied, the local health service, a significant local beach and settings in nearby Cairns. An understanding of how all the engagements aligned and intersected with each other were the drivers to facilitate design strategies and actions. It was hoped that the experiences with these engagements could also bridge the interface between non-Indigenous students and Smith's *twenty-five projects* to further enable ontological and epistemological exchange and synthesis. I envision the purpose of the *twenty-five projects* as a facilitator the can scaffold acknowledgement and equitable agency of Indigenous cultures that occupy spaces of engagement within the settler-colonising paradigm.

Example Personal Map

The student example shown from *week two*, *week seven* and *week thirteen* of the second semester in 2018, informed an immersive experience to understand engagement processes between Indigenous ways, an architectural approach and Smith's (1999) chosen *projects*. It must be appreciated that this was a second-year architectural studio and that the decolonising concepts of the *twenty-five projects* was new to the students. The personal maps ranged in degrees of detail and understanding of concepts, which led to variety in the qualities of the storymap outcomes. This will inevitably become factors of consideration when designing the processes of the next architectural studio exercise for August 2019. The iterations presented the evolving nature of the exercise and potential impactful and transformational qualities it may have on the student design qualities and personal positions.

The illustrations by Jeremy[1] that follow offer a student storymap through three iterations to support the discourse of this chapter, each adding layers of information from its previous iteration. It was noticeable from my point of view, as the tutor, that the level of detail promoted an understanding of the reasoning behind the map. The evolution of the design changed as the detail of the storymap continued to focus on the chosen *projects* and fostered a united methodological approach. From a subjective point of view, I certainly observed the added layering that the *projects* provided to the studio project.

First Iteration

This first iteration of the storymap was composed in week two with brief investigations of Yarrabah incorporated into the studio space. It illustrated an overall picture that starts in southern China, then to Singapore, then to Sydney to study architecture. (Fig. 1)

Zoom One into the top centre of the illustration, Jeremy explored his ancestral home in the southern Chinese province of Guangdong and described his community as Ethnic Chinese. Here he identified with the *naming* project. Smith (1999) quoted Paulo Friere (1970), the author of seminal work "Pedagogy of the Oppressed", who said "name the word, name the world." The reference to naming articulates the significance of language to culture and the retention of control of meanings. It is also significant to Indigenous communities as the loss of language has been detrimental to cultural expression. This illustration of ethnic minority language use in certain settings demonstrates negative stresses imposed by external events. It provides a common understanding with the issue of Indigenous community control of language and its position in relation to forces of colonisation. The storymap then illustrated the process of migration from this ancestral Country to Singapore in the 1880s. In Australia, this time corresponded with immense change in the cultures of Aboriginal communities around Australia through dispossession, forced migration off Country, loss of cultural practice and the impositions of new ways of living. (Fig. 2)

Zoom Two of the first iteration identified the *discovering* and *negotiating* projects. Here Jeremy describes *discovering* in reference to Smith's (1999) position of the influence of the west concepts of "science and technology." Smith's notion here is about

understanding these impositions and using in an advantageous way. In our context here, we are making inroads into how the science can be used and reframed to our advantage. The University of Queensland Spinifex Research is exploring the technologies of processes utilised by traditional Aboriginal knowledge systems in ways that could facilitate the creation of revolutionary materials.

The Project *negotiating* is about thinking strategically, what are the long-term goals? Smith noted that throughout time, Indigenous people have immense amounts of patience and have often been in cases taking one step back in the present in order to take two steps forward in the future. Perhaps Jeremy's story has been involved in these types of deals. (Fig. 3)

Zoom Three presents four projects as an illustration with great effect. The first project *representing* described a willingness to stand up and be counted despite lacking rights or being underrepresented. Exercises such as this enable an understanding representing, of cultures that are resilient and aspire to foster change.

The second Project is *connecting* and is supported by text that says – "looking back to roots." For the context of this comment, Smith stated that "looking back" is such a critical part of Indigeneity, creating relationships with others across space and time.

The third Project is *revitalising*, whereby the capacity to retain and practice language and culture with us is important. It is an obligation to oneself and to future generations that the revitalisation of culture is positioned at the fore to ensure the important qualities of one's being is kept alive and set up to aspire and thrive.

The final project is *sharing*, how the sharing of knowledge for collective benefit promotes wellbeing and reciprocated exchange. Jeremy has presented *sharing* across generations, a human quality that is important in communities. This notion facilitates the acknowledgement of cultural histories and also the foresight of future possibilities. (Fig. 4)

This first iteration was an important example of student exploration of self and how its enhanced understandings of community context. Interesting points of historical information were shared to communicate an understanding of self-positioning within a broader picture. It was envisaged that this first iteration provided a platform for further investigations and analyses of the intersections between self and the context of an Aboriginal community.

---

1. Jeremy John Sheng Jie Kum – Second Year Bachelor of Design in Architecture Student who participated in the Yarrabah Burri Gummin Affordable Housing Studio in the second semester of 2018.

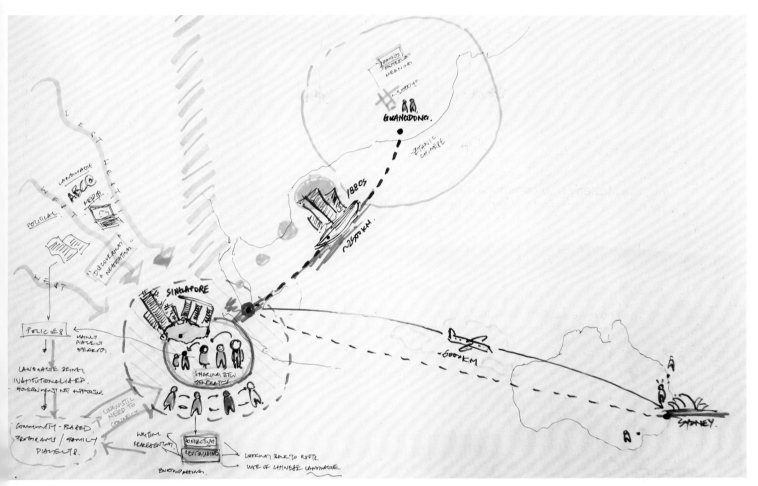

Figure 1. Iteration 1 – Shows the Restoring and Revitalising Projects. Illustration: Jeremy John Sheng Jie Kum.

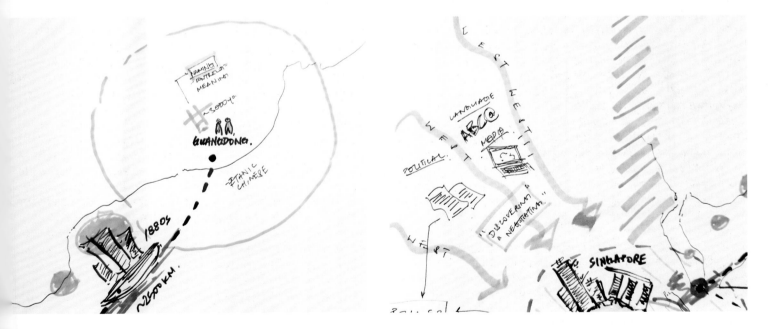

Figure 2. Iteration 1(a) – Zoom One | Shows the naming. Projects Illustration: Jeremy John Sheng Jie Kum.

Figure 3. Iteration 1(b) – Zoom Two | Shows the discovering and negotiating Projects. Illustration: Jeremy John Sheng Jie Kum.

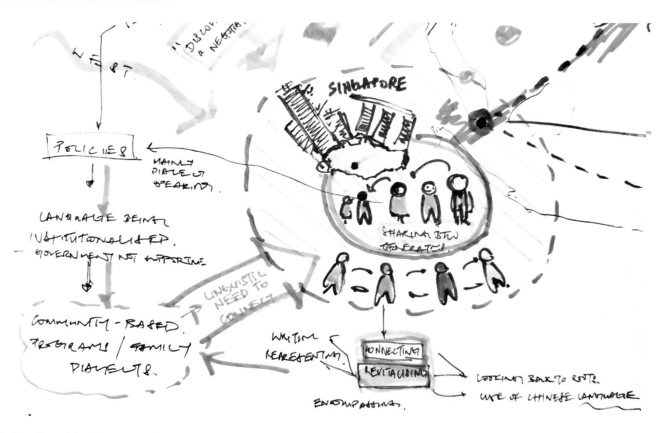

Figure 4. Iteration 1(c) – Zoom Three | Shows the connecting, revitalising and sharing Projects. Illustration: Jeremy John Sheng Jie Kum.

Second Iteration

As part of the interim presentation submission, the concept map shows more detail in the self-reflection with an emphasis on the intersections of the chosen projects, the multitude of locational contexts the author identified with the primary relational aspects of people and place. (Fig. 5)

This storymap was submitted at the interim submission in week seven prior to the visit on Country. It is here that more information was provided, particularly in relation to climate and architectural considerations. The relationship is connected between Yarrabah as a humid tropical environment with Jeremy's home in Singapore. It was envisaged that commonalities of this type could enhance design resolutions due to the intimate associations with self. The connection between self and Yarrabah focused on the elements of "PEOPLE" and "PLACE" with term "BONDS" leading to "PLACEMAKING." As the mapping exercise for second year architecture students, the collation of these terms of inquiry were advanced and provided a platform of understanding the studio context. (Fig. 6)

The Projects of *restoring* and *revitalising* were promoted with its positioning on this map close to the Yarrabah community. The *restoring* project notes that spiritual, emotional, physical and material wellbeing promotes a holistic approach beneficial to communities (Smith, 1999) Architecture and the way we design our environments can impact and transform these qualities of wellbeing to benefit communities. Revitalising builds on the first iteration storymap and its connections with Singapore and the promotion of culture for displaced migrant communities. These are critical notions that Aboriginal communities across Australia can relate to and, in turn, used to empower and benefit cultural practice. For example, the student investigations covered a range of issues outside of architecture that are critical in understanding the broader context of place. Revitalising through architecture is important in reframing the existing and historical conditions of the colonial and neo-colonial influences of building infrastructure on Country. It was observed that many of this infrastructure is ill-suited to the cultural context of a tropical environment so therefore requires a rethink of ideas that could alleviate this situation.

Jeremy also stated the following subheadings to further contribute to the *twenty-five projects* with lines of inquiry such as "economy", "climate", "sustainability", "future planning," and "comfort." Other offshoot topic such as "community growth", "beliefs", "public space", "vegetation", "tropical", and "materials" appeared to further encompass the magnitude of the investigative task.

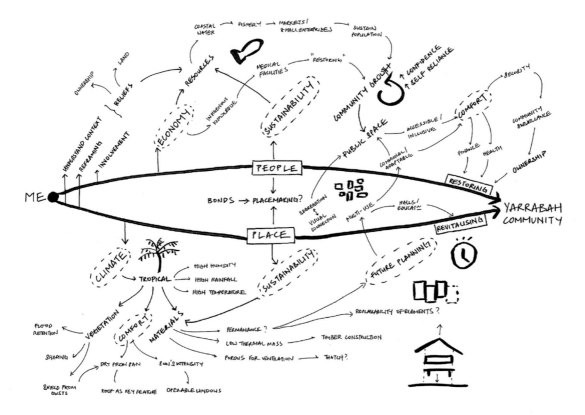

Figure 5. Iteration 2 – Shows the Restoring and Revitalising Projects. Illustration: Jeremy John Sheng Jie Kum.

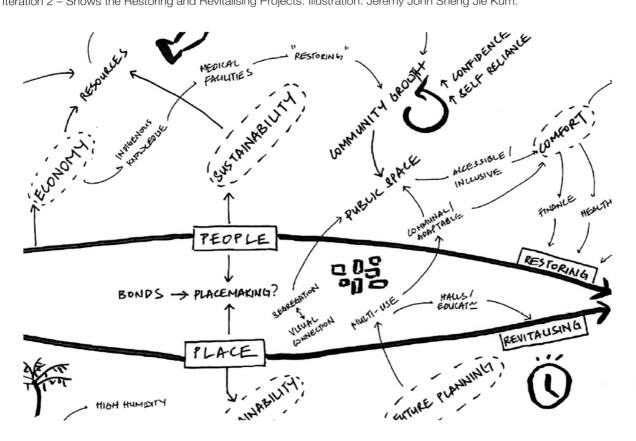

Figure 6. Iteration 2(a) – Shows the Restoring and Revitalising Projects along with the elements of "PEOPLE" and "PLACE". Illustration: Jeremy John Sheng Jie Kum.

Third Iteration

As part of the final presentation submission, the concept map showed more detail and clarity in the self-reflection with an emphasis on the intersections of the chosen *projects*. Both earlier iterations appear to be combined with the personalised histories adjacent to the architectural and community ideas and themes. The personal storymap has added a component titled "changing culture" along with "public housing" based on personal experiences of high density living. (Fig. 7)

An important element added to this context was "UNDERSTANDING CONTEXT" leading to "REFRAMING". This element was influenced by another addition – "CULTURAL COMPETENCY", a key exercise that was carried out by all students at the beginning of semester. Smith (1999) described *reframing* it as taking control about the way issues are defined, dealt with, and resolved in broader research environments. A reflective question could pose the question: how does the architectural education reframe ways of approaching contextualised issues? (Fig. 8)

More importantly, the question presented from the Aboriginal community was: how can architectural responses to an issue such as housing be reframed? Each student was required to complete the Cultural Competency online modules hosted by the Australian Centre for Cultural Competency It is important to acknowledge that local communities are the experts to inform the strategies around reframed conversations. The online modules, along with the methods of investigating self and context was critical in communicating the expertise that exists in community. This process was consistently reflected on throughout the semester process and provided lessons for future applications to these storymap exercises.

Student Statement

My analysis of Jeremy's storymap is subjective and influenced by my role as tutor, and my understanding of the processes that evolved during the semester long studio. There are many other ideas and possibilities incorporated into this personal storymap that provided an in-depth overview of the thoughts going on in Jeremy's mind. I would suggest that these thoughts would be less prominent if the storymap was not included in the program of requirements for the assessable tasks. The following is a written description by Jeremy that expresses his thoughts:

> The illustration is a storyboard which represents the interweaving of my personal identity and worldview with the indigenous communities through the studio project. It can be construed in two parts; firstly, understanding the climatic and cultural context of my place of origin in Singapore, and secondly how I reframe these knowledge

bases in designing housing for the community at Yarrabah. The exploration of Linda Smith's twenty-five Indigenous projects then allows me to consider the contextual histories, politics, and culture of indigenous communities towards formulating my design. Through the threads of people and place, I link key ideas from the twenty-five projects, expressing the desire to 'restore' community and 'revitalise' sense of place for the Yarrabah community. My design motivations therefore draw upon a similar tropical climate between Singapore and Yarrabah, and the experience of affordable modular housing in approaching the studio project. These then serve as key drivers in the crafting of tangible design strategies.[2]

It was with humility that I asked Jeremy to contribute in the form of this quote, and I am grateful for his willingness and effort to express his thoughts. I stand firm in activating the voices of students with the hope that their voices may one day contribute to understandings and conversations about marginalised community groups in the context of everyday practice.

Conclusion and Future Strategies

The *twenty-five projects* offer a method to decolonise thinking about how our contemporary environments are designed, and the affects architecture may have on Indigenous communities. The processes of architecture involve movement through space and time to always connect the occupier with current and historical events relative to their own experiences. The *twenty-five projects* promoted an opportunity for relationships between self and Indigeneity to be manifested into moments for critical exploration, realisation, analysis and dissemination. Smith (1999) argued that the *projects* are not offered as a definitive list, not the only method, but a way of starting a conversation that is complex and requires agency and advocacy.

This chapter has been an opportunity to share the processes and outcomes of this architectural studio. It promoted decolonising notions that engender understanding, collaboration and the creation of alliances, advocacies and agency critical to community needs. The *twenty-five projects* are indicative of potential engagement strategies, using terms to invoke thought from involved participants. The methods of engagement entailed a narrative building exercise which established and reinforced rapport, support and connections between cultures, communities and individuals. Enunciative statements relative to each project can harness ideologies from Indigenous and non-Indigenous

---

2. Quote from Jeremy John Sheng Jie Kum – Second Year Bachelor of Design in Architecture Student who participated in the Yarrabah Burri Gummin Affordable Housing Studio in the second semester of 2018.

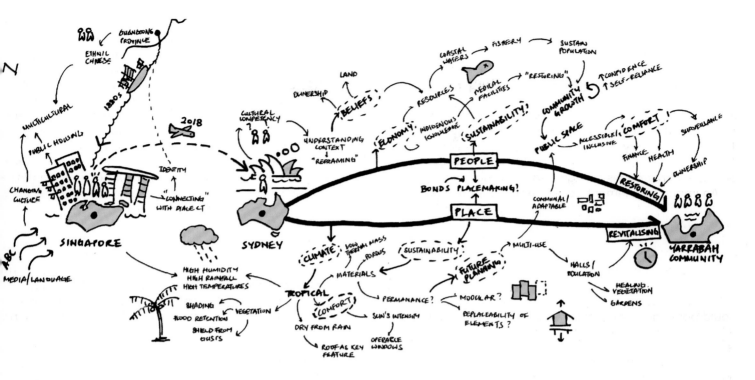

Figure 7. Iteration 3 – Shows the Restoring and Revitalising Projects. Illustration: Jeremy John Sheng Jie Kum.

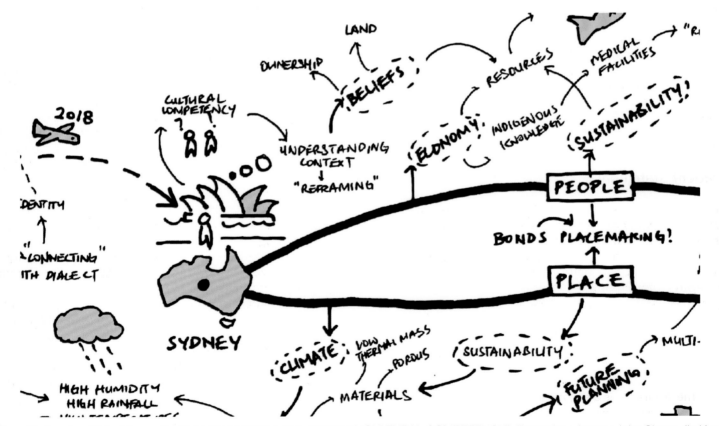

Figure 8. Iteration 3(a) – Shows the Reframing project in the context of "CULTURAL COMPETENCY". Illustration: Jeremy John Sheng Jie Kum.

worldviews. An important lesson taken away from the storymaps was to explore the stories with even more rigour and analyses to visualise the intersections with the twenty-five projects. This could be enhanced with more targeted briefing at the commencement of the studio as well as consistent returning to the exercise for student upkeep throughout the semester. It is important to remember that it is a constant learning experience for my own architectural educator self to apply for future studio iterations.

This studio exercise has challenged my own thinking to how architectural education can be inclusive and empowering of personal narratives and means to which it can be activated. This was the first instance that I was involved where the *twenty-five projects* were utilised as a process driver to enable the disruption and activation of mindsets. However, aspects of the exercise do indeed require investigation, such as emphasising the importance of layering the concept map with information. This strategy can be seen to continually evolve mindsets more rigorously and with greater intensity and constructive criticism. Initial iterations require detailed briefing to project an understanding by the students of why this task is carried out in the context of the studio. The layering of personal storymaps with the details of being present within a community provides as an opportunity to present the potential intersections of thought and being, while being immersed in the contextualised setting. Many opportunities have been established in how the method can be activated with more agency and understanding of the outcomes of the goals throughout the semester. It is my hope that this is seen as a strategic exercise that could be conducted in educational settings, and academic or professional environments. It is important to develop capacity for each of us to engage in our own concepts of self, Country, cultures and communities with that of others, and more specifically our First Nations.

gana ngayu gullina.

Bibliography

Coates, N. (2012) *Narrative Architecture*. West Sussex: Wiley & Sons Ltd.

Daley, B. (2004) *Concept Maps: Theory, Methodology, Technology Proc.* of the *First Int. Conference on Concept Mapping*. Pamplona: Spain.

Denigan, K. (2006) *Reflections in Yarrabah*. Department of Communications, Information Technology and the Arts: Australian Government.

Freire, P. (1970) *Pedagogy of the oppressed*. New York: Herder and Herder.

Kiddle, R., Stewart, L., & O'Brien, K. (2018) *Our voices: Indigeneity and Architecture* (First edition.) California, United States: ORO Editions.

Levin, M. & Greenwood, D. (2001) *Pragmatic Action Research and the Struggle to Transform Universities in Learning Communities* in Reason, P. & Bradbury, H. *Handbook of Action Research*. London: SAGE.

Massey, D. (2005). *For space*. London: SAGE.

Smith, L. T. (1999). *Decolonizing methodologies: Research and indigenous peoples*. London: Zed Books Ltd.

Tuck, E (2013) April 29 – *INQ13 | Linda Tuhiwai Smith and Eve Tuck – "Decolonizing Methodologies"* [Video file]. Retrieved from https://www.youtube.com/watch?v=rlZXQC27tvg.

Yunkaporta, T. (2009). *Aboriginal pedagogies at the cultural interface* (Doctor of Education), James Cook University.

Chapter 4.2: Navigating the gaps in Architectural education

Fleur Palmer – Te Rarawa, Te Aupouri

Dr Fleur Palmer is an Associate Professor of Spatial Design at Auckland University of Technology. As a registered architect, and active practitioner she uses her practical experience and involvement in architecture, exhibition and installation projects to inform her teaching practice. Fleur's award winning research is focused on addressing social inequity and developing ways of asserting self-determination and accessing affordable housing.

Spatial activism, the housing of displaced people, art and spatial practices based on community interventions, collaborative practices, participatory action research, social justice, ethics, emergent technologies, sustainability, Indigenous thinking, kaupapa Māori methodologies and food production form the principle components to Dr Palmer's practice based research interests.

Issues relating to internal displacement of Indigenous peoples through colonisation and access to housing are fraught with difficulties associated with conflicts over historical land transactions, tensions between different tribal groups, and control by territorial authorities, Land Courts and government entities that have historically been resistant to enabling Indigenous communities to develop thriving economic and political strongholds. To be an effective designer working in this space it helps if we have a clear understanding of how legislation that governs access to housing enforces restrictions that adversely impact on indigenous communities. But understanding how these restrictions are enforced and finding ways to resolve inequities that exist in relation to how indigenous communities gain access to housing within the legacy of a colonial regime isn't a subject readily taught in our design schools.

In this text, which draws on research undertaken for my PhD thesis, I discuss how I tried to find a way to overcome the way I had been educated within a Eurocentric system to effectively position my architectural research practice within a theoretical framework directed towards Indigenous thinking and Kaupapa Māori (a thinking that follows Māori philosophical beliefs and values). A shift that I believe is critical to the development of an inclusive practice that harnesses wisdom already present within Māori communities (G. H. Smith, 1997b; Tuhiwai-Smith, Linda 1999b; Palmer 2016).

When I trained as an architect in the 1980s, although there was extensive activity associated with Māori land rights, concepts of spatial justice were never on the agenda within the Architectural Schools, as there seemed to be little interest in projects that overtly interrogated how Māori had been displaced, or how they occupied our cities as internal refugees. There was no consideration of how our towns and cities had been socially and ethnically segregated through processes of colonisation. Nor was there any consideration of who was privileged to have a right to housing in Aotearoa, or who was excluded, and subsequently made homeless, as part of this process. Architectural practices as taught in our school was indifferent to the internal alienation from land that happened to Māori communities. The school's focus was disconnected to any commitment to interrogating social, political or environmental concerns that specifically related to indigenous peoples (Palmer, 2016; Barnes, Hoskins, Maher, 1994).

At the time I found this problematic. In terms of place-based struggles, a lot of things had transpired in Aotearoa. While civil rights movements were gaining traction in places like the United States of America, similar movements (with a history that stretched back to the signing of the Treaty of Waitangi) had also emerged in Aotearoa. In the late 1960s, groups such as MOOHR (Māori Organisation on Human Rights) were leading the fight against continued racism and injustice by advocating for a revolutionary change in people's thinking and actions to "rectify apartheid and all its evils," (Poata 2012, p.106) and fight back against years of significant racial oppression. Similarly, Ngā Taumatoa, formed by Māori students from Auckland University in the 1970s, also advocated for tino rangitiratanga (Māori control over Māori things), holding New Zealand's history of colonisation to account for the social injustices that affected Māori (A. Harris, 2004). Then in 1975, Māori land rights were further highlighted when Dame Whina Cooper (aged 75) set off from Cape Reinga and walked the length of the North Island to Parliament in the Māori land march to protest over loss of land. This was followed three years later in 1978 by the eviction from Bastion Point of Māori protestors who occupied the site in protest against government plans to develop it (Palmer 2016; A. Harris, 2004).

Within this context, I knew I had something to contribute but, I did not have the confidence to articulate my thoughts in an intelligible way. I also did not understand how to shape my practice to authentically resonate with ideas that related to thinking about place, alienation, consideration of protecting our rare local ecologies, and overcoming the ongoing effects of colonial oppression in response to the Māori experience to activate a transformation. I wanted to practice in a way that was ethically engaged, and specifically relevant to Māori communities that I knew had been excluded who had no voice within the academic context where my practice is situated. I also wanted to be able to address in a practical way how Māori might be able to determine their own futures in accessing affordable housing and generating change against an oppressive legacy of colonisation. This research required in-depth knowledge drawn from a broad range of fields and specialisations that is not well contained within the narrow scope of a traditional PhD Ideally this type of research should be undertaken collaboratively. But post graduate architectural programmes are set up competitively to support individual rather than collaborative long-term research practices which would better support indigenous communities (Palmer, 2016).

When I initially declared I was interested in doing research on Māori housing, the response from my Head of Research was "Why are you interested only in Māori housing? Don't Pākeha also have problems accessing affordable housing?" Of course, everyone has issues accessing affordable housing, so why is it different for Māori? It is hard to respond to a question like this if you are following a hunch drawn from family experience. I had no concrete evidence about the land loss and displacement of Māori. Without evidence, I did not know how to insist that my research topic was important. Aoetaroa's history of colonial occupation is never openly acknowledged or taught within our education systems, and unconscious institutionalised racism is systemic within universities. This culture of indifference towards Māori research has only changed recently when extra funding was allocated towards Māori research under the Performance Based Research Funding allocations.

In undertaking a Māori housing research project, I also had to re-educate myself. Nothing I had learnt during my undergraduate studies had developed my cultural competency in preparing me to undertake research that reinforced an indigenous world view. So, while I had a good grounding in philosophical traditions and methodologies that informed my practice within a Western framework, I had to start from scratch and re-educate myself to figure out what would be a culturally appropriate and authentic way to research Māori housing experience given my limited exposure to my own culture. It wasn't easy. While there are a lot of non-indigenous researchers who have positioned themselves as experts in supervising Indigenous research within our universities, I also did not want my research to be overly influenced or filtered by the unconscious bias of a non-indigenous lens. I wanted a supervisor who had an intimate understanding of the lived experience Māori communities' face, who implicitly understood why the issue of access to housing for Maori was important. It also took me a long time for me to overcome my own sense of imposter syndrome and find a way to position the work so that it would be reasonably grounded by an indigenous world view. Since completing my own research, I have noticed how difficult it is for other indigenous students to find their voice at a postgraduate level, especially if they have never had indigenous perspectives reinforced at school or at undergraduate level. I believe that if Māori students are researching their own culture it is also critical that they are looked after by Indigenous supervisors as within a covertly biased academic system, this is important for their own cultural safety.

One of the most fundamental differences between how I was educated within a Western system and te Ao Māori relates to how we perceive and operate in the world. Western world views traditionally follow a Cartesian mind/body split. This split encourages a distinct separation between nature and culture, or a separation between the thinking self and physical body. It is this split that enables the human self to be a "rational, free and self-determining agent" (Coole and Froste 2010, p.72). This separation has a direct influence on how we practice, and how we are able to exploit and control local resources in the name of progress and modernity. In contrast to this mind set, in the Māori world there can never be a separation between ourselves and the natural world. Instead of an 'us them' mentality or a nature/culture divide (Yates, 2008), Māori knowledge systems always consider the recognition of non-humans and other entities in the creation of our world. In the Māori world, the universe is perceived as a multidimensional field of ongoing and contingent negotiations between all things. Because everything is interconnected, the nature/culture divide becomes dissolved, as things and events become redistributed across a field of diverse entanglements. This interconnectivity between all things leads to a different way of thinking about how we build things, how we co-produce, how we share our world with all other things so that all things benefit (Palmer, 2016).

This belief in an interconnectedness between all things in turn raises ethical questions about how humans and all other things from microorganisms to climatic elements are organised and become complicit in the act of making the world. It is the shared interaction between things that enables our world to emerge. In turn, this leads to a different way of imagining the world in relation to how we build things, how we co-produce, how we theorise and share our world with all other things. The ontological thinking associated with Te Ao Māori is not dissimilar to Taoist and Buddhist practices and the belief systems of indigenous people from other parts of the world, who also share a belief in a deep connection to our world that entangles all things in such a way that nothing is inherently separate from anything else. As a framework for thinking about how we can all act in a more ethical and sustainable way, adopting this line of thinking is powerful, as whenever we take action, wider contexts must always be considered that extend well beyond the limitations of a practice reliant on human-centred paradigms (associated with the anthropocene) and exploitive practices (Palmer, 2016).

This fundamental difference towards how we imagine and relate to our world impacts on perceptions of land ownership. Prior to colonisation Māori did not conceive of outright ownership of land. Instead, their relationship to land was as kaitiaki (guardians). This role is intrinsically tied to a spiritual connection, linked to an ancestral genealogy that relies on an intimate alignment and interconnectedness to the natural world and spiritual world, where all forms of life were related by mauri (a spiritual life force). Emeritus Professor of Māori research and development, Sir Mason Durie writes that this interconnected relationship connects us to all things in such a way that "[p]eople are the land and the land is the people … we are the river, the river is us" (M. Durie 2011, p.139) This relationship endures "over centuries" through a collective, spiritual cultural knowledge and an ecological perspective, that provides the "basis for economic growth balanced against environmental sustainability for future generations" (Palmer 2016, p.236).

This deep "unity with the environment," (Rossouw, 2008) affects how Māori think and act in the world. As kaitiaki, or guardians of the natural world and everything that is related to them, the well-being of the community is intimately influenced by the protection of the natural environment. This relationship is defined by the term Mauri. Mauri refers to the "vital essence of a being or entity" and is dependent on a bond between humans and the physical world. This bonding between things frames all actions within a wider context and promotes an awareness of the importance of maintaining a sustainable balance between existing communities, all living things, and physical resources for future generations (M. Durie, 2011). The welfare of the environment depends on the galvanisation of collective rather than individual interests. If this link is broken and the natural environment becomes degraded, the vibrancy of mauri becomes diminished.

An interconnected perception of land radically conflicts with dominant Western perspectives, that regard land and all other physical entities as commodities that can be owned or exploited to support personal interests, and which are only marginally protected in New Zealand through legislation under the Resource Management Act 1991 (RMA) (Fisher, 1991; Palmer, 2016).

Over the last 150 years the vibrancy of our ecosystems has been seriously depleted. Māori have been physically displaced from their ancestral lands, our rare and ancient native forests have been destroyed leading to the rapid extinction of native bird species. An aggressive fishing industry has drained our abundant ocean reserves. Dairy and sheep farming has reinforced the depletion of our indigenous biodiversity and contaminated our atmosphere through excessive methane emission. Mono-cultural agricultural practices have also contaminated our rivers. According to a recent Environment Aotearoa report (2019), "two-thirds of New Zealand's rare ecosystems" face extinction. Coupled with this looming ecological catastrophe, Aotearoa also has the worst rate of homelessness in the OECD (Chamie, 2017). With extensive land loss and legislative constraints Māori have become internal refugees, with 95% physically displaced from their ancestral lands either through land loss or obstructive legislation aimed at preventing Māori strongholds to develop.

It is in the face of this looming ecological crisis and consideration of the on-going impact of social/cultural injustices experienced by Māori and things Indigenous to Aotearoa that we need to flex the contractual muscle of the Tiriti o Waitangi by shifting the way we are educated and think, so that we pay attention to considering how core values and wisdom that comes from Indigenous thinking can influence the way our future environments are designed in a more sustainable and non-exploitive way. We need to ensure that our deep, intimate and spiritual connection to our ancestors Papatāānuku (Mother Earth) and Ranginui (Sky Father) and in turn our deep affiliation to all things within the world is protected to support the health and well-being of our communities and future generations. It is core values that recognise Paptunuku's right to support life that enable us to shift our focus beyond short term thinking associated with the ownership of individual sites and protecting the accumulation of wealth linked to Western perceptions of land use and its exploitation to consider the long-term impact of everything we do. We urgently need to draw on the strength of Indigenous thinking to find better ways to educate architects to develop better tools to plan for a long-term sustainable future in response to the potentially catastrophic realities future Indigenous, marginalised and stateless communities face.

References

Barnes, M., Hoskins. R., Maher, P. "Relish the difference," *Architecture New Zealand*. March/April 1994, p.70.

Coole, D., & Frost, S. (2010). *Introducing the new materialisms: New Materialisms: Ontology, Agency, and Politics.* Durham & London: Duke University Press.

Chamie, Joseph. "As Cities Grow, So Do the Numbers of Homeless." *YaleGlobal* Online (2017) https://yaleglobal.yale.edu/content/cities-grow-so-do-numbers-homeless.

Durie, M. (2011). *Nga tini whetu: Navigating Māori futures*. Huia Publishers.

Environment Aotearoa 2019 | Ministry for the Environment. https://www.mfe.govt.nz/.../environmental-reporting/environment-aotearoa-2019.

Fisher, D. (1991). The resource management legislation of 1991: A juridical analysis of its objectives. Resource Management. Winter.

Harris, A. (2004). *Hīkoi: Forty Years of Māori Protest*. Huia.

Palmer, F. (2016). "Building Sustainable Papakāinga to Support Māori Aspirations for Self-determination." Unpublished Doctoral Dissertation. Te Ara Poutama: Auckland University of Technology.

Poata, T. T. K. (2012). *Poata: Seeing beyond the horizon*.

Rossouw, G. (2008). "Māori wellbeing and Being-in-the-world: challenging notions for psychological research and practice in New Zealand." *Indo-Pacific Journal of Phenomenology*, 8(2), pp.1-11.

Smith, G. H. (1997b). "Kaupapa Māori Theory and Praxis. Unpublished Doctoral Dissertation." Education Department: The University of Auckland.

Smith, L. T. (1999b). "Kaupapa Māori methodology: Our power to define ourselves." Unpublished paper presented to the School of Education, University of British Columbia.

Yates, A. (2008). "On nature culture and sustainable design" in C. Brebbia (Ed.) *Design and Nature IV: Comparing design in Nature with Science and Engineering,* pp. 191-200. Southhampton: WIT Press.

Chapter 4.3: Ngā Aho, Māori Design Professionals Inc Kaitiakitanga in Māori Design Industries

Desna Whaanga-Schollum – Rongomaiwahine, Kahungunu, Pāhauwera

Desna's work is connected through the exploration and articulation of cultural identity. Projects see her collaborating with a wide variety of communities, business and design professionals, artists and academics, to achieve results that effect change in people, practice and place. Desna is actively involved in Indigenous identity discourse, design, and stakeholder engagement, via: strategy, research, exhibitions, wānanga, speaking engagements, and governance roles. Chair of Ngā Aho Māori Design Professionals, Desna has come a long way from the dirt roads of Te Māhia-mai-Tawhiti, (but largely wishes she was back there).
Ku

Ka whiowhio mai te hau

Mai i te motu tapu o Waikawa

Pōrutu ana te tai

Rere ana te wai

Tū tonu te pā

Tū tonu tō mātou kāinga

Ko Taipōrutu

He uri au nō Rongomaiwahine, nō Kahungunu

The winds whistle

From the sacred isle of Waikawa

The sea resounds

The stream flows

The pā stands proud

Our home endures

It is Taipōrutu.

I am a descendant of Rongomaiwahine and Kahungunu

(Pepeha – Personal introduction written by Dr Mere Whaanga for Desna Whaanga-Schollum, 2019)

The following chapter is offered as a humble introduction to a powerful movement of Indigenous designers in Aotearoa, New Zealand. It is by no means the full wairua[1]-generating story of our journey to date. Many of the following words have been collectively articulated by our network of Māori design kaitiaki[2] over the years since our foundation, the chapter represents a weaving of the strands of our voices. Notable cultural elders, or Pou Ārahi[3] who guided the foundation of Awatoru, and subsequently what became Ngā Aho, were Paki Harrison,[4] Monte Ohia[5] and Trevor Moeke.[6] Whilst the stories of those aho[7] are not told here, Ngā Aho acknowledges that our work is built on the foundations created by many great cultural icons.

For our colleagues, mentors, whanaunga,[8] and gritty (designer) trench cohorts. Ka whawhai tonu mātou mō te āke, āke, āke!

Introduction

The name Ngā Aho, was gifted by Kaumātua Haare Williams, and denotes the weaving of many strands. Ngā Aho Inc. Soc. (Network of Māori Design Professionals) allows for the emergence, establishment and realisation of Māori potential in commercially focused creative disciplines such as Design, Architecture, Landscape Architecture, Planning, Engineering, Design-Thinking and Co-Design.

The Ngā Aho dialogue began with the Hui Kaihoahoa

———————————————

1. Wairua: (noun) attitude, quintessence, feel, mood, feeling, nature, essence, atmosphere (Maori Dictionary).
2. Kaitiaki: (noun) trustee, minder, guard, custodian, guardian, caregiver, keeper, steward.
3. Foundational leaders.
4. Pakariki Harrison. "Paki Harrison is widely regarded as one of the most accomplished people of his generation in the field of Maori art and was best known as a leading tohunga of carving." https://www.thearts.co.nz/artists/dr-pakariki-harrison.
5. Monte Ohia: https://researchspace.auckland.ac.nz/handle/2292/5730.
6. Trevor J Moeke: https://foma.conference.maori.nz/presenters/trevor-j-moeke/.
7. Aho: (noun) weft, woof – cross-threads of weaving.
8. Whanaunga: (noun) relative, relation, kin (Maori Dictionary).

Whare[9] at Hoani Waititi marae[10] in July 2001. Around 50 participants met to discuss recent developments in Māori architecture. The hui[11] acknowledged the need for a professional body representing the aspirations of Māori design professionals. This was progressed substantially in 2006, which saw the establishment of two landmark Māori design led initiatives:

Awatoru:

A Māori economic Development project funded under the Tertiary Education Commissions Growth and innovation Pilots Scheme. This built upon the Growth and Innovation Framework and 'Success by Design' strategy to develop design led businesses to increase export income. The Awatoru project brought together previously disparate sectors of Māori Arts and Culture, with Business and Design to develop a design enabled and culturally underpinned economic development model and tertiary education programme.

Te Aranga:

A cluster of Māori professionals spanning architecture, design, landscape architecture, engineering, planning, local government and environment convened to develop a national strategy for the reinstatement and development of our cultural landscapes and to seek the establishment of a professional cluster to compete commercially and function politically. Their inaugural national hui was convened at Te Aranga Marae in Hastings in November 2007 with the support of Ministry for the Environment and Te Puni Kokiri's Business Directorate and consequently resulted in a national Strategy being formulated and planned for its implementation.

Both initiatives have significant achievements under their belt, both are led by credible Māori professionals respected by their peers and clients and both have the necessary critical mass, stakeholder support and means to make a significant impact on Māori development and nation building.

Both initiatives have identified the need for, and desire of Māori professionals to establish, an accessible Network of Māori Design and allied professionals to progress these kaupapa and to pursue any future Māori design led initiatives (Wixon, me ētahi atu, 2007).

The early 21st century is a time of great challenges and opportunities for Māori design professionals and their communities. This chapter discusses the formative years for this distinct Māori design community in Aotearoa

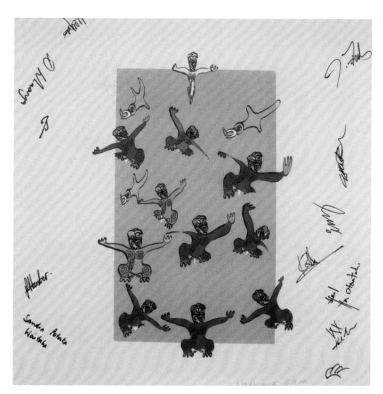

Figure 1. Nga Aho Awatoru Te Aranga, Tapu Te Ranga Marae, 2008.

New Zealand and some of the practices employed by Ngā Aho Inc. Soc. to acknowledge the mana[12] of Māori communities, build the capacity of Māori designers, and to develop methods which contribute to an active practice of kaitiakitanga.[13]

The information is structured by the five Ngā Aho Society objects or Whainga[14]:

TAHI (1): WHAKAMARAMA

Object: To raise awareness and increase knowledge, amongst members and their communities of interest, in respect to Māori issues, aspirations, methods, practices and knowledge in the Society's fields of interest.

RUA (2). WHAKAWHANAUNGATANGA

Object: To foster the development of productive relationships and networks between members and between members and their communities of interest.

TORU (3). MAHI TAHI

Object: To foster and facilitate collaboration between members and between members and their communities of interest.

---

9. Gathering of built environment designers .
10. Marae: the complex of buildings around a Māori community meeting house, where formal greetings and discussions take place.
11. Hui: (noun) gathering, meeting, assembly, seminar, conference (Maori Dictionary).

12. Mana: (noun) prestige, authority, control, power, influence, status, spiritual power, charisma – mana is a supernatural force in a person, place or object (Maori Dictionary).
13. Kaitiakitanga: (noun) guardianship, stewardship, trusteeship, trustee (Maori Dictionary).
14. Whainga: (noun) pursuit, aim, goal, objective, purpose (Maori Dictionary).

WHA (4). WHAKAMANA
Object: To increase the Profile and Standing of members and their communities of interest – particularly iwi[15] and hapū.[16]

RIMA (5). WHAKAHAERE KAUPAPA
Object: To do anything necessary or helpful to the above purposes.

TAHI (1): WHAKAMARAMA

Object: To raise awareness and increase knowledge, amongst members and their communities of interest, in respect to māori issues, aspirations, methods, practices and knowledge in the Society's fields of interest.

1.1 Cultural Landscapes

The world of human relations cannot be readily conceived anymore without its infrastructure of technological devices and heavily designed structural landscapes. Locating the identity of the individual or specific place, recognises the value the individual brings to the whole, the person within the community, the community within the town or city, these within the region and so on. Defining a cultural landscape in perceptive awareness, is nested within a series of experiential relationships, or understandings of specific meanings for place and connections to a cohesive whole identity. A conceptual structure which can cause either a feeling of "Insideness" or "Outsideness" for the individual (Sowers & Seamon, 2008). This structure is a combination of the physical attributes of the landscape, activities and events, and the individual and group meanings created through experiences and values or intentional relationships in regard to a place. A "cultural landscape" or "sense-of-place."

Connectedness to place is a challenge for everyone. For indigenous peoples it can be a struggle to see the identities of their ancestors in the landscape when physical features or natural resources have been destroyed or built

over. As a new resident, it requires effort and practice to learn someone else's narratives and connect them to the landscape and immediate people in day-to-day life. Within the developed New Zealand landscape, it can be a challenge to understand that Māori values and tikanga17 exist and persevere in contemporary realities (Whaanga-Schollum, Robinson, Stuart, & Livesey, 2015).

In recent history, local government organisations have acknowledged and formed relationships with Māori, tangata whenua[18] through formal consultation processes, advisory panels, and other processes including agreements as a result of Treaty of Waitangi claims settlement.[19] Through these relationships, awareness and understanding of Māori tikanga, including, but not limited to kaitiakitanga is growing. Contemporary practices of kaitiakitanga move natural resource guardianship beyond a preservationist view of culture and people as separate from nature, towards a more holistically integrated understanding of cultural landscape, guided by "sense-of-place."

The ethic of kaitiakitanga is becoming increasingly important as iwi and hapū assert their mana and respond to the obligations under current environmental legislation. … a 1997 amendment to the Resource Management Act definition now specifies that "kaitiakitanga" means "the exercise of guardianship by the tangata whenua of an area in accordance with tikanga Māori in relation to natural and physical resources; and includes the ethic of stewardship." The nature of tikanga Māori is therefore of direct relevance to the court's jurisdiction when considering kaitiakitanga issues" (Law Commission 2001, pp. 52-53).

Māori tikanga are further referenced in Section 6(e) and Section 8 of the *Resource Management Act* 1991.

Other than the concept of kaitiakitanga, a number of other philosophical concepts that form an important part of tikanga Māori are also referred to in the Resource Management Act 1991. Section 6(e) of the Act requires those with discretions under the Act to "recognise and provide for . . . the relationship of Māori and their culture and traditions with their ancestral lands, water, sites, wāhi

---

15. Iwi: (noun) extended kinship group, tribe, nation, people, nationality, race - often refers to a large group of people descended from a common ancestor and associated with a distinct territory (Maori Dictionary).
16. Hapū: (noun) kinship group, clan, tribe, subtribe – section of a large kinship group and the primary political unit in traditional Māori society. It consisted of a number of whānau sharing descent from a common ancestor, usually being named after the ancestor, but sometimes from an important event in the group's history. A number of related hapū usually shared adjacent territories forming a looser tribal federation (iwi) (Maori Dictionary).

17. Tikanga: (noun) correct procedure, custom, habit, lore, method, manner, rule, way, code, meaning, plan, practice, convention, protocol - the customary system of values and practices that have developed over time and are deeply embedded in the social context (Maori Dictionary).
18. Tangata Whenua: (noun) local people, hosts, Indigenous people – people born of the whenua, i.e. of the placenta and of the land where the people's ancestors have lived and where their placenta are buried (Maori Dictionary).
19. https://www.govt.nz/browse/history-culture-and-heritage/treaty-of-waitangi-claims/settling-historical-treaty-of-waitangi-claims/.

tapu, and other taonga." This provision cannot be applied without a knowledge of Tikanga Māori.

Section 8 of the Resource Management Act requires those with discretions to take into account the principles of the Treaty of Waitangi. The Treaty promises the protection of Māori custom and cultural values.

The Act pertains to an enormous area of law in which local government, central government and the mainstream courts have been required to understand and apply tikanga Māori" (Law Commission, 2001, p.54).

Through these layered opportunities, Indigenous protocols are increasingly applied to the management and development of the environment. The *Te Aranga Cultural Landscape Strategy* (Te Aranga), and it's operationalising through Ngā Aho, has been one such industry response to the contemporary application of Tikanga Māori.

1.2 Ngā Aho Founding Charter – Te Aranga, Cultural Landscapes Strategy

Acknowledgement of the "cultural landscape" is a recent phenomenon in Aotearoa New Zealand. In 2005, the Ministry for the Environment published the *Urban Design Protocol*. Few or no Māori had been engaged in the development of the protocol, and there was little recognition of Māori design concepts included. Māori professionals confronted the Ministry for the Environment, and from the 16th to the 19th of November 2006, a hui of Māori professionals and supporters spanning architecture, landscape architecture, planning, engineering, design, iwi and hapū development, education, arts and local and central government, gathered with the haukāinga[20] at Te Aranga Marae in Flaxmere to discuss and formulate a draft National Māori Cultural Landscape Strategy.

The hui reviewed case studies of local developments and attended presentations to help participants understand the need for recognition of Māori cultural landscapes in the built environment. Hui participants agreed on three areas that required national action and support. These included:

- Māori land under pressure
- Iwi / hapū / whānau with development aspirations
- Māori cultural landscape opportunities within shared landscapes / public spaces.
- Hui participants agreed to work toward the "development and articulation of the Māori cultural landscape" and agreed that this would "contribute to the health and well-being of all who reside in and visit Aotearoa" (Awatoru Project, 2008).

The response was the *Te Aranga Māori Cultural Landscapes Strategy* this strategy seeks to ensure iwi are well placed to positively influence and shape the design of cultural landscapes within their tribal boundaries. The first draft of the strategy and a plan for its implementation were completed in January of 2007. Between August 2007 and February 2008 the strategy was taken out for iwi consultation through eight hui from Te Tai Tokerau – Northland, Whanganui-a-Tara (hosted at Tapu Te Ranga Marae) to Murihiku - South Island, and gained unanimous support. Developed by Māori professionals and supporters spanning many areas of design, arts, iwi and hapū development, health, education, local and central government.

Te Aranga Māori Cultural Landscapes Strategy seeks to articulate a physical and metaphysical understanding of the cultural landscape, which hapū and iwi are committed to working towards reinstating and developing within contemporary Aotearoa. The collective which generated the strategy, asserts that,

> The development and articulation of the Māori cultural landscape will contribute to the health and well-being of all who reside in and visit Aotearoa – through realizing our unique Aotearoa and Pacific identity (Te Aranga Cultural Landscapes, 2008, p.4).

The concept of being tangata whenua, literally, "people of the land," is to know intimately your tūrangawaewae[21], the land that provides a place of standing and identity. This is the basis of environmental mātauranga[22] Māori, the Māori knowledge system. Mātauranga Māori can be understood as differing from "Western Knowledge" systems, due to connectivity being both the defining quality and objective.

> The key distinction between Mātauranga Māori and Western Knowledge is that Mātauranga Māori has evolved over centuries of interaction between people and a specific environment (that of the waters, lands, forests, and creatures of Aotearoa) and is fundamentally designed to *bond people into a community,* whereas Western scholarship and beliefs are based on the application of unrestricted criticism and scrutiny of all beliefs towards obtaining *the best possible knowledge of the world* we inhabit (Te Tau-a-Nuku, Ngā Aho, 2014).

Place-based narratives can be very specific to each whānau and hapū, as this is knowledge generated through long-term occupation of an environment. It is this living with, and knowing of the environment that

---

20. Haukāinga: (noun) local people of a marae, home people (Maori Dictionary).

21. Tūrangawaewae: (noun) domicile, standing, place where one has the right to stand – place where one has rights of residence and belonging through kinship and whakapapa (Maori Dictionary).
22. Mātauranga: (noun) knowledge, wisdom, understanding, skill – sometimes used in the plural.

is the wairua[23] of iwi and hapū identities. Area-specific experiences, spiritual beliefs, and ancestral narratives are woven together to create a unique and wholly integrated connection and responsibility to place and people.
Te Aranga Cultural Landscape Strategy articulates a mātauranga Māori view of the cultural landscape as an environment which encompasses history, nature and people, territory and rights, and the language, art and design forms which connect, inform and sculpt our identities. The following aspirational statement leads into the strategy and communicates the cultural creative relationship between tangata whenua design and arts practices and the environment – a concept of creative mauri.[24]

> As Māori we have a unique sense of our 'landscape'
> It includes past, present and future.
> It includes both physical and spiritual dimensions.
> It is how we express ourselves in our environment.
> It connects whānau and whenua, flora and fauna,
> through whakapapa.
> It does not disconnect urban from rural.
> It transcends the boundaries of 'land'scape into other
> 'scapes'; rivers, lakes, ocean and sky.
> It is enshrined in our whakapapa, pepeha [tribal saying],
> tauparapara [incantation to begin a speech], whaikōrero
> [a formal speech], karakia [ritual chants], waiata [song,
> chant], tikanga [correct procedure, custom, lore, method],
> ngā korero a kui ma, a koroua ma [the words of our elders]
> and our mahi toi [art and architecture].
> It is not just where we live – it is who we are!
> (Te Aranga Cultural Landscapes 2008, p.1)

In July of 2007, saw a hui convened at Apumoana Marae in Rotorua entitled "Designing Māori Futures" to progress the establishment of a network of Māori Design Professionals to progress aspects of the Te Aranga Cultural Landscape Strategy. The hui secured 25 founding members and a further 28 registrations of interest to join, the formation of the Ngā Aho Incorporated Society.

Teams were identified at this hui to work on the Society business structure, communications and branding. A number of working group hui were held to in subsequent months, developing what became Ngā Aho Inc Soc. The following are excerpts from a hui of the branding team, held at Awataha Marae, Auckland, regarding the naming and brand or purpose of Ngā Aho.

The discussion with Arnold[25] was pretty important and

came at just the right time for me because it clarified the role we have as designers to accept that we have skills and insights that are different to the skills and insights others have. That we are often in situations that are the nature of our occupation and place in the mix of things where we need to make decisions and determinations that mark our world and landscape and while this is a huge responsibility we do it using the best of our knowledge within the given circumstances with awareness of the things we know and don't know and because of this we explore the possibilities and the implications at a number of levels and then get on with making the mark. The ability to intuit is what it is all about and that basic freedom is what we would like to celebrate – after all it's about being alive and making life – creation (Scott, 2007).

We were reminded of the importance of the whakatauki 'MAI TE KOREKORE KI TE AO MARAMA'. I believe we saw the initiative in drawing maori professionals under the collective banner 'Tuia'[26] somehow being a progression in organising ourselves in response to a process that began at the signing of the Treaty. A concept evolved whereby we recognising that mark-making in some way is an important reflection of what we do collectively – making marks on the landscape, marks in the urban environment, impressing and/or leaving marks on the culture of Aotearoa.

- We are interested/involved in designing or intervening in a wide-ranging set of processes that involve making or leaving marks on the landscape
- We accept that our collective skills enable a contribution toward keeping the wairua and mauri intact
- Te Tiriti has established a precedent/ a set of principles that may often influence or govern the outcome of these processes
- Our tupuna participated in the enshrining of te tiriti in some essential practices around governance (Wilson, 2007).

Te Korekore – The nothingness – unlimited potential/ possibility
Te Po – The dark ages
Te Ao – The light – actual form
Whakapapa connects you to the creator – to be like the creator to create – to wairua – to mauri. Tohu is expression of you in all your states of being – all of your tipuna – combined then it is an expression of our tinorangatiratanga – manamotuhake (Wilson A. , 2007).

I felt we drew a particular connection between Maori design professionals – in that we often transcend boundaries in terms of the practices we cover. The ability to do so is through seeing all creativity coming from

---

23. Wairua: (noun) attitude, quintessence, feel, mood, feeling, nature, essence, atmosphere (Maori Dictionary).
24. Mauri is an energy which binds and animates all things in the physical world (Royal T. A., updated 22-Sep-12).
25. Arnold Manaaki Wilson, MNZM "… a major presence on the contemporary Māori art scene for half a century. He was among

---

the Māori art educators who joined forces to present the first exhibition of contemporary art by Māori artists."
26. This later changed to 'Ngā Aho', after research into the use of 'Tuia' established its prominence elsewhere.

Figure 2. Hui-a-Tau, Rongopai Marae, Haare Williams and Jamaine Fraser, 2011.

Figure 3. Hui-a-Tau Hikoi, Maketu Awa, 2012.

Figure 4. Hui-a-Tau Hikoi, Maketu Marae, 2012.

Figure 5. Matariki Kora Session, Auckland, 2012.

Figure 6. Para-Matchitt Studio-visit, 2016.

Figure 7. I-Te-Timatanga Hikoi-Heretaunga-Pou, 2016.

the same space within us – that the "physical" project outcomes were not constraining or defining for us as design practices as they all draw from the process. The concept of 'Te Kore – from nothing, comes creation', felt a relevant and meaningful cultural explanation of the space we come from and stand within as Māori (Whaanga-Schollum, 2007).

Ngā Aho and the Te Aranga Māori Cultural Landscapes Strategy national steering committee, were immediately active in advocating for "Seeing our faces in our places" [27]via consultation with the Ministry for the Environment. Te Manatū ō te Taiao.[28] An expectation and level of activity which has continued over subsequent years.

On the 12th and 13th of September 2008 a hui was held at Tapu Te Ranga Marae in Island Bay Wellington to review, and formulate a response to, the proposed National Policy Statement (NPS) on Urban Design. The hui was convened by members of the Te Aranga Māori Cultural Landscapes Strategy (MCLS) national steering committee and Ngā Aho – the national society of Māori design professionals. Invitations were sent widely throughout the country to Māori design professionals and iwi…

The hui was already being convened for members of Ngā Aho through the Awatoru project and when MFE approached the Te Aranga Strategy Steering Committee for comment on the proposed NPS, it was suggested that the planned hui provided a good opportunity to seek and formulate a Māori response to the proposal.

It must be noted, the first concern expressed by the Te Aranga Steering Committee, was the absence of Māori in the 45 organisations consulted prior to release of the

discussion paper. This was viewed as an indictment upon the Ministry and the consulted organisations – in that none evidently raised this as a key concern. This was also particularly concerning given the same response had been provided in regard to the lack of Māori involvement in development of the Urban Design Protocols – a fact which later resulted in MFE supporting development of the Te Aranga Māori Cultural Landscapes Strategy (Proposed National Policy Statement on Urban Design – Hui Response, 2008).

1.3. Ngā Aho, Māori Design Professionals – Who are we?

Ngā Aho, Māori Design Inc. aims to apply design skills to achieve Māori aspirations in envisaging, designing and realizing a future Aotearoa. Ngā Aho translates to "the many strands," communicating a concept of bringing together the many strands of the Māori design world to explore and articulate Māori culture through Design, Architecture, Landscape Architecture, Planning, Design-Thinking and Co-Design. Ngā Aho exists as a multi-disciplinary professional cultural advocacy network, tackling complex Māori cultural issues which span across economic, social and ecological concerns.

Within the professional design industries, Ngā Aho is perceived to sit alongside other design institutions such as DINZ,[29] NZILA,[30] NZIA[31] and NZPI,[32] however, the focus of Ngā Aho is primarily driving positive change for the wellbeing of Māori community, rather than development purely for industry or commercial gains. Central to this approach is actively maintaining reciprocal relationships with the Māori communities and therefore, an immediate responsibility, awareness, and knowledge of what is needed. Research, development and industry within Ngā Aho membership seeks primarily to be led by community-needs. Ngā Aho therefore, is technical and analytical in the professional experience and "tools" that we utilise, however, this way of working is based on social-political processes. The stakeholders are whānau,[33] hapū, and iwi. Ngā Aho has a broad-based interdisciplinary design agenda, with respect to the development of cultural goals through social, ecological and economic dimensions. We promote the development of policy and structural industry approaches leading to the regenerative presence of Māori culture in the designed landscapes of Aotearoa. This

---

27. Seeing our faces in our places" national hui. 12th & 13th September, 2008 Tapu Te Ranga Marae. Wellington. Jointly convened and funded by Te Wānanga o Aotearoa through the Awatoru Growth and Innovation project and the Ministry for the Environment. Initiated by members of the Te Aranga Māori Cultural Landscapes Steering committee and Society of Māori Design professionals through the Awatoru Project. The first phased initiated by Māori designers Jacob Scott and Karl Wixon, later joined by Carin Wilson, resulted in the development of a unique kaupapa Māori model for design enabled business development. It was trialled through a pilot project with Hokotehi Moriori Trust with stunning results and in turn informed the development of a proposal to establish a unique MBA (design) programme. In addition the project, in partnership with the Te Aranga Māori Cultural Landscapes Strategy Steering Committee, convened an inaugural hui to establish a society of Māori design and design related professionals spanning design, architecture, engineering, landscape and environment. It was convened under the kaupapa 'Designing Māori futures.' The first phase of the Awatoru project finished in July 2007.
28. https://www.mfe.govt.nz/.

---

29. DINZ: Designers Institute of New Zealand.
30. NZILA: New Zealand Institute of Landscape Architecture.
31. NZIA: New Zealand Institute of Architecture.
32. NZPI: New Zealand Planning Institute.
33. Whānau: (noun) extended family, family group, a familiar term of address to a number of people – the primary economic unit of traditional Māori society. In the modern context the term is sometimes used to include friends who may not have any kinship ties to other members (Maori Dictionary).

regenerative presence is driven through capacity building of Māori design practitioners in collaboration with their communities of interest.

RUA (2): WHAKAWHANAUNGATANGA

Object: To foster the development of productive relationships and networks between members and between members and their communities of interest.

It is the expectation of Māori communities that any person working with Māori tikanga and mātauranga, will retain a personal responsibility for ensuring that knowledge is respected and a reciprocal relationship of trust with the guardians of that knowledge. Being aware of culturally bound concepts of identity and consequently personal subjectivity, is central to developing a design process which demonstrates integrity.

2.1 Building Connections – Hui-A-Tau and Wānanga

One of the regular practices Ngā Aho has employed to keep a tangible and transparent connection with the community is through the *Hui-a-Tau* (Annual General Meeting), which is formed around a three-day wānanga[34] at a marae. Alongside the mechanical business of an Incorporated Society, the wānanga is an opportunity for members from across Aotearoa to connect with each other, share their experiences, discuss projects and challenges in cultural, educational, professional and political sectors which are pertinent to Māori design. The wānanga often includes hīkoi[35] to significant sites with the hapū of the hosting marae, providing an opportunity to learn about the relevant cultural history of the area and also to discuss site specific issues which Ngā Aho members may be able to assist with. Design requests from haukāinga have ranged from wharenui restoration, marae buildings, environmental regeneration, cultural site markers, murals (depicting local histories), to educational programme input and a wide range of other design and culture connected initiatives.

Wānanga bring together a wide range of people for deliberative working dialogue on a specific subject or initiative, to arrive at a deeper understanding. To describe this within the Ngā Aho design context, "Co-design wānanga can be an effective focused methodology when utilized as the 'container' for aligning purpose and generating new knowledge. An intentional mauri[36]

ora[37] process can become embodied in design wānanga to create a resonant 'container' for place-based co-design, valuing personal contribution and identity, as well as establishing and sustaining strong relationships" (Whaanga-Schollum, Robinson, Stuart, & Livesey, Regenerating Urban Mauri, 2015).

Each year an invitation is extended by one of the Ngā Aho members to hold the next year's wānanga at their home marae. This invite is termed a tono. A tono is an invite considered and extended through a collective decision, and promises an undertaking of respectful, reciprocal working relationships for the kaupapa at hand.

> An invitation to an individual by an institution promises a relationship. The relationship promises to value what everyone brings to the kaupapa... A tono recognizes the taonga shared by tāngata when they participate, attend, and give voice to their thoughts (Livesey, 2015).

Workshops are run during the gathering to immediately address the identified site-specific issues for the hapū, providing an opportunity for whakawhanaungatanga[38] between members and building a practice of genuine practical reciprocity with Māori communities. Hui attendees interacting with the haukāinga in this way, are able to learn in an immediate and experiential manner from people with ahikā[39] mātauranga.[40] Ahi kā brings a knowledge of intergenerational lived experience to the place identified as tūrangawaewae ("a place to stand"). This way of "briefing" and working together with the community on their identified needs, is an opportunity for the designer to produce meaningful work that creates immediate real-world impact. An approach which focuses on social, and cultural drivers within a sector that historically has primarily been driven by global commercial imperatives.

The Ngā Aho *wānanga-a-tau* have particular value for the large contingent of attending tertiary students and early career practitioners, who may have limited opportunity to integrate Māori cultural experience in their institutional study or early career roles. Through the

---

34. Wānanga: (noun) seminar, conference, forum, educational seminar (Maori Dictionary).
35. Hīkoi: (verb) (-tia) to step, stride, march, walk. (Maori Dictionary) In this case – referencing visiting cultural sites of significance.
36. Mauri: (noun) life principle, life force, vital essence, special

nature, a material symbol of a life principle, source of emotions – the essential quality and vitality of a being or entity. Also used for a physical object, individual, ecosystem or social group in which this essence is located.
37. Ora: Well-being.
38. Whakawhanaungatanga: (noun) process of establishing relationships, relating well to others (Maori Dictionary).
39. Ahi kā: (noun) burning fires of occupation, continuous occupation - title to land through occupation by a group, generally over a long period of time. The group is able, through the use of whakapapa, to trace back to primary ancestors who lived on the land (Maori Dictionary).
40. Mātauranga: (noun) knowledge, wisdom, understanding, skill (Maori Dictionary).

wānanga-a-tau, professional cultural capacity is grown. Students and early career practitioners are provided an opportunity to form relationships with experienced Māori design professionals, gain an understanding of how their work might assist with Māori community development, and experience real world cross-sectoral collaboration. These annual gatherings have become a key tool for Ngā Aho in fostering cultural awareness within the design community and connecting professional practice to community needs.

2.2 Inaugural International Indigenous Design Forums

In 2016, Ngā Aho undertook the design and delivery of the inaugural International Indigenous Design Forum. *I Te Timatanga | In the Beginning |* was a successful pilot four-day wānanga in Ngāpuhi territory, at Whakapara Marae,[41] Te Tai Tokerau. This event elevated the Ngā Aho (Māori Design Professionals) Hui-ā-Tau wānanga (2007) to a new international audience. The Forum and post-event tour of studio, and sites of significance for Māori across the North Island, established important international relationships in the Indigenous design fields, shared skills and knowledge and built a foundation of positive shared experiences from which to grow the field of Indigenous design practice.

Foundational relationships were established between tangata whenua and multicultural manuhiri,[42] experienced and fledgling practitioners, professionals and community.

International practitioners that attended and presented included Indigenous from Gunditjmara, Australia; Tlicho First Nation, Canada; Nisga'a, Canada; Samoa; Tokelau; Nigeria; Apsaalooke – Crow, United States; Ojibway – Peguis First Nation, Manitoba, Canada; Mayan, El Salvador. It is well recognised in contemporary urban design practice that communities want to be, and already are, involved in the design of their spaces, places, and services. New knowledge was created by connecting at the deeper level of what is core to Indigenous people, across worldviews, across disciplines, and across experiences.

> Indigenous peoples' struggles are against the government of individualization...It takes more than just one or two people to work on this, everyone has a role to play (Stewart, 2016).

> We mirror what we see in the stars, we mirror this back into our cities... The blood we carry is our bodies is borrowed. We carry the blood down through to the next generations...We must remember that blood has been shed in these places we build cities (Laotan-Brown, 2016).

> Quality of life on our planet has been adversely affected by ongoing siloed production of places / tolls / living. The future is working across disciplines, understanding that life is connected.... Māori have been dragged into urbanity. What is the indigenous basis? We need to look to indigenous ancient knowledge (Kiddle, 2016).

In 2018, a cohort of Ōtautahi (Christchurch) based Ngā Aho members took up the challenge of hosting the second International gathering Nā Te Kore.[43] Hosted by Ngāi Tūāhuriri[44] and Ngāti Wheke[45] welcomed an attendance of over 150 delegates across the four days of the wānanga. Internationally significant to Indigenous peoples, Nā Te Kore provided an opportunity to discuss approaches to design, share thoughts, and stories-of-place, whilst evolving ideas and concepts about integrating Indigenous design narrative and values into the public realm.

> Architecture, urban design, landscape architecture and planning have always been used as colonial tools every bit as effective as military conquest, land confiscation, imposition of private property etc. – in erasing the materiality, memory and humanity of indigenous communities. Ōtautahi/Christchurch, Aotearoa/New Zealand is no exception.
> In this presentation, I talk 'around' these issues and in particular the need to theorise indigeneity back into architecture, planning and urban design – which by the way, had never left but had simply been paved and boarded over during the colonial project (Matunga, 2018).

TORU (3): MAHI TAHI

Object: to foster and facilitate collaboration between members and between members and their communities of interest.

3.1 Mauri – Life Principle and Creative Practice

Strengthening confidence in identities and working relationships, provides an opportunity for a much deeper collective understanding of the unique way that 'life works' in each place. This process of building integrity

---

41. https://maorimaps.com/marae/whakapara.
42. Manuhiri: (noun) visitor, guest.

---

43. https://www.natekore2018.com/.
44. https://ngaitahu.iwi.nz/te-runanga-o-ngai-tahu/papatipu-runanga/ngai-tuahuriri/.
45. https://ngaitahu.iwi.nz/te-runanga-o-ngai-tahu/papatipu-runanga/rapaki/.

through recognizing the value in all interactions, tangibly informs how to nourish mauri, life-essence, through design practice (Whaanga-Schollum, Robinson, Stuart, & Livesey, 2015). Mauri is a central concept to creative practice and design. In Te Ao Māori[46], mauri connects people and spirit to all within the natural physical world, and taonga in the form of highly-valued man-made objects, carry the mauri of the maker. Art forms and products are seen as having an intimate relationship with environment and people, with mauri being the connective life-essence that flows throughout all.

Changing societal laws and geographical occupation patterns in New Zealand have led to many Māori becoming disconnected from their Indigenous philosophies. In *Urban Mauri*, an article produced by Ngā Aho members, the negative impacts of colonisation and industrialisation on the mātauranga Māori concept of mauri were discussed.

> Marsden (2003) contrasted the Māori world with what he called 'metropolitan culture,' characterized by macroscale aggregation of people, and by secular and spiritual disconnection. Contemporary communities are infinitely larger than anything our ancestors envisaged; Māori may not be principally connected by common ancestry, as was the case in early Māori settlements, but rather through contemporary societal structures such as industrialisation. Education, work, or cultural interests are more likely to be the connection than whānau or natural resources in the contemporary societal landscape (Whaanga-Schollum, Robinson, Stuart, & Livesey, 2015).

The *Urban Mauri* article asked "What culturally grounded methods might be utilized in professional practice to regenerate mauri in an ephemeral existence, where social, cultural and environmental disconnection is prevalent in day-to-day life?" (Whaanga-Schollum, Robinson, Stuart, & Livesey, 2015).

In November 2014, the Auckland Council's Auckland Design Manual team partnered with Ngā Aho to host an *Urban Mauri, Co-Design Wānanga*, to explore further opportunities for understanding Māori design processes. The wānanga attendees were called together under the kaupapa[47] of Designing Tāmaki Makaurau – connecting cultures. The focus was to, "integrate arts and culture into our everyday lives. Support sustainable development of Māori outcomes, leadership, community and partnerships. Acknowledge that people and nature are inseparable" (Ngā Aho Inc, 2014).

The gathering integrated cultural art practices such as karanga,[48] contemporary dance, drawing, music, whaikōrero,[49] manaakitanga,[50] recognition of the value of place via architecture and location, in order to produce more substantial knowledge sharing experiences. Artists and designers from many walks were more able to contribute to the questions at hand, and also draw personal benefit from the experience - rather than a consultation process which is often seen as a one-way street.

The wānanga was led by a session delving into the perceived barriers for Māori to connect to a sense of place, and expressing these understandings in professional practice. The participants felt that within professional situations, they often operated in isolation; invitations to become connected weren't obvious. Furthermore, engaging in relationship-building takes too much time and resources for the infrastructures of these professional contexts and the willingness to connect isn't always there. Some Māori felt that it's easier to "do the Māori thing" outside the urban context, where communities and the environment may be more obviously connected. They felt that non-Indigenous practitioners needed to spend more time building reciprocal relationships to connect with the sense of place held by Māori communities, and to express these connections (Whaanga-Schollum, Robinson, Stuart, & Livesey, 2014).

A common theme that emerged from the wānanga, was that Māori communities need to feel they are invited to participate. A process that does not invite people to participate wholly will become combative and result

---

46. Māori world view.
47. Kaupapa: (noun) topic, policy, matter for discussion, plan, purpose, scheme, proposal, agenda, subject, programme, theme, issue, initiative (Maori Dictionary).
48. Karanga: (noun) formal call, ceremonial call, welcome call, call – a ceremonial call of welcome to visitors onto a marae, or equivalent venue, at the start of a pōwhiri. The term is also used for the responses from the visiting group to the tangata whenua ceremonial call. Karanga follow a format which includes addressing and greeting each other and the people they are representing and paying tribute to the dead, especially those who have died recently. The purpose of the occasion is also addressed. Skilled kaikaranga are able to use eloquent language and metaphor and to encapsulate important information about the group and the purpose of the visit (Maori Dictionary).
49. Whaikōrero: (noun) oratory, oration, formal speech-making, address, speech – formal speeches usually made by men during a pohiri and other gatherings. Formal eloquent language using imagery, metaphor, whakataukī, pepeha, kupu whakaari, relevant whakapapa and references to tribal history is admired. The basic format for whaikōrero is: tauparapara (a type of karakia); mihi ki te whare tupuna (acknowledgement of the ancestral house); mihi ki a Papatūānuku (acknowledgement of Mother Earth); mihi ki te hunga mate (acknowledgement of the dead); mihi ki te hunga ora (acknowledgement of the living); te take o te hui (purpose of the meeting). Near the end of the speech a traditional waiata is usually sung (Maori Dictionary).
50. Manaakitanga: (noun) hospitality, kindness, generosity, support – the process of showing respect, generosity and care for others (Maori Dictionary).

in compromise. Further, design processes are needed to create a space for reconciliation and alignment of different worldviews. For Māori design concepts to be employed with integrity, Māori professionals and communities need to be leading the process.

Authors Allan and Smith, (2013) in their discussion of a New Zealand bi-cultural studio practice, emphasise the need to move away from "superficial" outcomes, through having cultural integrity in landscape design.

> If a country's designed landscapes reflect superficial attributes rather than deeper values, it may mean that the sharing and blending between cultures is far from equal, or that designers are not yet fully conversant with the appropriate design modes and practices necessary to make meaningful cultural exchange work (Allan and Smith 2013, p.134).

3.2 Building Relationships – Keeping the Discussion and Cultural Context Responsive and Evolving

One of the key observations from *Urban Mauri* Wānanga participants was that wānanga are a space for ongoing knowledge exploration and building of relationships.

> In this conversation it is emergent. We are not getting somewhere. It is not outcomes driven. It's a relational discovery. Discovering things together (Tamati Patuwai, Cultural Creative Practitioner, Community development – Mad Ave cited in Whaanga-Schollum, Robinson, Stuart, and Livesey, 2014.)

Similar to the legal employment of the Treaty of Waitangi, the ability for the discussion and continuing relationship to be open ended, and therefore continually evolving as suited to context, is a frequent request from Māori communities when forming contemporary agreements in resource management, design and development (for example Memorandums of Understanding (MOU), Strategic Partnerships, resource Co-Management agreements).

> The Waitangi Tribunal has made it clear that the Treaty of Waitangi encapsulates a mutual exchange to benefit the nation as a whole. Thus, the Treaty must be applied to today's circumstances. At times, compromise is required to adjust to an evolving society. The Waitangi Tribunal has consistently stressed this point which lies behind and is acknowledged in the phrase: "Principles of the Treaty... with the passage of time, the 'principles' which underlie the Treaty have become much more important than its precise terms" (Law Commission, 2001, p79).

In essence, it is important to note, that the agreements are largely seen as guidance frameworks, rather

than prescriptions – all iwi are different, and projects are different. Knowledge is built from collecting and communicating learning from successive projects, rather than a set traditional approach. Cultural approaches, if seen in this light, can be given the room to be dynamic and globally connected through the different viewpoints that might be brought to any given conversation by an individual, balanced by the contextual knowledge that comes from long-term occupation and guardianship of place.

This approach to Māori tikanga is recognised in the Treaty principle of "development."

> This principle recognises that culture is not static. The integrity of tikanga Māori is not threatened, rather it is enhanced, by its ability to adapt and evolve as society changes (Law Commission, 2001, wh. p.81).

WHA (4): WHAKAMANA

Object: to increase the profile and standing of members and their communities of interest – particularly iwi and hapū.

Historically, the relevance of Māori concepts to design have not been acknowledged by "mainstream" design industry bodies. Ngā Aho has sought to change the industry status quo through forming strategic partnerships with other professional design industry bodies, and via awards.

4.1 Awarding Best Practice

Industry awards are used as a platform for increasing awareness of specialist areas of practice and recognising excellence in practice. They can be useful platforms for encouraging critical dialogue and progressing professional practices through peer analysis. Recognising this as an essential need for the growth of Māori design, in 2012 Ngā Aho partnered with the Designers Institute of New Zealand (DINZ) and brought a new Ngā Aho Award to the annual Best Design Awards. The Designers Institute of New Zealand was formed in 1991 by the merger of the New Zealand Society of Industrial Designers (formed 1960), and the New Zealand Association of Interior Designers (formed in 1968). The Best Design Awards represents over 1000 design professionals across spatial, graphic, and product design (Designers Institute of NZ, 2015). The Ngā Aho award showcases and celebrates design work that articulates a strong sense of Aotearoa, New Zealand identity, and design that results from meaningful collaboration. The award parameters[51] were

---

51. Ngā Aho Best Award parameters were authored by Past DINZ

Figure 8. I-Te-Timatanga Hikoi-Treaty Grounds, 2016.

Figure 9. I-Te-Timatanga Whakapara Marae, 2016.

Figure 10. Hui-a-Tau Omaka Marae, 2017.

Figure 11. Nga Aho Study Tour, Evergreen State College, Pacific Northwest, 2017.

Figure 12. Na-Te-Kore, International Indigenous Design Forum, 2018.

Figure 13. Nga Aho Co-Design, Wananga, Auckland, 2019.

described as:

1. Aotearoaness:
Design that reflects a clear understanding of who we are and where we are in our unique corner of Moana nui a Kiwa, the Pacific Ocean, by responding to our Indigenous culture, heritage and sense of place.

2. Collaborative practice:
Design that results from meaningful collaboration. Ngā Aho recognises the collaborative practice of "co-design," requiring an effective and measurable engagement between designers and clients, as best practice when working within and between cultures, whether that be:

- Māori or non-Māori Designers working with Māori clients, or;
- Māori and non-Māori Designers working with one another to express uniquely NZ design that exudes Aotearoaness, or;
- Non-Māori designers engaging with Māori people, culture and identity to develop work that seeks to expresses Aotearoaness (Ngā Aho Inc, Designers Institute of NZ, 2012).

Since establishment, the Ngā Aho award has progressively gained interest and support from an industry that historically has had little Māori identity presence. Designers submitting work for the Ngā Aho award, have commented on their growth of understanding in projects which have pursued solid cultural connection with iwi, via a whakawhanaungatanga or relationship development and "co-design" process. This is described in the award parameters as "designers and clients working effectively Kanohi ki te Kanohi – Pakahiwi ki te Pakahiwi – Face to face and shoulder to shoulder, exhibiting trust, respect and rapport" (Ngā Aho Inc, Designers Institute of NZ, 2012). This is a significant shift in mindset for the New Zealand design industry, both in championing a New Zealand design vernacular, and encouraging designers to challenge the commonly held assumption that the designer knows best, and within a project, is primarily in the role of educating the client. The co-design proposition opens up communication and value channels that support genuine dialogue and respect each party's needs within a project, creating new opportunities for unexpected outcomes or solutions to design problems.

4.2 Industry Partnerships

In August of 2014, Te Tau-a-Nuku (a Landscape Architecture constituent group of Ngā Aho whose activities are based on the *Te Aranga Māori Cultural Landscape Strategy*) provided a submission on the review of the New Zealand Institute of Landscape Architects (NZILA) documents, *Landscape Architecture Education Policy* and *Landscape Architecture Accreditation Procedures*. The submission noted that landscape education and the practice of landscape architecture in Aotearoa / New Zealand is predominantly based on western values and constructs. The submission is a clear reflection of the difference of "mātauranga Māori" being based on "rootedness" and "Western scholarship" as a broader, more mobile knowledge focus.

These "two types of knowledge" were acknowledged in March 2015, when Ngā Aho signed an MoU on behalf of Te Tau-a-Nuku with the NZILA. This was reflective of NZILA recognising the importance of Māori cultural values integration with landscape architecture practice as appropriate to place. The MoU outlines several key points in the statement of intent, including:

Reciprocating in the provision of information, advice and support to one another on the recognition of individual and shared knowledge and beliefs, fields of expertise and spheres of interest; Positively contributing to the social, cultural, environmental and economic development of Aotearoa/New Zealand (Ngā Aho Inc, NZILA, 2015).

The industry partnership agreements between Ngā Aho and NZILA MoU, is significant in its acknowledgement of people and culture as an important element of the landscape. Indeed, it has been noted that for the most part, landscape is understood solely as an object, rather than a concept that is developed through social cultural power networks (Menzies, 2015).

The most recent industry partnership agreement which Ngā Aho has developed, is with Te Kāhui Whaihanga – The New Zealand Institute of Architects (NZIA). With Ngā Aho Kaumātua Dr Haare Williams[52] leading the tikanga, an agreement of aligned values was developed with members of the NZIA and Ngā Aho practitioner communities, and a draft presented at Waipapa Marae in Auckland on 19 February 2016.

Haare Williams... he's such an orator, and he's of such the old way that we had to, every, literally if there was a grammar change, there was a comma put it, or one hair was put in, we had to say the whole sentence out loud, again. It was amazing. But what it did is it really taught me about where he was coming from and what he was trying to instil, from his point of view, within the language of the kawenata. For me, that was really about establishing, again, a Treaty-based relationship between

presidents, and Ngå Aho founding members Karl Wixon and Carin Wilson; Ngā Aho Kāhui Whetū and founding member Jacob Scott, and Ngā Aho founding member and Chair Desna Whaanga-Schollum.

52. Haare Mahanga Te Wehinga Williams 1936 – (Te Aitanga-a-Māhaki, Rongowhakaata, Ngāi Tūhoe, Te Whakatōhea). https://www.ngataonga.org.nz/set/item/448?lang=en.

two organisations who have otherwise not had a formal relationship set up... That relationship is going to be based on all the good stuff – respect, and we're going to honour mātauranga Māori, we're going to honour mana whenua, we're going to think about sustainability. And from that, our memberships, both Ngā Aho and the NZIA, have such a solid foundation from which to interrogate ourselves, in a positive way. Be self-aware (Heta & Kake, 2018).

The final agreement was signed in February of 2017, in the form of Te Kawenata o Rata,[53] a covenant which formalizes in a Treaty styled format the collaborative relationship between the two entities.

The kawenata is a values-based agreement, deliberately kept simple, and based around five articles that set out the relationship between the NZIA and Ngā Aho in the spirit of partnership under the mana of the Treaty of Waitangi. The five articles refer to: Respect – Whakaritenga; Authority and Responsibility – Rangatiratanga; Knowledge and Tikanga – Mātauranga Whaihanga; Cooperation – Mahi Kotahitanga; and Representation – Kanohi Kitea (NZIA, 2017).

A Ngā Aho member is co-opted for two-year term onto the NZIA Council, as an intermediary between the two entities, leading on the workstream of effective development and implementation of Te Kawenata o Rata intent.

4.3 Auckland Design Manual – Te Aranga Principles

In 2014, the Auckland Council developed an online resource, the Auckland Design Manual (ADM). Intended as a source of inspiration, the online platform provides examples of good design practice supported by design guides that give a more detailed account of how high-quality results can be achieved. The website builds awareness of design as a problem-solving process as well as an outcomes-oriented industry. Factors such as social needs, environmental aims, budget, time and quality of outcomes are addressed in various project examples, aiming to involve the residents of Tāmaki Makaurau in the development of their city (Auckland Council, 2015).

Māori design has been represented by the Te Aranga Principles in the ADM. Derived from the Te Aranga Cultural Landscape Strategy, the Te Aranga Principles are accessibly articulated through a set of core Māori values. These are rangatiratanga,[54] kaitiakitanga,[55]

manaakitanga,[56] wairuatanga,[57] whanaungatanga,[58] mātauranga[59] as well as kotahitanga[60] (Auckland Council and Ngā Aho Inc Soc, 2014).

The application of the values is then explained through seven outcome-oriented principles:

1. Mana: The status of iwi and hapū as mana whenua is recognised and respected.
2. Whakapapa: Māori names are celebrated.
3. Taiao: The natural environment is protected, restored and / or enhanced.
4. Mauri Tu: Environmental health is protected, maintained and / or enhanced.
5. Mahi Toi: Iwi/hapū narratives are captured and expressed creatively and appropriately.
6. Tohu: Mana whenua significant sites and cultural landmarks are acknowledged.
7. Ahi Kā: Iwi/hapū have a living and enduring presence and are secure and valued within their rohe (Auckland Council and Ngā Aho Inc Soc, 2014).

Lucy Tukua (a Ngā Aho founding member) as mandated Mana Whenua design representative alongside Hana Maihi and Rau Hoskins of Design Tribe (Past Chair Ngā Aho) first proposed a Te Aranga matrix for Auckland's City Rail Link project in 2012.[61] These Māori design principles are now widely throughout Auckland Council procurement processes.

The principles are used as a guideline by the Auckland Council - Auckland Urban Design Panel (AUDP) in assessing Te Ao Māori presence through Mana Whenua mātauranga and more general Māori design in proposed developments. The AUDP provides governance and advocacy. The Auckland Urban Design Panel Terms of Reference note: Te Aranga Māori Design Principles are intended to inform the design community how to incorporate Māori design thinking into design guidelines and are an effective tool for delivering on Māori design aspirations (Auckland Co-Design Lab, 2018).

The visibility of the Te Aranga Principles has been a significant step forward for Māori design, raising awareness of the relevance of Māori concepts to the

---

humans are part of the natural world.
56. The ethic of holistic hospitality whereby mana whenua have inherited obligations to be the best hosts they can be.
57. The immutable spiritual connection between people and their environments.
58. Explained as a relationship through shared experiences and working together which provides people with a sense of belonging.
59. A relationship through shared experiences and working together which provides people with a sense of belonging .
60. Explained as unity, cohesion and collaboration.
61. https://www.cityraillink.co.nz/.

---

53. https://www.nzia.co.nz/explore/te-kawenata-o-rata.
54. The right to exercise authority and self-determination within one's own iwi / hapū realm.
55. managing and conserving the environment as part of a reciprocal relationship, based on the Māori world view that we as

design process and the existence of a differing worldview from the prevailing paradigm. Clearly stating some simple culturally grounded concepts of the environment and community place within it, the *Te Aranga Principles* are a platform for understanding New Zealand identity, generating a sense of positive belonging, through clear sense of place.

4.4 Ngā Aho Kāhui Whetū

The Ngā Aho "Kahui Whetū"[62] were established at the inaugural international indigenous design forum, celebrating the considerable contribution, leadership, and excellence senior Māori design practitioners. To date these are: Jacob Scott, Carin Wilson, Ross Hemera, Alan Titchener[63], and Dr Diane Menzies. The name 'Kāhui Whetū' was gifted to Ngā Aho by our Kaumātua Haare Williams. The story of name (as related by Phil Wihongi of Te Tau a Nuku):

> To mark the ascension of Ngā Aho's Kahui Whetū, each new member will receive a tohu which has been named Whakaahu rangi by our beloved kaumātua, Haare Williams. Whakaahu rangi is the Māori name for one of the two main stars of the Gemini constellation. Kahui is the brighter of the two, however it is to Whakaahu rangi that we turn. Whakaahu rangi was the star that our tūpuna turned towards when faced with storm conditions. Whakaahu rangi is the ever-present marker that delivered our tūpuna to their destination Aotearoa, and which has delivered us to our destiny as tangata whenua here in Aotearoa (Wihongi, 2016).

The establishment of the Kāhui Whetū is a significant move forward for Ngā Aho, acknowledging the lifetime of leadership our senior practitioners have given to our design communities. The Kāhui are recognized not for a single project, but are awarded for a history, ongoing work, and demonstrable strength of kaupapa commitment to our Māori creative communities. Their leadership has enabled the growing body of Māori and indigenous designers we see making change in Aotearoa today.

> Their commitment to advancing kaupapa Māori design, to toi mahi, to the enhancement of Māori outcomes through engagement and design, backed up by their all-round taniwha-nacity is celebrated by us all tonight... (Wihongi, 2016)

> I just wanted to touch base about how humbled I was to receive the taonga pounamu at the Ngā Aho hui in February. It was a considerable honour and am very proud to have received such a prestigious acknowledgement. For me it means so much to be recognised by our wider whānau of Māori design professionals. And I have to say that one of the significant aspects to the award is the mana an esteem that it brings to the Ngā Aho as a network and as an organisation. So, this is just a short note to say how important such recognition is and the important role that Ngā Aho has taken on (Hemera, 2016).

RIMA (5) WHAKAHAERE KAUPAPA

Object: to do anything necessary or helpful to the ngā aho purposes.

At the forefront of design development in Māori cultural landscapes, is a steadily growing body of work focusing on the articulation of Māori values and methodologies that centre upon respectful, reciprocal and dynamic (rather than static) relationships. The basis of these is recognising, recording and understanding historical concepts of place.

> If society is truly to give effect to the promise of the Treaty of Waitangi to provide a secure place for Māori values within New Zealand society, then the commitment must be total. It must involve a real endeavour to understand what tikanga Māori is, how it is practiced and applied, and how integral it is to the social, economic, cultural, and political development of Māori, still encapsulated within a dominant culture in New Zealand society.

> However, it is critical that Māori also develop proposals which not only identify the differences between tikanga and the existing legal system, but also seek to find some common ground so that Māori development is not isolated from the rest of society" (Law Commission, 2001, p.95).

Treaty based relationships between Ngā Aho and other design industry bodies, developing methods of Indigenously grounded co-design, and *Te Aranga Principles* design guidelines are nurturing a dynamic approach to the development of cultural landscape in Aotearoa, New Zealand. The Ngā Aho "movement" illustrates the importance of networks and shared tools in enabling Indigenous practitioners to engage critically in designing our Indigenous futures.

---

62. Kāhui Whetū: (noun) constellation.
63. "We need to explore and recognize the essence of our respective cultures and find new ways of expressing them in the world we live in. Identifying, protecting and, where appropriate, restoring and rejuvenating our cultural landscapes is an essential part of this. The Asia Pacific is richly endowed with cultural landscapes of breathtaking beauty and profound sacredness. Landscape architects need to be at the forefront of these processes, working alongside historians and archaeologists to ensure that the past is recognized, valued and respected.... The lessons learned from these places also need to be applied to the ordinary places that we frequent." Alan Titchener, NZILA – AILA 50th World Congress in Auckland in 2013. https://nzila.co.nz/news/2017/04/alan-titchener.

Conclusion: Designing Māori and Indigenous Futures:

Maree Mills noted in her keynote address at Nā Te Kore, an overall sense of increased speed in change:

> In recent times, I have been confronted by speed, rather than slowing down, the years zip by faster and faster, bringing environmental, social and personal challenges alongside exponential change. I remind myself that Māori have survived a predicted demise and overcome what might have been insurmountable change over the last two centuries. We have adapted, reclaimed our languages, our education and research. Our indigenous knowledge is sought after to develop new foods and medicines. It is Māori art and design that represents our nation on the international stage. In many instances we have led the charge regarding sustainability and are to be found in all levels of leadership (Mills, 2018).

As we move into the new decade, our members are now looking to broader horizons more frequently through our international networks. In the face of climate crises, the need to weave our Indigenous skills and realities across waters, becomes increasingly urgent.

> To weave established indigenous (design) communities from key regions to lead a truly authentic global initiative, creating a self-sovereign International Indigenous Design Circle flowing across international waters without colonial or political boundaries; its highest purpose toward becoming the guardians of mother earth's codes of visual, tangible and intangible knowledge (Larios, Wilson, & Whaanga-Schollum, 2019).

The future potential that sits in the weaving of our Indigenous design communities looks to continue to seek to address kaupapa such as Indigenous design/creative activists' response to climate change; diversity in design/creative leadership; building capacity and accessibility in design; connecting with colonized, and frequently under-represented peoples and places.

Significantly, our designers recognise the environment as an active living entity within design and creative practices, as is commensurate with Indigenous ways-of-being. In doing so we recognize our roles and responsibilities as kaitiaki for future generations.

Works Cited

(n.d.). Retrieved from https://maoridictionary.co.nz/

Allan, P., & Smith, H. (2013, Dec). "Research at the Interface. Bi-cultural studio in New Zealand, a case study." *MAI Journal, 2*(2), p.133-149.

Auckland Co-Design Lab. (2018, May). *Policy by Design: Exploring the intersection of design & policy in Aotearoa NZ: 7 case studies.* Retrieved from Auckland Co-Design Lab: https://static1.squarespace.com/static/55ac5ee5e4b08d4c25220f4b/t/5c58b602ec212da21e45a72a/1549317656958/Policy+by+Design+-+7+cases+studies+from+Aotearoa+NZ.pdf.

Auckland Council. (2015). *About the ADM.* Retrieved Sep 2105, from Auckland Design Manual: www.aucklanddesignmanual.co.nz

Auckland Council and Ngā Aho Inc Soc. (2014). *Te Aranga Principles.* Retrieved Sep 2015, from Auckland Design Manual: www.aucklanddesignmanual.co.nz

Auckland Council, Ngā Aho. (2015, Oct). Mana Whenua Co-Design Wānanga. *Wānanga notes.* Auckland, NZ: Unpublished.

Awatoru Project. (2008, September 04). Seeing our faces in our places - national hui. *Seeing our faces in our places – hui programme.* Tapu Te Ranga Marae. Wellington.

Blackhurst, M. D. (2003). *Iwi interests and the RMA: An evaluation of iwi and hapū participation in the resource consents processes of six district councils.* Hamilton, NZ: The International Global Change Institute, University of Waikato.

Designers Institute of NZ. (2015). Ngā Aho Award – sponsorship. Auckland, NZ: Unpublished.

Hemera, R. (2016). *Private correspondence – email to Ngā Aho Inc Soc.*

Heta, E., & Kake, J. (2018, August 3). Retrieved from Indigenous Urbanism: https://indigenousurbanism.simplecast.com/episodes/in-conversation-with-elisapeta-heta.

Kiddle, R. (2016). I Te Timatanga. Ngāti Porou, Ngāpuhi. New Zealand.

Laotan-Brown, T. (2016). I Te Timatanga. Nigeria.

Larios, F., Wilson, C., & Whaanga-Schollum, D. (2019, December 02). Invitation. *INDIGO – International Indigenous Design Circle.* Vancouver, Canada.

Law Commission. (2001, March). Māori Custom And Values In New Zealand Law. *Study Paper, NZLC SP9.* Wellington: Law Commission.

Livesey, B. (2015). A collection of words to use with each other – wānanga reflections. *Unfolding Kaitiakitanga. Shifting the insitutional space with biculturalism.* Auckland: ST PAUL St Publishing, Aut University.

Malin, N. (2005). The Mindset Thing: Exploring the Deeper Potential of Integrated Design . In *Environmental Building News* (Vol. 12). Building Green, Inc.

Maori Dictionary. (n.d.). Retrieved from https://maoridictionary.co.nz/.

Maori Dictionary. (n.d.). Retrieved from https://maoridictionary.co.nz/.

Matunga, H. (2018, March 3). A Discourse on the Nature of Indigenous Design. *Nā Te Kore*. Ōtautahi, Christchurch.

Menzies, D. D. (2015). East-West: Driving integration and innovation in Landscape Architecture. *52nd World Congress of the International Federation of Landscape Architects Congress proceedings.* Saint-Petersburg, Russia: Unpublished.

Mills, M. (2018, March 3). *E Rere Ana I Te Hau Tere - Riding the Wind Fast*. Retrieved from Nā Te Kore: https://www.natekore2018.com/keynotes/maree-mills-87yym-fzwxx.

Ngā Aho. (2006). Retrieved from http://www.ngaaho.maori.nz/.

Ngā Aho Inc. (2014, Nov). Urban Mauri Co-Design Wānanga. Auckland.

Ngā Aho Inc, Designers Institute of NZ. (2012). Ngā Aho Best Award parameters. Auckland, NZ.

Ngā Aho Inc, NZILA. (2015, March 18). Memorandum of Understanding. NZ: Unpublished.

NZIA. (2017, February). Retrieved from NZIA: https://www.nzia.co.nz/explore/news/2017/new-zealand-institute-of-architects-and-ng%C4%81-aho-sign-te-kawenata-o-rata

Proposed National Policy Statement on Urban Design – Hui Response. (2008, September 29). *Submission to: Ministry for the Environment. Te Manatu Taiao*.

Scott, J. (2007, August 21). *NOTES FROM BRAND TEAM MEETING*. Auckland, Awataha Marae.

Sowers, J., & Seamon, D. (2008). In R. K. P. Hubbard, *Key Texts in Human Geography* (pp. 43-51). London: Sage.

Stewart, P. (2016). I Te Timatanga. Nisga'a. Canada.

Tau, T. M., Ormsby, D., Manthei, M., & Potiki, T. (2003). *Treaty-based guidelines and protocols: For Tertiary Education institutes.* Dunedin, Otago, NZ: Te Tapuāe o Rehua Ltd; University of Otago Press.

Te Aranga. (n.d.). Retrieved from http://www.tearanga.maori.nz/cms/resources/TeArangaStrategy28Apr08_lr.pdf.

Te Tau-a-Nuku, Ngā Aho. (2014, Aug 11). NZILA Education Policy and Accreditation Policy Review. NZ.

Whaanga-Schollum, D. (2007, August 7). *NOTES FROM BRAND TEAM MEETING*. Auckland.

Whaanga-Schollum, D. (2007, August 21). *Notes from Brand Team Meeting*. Auckland, Awataha Marae.

Whaanga-Schollum, D., Robinson, C., Stuart, K., & Livesey, B. (2014, Nov 10). Urban Mauri Wānanga. Auckland, NewZealand: Ngā Aho, Unpublished.

Whaanga-Schollum, D., Robinson, C., Stuart, K., & Livesey, B. (2015). *Regenerating Urban Mauri*. (L. Foundation, Producer) Retrieved 2015, from Landscape Foundation Journal: http://www.landscape.org.nz/regenerating-urban-mauri.html.

Wihongi, P. (2016, February). *I Te Timatanga - International Indigenous Design Forum*.

Wilson, A. (2007, August 21). *Notes from Brand Team Meeting*. Auckland, Awataha Marae.

Wilson, C. (2007, August 21). *Notes from Brand Team Meeting*. Auckland, Awataha Marae.

Wixon, K., Wilson, C., Scott, J., Hoskins, R., Mills, M., Titchener, A., . . . Wilson, A. (2007, June 11). *Network Entity Establishment Proposal.* Aotearoa, New Zealand.

Chapter 4.4: Developing Indigenous design principles – Lessons from Aotearoa

Edited by Jade Kake – Ngāpuhi, Te Arawa, Te Whakatōhea and Jacqueline Paul – Ngāpuhi, Ngāti Tūwharetoa, Ngāti Kahungunu ki Heretaunga

Jade Kake is a designer and writer. Her practice supports Māori communities and organisations to develop marae and papakāinga projects, and to express their cultural values and narratives within the public realm through urban design, landscape, and architecture. She lives and works in Whangārei.

Jacqueline Paul
Māori Landscape Architect, Lecturer at the School of Architecture and Researcher at Ngā Wai a Te Tūi Māori and Indigenous Research Centre at Unitec. Key research interests focusing on building better homes towns and communities, Māori housing, mobilizing rangatahi and Māori voices, transformative policies, improving architecture and urban planning.

Introduction

Over the past decade or so, Māori-built environment practitioners in collaboration with Tāmaki Makaurau (Auckland) mana whenua have developed the Te Aranga principles – a set of seven outcome-based Māori urban design principles founded on core Māori cultural and spiritual values. The principles have arisen from a widely held desire to enhance mana whenua presence, visibility and participation in the design of the physical environment, and to assist mana whenua to engage in urban design along with architecture within their local rohe in a meaningful way. Underpinning the principles from inception has been the intention for the principles to be flexible and adaptive. With widespread interest in the Te Aranga principles, growing both within New Zealand and internationally, there is a need to tell the story of their development.

This chapter seeks to draw on a diverse range of voices to reflect on the evolution of the Te Aranga principles (starting with the development of the Te Aranga strategy in 2006), to reviewing work completed on early projects (in collaboration between Māori designers and mana whenua in Tāmaki Makaurau), through to their subsequent adoption and greater integration into Auckland Council policies, plans, and processes. We will review their later application to major urban projects across both the public and private sector in Tāmaki

Makaurau. We will then identify alternative approaches developed in other regions. Finally, we will discuss some of the ongoing challenges and opportunities to their implementation and consider strategies to evolve and extend their scope to integrate and encourage sustainable cultural design practises.

Background – Development of the Te Aranga Māori Cultural Landscape Strategy and the Emergence of the Te Aranga Principles

Rau Hoskins, nō Ngāti Hau, is the co-author of the Te Aranga Māori urban design principles and a pivotal figure in the development and application of the principles in Tāmaki Makaurau.

Rau Hoskins: Nō Whakapara marae, Ngāti Hau, Ngāpuhi. Whangaruru te moana, Whakapara te awa, Huruiki te maunga. Tū i te pō, tū i te ao.

Jade Kake: What was the driver behind the emergence of these principles? Where did they come from?

RH: So, in 2005 we had the urban design protocol released by the Ministry for the Environment (MfE), and they had developed this protocol with its seven C's. Interestingly, none of those C's were culture. Wayne Knox who was then working for Te Puni Kōkiri, approached me and said, would I like to comment on this, or think about how Māori design professionals might wish to respond to this. And I think MfE was thinking that we might become a chapter in their protocol. I organised a hui in Waitakere City, in July of 2006, and then a larger hui in Te Aranga marae in Flaxmere November of 2006, and we collectively developed the Te Aranga Māori cultural landscape design strategy. Now that was then, that strategy document was then taken around the motu and given good support. But what was effectively missing from that strategy was a concise set of principles which would inform the engagement of landowning groups – mainly local government, central government, hapū/iwi, and their design experts. So, that's really where the Te Aranga principles came from. They came from a distillation of the Te Aranga Māori cultural landscape design strategy, but the desire to have a tool which could be readily communicated to user groups, and readily adopted.

I began developing the principles where there were four principles, and I remember going to a conference in Christchurch well before the earthquakes, and effectively the theme of my presentation was: What makes a difference to Māori in the built environment, or the urban environment? There were four principles: What we did, working with mana whenua, from 2012 onwards, 2012-2014, on some Auckland Transport projects, including CRL, was to say start with those four principles and then to work with them to look for a) the application of those principles, but b) the extension of the principles, and we actually did arrive at seven. With the last principle being the ahi kā principle, which really talks about that living presence, and that last principle came last, and it came from a reflection on some other projects, saying well okay, we've got good outcomes in all these other areas, but if iwi aren't naturally using those spaces, making them their own on a day to day basis, then we actually can't call that a truly successful project.

From 2006 through 2014, we began to anchor the principles and then get them adopted within the Auckland Design Manual. There were quite a few twists and turns along the way. It also came from the former Auckland Council urban design framework, which had five principles. They only had four to begin with, which from memory they were: a green city, a beautiful city, a connected city, and a compact city. I managed to add the fifth principle, which was: a distinctive city. And by adding the distinctive term, I was really saying, well, the distinction is actually mana whenua. At that time, between 2006-2007, it wasn't politically tenable to overtly talk about Māori things and expect them to get through the processes that existed at that time.

Auckland Design Office advocacy – integration of the principles into Te Kaunihera o Tāmaki Makaurau / Auckland Council policy, plans and processes

Auckland Design Office advocacy

In 2013, Ngā Aho worked alongside Auckland Council to develop a Te Aranga business case. The business case provided a set of strategies for embedding the Te Aranga principles within Auckland Council policy and processes.

Carin Wilson, a Ngāti Awa artist, designer and craftsperson with studios in Te Tai Tokerau and Tāmaki Makaurau, has been another leading figure within Ngā Aho who has contributed to the development and implementation of the principles.

Figure 1. Hui at Apumoana 2007 (Photo credit: Carin Wilson).

Figure 2. Hui at Rongopai 2010 (Photo credit: Carin Wilson).

Carin Wilson: Ko Pūtauaki te maunga, Ko Mātaatua te waka, Ngāti Awa te iwi, Ko Te Awa o Te Atua te awa, Ko Moutohorā te motu, Ko Te Rangihouhiri te hapū, Ko Tiaki Mahiti Wirihana or Wilson tōku papa, Ko Nina Estarina Bianca di Solma tōku mama, Ko Carin Wilson ahau.

JK: What are some of the positive changes and challenges you see currently, in terms of integrating Māori cultural values and narratives into the built environment?

CW: I guess the obvious one is the Te Aranga principles, and the way those principles have been adopted by the new Auckland Council. So, that journey I think, for us as Māori working in the design world, has been one of the most important journeys that we've travelled in my time as an artist and designer. To have a city respond in the way that it has, to principles like those seven Te Aranga principles, has been amazing. To have that conversation facilitated by the Independent Māori Statutory Board, in the way that it has, has been equally important, and now, we're moving at a pace that we've never seen before, around achievement of those principles of participation in the development of this society, as Māori. There is iwi consultation happening at a level that I haven't seen it happening before. Decisions aren't made without at least an informing discussion with iwi, and if it's taken a step further, then we even go to generating an opportunity for participation. In other words, it's not just a token dialogue, the dialogue has progressed to one where there's the opportunity for actual engagement.

If we now were able to document or charter – and nobody has done it yet – but every single project in the city, and the level at which there's integration of concepts, imagery, there's been a narrative happening in the background. It's huge. It's like an explosion. It's not like, well, this is ten times what it was ten years ago. It's like fifty times. Comprehensive change.

JK: You know, it was pretty amazing for me way back in 2013 when we had all of those meetings with the Auckland Design Office, and to be working with you on that along with Rau. I don't think that I, at that time, could have anticipated... well the contribution that many of us have made, but the impact that that would have now, years later. I really liked hearing you say that it was one of the most important things, because for me, I think it might be the most important thing I've done so far, to be someone who's contributed to that. Because it's had a huge impact. Talk me through it – how did this come about? What were the steps that led to Ngā Aho and Auckland Council working together to develop a Te Aranga business case?

CW: It was largely driven by Council's way of doing these things, but my recollection is that we were advised that to get something heard, we needed to produce a business case. At that time, I was running around individual departments trying to get commitment to the allocation of funds, so that we could put the pātaka (a toolkit of Māori design resources) together. What I'd seen was that there wasn't much inter-departmental communication going on. Auckland Council was established in 2011, and it went going through this long-winded process of developing the Auckland Plan, and we were getting drip-fed bits of information that were coming to light as the assembly of that plan came together. And it really was a long and protracted engagement with questions about what do we want this city to be, now that we have seven local and one regional council all wrapped up as one?

JK: And keeping in mind that the different legacy councils were in different spaces and further progressed with this kind of work, others less so.

CW: They were all in different spaces, and Manukau in particular had the best grasp of how to engage with tangata whenua. They had good relationships with tangata whenua in their rohe, and I think that the opportunities for community feedback into the Council were quite fluid. The route map for community to contact the Council was also reasonably well-established with Manukau. Waitakere also, most likely. North Shore would probably have been at the bottom of the list at that time – both in terms of communication with tangata whenua, and the understanding of who tangata whenua were on the North Shore. So we knew that we had to work within a new framework, and to ensure that the valuable relationships that had been generated in Manukau and Waitakere, and the supportive environment that Māori were working in there, transferred across. And what we began to see was that the best way to achieve that was to strongly advocate for a Māori voice as the Auckland Plan (Auckland's primary long-term high-level planning, and strategic document, the production of which is required by legislation) came together.

At that time, there were Māori interests on one side, and Council processes on the other, and those lines of sight didn't even exist. Māori were busy articulating their value and priorities, and Council meanwhile was just going through its regular routine, and they weren't connecting. But, what we saw, was that there were obligations to local bodies. So all the time we were learning as well. We saw those obligations to local government, to engage in these questions, were being ignored, or certainly being overlooked. The Independent Māori Statutory Board was established in 2009 to represent Māori interests in Auckland following the amalgamation. Early on, the Independent Māori Statutory Board were moving strategically to call for the Te Tiriti o Waitangi audits, of which the PricewaterhouseCoopers audit in 2011 was the first. They were actively looking for external feedback on how well Council was performing and hearing the voice of its tangata whenua constituents. I've been through quite a lot of the documentation from Māori interests pre-2011 and they're quite well articulated. Here's the thing - Māori knew what they wanted and needed, but as the audits revealed, they were just not finding access within Council to have those concerns heard.

Once Brandi Hudson was appointed to the role of CEO of the Independent Māori Statutory Board then we had a point through which we could – instead of having to talk with all of the disparate Council-Controlled Organisations (CCOs) and departments in Auckland we could bring these questions to Independent Māori Statutory Board and then use or allow the Independent Māori Statutory Board to make our voice heard in the overall context of the Council. One of the things that Brandi and I devised as part of our strategy was to generate a presentation that asked, what would Auckland look like if Māori were isible in the planned development of Auckland City? And his was also a way for the Independent Māori Statutory Board and Brandi to say to key people in the Council, his is what we're here for, this is the interest group hat we represent, and this is the kind of work that you an expect to see us engage in, and you'll be hearing rom us again in future. So, together we generated this resentation which we co-presented in December 2012, oon after the amalgamation of the Councils. A lot of ouncil-controlled organisation chief executives were n the room, and a lot of developer interests and so n, and we painted this picture. It's from there that we hen started to develop a really active dialogue with the ndependent Māori Statutory Board and expressed to hem what we saw were shortcomings in process and ngagement.

K: So we're at the point where we've been working longside the Independent Māori Statutory Board on this ātaka proposal. How did that proceed to the meetings hat we had with the department within council – I don't now if it was called the Auckland Design Office by then r maybe that was its later name – but how did that evelop?

W: It was before the establishment of the Auckland Design Office. There was an amalgamated group of esign capacity among all seven Councils, and it was ecided that that would all be assembled around the North Shore offices. It was just convenient - the individual Councils all had these commitments to premises, and efore they could bring everybody together in one place, hey were still occupying those premises. So, again hrough the dialogues with Brandi and Independent Māori Statutory Board, an opportunity came up around commentary on a new streetscape for Hurstmere Road n Takapuna, to go into the offices of the predecessor to he Auckland Design Office and talk with the team there. hey were anxious that they should begin to establish a rocess whereby at least a Māori contribution could be nade to that planning process, and The Hurstmere Road treetscape was the first. Inevitably, because they all at together in the same offices, and we were agitating or integration of the Te Aranga principles, through that roject, that it then led to a progression at a wider level.

K: I think that maybe it all started with getting the Te ranga principles on the Auckland Design Manual, which hey were developing at that time. And then, once that vas in place, we said well actually, we've got some nore ideas about how you might really integrate these rinciples into what you're doing, into your policy and rocess.

W: Even today, I see the enabling of our contribution to he Auckland Design Manual was a roundabout response o our call for the pātaka to be funded one way or another

Figure 3. Hui at Rongopai 2010 (Photo credit: Carin Wilson).

as a kind of design manual for use right through the organisation. Having hit walls around securing direct funding, the people that we were talking to in Auckland Council said well, let's try going about this in a different way. We'll create a business case, and we'll see if we can get the funding to you that way. So I guess we could acknowledge that they were trying to support us.

JK: I remember when the business case we produced was not accepted into the long-term plan, and I felt terribly disappointed, because I thought well what the heck, we've spent all this time and energy just for someone at some level to go, nope. But actually, everything that was in there has happened since then. Although the business case wasn't adopted through the Long-term Plan process at that time, it has informed a number of work programmes within Auckland Council, including the establishment of a Senior Māori Design specialist role within the Auckland Design Office, formation of a mana whenua steering group for the Māori Design Hub within the Auckland Design Manual, Ngā Aho (Māori design) appointments to the Auckland Urban Design Panel, and cultural competency training to upskill Auckland Urban Design Panel members. So now I go, "Well okay, it definitely wasn't a waste because they ran with the idea." That's a bit of hindsight, I guess.

CW: Yeah. And thank you, thank you for the opportunity to work on it together with you, because I really enjoyed that time we were working together, bringing that stuff to some sort of form that we could have other people understand it.

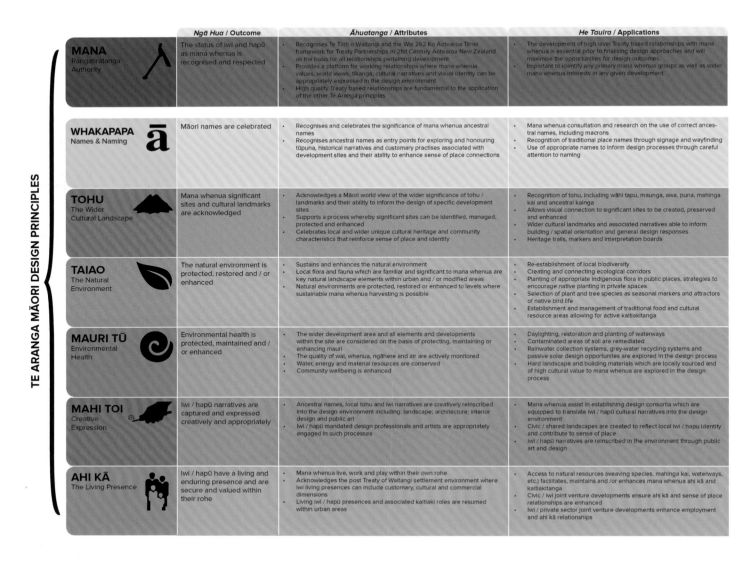

TE ARANGA MĀORI DESIGN PRINCIPLES

	Ngā Hua / Outcome	**Āhuatanga / Attributes**	**He Tauira / Applications**
MANA Rangatiratanga Authority	The status of iwi and hapū as mana whenua is recognised and respected	• Recognises Te Tiriti o Waitangi and the Wai 262 Ko Aotearoa Tēnei framework for Treaty Partnerships in 21st Century Aotearoa New Zealand as the basis for all relationships pertaining development • Provides a platform for working relationships where mana whenua values, world views, tikanga, cultural narratives and visual identity can be appropriately expressed in the design environment • High quality Treaty based relationships are fundamental to the application of the other Te Aranga principles	• The development of high level Treaty based relationships with mana whenua is essential prior to finalising design approaches and will maximise the opportunities for design outcomes. • Important to identify any primary mana whenua groups as well as wider mana whenua interests in any given development.
WHAKAPAPA Names & Naming	Māori names are celebrated	• Recognises and celebrates the significance of mana whenua ancestral names • Recognises ancestral names as entry points for exploring and honouring tūpuna, historical narratives and customary practises associated with development sites and their ability to enhance sense of place connections	• Mana whenua consultation and research on the use of correct ancestral names, including macrons • Recognition of traditional place names through signage and wayfinding • Use of appropriate names to inform design processes through careful attention to naming
TOHU The Wider Cultural Landscape	Mana whenua significant sites and cultural landmarks are acknowledged	• Acknowledges a Māori world view of the wider significance of tohu / landmarks and their ability to inform the design of specific development sites • Supports a process whereby significant sites can be identified, managed, protected and enhanced • Celebrates local and wider unique cultural heritage and community characteristics that reinforce sense of place and identity	• Recognition of tohu, including wāhi tapu, maunga, awa, puna, mahinga kai and ancestral kainga • Allows visual connection to significant sites to be created, preserved and enhanced • Wider cultural landmarks and associated narratives able to inform building / spatial orientation and general design responses • Heritage trails, markers and interpretation boards
TAIAO The Natural Environment	The natural environment is protected, restored and / or enhanced	• Sustains and enhances the natural environment • Local flora and fauna which are familiar and significant to mana whenua are key natural landscape elements within urban and / or modified areas • Natural environments are protected, restored or enhanced to levels where sustainable mana whenua harvesting is possible	• Re-establishment of local biodiversity • Creating and connecting ecological corridors • Planting of appropriate indigenous flora in public places, strategies to encourage native planting in private spaces • Selection of plant and tree species as seasonal markers and attractors of native bird life • Establishment and management of traditional food and cultural resource areas allowing for active kaitiakitanga
MAURI TŪ Environmental Health	Environmental health is protected, maintained and / or enhanced	• The wider development area and all elements and developments within the site are considered on the basis of protecting, maintaining or enhancing mauri • The quality of wai, whenua, ngāhere and air are actively monitored • Water, energy and material resources are conserved • Community wellbeing is enhanced	• Daylighting, restoration and planting of waterways • Contaminated areas of soil are remediated • Rainwater collection systems, grey-water recycling systems and passive solar design opportunites are explored in the design process • Hard landscape and building materials which are locally sourced and of high cultural value to mana whenua are explored in the design process
MAHI TOI Creative Expression	Iwi / hapū narratives are captured and expressed creatively and appropriately	• Ancestral names, local tohu and iwi narratives are creatively reinscribed into the design environment including: landscape; architecture; interior design and public art • Iwi / hapū mandated design professionals and artists are appropriately engaged in such processes	• Mana whenua assist in establishing design consortia which are equipped to translate iwi / hapū cultural narratives into the design environment • Civic / shared landscapes are created to reflect local iwi / hapū identity and contribute to sense of place • Iwi / hapū narratives are reinscribed in the environment through public art and design
AHI KĀ The Living Presence	Iwi / hapū have a living and enduring presence and are secure and valued within their rohe	• Mana whenua live, work and play within their own rohe • Acknowledges the post Treaty of Waitangi settlement environment where iwi living presences can include customary, cultural and commercial dimensions • Living iwi / hapū presences and associated kaitiaki roles are resumed within urban areas	• Access to natural resources (weaving species, mahinga kai, waterways, etc.) facilitates, maintains and /or enhances mana whenua ahi kā and kaitiakitanga • Civic / iwi joint venture developments ensure ahi kā and sense of place relationships are enhanced • Iwi / private sector joint venture developments enhance employment and ahi kā relationships

Figure 4. Te Aranga Māori Design Principles - outcome, attributes, and applications (Image credit: Jade Kake, Rau Hoskins).

A Māori Design Leader role within Auckland Council

Phil Wihongi, nō Ngāti Hine, is a roof tiler, landscape architect and planner and was appointed to the role of Māori Design Leader within Auckland Council in 2016.
Phil Wihongi: Ko Hikurangi te maunga, Ngātokimatawhaorua te waka, Ngāpuhi me Ngāti Hine ngā iwi, Kawiti Te Ruki te tangata, Motatau te marae, Ngāti Te Tarawa te hapū. Ko Phil Wihongi tāku ingoa. Kia ora.

One of the main kaupapa that Council's Māori Design programme leans on is the concept of moving from Auckland to Tāmaki Makaurau, a concept that is beginning to be picked up by the local design industry. We all know what Auckland is and the urban form that has developed. Most of us aren't happy with what is essentially a mash-up of post-colonial, Anglo-settler traditions heavily garnished by globalisation which hasn't listened particularly well to our founding culture or to natural systems: to here. The flip is that nobody knows what Tāmaki Makaurau is or what that looks like in a contemporary sense. Implicit in the name however is that unlike as Auckland's history tells us, Mana Whenua are present and flourishing, Māori culture is strongly present, and this is manifest in our urban form, function and cadence. It gives us something to aim towards and to work together to figure out. In short, exciting!

The Te Aranga principles are definitely the pre-eminent Māori design tool in use across Council. It's a tool that is very familiar to Mana Whenua, and there's a degree of comfort and understanding that Mana Whenua have in the application of the principles. So, the principles are very useful, but as we hear regularly from our Mana

Whenua partners, are only one tool. The intent of the principles when they were developed from the Te Aranga strategy here was that they would be further refined with Mana Whenua groups to access a finer grain of detail and nuance and specificity based on the takiwā that they would be applied within. This is something we're continuing to work towards, but in the meantime the principles are an effective placeholder which has delivered a range of interesting outcomes within our built environment.

Through Council projects, we are in a position, and I would argue that we have a responsibility to Mana Whenua and broader Māori communities that we incorporate the principles within our project works. Alongside the need to bring Mana Whenua closer to help shape public developments, a core rationale is that through public development Council is able to demonstrate very clearly what the outcomes of applying the principles are, and to highlight processes have been developed and applied in project delivery. Doing this offers tangible precedent and outcomes for the private development sector to be able to pick up and run with, on their terms within their developments.

The most visible private development to incorporate the principles to date has been Commercial Bay, a full downtown block development right on the waterfront. The developers went through a lengthy and robust engagement process with Mana Whenua facilitated by one of our leading Māori designers, which has resulted in a number of outcomes that speak clearly to the influence of this engagement. That development is the private development exemplar that we have currently, and we are looking at how we can incentivise uptake of the principles as a design engagement tool for the private development sector.

We currently have a significant programme of works on the waterfront where we have introduced new ways of "doing" things. All of the innovation we are trying out aims to considerably raise expectations from a Māori design perspective. The aspiration for that programme is it will result in a thicker, deeper expression of what a Māori identity for Tāmaki Makaurau might be, worked through the mana whenua design partnership approach that the programme has adopted. This is an indication of thinking, processes and relationships maturing – progress.

Promoting outcomes that result in mana then is a focus. A very dear colleague has helpfully made me aware of a kōrero provided by Ngāpuhi tohunga Reverend Māori Marsden, which describes mana as the delicate balance of power and authority. A traditional function that occurred was that of takawaengatanga, effectively an emissary or broker role between groups coming together to try to ensure that all was in place to make the most of the opportunity presented by the groups coming together. A conscious effort to try to balance the power and authority of those coming together to benefit the kaupapa in common focus in order to generate outcomes of mana.

What has become apparent through tenure in my role is that there are similarities to that traditional takawaenga role. In a contemporary sense it is working to negotiate the power that well-resourced groups like local and central government and the design industry hold, with the authority of the whenua that mana whenua hold – in the pursuit of promoting outcomes that result in mana. So that's where a lot of our work actually occurs, in the bridging between cultures, in the bridging between groups.

Experience highlights that by working collaboratively across sectors, behaviour-based matters can begin to be resolved in shorter time frames. However, if we are to address broader issues of power, authority, capability, and capacity, these will require longer build periods, and the application of commitment and investment across sectors.

But we're moving. Steadily. Relentlessly. Towards Tāmaki Makaurau.

Auckland Urban Design Panel

The Auckland Urban Design Panel was established in 2003 to provide independent design review of significant projects across the Auckland region. Recent appointments have strengthened Māori representation on the panel, and Māori design training has been offered to support and upskill panellists.

Rau Hoskins shared his insights into the use of the Auckland Urban Design Panel as a mechanism to ensure better integration of Te Aranga principles.

Jade Kake: Rau, you're on the Auckland Urban Design Panel, have you found that to be a useful mechanism to support the quality integration of Te Aranga principles into projects?

Rau Hoskins: I think one of the issues is that we've got over 40 panellists and five or six Māori panellists (there used to be just one or two). We've had a few more added recently which has been really good. The challenge has been that you're only considered on so many panels, and you're only invited to sit on so many panels, and from my perspective each panel would benefit from somebody who is proficient with the application of those principles. So there's an issue around capacity, and there's an issue around the allocation of projects and allocation of roles on various panels that I think needs further work.

The urban design panel gets to see a project when it's just prior to resource consent, so there's a lot of work that's gone on prior, so it's a little bit ambulance at the bottom of the cliff, in a way, because you can certainly express concern or give directive in terms of engagement, but if there is an issue, it'll only be retrospectively corrected, which is not ideal for trying to establish a relationship with a mana whenua group, for instance, where you have to say, well, by the way we're this far down a track, and we've been told to come and see you, or it's been suggested that we should come and see you. So that's not ideal.

The urban design panel is a check, and a guide, but ideally there would be better guidance at the outset of each of these projects. For instance, there was a requirement for a pre-briefing with the appointed designers and/or developers to say, "Okay, before you even begin, let's have a conversation around a whole lot of compliance issues," not least of all which includes the Te Aranga principles and engagement with mana whenua.

JK: I guess the more that these firms – and a lot of them would be the same ones – if they start engaging in this way, then they'll know next time that that's the right point to engage for better outcomes.

RH: It's fair to say that the larger urban design, landscape, and architecture firms are all reasonably au fait with Te Aranga now and are reasonably competent at applying the principles or ensuring that they develop the working relationships necessary to apply the principles, that has been very helpful.

Further Development of The Principles through Key Projects in Tāmaki Makaurau Auckland

Development of the principles through projects – a practitioner perspective

Rau Hoskins has been involved in a number of significant infrastructure projects in Tāmaki Makaurau, which have been critical to the development and application of the principles. We asked him to discuss the City Rail Link and Commercial Bay projects in the downtown Tāmaki Makaurau.

JK: You've been involved in the City Rail Link (CRL) project, which has been going on for quite a long time in terms of planning and is under construction now. So, what was the process like? How have the Te Aranga principles, or how will the principles be manifest in the physical environment upon completion?

RH: Well, I was brought onboard by Jasmax at the time, and Jasmax were successful in being appointed as the urban designers who were developing the urban design framework for the CRL. So effectively that was looking at all of the different station environments and routes, applying a framework to the Notice of Requirement (NOR) – which is effectively the use of the Public Works Act to compulsorily acquire the land for the CRL. So we managed to write the Te Aranga principles into that urban design framework. From there, I was separately

engaged directly by Auckland Transport, and then CRL, to work directly with mana whenua in an ongoing capacity to apply the Te Aranga principles to each of the station environments.

So that's been about an 18-month process, and we are probably coming to the tail-end of that now. And so we've been working with six or seven mana whenua groups meeting weekly or fortnightly, and responding and giving input to design coming through from the architects on the station environments and public shared landscape environments in proximity to the station environments. So, for instance, the Waitematā station, which is an extension of the current Britomart station, has significant number of above ground environments that are being developed alongside the CRL, so we have Lower Queen St, and we have some work on up Albert St, and so on and so forth. So, there's a range of different above and below ground environments where mana whenua are having direct input into the design themes and the design responses for those station environments. That has been a really important project to really ground the principles.

The Britomart / Waitematā station is closely intertwined with the Commercial Bay development, and the Commercial Bay development has been designed to respond directly to the tunnels beneath it, that go up Albert St. Part of the requirement for them purchasing that piece of QEII Square in Lower Queen St, was that they were required to apply the Te Aranga design principles. I've also worked in a similar way, working between the architects and landscape architects - that's Warren and Mahoney and LandLAB – with a similar group of mana whenua representatives. And so, it's been useful to be working in contiguous design locations and being able to respond to narratives which have been applied in one area, and how they may be appropriately reflected in a neighbouring environment.

I guess the other key location that the principles have been applied is in the Wynyard Quarter. So those principles through Waterfront Auckland and then Panuku have been applied across six or seven different urban design projects in that area, including on private developments; medium density housing, retrofitting of heritage buildings, park landscapes, hotel frontages and so on.

One more project which I think has been pretty successful has been the Ōtāhuhu bus route interchange, and that was an opportunity to try and bring iwi and the design group together – primarily Jasmax - and to help refine and guide that design process and design outcomes, to make sure that mana whenua culture narratives were privileged, that they were identifiable, that they were faithfully represented in the built environment there, and also that their artists were directly involved in the design of various elements and treatments.

JK: Māori are so often categorised as being rural, or have been for a long time, Māori spaces are the marae and papakāinga on our ancestral land, and absolutely those places are very important for our identity and for our culture and for our social structures, but the reality is that in this day and age, the majority of Māori now live in urban environments, and they often live away from their ancestral areas. For those of us who are living outside our ancestral rohe, how do we conceive of ourselves as urban people, and how do we as Māori designers work effectively in spaces where we do not hold mana whenua status?

RH: I think it's an interesting perspective, and if you say, "Okay, 88% of Māori are urbanised, and in Tāmaki, 85% of Māori are not from Tāmaki," so only 15% are actually from here. I've argued in the past, and still strongly believe, that mataawaka sense of place, in urban environments that are obviously not their own, is via the cultural lens of mana whenua. I think the more familiar you are with where you are from, the more likely you are to want to make sure that local mana whenua cultural histories are strongly represented, as you would hope yours would be back home. There's often a question: what about mataawaka identity? How do you allow for their aspirations and needs in the built environment? And that's my answer. So, if you are privileging their aspirations separate to mana whenua, then you are recolonising that environment.

Development of the principles through projects – a mana whenua perspective

In recent years, mana whenua participation in development has increased exponentially. Tools like Te Aranga have supported mana whenua to work collaboratively as part of project teams to creatively reinterpret their own narratives and histories, and to apply these to the construction of new buildings and landscapes.

Lucy Tukua, nō Ngāti Paoa raua ko Ngāti Whanaunga, has been a driving force behind the application of the principles from a mana whenua perspective.

Lucy Tukua: Tēnā tatou katoa, i tū ana, maua i runga i te maunga a Maungarei, te tihi maunga o Tāmaki Makaurau. E whariki nei, ngā maunga e maha, ngā maunga i rongonui o Tāmaki, i te taha nei, ko te Wai-o-Taiki, e rere atu ra ki te Waitematā. Āe, me mihi hoki ki ngā tangata ngā tūpuna, ngā wāhi tapu, kei waenganui. He uri o hau o Ngāti Paoa, Ngāti Whanaunga. I noho ana au e Papakura. Ko Lucy Tukua ahau.

In my capacity as the Environment Manager for Ngāti Paoa I was involved in the Panmure Station quite closely,

and the mana whenua that were involved on the project basically supported Ngāti Paoa being the lead on this particular project. And because of our close association to this area, and the pā site being a Km up the road, down to the mouth of the lagoon, we were able to work closely alongside Auckland Transport.

In terms of the biodiversity and those environmental taiao matters, mana whenua have been really strong advocates in terms of returning native plantings where possible. So, nine times out of ten, with developments and stuff that are going on, it's always going to be kind of, it's a standard now, which is really cool. And also, in terms of how do we green up this infrastructure? So, there's plantings up the side of the wall. So that's been really good.

One of the things for Auckland Transport is really around the maintenance, and the stuff that you can't see. Where are all the heavy metals going? That kind of stuff, and so mana whenua are always happy to push those boundaries. So, where you have the various standards in Council, mana whenua are always saying to the likes of Auckland Transport and others, we actually don't like the standards, we actually want you to do better.

The Panmure Station was kind of the first part, and now the work that's happening with that particular project is from Panmure through to Pakuranga. My particular role on this project is the cultural design and mana whenua advisor on the project. So, we've been able to have our artists closely working with the BECA landscape architects, designers, engineers. So, this place where we're standing now, beside the station, bus station, there's going to be a carved waharoa. So that carved waharoa is going to acknowledge - cause, waharoa is an entry point - so, it's going to, in terms of its functionality, it would be an opportunity to not only function as a waharoa for the Pā site, which is South-East of the station, but also back to the maunga. So, it'll work as a double function. And, the scale of it is quite huge. So, we've had to get engineers onto that stuff. But right through this particular part of the AMETI project, we've been able to have three mana whenua artists involved in the programme, and so I've been working specifically with mana whenua, the consultants, and Auckland Transport, about that cultural narrative and how mana whenua see it.

This area here, specifically where we're standing, the significance is Maungarei. And as we go down through the project, it then becomes Mokoia, and then Wai Mokoia, so the part of the Tāmaki River that's just at the mouth of the Panmure Lagoon, is referred to by mana whenua as Wai Mokoia, as opposed to Wai o Taiki, which is at the opening of the river. And then the next part after that is really around the southern side of the river, or the eastern side of the river being more associated with waka landing, and occupation, and those kinds of things.

Figure 5. Ōtāhuhu Station, Ōtāhuhu, Tāmaki Makaurau (Photo credit: provided by Phil Wihongi / Auckland Design Manual).

So we've been able to develop that narrative, and the artworks that are going along this particular stretch are in relation to that narrative.

When we talk about the importance of this area as a māra, as a garden, that fed a lot of Tāmaki, the patterning on the retainers are the rau kumara, the leaf of the kumara vines, and [we're] just trying to bring that narrative back so that it's visual, and people will have an appreciation, if we start to peel back the layers, kind of what was here before.

JK: The Te Aranga principles have obviously been something that has been useful to mana whenua engaging in development projects, and I'm just wondering now that they're getting a lot of uptake, and everyone's kind of talking about them, what do you think is the next step to kind of evolve and progress and make them continually be useful?

LT: If we were to review that beginning point to where we are now, and how those principles have really taken shape, I think [it would be important] to acknowledge the work that's actually been done in Tāmaki, as opposed to other parts of the country. I was at a water-sensitive cities

workshop in Wellington, and people were talking about the Te Aranga strategy and the principles, but they didn't really know what it was. And they were like, you know, Auckland are using it, and it's really cool, but you know we don't really know what it is. And I'm like, but it's so simple. It's a process that I feel is easily transferable. But I'm always anxious about people just kind of defaulting to the principles, because what really underpins them are the values, and we always need to be cognisant of, the values are the ones that actually underpin and hold that space for those principles. And they're also very much place-based. You can't talk about Tāmaki cultural narratives in Tauranga. Or designing for an environment like Auckland in Wellington. You know, so, it does require a little bit of work to really understand what they are and then how to work with them.

In thinking about the future, it would be awesome if we could actually review those values and principles from a Tāmaki Makaurau sense of place, and story of place, so that they become the Tāmaki strategy for design, or whatever. Maybe design, because then design covers absolutely everything, it's not just about infrastructure or architecture. Yeah, so I think that's kind of the next challenge for us as mana whenua is being able to articulate our own design narratives within a framework.

An Alternative Approach - The Ōtautahi Model

Matapopore Trust emerged during the Christchurch rebuild process as a vehicle to ensure Ngāi Tūāhuriri and Ngāi Tahu values, aspirations and narratives were appropriately recognised and understood within the recovery. The Trust worked with Karl Wixon in 2015 to develop a set of design principles founded on Ngāi Tahu and Ngāi Tūāhuriri values.

Debbie Tikao is a landscape architect of Cherokee and Pākehā descent and the General Manager of Matapopore Trust.

Debbie Tikao: Kia ora koutou, ko Debbie Tikao tōku ingoa, I'm the General Manager of Matapopore Charitable Trust. I'm also a landscape architect, and mother of two beautiful little girls.

JK: Now I've heard a bit about the design principles that have been developed, and I thought that was really exciting because I've had a fair bit to do with Te Aranga. And it's quite cool because a lot of the outcome areas are very similar, but it's coming from absolutely that mana whenua perspective and basis, and what's right for the people there. So, I'm just wondering if you could tell me a little bit about how they emerged and developed and that process?

DT: They came out of, I suppose, the grand narrative. I suppose one of the very first exercises was to develop the stories that we were going to thread through the city. Once we had those stories from those, we could see that there were a number of main, I suppose kaupapa, that would, that we really needed to explore some more. And so, they became the basis of the urban design guidelines.

We identified five kaupapa, and we carried on with storytelling as a way to communicate and describe and explain what those kaupapa meant. Because we want these guidelines to be accessible to everybody, and sometimes we are talking about reasonably complex concepts. Our approach to these five kaupapa was more that we would take people on a journey, explain them in a way, and provide a context so they could be grasped more easily, and therefore be more effective. We also provided examples of the types of traditions and concepts that may relate to particular kaupapa, plus also we gave examples of some types of outcomes might be. So they were a starting point for a conversation, for a creative process.

JK: I was in Christchurch in 2012 when Ngā Aho held the symposium, Ōtautahi Revealed, and it was, you know, not too far after the earthquake, and there was all these aspirations of what might be possible. So, I guess having come from that point to now, I'm just wondering how you feel about where things are, and the things that have happened since that time?

DT: Well it's been a ride. It's been definitely a journey; a lot of lessons have been learned along the way. It wasn't straightforward. From that point, to where we are now, where we actually are delivering on those objectives. You know that path has been an awful lot of work that's occurred to get to this point. And it hasn't, we didn't have all the answers at the beginning. You know, we had to work through a number of different processes. We tried different things. We worked out that providing cultural advice, pretty much got us nothing. Because what was happening is that, you know, you were really leaving, you were providing information, you were handing over cultural narratives to Pākehā organisations to interpret, and that wasn't getting the results that we wanted to see. It was certainly, you would certainly go part way. What we realised is that we needed to be sitting at the table, working with them in a design capacity. The interpretation of narratives needs to be coming from ourselves. You know, you can't hand that over to others to do. You can work with them, you know, to develop some of those outcomes, but that interpretation needs to really come from ourselves. And we developed a process, and part of that process, particularly for the larger projects, included, I suppose, the preparation or writing of a cultural design strategy, that allowed us to consider what that narrative was, or what element of that narrative we were wanting to really explore through design in relation to the kaupapa, the values identified within the urban design guidelines. We brought two things together, and we applied them to a place or project. And, you know, we also would, part of that process is, we would also look at that cultural context. The cultural context of that land, that landscape, and look at all those connections and start to work through and develop a cultural framework, that we would then develop outcomes from. And so, when you apply a design language, it allows for design teams to understand these concepts, and we were then getting the results, by working with them.

JK: I was recently in Christchurch and I went on a wonderful tour through some of the projects you've been involved with, and particularly Tākaro-ā-Poi and Te Omeka Justice and Emergency Services Precinct. And I was just wondering if you could tell me a little bit more about those two projects.

DT: Probably the first point I want to make is that all the projects we are involved in are connected through narrative. So, there's an overriding story that we're weaving throughout the city. So, each project relates to the other projects. None are in isolation. And it's not really until you actually go on one of those tours that you, or go for a walk around, that you really experience and get a sense of what it is that we're doing. If you look at any one element, or any one piece, or any one project, it's beautiful and it's fantastic, but it's not until you get a sense of them all together as a collective that you realise there's something quite incredible that's happening here. You know, and it all relates back to storytelling.

So Tākaro-ā-Poi is at the base of that narrative. We're telling two stories – one, based on mahinga kai and the other, really about our migration stories. So, we had an artist, Piri Cowie, involved in that project and she did a beautiful job, she worked on a number of projects. With Tākaro-ā-Poi, by embedding our stories into that playground through predominantly art elements, we're trying to, I suppose, educate our kids. And so our kids have got that strong connection to, or get to learn more about their stories, their migration stories, and also have that stronger connection to the natural environment and familiarise themselves with concepts such as mahinga kai.

JK: And engage in a way that's meaningful and natural to them.

DT: And through play. So, there's a story arc, and within that story arc there's a lot of images that they'll be familiar with. A lot of images about, I suppose, species, some from Pacific islands, that connect Aotearoa to the Pacific islands. There are images of waka. There are also images of European vessels. So, it's all of our migration stories. And, there's also waiata. So, the kids can actually, you know, there are songs that they can sing, that they'll be familiar with. It's also very much about the language. You know, having a language – te reo Māori – within our play environments, within the urban environment, by making that more accessible, it's really so that our kids, when they're out there playing, potentially are going to feel more comfortable using and speaking te reo. Cause often, they only really speak it on the marae, or at school where they're learning it. So, it's really encouraging them to speak it, when they see it out there, to know that they can speak it out there too.

DT: That project [the Te Omeka Justice and Emergency Services Precinct], we actually came into that project quite late. But even though we weren't involved in that project from the conception, and we weren't able to embed those core values into the, I suppose into the guts and the bones of that building, we were able to still provide that narrative on the outside. And that narrative within that, within those stories, there's layers and layers and layers of meaning.

JK: And these narratives, as you said, are threaded throughout the city, so it's a part of the urban fabric. So, it's not confined to a single site. So even if in some places it just seems like a surface treatment, it doesn't stand

there alone, it's threaded through. Is there anything from your learnings that you do, or are able to share with other mana whenua groups who are looking to do similar things in their rohe?

DT: You really need to, you need to develop an organisation, and in that you need to have design professionals as well. Your design professionals. You need to work; you need to team up with those that hold that cultural knowledge as well. The components of what you need may not be housed within the one person. And it's so critical that you've got a robust endorsement process in place. You need to make sure that what outcomes, you need to know that the stories that you're putting out there are the right stories, that you've interpreted those stories correctly.

Applying Learnings to Develop Principles in other Rohe and other Indigenous Contexts

The Te Aranga principles have had a significant impact both locally and internationally and have been been considered for adaptation in places as far away as Seattle, Vancouver, and Montreal.

Rau Hoskins shared some insights into how the principles might be further developed and adapted for use in other cities.

Rau Hoskins: It's been encouraging to see the uptake and adoption of the Te Aranga principles, particularly the last five years, to see them being normalised in design processes around Auckland and increasingly outside of Auckland. A few weeks ago, I was in Tauranga working with mana whenua there on the adoption of the Te Aranga principles, and the renaming of the principles as the Tauranga Moana design principles. As we envisaged, if we could create a set of more generic Māori design principles, then they would act as a platform for our iwi groups, hapū groups, to customise those principles for their particular processes, and to ground them in their particular cultural landscape, and within their own mātauranga-ā-hapū, -ā-iwi. I think the key thing about Te Aranga principles, it's about the kaupapa. It's not about the IP, it's not about locking them in stone, it's about saying, "Hey, there's value to the Indigenous world within this approach." Take it, adapt it, customise it, rename it, try, and extract value from it.

We've all got a role – Ngā Aho's got a role – to continually clarify those issues. To take them out to other parts of the motu, and also just to apply them. You may be doing quite a humble project, in a rural community. Without even necessarily making a big deal out of it, just using a simple foundation that they provide as a way to help maximise outcomes. I often find myself, we're involved at designTRIBE with multiple projects, from very humble to some large projects, and sometimes I have to remind myself, oh actually if I just mentally go through the Te Aranga principles and make sure I raise them with this particular group, then there will be more opportunities than I've seen at first glance to embed layers of meaning and appropriate design resolution in the project.

Jade Kake: There's been a huge amount of interest, not just in Tāmaki where there's been an explosion, but in other areas the country with smaller Councils, but even as far afield as Canada and the US, as we discovered last year. Could you talk a little bit more about that kind of expansion, and what that might mean in other contexts?

RH: In 2014 I went to Winnipeg to speak at a symposium to do with the development of the University of Manitoba Fort Garry Campus. At that time I talked about experiences in tertiary education and other master planning work that we'd done here, and I did talk about the Te Aranga principles and the fact that we did feel that they were able to be adopted and customised around the Indigenous world. I know Phil Wihongi went over in, I think 2016, to a gathering in Seattle as well, and I think that his presentations had a lot of impact there as well. So, I understand that in Seattle and in Vancouver in particular there are moves afoot to develop a version of the Te Aranga principles, and of course in Arizona and other locations as well, there's a lot of interest.

I think the stumbling block in those countries, as it was here in Auckland, was first of all mana whenua have to have the appropriate status, or a certain degree of status, within their own local government areas for this conversation to really be taken to the next level. In other words, respect. If there is no respect, then there is no foundation for the application of Indigenous design principles. And that's not something you can magic up. The Treaty journey that we've been on here, particularly the last fifty years, you can't replicate that, and you can't necessarily fast track that. From this distance, that appears to be one of the stumbling blocks to versions of the Te Aranga principles being developed and adopted elsewhere. Notwithstanding that, there are certainly things that we've done here which I think can provide guidance to Indigenous groups around the world, and also maybe enable them to do things a bit more strategically to make sure that they get better outcomes sooner.

Daniel Glenn is an architect from the Crow tribe of Montana who leads a firm based in Seattle, Washington specialising in culturally and environmentally responsive architecture and planning. Daniel shared some insights into the challenges and opportunities of developing Indigenous design principles in Seattle, Washington.

Daniel Glenn: I'm Daniel Glenn, I'm an architect based

in Seattle now, originally from Montana, the Crow Reservation. Crow, we call ourselves Apsáalooke in our language. I've really been focussing on tribal work for most parts of my career. Starting very young. My current firm, it's called 7 Directions Architects and Planners. We're a small firm, and we're working with tribes around our region in Washington, but also, we have projects in California, we have a new one in Alabama. So, we work in many parts of what we call Indian Country in the United States, primarily.

Jade Kake: When our Ngā Aho rōpū visited Seattle, we learnt that people there they were already looking at Te Aranga and developing a similar model relevant to them, and they'd already been talking with some of our key people here, as well as, of course, these ideas getting traction in other cities around the country. Could you tell me a bit more about that?

DG: Well, we're actually in the process of trying to learn again from your communities, like the experience in Auckland with the Māori design principles that are being put in place there, and we're very interested in trying to bring similar approaches to decolonising our cities.

In the United States, the majority now of the Native community lives in cities. Part of that was by design, in the 50s and 60s there was a whole effort to get people off the reservation and move them to cities, and so there was this big internal migration. Myself now as an urban Indian living in Seattle Washington, far from my traditional land, connecting with all these, there's many different tribes living in Seattle and places like that. So, there's two things there.

It's the challenge of creating places that feel like home for urban Indians, and dealing with the challenges, like homelessness, which is significant, the Native community is the highest representative population of homeless in Seattle. But, also having an impact on the City as a whole, and saying, how do we demonstrate and celebrate, make a strong presence, of that Salish culture that's been there for thousands of years, and has largely been erased by the settlement process. So, I think that that's something, it's a part of our job, in our own communities, is bringing that voice back to our cities, and having that presence.

When I've met with the City of Seattle, and planning leadership and talked about this, it's a challenge, because planners think in numbers. Like, whoever shouts the loudest. So, if you have a majority of people, that's who tends to get listened to. And we don't have those numbers. We don't have those numbers, so there's very small numbers in urban, comparatively to the larger,

Figure 6. Daldy St Play Structure, Wynyard Quarter, Tāmaki Makaurau (Photo credit: Jade Kake).

Figure 7. Kahu Matarau by Lonnie Hutchinson, Ōtautahi (Photo credit: Jade Kake).

Figure 8. Waharoa by Blaine Te Rito Te Wero Bridge, Viaduct Basin, Tāmaki Makaurau (Photo credit: Jade Kake).

Figure 9. Paving detail, Tākaro-ā-Poi Margaret Mahy Family Playground (Photo credit: Jade Kake).

majority population.

So, what I try to talk about, is that we don't have numbers, but we have centuries, and millennia of time. So, this notion of the weight of time, that presence sort of supersedes the small numbers that we currently have. And say, how can we bring the power of that ten thousand years, or 15 thousand years of presence, to the forefront in our cities. And I think it will profoundly affect not only the Indigenous communities, but for the Pākehā people in our communities. The idea that it's a wonderful thing, that they'll know that they're in a special unique place, and that's part of what gives it uniqueness, and moves beyond the sort of sameness, this kind of overriding sameness of consumer culture and colonial spaces.

Towards The Future – Challenges And Opportunities

Growing iwi and hapū capacity and capability to engage in design

Jacob Scott is a Ngāti Kahungunu and Te Arawa designer and was part of the core group involved in the development of the Te Aranga strategy. Desna Whaanga-Schollum (Rongomaiwahine, Ngāti Kahungunu, Ngāti Pāhauwera) – artist and designer, and current Ngā Aho Chairperson – discussed with Jacob about some of the ongoing challenges to, and opportunities for, the implementation of the Te Aranga principles.

Jacob Scott: It's great that the Te Aranga principles have found such traction. So, I think the opportunity is there to inform them. The Te Aranga principles kind of need to be activated and activating them is another whole ball game. Because, what does that mean? And it is sort of a process that needs to happen, I think, more than just some of the things in [the implementation of the] Te Aranga principles that have just come down to names, and things like that. I think that's too simplistic, too easy to achieve. It's process that wants to be implemented or described.

We've learned a lot about them. And we've learnt enough about them to understand that it is process that needs to happen. But now we've got these principles that are too outcome oriented. So, they kind of provide the answer, whereas originally, in the Te Aranga work to establish it, what was described as, what would be good relationships? What does a good relationship look like? I think what happened with the Te Aranga principles was that they were principles that wasn't really strategy, but it was put out as being a strategy, and originally it described relationships, and that was what got bandied around the country for iwi sign-off, I guess. But then it got interpreted by the landscape architecture fraternity into

this simplistic Te Aranga principles that we've got now. And I think it suited them to do that, for themselves, but it doesn't fully suit the bigger picture of development and social development.

Desna Whaanga-Schollum: So, the principles have demystified the whole design concept somewhat, but it's still a really once over lightly, there's still a long way to go between understanding.

JS: Well they've provided some tick boxes to get done, but they're not really process-oriented or relationship-orientated. And I think the thing that should be interesting in them is that each hapū or iwi or wherever the situation is, is that somehow, they need to be informed enough to be able to interact in that space. And there's been no educational... people haven't been walked into the space of thinking about the environmental, the physical built environment, the articulation of all of the things that can connect people. We haven't had that. And so, the whole, really that whole visual arts scene, the tertiary institutions have let us down, I think. There's nobody practised in it, and nobody's got any skills in it, except, I think, the Ngā Aho lot.

Because the counterculture, the dominant culture, is for project procurement, is one where you need to respond to an RFP or request to participate in a job, and you have to define what it's going to look like, the outcome, before you even start. And before the job's even (given) to you. And so, you're in a competitive kind of position, trying to win the opportunity to begin the thinking and work with the people through to evolve an outcome. You're expected to do that before you start. So, they all want the idea, within two or three weeks of putting out the request for work, and you haven't even begun to research. That's what the design process is, that's what you should be getting paid for. That's where the work is. And this thing that expects the outcome to be defined, completely, visually. They don' know what a concept is. It would be better to be able to present the concepts for procurement that consider this, this, and that proposition. And we'll work like this. Not, "It's going to look like this." It's too early.

DWS: If we considered the Te Aranga principles as basically a trigger or a platform to be able to elevate Māori design, they were one form and one way of doing that, and the culture landscape, the strategy talked about the bigger picture of telling our stories. If you're looking at relationships, if you're to place some effort about where it went next, would you think that you would get more traction from spending time with iwi and educating them about what good Māori design looks like? So, from that relationship side of things? Or is it? Because Te Aranga principles has mainly taken hold because we've worked closely at the Council end of the scale. I mean, not that it has to be an either or, but if you were to focus do you think you'd have a preference on direction?

JS: Yeah, I think it's iwi. I think it's our own that need
the skills, and the understanding of how to tap into the
skills that exist. I think, we know our people are there,
within Ngā Aho, but they don't know, I don't think. If they
would hand over that responsibility to perform in that
space, to others who have developed skills to do that,
it would make a big difference. I see it all the time with
papakāinga. You know, we do the feasibility studies for
them. And then what happens is, some project manager
on the Māori side comes in, and he just goes to a dial-up
volume builder who just gets the job done. And it's just
terrible.

DWS: So, relating that back to what you were earlier
saying, about the fact that we need to look at the process
and the relationships. It's a relationship, not just between
Māori and non-Māori, it's actually Māori practitioners and
their iwi, like that relationship is a fundamental part of
our process. If you were forming that relationship from
a Māori design practitioner's viewpoint with iwi, what
kind of conversations do you think are needed? Or, what
would that look like?

JS: It's an interesting question, because you have a look
at the scholarships that iwi support. They're all in health,
or fisheries, or forestry, or something like that. Nothing
in design. Architect's Institute don't really promote or
describe what they do either, to anybody. People don't
realise that architects work in that social, historical, future
context. To them, architecture is just, a draughtsman can
do it, do a better job. Or quicker. Cheaper. They don't
understand the range of things that need to be thought
about in a project.

DWS: I think we've created the desire from the Council
kind of things, to want to have something, or they can see
the Te Aranga principles as a possible way that they start
to work with mana whenua, but then it's whether mana
whenua are in the right place to be able to, whether mana
whenua themselves understand enough about design to
be able to realise that opportunity.

JS: I don't think they really know how to create an
environment for the kind of wellbeing we're talking about.
They've lost the belief that you can make change in that
space from the status quo. The whole process, further
down the procurement process of getting a house, and
getting a property, and getting it launched, is so fraught
with compliance and it's huge now, isn't it? Normal
people just don't know where to go in that anymore, so
they do the volume builder thing. But collectively – really,
Māori – which is how we can work, is that the capability is
here if they come to the right people.

Ensuring appropriate application of the principles by practitioners

Rau Hoskins also shared his perspective on the future of Te Aranga.

Jade Kake: You've can't seem to go anywhere without
people talking about Te Aranga, and how it's been
applied, and how you need to work with these principles,
but we're also still hearing examples where developers
and architects are not properly engaging with mana
whenua, or not early enough. So, I guess, how do we
keep up the good work and the progress that has been
made, and how do we ensure with this kind of explosion
of growth that these principles and these processes are
being done correctly?

Rau Hoskins: Well I think one of the key things is
that mana whenua themselves are requesting that
the Te Aranga principles be used as the basis of their
engagement. So, I think that's probably a critical success
factor for the development of the Te Aranga principles,
is that they are not only owned by mana whenua, but
they are promoted by mana whenua. There is a process
happening at the moment for those principles to be
re-grounded in Tāmaki. And that's another important
dimension, that they were never designed to be set in
stone. And they were there as a kind of a springboard for
robust discussions which could maximise outcomes in
the built environment. I think lots of people quote the Te
Aranga principles, and people that don't know that you
co-developed them, talk to you about them. Interesting to
see, I mean it's gratifying to see that they have become
embedded in the way that urban design is practised in
Tāmaki at least, but there's always ongoing professional
development required to assist people who have got a
kind of passing knowledge of the principles.

I think the problem arises when a group come across
the principles and see them as a good resource, Google
them, and then have a go, and don't actually really read
or understand the very first principles. And don't really
know how to go about developing a working relationship
with one or more mana whenua groups. I think there's
vigilance required from the Māori design community,
just to make sure that principle number one, the mana
rangatiratanga principle, is really understood. There is
no application of the Te Aranga principles until a working
relationship with mana whenua has been established to
the satisfaction of mana whenua. And when and if they
are satisfied with the working relationship, then you can
start to progress an investigation into the other principles,
or the opportunities that the other principles signal. It's
moved further than I would have hoped, in the last 3-4
years in particular. So that's really encouraging, but I
think the key thing is to keep the quality application of the

principles up there, as opposed to a cursory application and/or misapplication of the principles.

Reference List

Matapopore Trust. (2015). *Matapopore Urban Design Guide.* Retrieved from https://matapopore.co.nz/wp-content/uploads/2016/05/Matapopora-UDG-Finalv3-18Dec2015.pdf.

Ministry for the Environment. (2005). *New Zealand Urban Design Protocol*. Retrieved from http://www.mfe.govt.nz/publications/towns-and-cities/new-zealand-urban-design-protocol.

Ngā Aho. (2013). Te Aranga Principles. *Auckland Design Manual* [website]. Retrieved from http://www.aucklanddesignmanual.co.nz/design-thinking/maori-design/te_aranga_principles.

Ngā Aho. (2016). *Te Aranga Māori Cultural Landscape Strategy.*

http://www.tearanga.maori.nz/cms/resources/TeArangaStrategy28Apr08_lr.pdf.

Chapter 4.5: Guiding Decolonial Trajectories in Design: An Indigenous Position

Brian Martin – Bundjalung, MuruWarri and Kamilaroi and Jefa Greenaway – Wailwan and Gamillaray

Dr Brian Martin is Associate Dean Indigenous at Monash University Art, Design and Architecture and is from Bundjalung, MuruWarri and Kamilaroi ancestry. As a practising artist, Brian has been exhibiting his work for approximately 27 years, both nationally and internationally. His research has investigated the relationship of materialism in the arts to an Indigenous worldview and Aboriginal knowledge framework and epistemology. His work reconfigures understandings of culture and visual practice from an Aboriginal perspective. He is also an honorary professor of Eminence with Centurion University of Technology and Management in India.

Jefa Greenaway is an academic at the University of Melbourne, a Director of Greenaway Architects, an advocate as Chair of the not-for-profit organisation Indigenous Architecture + Design Victoria (IADV) and a regular design commentator on ABC Radio. For over 25 years, he's championed Indigenous-led design, particularly through the International Indigenous Design Charter, as Regional Ambassador (Oceania) of INDIGO (International Indigenous Design Alliance). As part of the first generation of urban Indigenous registered architects in Australia, he has sought to reveal layers of history and memory through connections to place, demonstrating the value of people centred design which interrogates one's own philosophical or ethical underpinning and design responsibilities. His award winning Ngarara Place was exhibited in the Australian pavilion of the Biennale Architettura 2018 in Venice.

This chapter considers the current dynamic surrounding de-colonising/Indigenising structures that have been created under the premise of coloniality. It specifically looks at the de-colonialization process of curriculum in universities and its aim to challenge post-colonial norms and "whiteness" within disciplines. In this aspiration, we have found it is necessary to provide support to non-Indigenous peoples and systems in the process of decolonisation. Therefore, this chapter presents a set of guidelines that others can use in a pragmatic way to decolonise/Indigenise curriculum.

The authors, both Indigenous Australians, explore the importance of Indigenous voice, agency and leadership including ways of knowing that underpin this destabilization of the centre of coloniality. This chapter examines the dynamic of being Indigenous within colonial structures, such as universities, that now want to follow the agenda of decolonisation and questions what this means for them.

In looking at these specific spaces, institutions, and their strategic approaches, we argue that the only way to subvert and disrupt these places is that these projects are Indigenous-led and if non –Indigenous peoples have an immersive and embodied experience with Indigenous peoples. We posit that for any success in the plight of a successful de-coloniality, then the first point of departure is an Indigenous one. Any other approach than this returns to the habitus of an imagined post-colonialism and therefore continues the redundant discourse of colonisation. We also postulate that this trajectory is not only about increasing Indigenous peoples' participation in these spaces and combats the dilemma of under-representation, but also presents Indigenous ways of knowing and practise as a way of reconfiguring ontologies and epistemologies in the general knowledge economy of institutional spaces.

The authors acknowledge and pay respects to the traditional and sovereign territories of the Wurundjeri, Boon Wurrung and Wathaurong peoples and communities. We pay respects to elders, past, present and emerging and to the numerous Indigenous peoples who have crossed these lands throughout millennia. We further extend that respects to creation ancestors across these ancestral Countries.

> The goal of Decolonial thinking and doing is to continue re-inscribing, embodying and dignifying those ways of living, thinking and sensing that were violently devalued or demonized by colonial, imperial and interventionist agendas as well as by postmodern and altermodern internal critiques.[1]

---

1. Anonymous. 2013. Decolonial Aesthetics.*Fuse Magazine;* Fall. 36, 4; ProQuest Central p. 10.

There is a strong aspiration for institutions in various countries to "decolonize" things like curriculum and colonial structures and to be inclusive of Indigenous content in these. Regardless of such motivations to achieve this ambition the are a number of issues that arise due to the complexities surrounding colonial states- both in the physical and metaphysical sense. Ever since the renewed interest in Indigenous ways of knowing the following question is raised: "But what happens, or what do we need to consider, when Indigenous Knowledge is brought into relation with the disciplines in the academy?"[2]

Although Martin Nakata is referring to Indigenous ways of knowing in terms of research, this still applies to the trajectory of decolonising or Indigenising curriculum and structures. What is decolonisation? It must be located into the context of coloniality for it to be de-contaminated and therefore we ask can things like curriculum, research or structures be decolonized because their very premise is colonial in-of-itself?

Institutions exist within a continued habitus of coloniality as this is often how they have been formed and they carry their colonial baggage "when" ever they go or turn. Underlying the ambition to decolonize, is a sense of this baggage and all its trimmings facing a possible redundancy. We risk the process of bringing our knowledges into this mess. However, it is easily recognized that we are in this "mess" already. Curriculum, research, institutions and structures can be a platform where we find possible distinct ways in creating voices of self-determination and self-definition. Therefore, it is necessary to subvert and reconfigure this platform and create spaces away from its original formation. This chapter examines this dynamic and proposes simple guidelines in draft form to establish the beginnings of Decolonising and therefore Indigenising curriculum, research and colonial structures.

A Starting Point

For Nerida Blair, "It is our challenge as Indigenous peoples and communities to break our silence and create and engage in new terrains of not only resistance and survival but enrichment through the centring and privileging of our own Knowings."[3] Blair sees decolonisation as a strategic discourse, yet as "one of the bricks in the Eurocentric wall." We need to remember this- where it comes from and keep a healthy suspicion about the risks that threaten memory and reconstitute

amnesia that suppresses our voice and ways of knowledge production.

It is this positioning of Indigenous self-determination as outlined by Linda Tuhiwai Smith (1999) that underpins the approach here. But it goes deeper than this. The process of decolonisation is about *un*learning the past. The premise here is to examine the relationship between this voice as it interacts with the cultural interface of colonial structures.

So, what is decolonisation?

We have stated that there is a strong desire for various modes of thought to "decolonize" established narratives of the past, and through this motivation, history is critically analysed through and by an Indigenous lens. In examining Smith's disruption to the research game, what falls into question is:

What is our role as Indigenous peoples to lead and care for Indigenous ways of knowing within these constructs?

And more importantly, how do we balance the spaces between the construct of research and institutions with the obligation to protect the agency of our ways of knowing?

And furthermore, what role and responsibilities do non-Indigenous people have or take on in this positioning?

Decolonisation is about developing the counter-story, the shifting position where we can write our own narratives. For Smith, it is about critiquing the collective memory of imperialism that has propagated the ways in which Indigenous peoples have been classified and represented.[4] For Smith, it is about creating spaces to operate in and from.

To resist is to retrench in the margins, retrieve what we were and remake ourselves. The past, our stories local and global, the present, our communities, cultures, languages and social practises – all may be spaces of marginalisation, but they have also become spaces of resistance and hope.[5]

This trajectory is about decolonising structures, views and agendas. For Indigenous peoples, the critique of history is not unfamiliar and has been claimed by various contemporary modes of thinking and theories. We can translate Indigenous ways of knowing through other platforms of knowledge such as feminist and practise-led discourses. What is vital here is that this is done not

. Nakata, M. 2008. *Disciplining the Savages; Savaging the Disciplines.* Aboriginal Studies Press, Canberra ACT. P. 183.
. Blair, N. 2015. *Privileging Australian Indigenous Knowledge: Sweet Potatoes, Spiders, Waterlilys, and Brick Walls.* Illinois, USA. Common Ground Publishing. P. 176.

4. Smith, L. T. 1999 *Decolonising Methodologies: Research and Indigenous Peoples.* Zed Books Ltd. London & New York. University of Otago Press, Dunedin. P.1.
5. Ibid P. 4.

to validate Indigenous ways of knowing, but to do so as a platform of thinking that is accepted in the wider knowledge economy.[6] It is here that we have to disrupt the narratives that exist.

Norm Sheehan refers to this dynamic and narrative as a construction to marginalize Aboriginal culture whilst at the same time not revealing its own unworthiness.[7] It is our role here to challenge what structures have created in terms of the power dynamic and how value is ascribed to certain knowledge systems.

In this Imagined Moral Centre, forms of discipline were constructed in order to perpetuate an imagined consciousness. For Smith:

> The most obvious forms of discipline were through exclusion, marginalization and denial. Indigenous ways of knowing were excluded and marginalized. This happened to Indigenous views about land, for example, through the forced imposition of individualized title, through taking land away for "acts of rebellion", and through redefining land as "waste land" or "empty land" and then taking it away.[8]

For Smith, this form of discipline also worked at the curriculum level. Normative tests designed around the language and cultural capital of the white middle classes. It is here that institutions postulated their colonial structures that in turn created a type of Moral Centre that excluded all forms of "otherness". At a more exclusively physical, cultural and emotional level, "The deepest memory of discipline, however, is of the sheer brutality meted out to generations of Indigenous communities. Aboriginal parents in Australia had their children forcibly removed, sent away beyond reach and "adopted".[9]

These forms of discipline have been instrumental in Indigenous peoples" self-determination and reclaiming voice. It also about reclaiming and reordering those ways of knowing which were submerged, hidden or driven underground. This is where a promise of (de)colonisation occurs and is attractive to Indigeneity.

The Finishing Line

What is the desired outcome for us- for "them"- to create a type of equilibrium? To (re)concile the past there needs to be a time where there was balance? In Australia- this balance never existed. The desired outcome for Indigenous peoples from our positioning is about reconfiguration.

For Smith, the *Native Intellectual* is related to their abilities to reclaim, rehabilitate and articulate Indigenous cultures and to their implicit leadership over the people as voices which can legitimate a new nationalist consciousness.[10] However, Smith warns, these same producers are a group most closely aligned to the colonizers in terms of their class interests, their values and their ways of thinking. It is here that we need to head with caution as we can become estranged with ourselves and face a type of de-Indigenisation.

"There were concerns that the native intellectuals may have become estranged from their own cultural values to the point of being embarrassed by, and hostile towards, all those values represented."[11] We need to be careful to not de-Indigenise ourselves.

The level of self-analysis and critique becomes particularly relevant in the context of both design practise which engages with cultural expression as well as how pedagogical structures equip non-Indigenous people in developing skills towards disciplines which interface with the built environment and design practise.

The relevance of intellectual interrogations of how Indigenising motives can empower Indigenous voices, becomes particularly relevant in the age of Treaty conversations – recently accelerated in the Australian context. Given the limitations of Indigenising curriculum, as often starting from a position of privileging non-Indigenous priorities, the notion of Indigenous agency becomes more acute. As Jenny Williams states, "I cannot think of one are of our arts and creative industries that is not owned, defined and represented through the lens of the white gaze."[12]

The simple act of facilitating an Indigenous led approach is a pivotal priority, as it foregrounds *our* voices on *our* terms. In other words, the formulation of an embedded Indigenising act is enhanced by being centred from ideation to implementation – unfiltered or culturally authorized by non-Indigenous overseers.

This comes with a number of challenges, not least being the necessity to assist the vast majority of non-Indigenous colleagues towards an understanding an acceptance of Indigenous ways of knowing, as well as avoiding "another diversity casualty."[13]

This initial challenge centres on a tension of being led by Indigenous interlocutors, to come on a journey of discomfort, that can lead to a realization that one does

6. Martin, B. 2018. Platforms of Indigenous Knowledge Transference in Oliver, J. (2018) *Associations: Creative Practise & Research.* Melbourne University Press..
7. Sheehan, N. (2001). Some call it culture: Aboriginal Identity and the imaginary moral centre. In *Social Alternatives* (Vol. 20, pp. 29–33). Queensland: Sunshine Coast University.
8. Smith 1999 Ibid p. 68.
9. Smith 1999 Ibid p. 68.
10. Smith 1999 Ibid p. 69.
11. Smith 1999 Ibid p. 69.
12. Williams, J. c.2010 "Black leadership and the white gaze" in A Cultural Leadership Reader eds Kay, S., Vanner, K., Burns, S., and Schwarz, M. Creative Choices, London P.41.
13. Williams, J. c.2010 "Black leadership and the white gaze" in A Cultural Leadership Reader eds Kay, S., Vanner, K., Burns, S., and Schwarz, M. Creative Choices, London P.42.

ot necessarily know what they do not know. The need to build cultural intelligence compels one to acknowledge that this is part of a learning journey, of ongoing professional development that places non-Indigenous voices secondary to those with the cultural authority or with the cultural permission or lived experience that often requires the ego to be parked and to be open to what is often regarded as *deep listening.*

This second issue points to the common experience of cultural burnout resulting from the responsibility and expectations of Indigenous leadership, while balancing what Richard Franklin calls the "cultural load" or the difficult and unrelenting balancing act of keeping all the competing cultural balls in the air, above and beyond the role expected within the normal workplace environment. The challenge rests with organizational leaders to provide the requisite support, resource scaffolding along with the adequate time and space to become a true enabler of success.

Indigenous led in the context of Indigenising curriculum or for that matter design practise is the only meaningful and authentic means towards Indigenous empowerment and agency. That said, the experience towards implementation has many potholes along the way. Not least the need for a sustainable foundation which is challenging, avoids the typical tropes of a deficit discourse approach and pivots to an embrace and pride towards our shared connections are but a few of the considerations that are now being explored.

An approach that has been developed over recent years at the University of Melbourne's Faculty of Architecture, Building & Planning in their quest to embed Indigenous perspectives, sensibilities and knowledge systems into their design degrees has focused attention across four key domains. These areas have become the building blocks required before any consideration of tweaks to the curriculum could even be considered. Driven by Indigenous voices the focus was framed as follows: cultural competency, capacity building, partnerships, cultural visibility. These areas have become a springboard to liberate the focus on the individual towards the responsibility of the majority to take ownership of their own cultural limitations.

Firstly, it became clear from the outset that developing the language, the confidence and the tool kits or resources for those who would actively be required to implement, teach into and engage with are more culturally complex terrain could not be undertaken without a baseline of knowledge, to navigate cultural blind spots or to manage the nuances of Indigeneity. Secondly, the practical resources to access were required to be built on. Thirdly, a more concerted and deliberative effort to engage with those who are the cultural custodians of Indigenous knowledge – Traditional Owner Groups, elders and the local Indigenous community, would be paramount to co-designing a culturally responsive approach. Finally, an often overlooked yet important aspect was to build

cultural visibility, particularly where little evidence or practical sight of Indigenous culture was the norm.

In totality, these four guiding steps have enabled the beginnings of a long walk towards normalising a sense of cultural respect which will enable future prospect to fundamentally inform the structures and practical consideration of Indigenous culture to inform curriculum as part of the DNA of the faculty, as opposed to an add-on or retrofitted solution which avoids tackling some of the difficult questions previously cited. Furthermore, of equal importance if this methodology has been underpinned by values, as opposed to compliance, which gives legitimacy to thicken that box thinking KPI approach can never meaningfully raise the bar and meet the needs and expectation of such ambition. In other words, in order to the tick the box, one needs to open it. The act of engagement invariably leads to broadening the frame of reference in which one typically encounters the unfamiliar. The Indigenising premise starts with a premise – who benefits, and what is the intention?

The context of how such thinking informs design pedagogy becomes further nuanced, as it talks to how we avoid the clichés, stereotypes, or simplistic approaches while seeking to tease out what is distinctly Indigenous design. There is indeed a richness of academic enquiry here, as it will invariably intersect with cultural expression, connections to Country, the sophisticated and diverse relationship with people, language, and place while being inextricably linked to history and memory. This lens further reinforces the need for Indigenous facilitators.

This approach reiterates the maxim, *not about us without us.* Critically this presupposes an ongoing dialogue with Indigenous voices. It ensures that through deep and immersive, collaboration, knowledge exchange and reciprocity we can move some way towards unlocking the power dynamics that have too often under-appreciated or seldom acknowledged the critical role, contribution and wisdom that resides in Indigenous knowledge. As each new discovery attests, deep Indigenous understandings are being constantly validated. However, the flawed expectation that Western knowledge needs to validate Indigenous knowledge to give it veracity should not be forgotten is no more than a throwback to the colonial mindset that has subjugated Indigenous voices for millennia. As Indigenous peoples ascertain their agency the edifice of colonial thinking will crumble and reposition the intellectual building blocks towards equity.

A similar trajectory is occurring and is active across various institutions in Australia, including Monash University's Art, Design and Architecture Faculty. The most vital point of reconfiguring curriculum in Art, Design and Architecture is the onerous task this would be for Indigenous academics. In this instance, not only is cultural burnout a significant issue, but the premise to decolonize curriculum and structures is everyone's business. It is about holistic ownership of the issues at hand. Seeing the aim to decolonize curriculum at Monash Art Design and Architecture and this potential clearing, allows for Indigenization to occur. The two are distinct but are significantly relational- as they can platform off and for each other.

In both contexts, we need to remember that Western modes of thought are facing a type of redundancy and have for some time. Therefore, we do move from a new materiality to a type of Indigeneity. Recognize that these are redundant and move aside please. This contributes to the journey of discomfort and the need for building cultural intelligence. Furthermore, this trajectory creates a tenuous space and tense relationality for Indigenous intellectuals.

In George Sefa Dei's *Indigenous Knowledge, Studies, and the next generation: Pedagogical Possibilities for Anti-colonial Education,* we see an exploration of epistemological equity through the reclamation of identity knowledge and politics of embodiment. Sefa Dei states that within institutions, the production of knowledge is institutionalized on a "production-line" model. When considering this in terms of trading the other, we need to reconfigure the structuring of the institution. It is here that he claims we must Indigenize our institutions. We argue we can do this through "practise". Practise is a Platform for Indigenous way of knowing to enter the institution. Real lived experience-practise is real-practise is tacit knowledge. It is here that we can speak back to the institution and significantly shift the colonial parameters they construct.

Indigeneity: A "New" Paradigm

As with Nakata's statement in terms of what happens to Indigenous knowledge when brought into the institution, we need to question why this happens again and again, as this is a continual recurrence. The colonial settlers need deep self-reflection, to build relationality, seek experiences that are immersive and embodied acts in order to develop "deep listening". This is how we all can achieve a curriculum/structure that can be possibly decolonized. However, for this to occur, we as Indigenous peoples need to lead the charge and although once again it seems like the onus is on us, we cannot forget that with resistance comes responsibility. For example, David Garneau states, "Cultural decolonisation in the Canadian context is about at once unsettling settlers and, ironically, helping them to adapt, to better settle themselves as noncolonial persons within Indigenous spaces" (Garneau 2013, p.15).

We need to be mindful that we as Indigenous peoples need to tread with caution. We need to ensure that this is not a ploy to subsume Indigenous ways of knowing within the discourses of institutions and western thinking. Part of this is to attempt to ensure that there is a significant shift in reconfiguration of the premise of colonial settler statehood.

For Sefa Dei, "Bringing a humility of knowing and acknowledging the power of the "not knowing" is a critical component of Indigeneity".[14] This is also the inquisitive nature of practise and design led research. Practise is not knowing- practise is revealing knowing and it is in this that the journey of discomfort can operate from.

Furthermore- we must challenge binarism's and dualistic modes of thought. "We must evoke Indigenous knowledge to challenge the linearity of Western paradigms privileged in the academy."[15] In creating these spaces, Sefa Dei gives words of caution in terms that we need to ensure that we do not theorize ourselves out of our identities.

So here lies the tenuous space. It is here that we need to position ourselves and furthermore- not do it alone- we need a global Indigenous network. As there still exists deep scepticism towards Indigenous knowledge, we need to claim space. It is here that we must maintain an independence and sovereignty to have identity. For Sefa Dei, "An Indigenous framework with its interconnections of self, group, community, culture and nature can provide compelling arguments against racism, colonialism, and imperialism that have ensured divisions, fragmentation, and inequities in communities."[16]

This is the main difference between decolonisation and Indigenization. Indigeneity can become the platform for this reconfiguration. This is reconfiguring the position by positioning and situating the Decolonial. The approach of building relationality is an Indigenous one. The difference in this process is there is a rightful expectation on the colonial settler to immerse themselves in this dynamic, as they are the ones that hold the majority in institutions. The deal is we, as Indigenous peoples, can lead the process as long as there is a commitment for an unequivocal immersion from our counterparts. This is how we start the process and we hope for it to spread in a way that the majority "deeply" learns the privilege of Indigenous ways of knowing. Let's wait and see (again).

These guidelines create a relational narrative within the research epistemology, where the researcher, participants and entities coexist and claim their agency. If any researcher follows these guidelines regardless of the qualitative research participants, different narratives will appear. These relational narratives not only enrich the research process but shift the content of the research by revealing different knowledges. These knowledges assert

---

14. Sefa Dei, G. 2008. Indigenous Knowledge Studies and the Next Generation: Pedagogical Possibilities for Anti-Colonial Education. *The Australian Journal of Indigenous Education.* Volume 37. P. 8.
15. Sefa Dei, G. 2008. Indigenous Knowledge Studies and the Next Generation: Pedagogical Possibilities for Anti-Colonial Education. *The Australian Journal of Indigenous Education.* Volume 37. P.8.
16. Sefa 2008 Ibid p. 11.

their agency within this zone.

Relationality has agency. Indigenous Australian methodological approaches operate in their own right, and at the same time they accept existing binaries and ambiguities, as they are not linear in their worldview and epistemology. The methodological approaches to research are the content of the research and vice versa. They have a two-way agency. These are inseparable in an Indigenous worldview and it is in this light that we not only reassign axiology to this framework but offer a relational way of reconfiguring research within the general knowledge economy. Any guidelines pertaining to decolonising or Indigenising curriculum need to share this premise of relational agency.

The Cultural Interface

Let us return to Nakata and look at the intersection of knowledge production between western discourses and Indigenous ways of knowing. For Nakata:

> Indigenous knowledge systems and Western knowledge systems work off different theories of knowledge that frame who can be a knower, what can be known, what constitutes knowledge, sources of evidence for constructing knowledge, what constitutes truth, how truth is to be verified, how evidences becomes truth, how valid inferences are to be drawn, the role of belief in evidence and related issues.[17]

In this instance, we cannot "do" Indigenous knowledge in the curriculum and therefore structures. It needs a deeper configuration, a "deep listening". It is this space that decolonising and Indigenising curriculum should and needs to operate from. Nakata speaks about the cultural interface- this is the contested space between two knowledge systems. He states that much of what Indigenous peoples bring to this space is tacit and unspoken knowledge. However once in this space western knowledge and epistemic discourse cannot help itself to separate and categorize. This is the antithesis of Indigenous knowledge traditions and technologies. This is why the process is a concerted effort together. Nakata introduces a way to position Indigeneity in this space if through standpoint theory – which we will not go into here. There are issues with it as it is located with imagined ideas of the post in post-structuralism and post-modernity.

Let us turn to Nakata. It is in the cultural interface that these guidelines can operate:

- Indigenous led
- Locating and positioning oneself
- Building relationality
- Immersive and embodied experience
- Developing clarity and being explicit
- Valuing Indigenous knowledge
- Aboriginal Terms of Reference and ethical principles

Indigenous-led

This approach recaps the maxim, *not about us without us.* It is here that Indigenous voices need to be privileged and valued from the onset. This underpins the premise of reconfiguring curriculum as it is premise on presupposing an ongoing dialogue with Indigenous voices. It ensures that through deep and immersive, collaboration, knowledge exchange and reciprocity we can move some way towards unlocking the power dynamics that have too seldom under-appreciated or acknowledged the critical role, contribution and wisdom that resides in Indigenous knowledge. As each new discovery attests, deep Indigenous understandings are being constantly validated.

Locating and positioning oneself

Non-Indigenous peoples have to position themselves clearly in the trajectory of decolonisation. This initial questioning of self is the first instance of decolonising one's own self. A significant part of positioning oneself, is about locating one's own origins and location in terms of Place.

Building relationality

In terms of positioning oneself, the idea of locating is about building relationality with Place and people. This builds on the first two principles.

Immersive and embodied experience

Similar to acknowledging an oncological deep listening, people should immerse themselves into a deeper understanding of Indigeneity and Indigenous culture in general. This positioning is not an anthropological understanding of Indigenous culture as an objective study, but as a culture that is relational and invites non-Indigenous people to participate within it.

Developing clarity and being explicit

In developing curriculum and the motivation of including a decolonial and furthermore Indigenising content, there needs to be absolute clarity, conviction, and explicitness in what is being transmitted to others in the curriculum.

---

7. Nakata, M. 2008. *Disciplining the Savages; Savaging the Disciplines.* Aboriginal Studies Press, Canberra ACT. P. 8.

Valuing Indigenous knowledge

Whilst this may be obvious in the trajectory of decolonising and Indigenising curriculum, valuing Indigenous ways of knowing is vital to its substantiation of a significant way of looking at the world. This is vital to shifting the construct of how knowledge is valued within academia.

Aboriginal Terms of Reference and ethical principles

Each person should construct a set of principles themselves in their striving for the reconfiguration of curriculum. This also should be localized – specifically for Country and also for the discipline area.

Concluding remarks

There exist difficult roles for both Indigenous and non-Indigenous peoples in the plight to reconfigure and reconstruct curriculum as this has been foremost set by colonial constructs. It is clear that our voices need to be privileged in this space, however, we cannot do this alone.

This relationality operates at the cultural interface which moves between the space of the axiom *not about us without us.* This tenuous space need to value our value and leadership but also to support it by resourcing its tenor and proceeding this by way of the "system" ceding its power. Indigenous peoples in Australia have been standing for a long time, awaiting for the interface to do things properly. We are waiting once again, arms open but with learned caution and suspicion for a (de)colonial promise that we encourage to happen.

References

Agrawal, A. (1995). Dismantling the Divide Between Indigenous and Scientific Knowledge. *Development and Change.* Vol. 26. Institute of Social Sciences. Blackwell Publishers: pp. 413-439.

Bond, C. et al. (2016). *Great Guide to Indigenisation of the Curriculum.* Office of Indigenous Engagement, CQ University: Rockhampton, Australia.

Anonymous (2013). Decolonial Aesthetics. *Fuse Magazine;* Fall. ProQuest Central: p. 10.

Blair, N. (2015). *Privileging Australian Indigenous Knowledge: Sweet Potatoes, Spiders,*

Waterlilys, and Brick Walls. Illinois, USA. Common Ground Publishing.

Brown, C. and Archibald, J. (1996). Transforming First Nations research with respect and power. *Internal Journal of Qualitative Studies in Education.* Routledge: pp. 245-267.

El Zoghbi, M. (2008). Inclusive Pedagogies: the development and delivery of Australian curricula in higher education. *Learning and Teaching in Higher Education.* Issue 3. pp. 33-48.

Garneau, D. (2013). *Extra-Rational Aesthetic Action and Cultural Decolonisation* in *Fuse*

Magazine. Fall 2013, 36, 4. ProQuest Central: pp. 14-23.

Haraway, D. (1988). Situated Knowledges: The Science Question in Feminism and the Privilege of Partial Perspective. *Feminist Studies.* Vol. 14, No. 3 Autumn. pp. 575-599.

Martin, B. et al. *International Indigenous Design Charter: Protocols for sharing Indigenous knowledge in professional practise design.* Deakin University: Geelong.

Kēpa, M. and Manu'atu, L. (2008). Pedagogical Decolonisation: Impacts of the European/Pākehā Society on the Education of Tongan People in Aotearoa, New Zealand. *American Behavioral Scientist.* Volume 51. Number 12. Sage Publications: pp. 1801-16.

Mackinlay, E. and Barney, K. (2014). Unknown and Unknowing Possibilities: Transformative Learning, Social Justice, and Decolonising Pedagogy in Indigenous Australian Studies, *Journal; of Transformative Education.* Vol. 12. SAGE Publications: pp. 54-73.

Martin, B. (2018). Platforms of Indigenous Knowledge Transference in Oliver, J. *Associations: Creative Practise & Research.* Melbourne University Press.

Moreton-Robinson, A. (2004). *Whitening Race: Essays in social and cultural criticism.* Aboriginal Studies Press.

Nakata, M. (2007). The Cultural Interface. *The Australian Journal of Indigenous Education.* Volume 36: pp. 7-14.

Nakata, M. (2008). *Disciplining the Savages; Savaging the Disciplines.* Aboriginal Studies Press, Canberra ACT.

Rigney, L. I. (1997). Internationalisation of an indigenous anti-colonial cultural critique of research methodologies: A guide to Indigenist research methodology and its principles. *(Conference proceedings). Advancing international perspectives: The internationalization of higher education in Indonesia Conference,* pp. 632-639. Adelaide, South Australia, http://www.herdsa.org.au/wpcontent/uploads/conference/1997/rigney01.pdf.

Sefa Dei, G. (2008). Indigenous Knowledge Studies and the Next Generation: Pedagogical Possibilities for Anti-Colonial Education. *The Australian Journal of Indigenous Education.* Volume 37: pp. 5-13.

Sheehan, N. (2001). Some call it culture: Aboriginal Identity and the imaginary moral centre. In *Social alternatives* (Vol. 20). Queensland: Sunshine Coast University. pp. 29-33.

Smith, L. T. (1999). *Decolonising Methodologies: Research and Indigenous Peoples.* Zed Books Ltd. London & New York. University of Otago Press, Dunedin.

Walby, S. (2000). Beyond the politics of location. The power of argument in a global era. *Feminist Theory.* Vol. 1(2). SAGE Publications. pp. 189-206.

Williams, J. (2010). "Black leadership and the white gaze" in *A Cultural Leadership Reader* eds Kay, S., Vanner, K., Burns, S., and Schwarz, M. Creative Choices, London.

Chapter 4.6: #dickdesigner – How not to be one (The devil is in the detail)

Rebecca Kiddle – Ngāti Porou and Ngā Puhi

Dr Rebecca Kiddle's iwi are Ngāti Porou and Ngā Puhi. She is a Senior Lecturer at the School of Architecture at Te Herenga Waka Victoria University of Wellington and has a PhD and an MA in urban design from Oxford Brookes University. And an undergraduate degree in politics and Māori studies. She is the co-chair Pōneke for Ngā Aho Network of Māori Designers. Current research includes: Decolonising Aotearoa New Zealand cities and Indigenous place identities; Māori housing and urban design; Spatial Justice; Rangatahi (youth) involvement in built environment decision-making; Urban and suburban spaces for community building and third places; and, the politics of the production of place.

There have been positive inroads to reinstating the mana (value) of Indigenous design in both Aotearoa New Zealand, and other countries represented in this book. In our Aotearoa context, the Te Aranga principles[1] have become influential in design processes, at least in Auckland, New Zealand's largest city. These principles sit in the Auckland Design Manual setting out a set of guiding values that offer a sort of road map on which to develop urban and architectural design grounded in Māori identities and worldviews. In civic projects these have held much weight.

Treaty settlements have also acted as a catalyst for the reinvigoration of Māori design. Te Tiriti o Waitangi,[2] the Māori-language version ensured the Queen of England would protect the ability of Māori to exercise chieftainship over their lands, villages and things they treasured and ensured that Māori would have the same rights and duties of citizenship as settlers. Māori allowed for the Queen of England to have governorship over their land, though importantly, not sovereignty. The Queen and her subjects did not live up to all promises. And only recently, (the 1970s) a process that allowed Māori to receive recompense for their land and other loses was set up.[3] Since that time approximately 59 claims[4] have been settled and Māori groups or tribes have received compensation often made up of land and money. Some have chosen to develop housing or tribal buildings on their land and have worked to ensure their tribal identities and values are present in the resultant architecture (See for example: Tuhoe's Living Building developments[5]).

Concurrently, larger architecture and design firms are building "Māori" capacity by recruiting Māori practitioners and setting up dedicated teams within these firms to focus on providing Indigenous expertise on projects and a smaller number of Indigenous-led firms have started up in their own right.

In the academic world, there is starting to be a good body of written work about Indigenous architecture and design, albeit much of it is still being written by non-Indigenous writers.

However, one might argue, as I do, that all is not yet well, and colonisation continues in small, often obscured ways. Some examples of this are discussed below. To get ironically biblical (given the gross injustices oftentimes inflicted by the Christian church on Indigenous people all over the world), I imagine my non-Indigenous colleagues "do not know what they do" (Luke 23:34). This chapter seeks to illuminate that colonising small detail that goes unnoticed and unchecked in everyday practice. These small acts of colonisation work to reinforce non-Indigenous "norms" and power imbalances.

Conversely, decolonisation, I argue, is not just in the overt grand gestures, but also in the small and concealed ones. That is, **decolonisation is also in the detail.**

The following observes six "dick moves" that are

---

1. Auckland Council (n.d.) Te Aranga Principles, Accessed from: http://www.aucklanddesignmanual.co.nz/design-subjects/maori-design/te_aranga_principles.
2. The Treaty of Waitangi signed between the Crown and Māori chiefs in 1840.

---

3. Waitangi Tribunal (n.d.) About the Waitangi Tribunal, Accessed from, https://www.waitangitribunal.govt.nz/about-waitangi-tribunal/.
4. Te Arawhiti (2019) Te Kāhui Whakatau (Treaty Settlements), Year-to-date progress report, 1 July – 30 September 2019, Accessed from : https://www.govt.nz/assets/Documents/OTS/Quarterly-report-to-30-September-2019.pdf.
5. Tūhoe (n.d.) The Living Building Challenge, Tūhoe website, Accessed from https://www.ngaituhoe.iwi.nz/sustainability-and-the-living-building-challenge.

ideas, experiences, or observations that might seem innocuous but actually sustain colonisation. It also offers suggestions around how non-Indigenous designers and scholars can better support a decolonising ethic of practice and theory-making.

1. Engaging Indigenous groups after key decisions have been made

I feel a bit tired even mentioning this one given much has been written on this but unfortunately it is still so common. Good engagement starts at the beginning of any project - ideally before the beginning – to ensure Indigenous people are involved in setting design priorities. Either way, before designers commit to any decisions one should ask, how can I best engage those who are "of this place", who will be directly affected by the design decisions that are being made here? And what biases might be playing out here if design is left just to non-Indigenous designers?

Perhaps you've made moves to try to engage with Indigenous groups and you've received a knock back with communities being unresponsive or even unwilling to talk. This could be for a number of very legitimate reasons. They may not have capacity to engage with what you are doing given Indigenous groups can be inundated with requests for Indigenous knowledge, views, and decisions on a multitude of projects and activities. They may feel it's not something they know about, in which case the request was communicated badly and, in a way, that doesn't make clear the value of their Indigenous knowledge. Or, they may simply not be interested or like the project you're proposing. We're all allowed to have our likes and dislikes and perhaps your project is not an attractive enough proposition. Whatever the reason, the fundamental point here is that relationship building is key and really guides all else. If you don't put effort into building and maintaining relationships, there's not much point doing much else. It's scary, but you've just got to step out of your comfort zone and make the first move, whatever that looks like.

2. Engaging with Indigenous groups and forgetting to name them on the team when you go up for awards

I've written about this previously[6] and so have others[7] but this point is short and sweet: Indigenous expertise counts. It counts alongside the engineers, the landscape designers, the plumbers, it counts. Arguably it counts even more than other contributions given the scarcity, due to colonisation and, thus value of Indigenous knowledge and the role of Indigenous Peoples as First Nations Peoples in these lands. Don't let your marketing teams miss them off the list of contributors when you submit your building or space for an architectural award.

3. Asserting your right to lead on Indigenous kaupapa[8]

I feel pretty incredulous about this, particularly given the wealth of talent in the Indigenous design world today. This book, and the last[9], is proof enough that there is a large, and growing group of Indigenous people now with design esteem, that non-Indigenous people should hesitate to put themselves forward to lead on Indigenous projects. Offer support, yes please, but go in for the glory (and I guess the demise if it all goes wrong) of leadership, no. I've seen this happen both in the academic world and the architectural practice world and it's disrespectful at best and re-colonisation at worst. These acts also have ongoing extractive implications with non-Indigenous people drawing on their efforts in this regard to underpin promotions and awards. My non-Māori co-editor in a book on decolonisation in Aotearoa New Zealand puts it well in her chapter "Pākehā and doing the work of decolonisation" when she says:

> At its base, decolonisation means Pākehā [non-Māori New Zealanders] giving up some power – particularly the power of deciding what our country should look like and how it should be organised, at the exclusion of Māori visions, dreamings and restorations. This is going to mean discomfort for us non-Māori.[10]

So even if you're in a position to lead something Indigenous, please ask whether you should. Who wins when you are leading? Or, are you willing to get a little uncomfortable and share power and perhaps even work to promote and promulgate Indigenous colleagues who are perhaps overlooked by existing power structures that privilege non-Indigenous worldviews?

4. Claiming others" Indigenous whakapapa[11] to

6. Kiddle, R. (2019) The buildings are "uniquely Aotearoa". Their Māori designers are ignored, in The Spinoff, Accessed from: https://thespinoff.co.nz/atea/24-06-2019/the-buildings-are-uniquely-aotearoa-their-maori-designers-are-ignored/.
7. McDonald, K. (2019) Māori artist annoyed at awards snub, in Te Ao Māori News, Accessed from: https://www.teaomaori.news/maori-artist-annoyed-awards-snub

8. Kaupapa means in this case platform, programme of work, or even project.
9. Kiddle, R., O'Brien, K. and Stewart, P. (2018). Our Voices II: Indigeneity and Architecture. ORO Editions, San Francisco.
10. Thomas, A. (2020) Pākehā and doing the work of decolonisation in Imagining Decolonisation, R. Kiddle et al., Bridget Williams Books, Wellington.
11. Whakapapa means geneaology.

suggest authenticity when working in Indigenous spaces

When I read this one out to my mother she said, "Whaaat, do people actually do that?" I have seen non-Indigenous people stand up in conferences and talk of being "accepted into a tribe or mob," with the inference being therefore that this acceptance gives them the right to talk on behalf of that group of Indigenous people. Now Indigenous people are generally very generous types, even after the evils of colonisation. And, if a non-Indigenous academic or designer spends time getting to know that community, learns the language or supports initiatives that might even be seen as decolonising in and of themselves (e.g. retention and reclamation of land or celebrating Indigenous knowledge in some way in their building design) you still should not claim to speak on behalf of, or potentially even about that community.

The community may even say, "you are one of us" if you're really doing things well. Or, you might have a family member that's Indigenous and you respect their ways of doing things an awful lot. Even if all that happens, it is still not your place to claim Indigeneity or suggest you have the right to speak on behalf of Indigenous communities because a group has generously brought you into their circle of trusted allies.

5. Bringing on board an Indigenous colleague to superficially "brown up" your team

So, this one I get a lot and I know my Māori friends in architectural practice or working as built environment academics get this a lot too. Projects, both research or practice-based ones come up and a non-Indigenous designer or academic thinks "We'd have a much better chance of winning the bid if we had some Indigenous input" and so out goes the invitation to a "brown person" to be on the team. Now don't get me wrong, I am sure not all non-Indigenous "procurers" are thinking about this in quite such extractive ways, and it is indeed important that Indigenous designers are involved in key projects that re-inscribe Indigenous values, identities and knowledge sets on our landscapes. However, one would do well to really scrutinise the motivations for asking: What value are we bringing to Indigenous communities by bidding for, or doing this project?; What value are we contributing to building Indigenous design and research capacity and expertise?; How are we upskilling ourselves so the weight of the work around celebrating Indigeneity does not rest on the shoulders of the "brown person"? ; and How are we ensuring that we as non-Indigenous architects and designers do the heavy lifting needed to maintain enduring relationships with the Indigenous communities who are our clients? Finally, in the spirit of the previous section, are we ready to let go of some of the power around project decision-making to enable us to truly "collaborate" in these design discussions? Sharing or relinquishing power may, for example, mean not claiming authorship, or at least sole authorship when we hold the pen.

6. Appropriation of Indigenous knowledges in superficial and unsophisticated ways

A final "dick" move in the list is the good ol' ever present and ongoing appropriation of Indigenous knowledge. Most people are "woke" enough to understand this is a crap thing to do. We gasp and splutter when we hear about Jean-Paul Gaultier using a moko kauae (a traditional Māori tattoo on the chin and lips of women) in his 2007 collection,[12] but things get blurry when it comes to less clear-cut examples. Is the designer celebrating Indigeneity or appropriating culture? A recent article in the *New Zealand Herald*, "heralded" the design of a new museum to "celebrate the "legends" of "New Zealand history".[13] The architect talks of a building which has the look of a waka (traditionally meaning a Māori canoe) being a "universal vessel". That is, "it could be any kind of boat" the architect says "including a waka huia, a canoe, a yacht or a ship."[14] Well if that's not a "catch all, could be almost anything kind of a design rationale" that superficially draws on Māori traditions, I don't know what is. A waka huia, literally translated as a treasure box (a favourite source of inspiration amongst non-Māori designers I might add – I've heard it used many a time) is very different in form and meaning from a canoe/waka, which is different again to a yacht or a ship. Jade Kake (pers.comm., 2019) responds:

> Pākehā [non-Māori New Zealanders] have a history of appropriating Māori cultural concepts under the guise of a generic Kiwi identity that incorporates aspects of Māori culture in a generalised sense. Under the misguided notion that it isn't cultural appropriation, provided it is watered down, and sufficiently generic so as to fall into the realm of national cultural property. This is insidious and harmful, playing into ideas of a shared national identity that ultimately justify (ongoing) colonialism. Under Te Tiriti o Waitangi, hapū [kindship group] have the right to control access to their narratives, and their application. As Māori, our narratives, our pūrākau [narratives/stories], are taonga [treasures]. Not everything is fair game or material for

---

12. Hawkins, N. (2018) You can't copyright culture, but damn I wish you could, in Ātea, The Spinoff, Accessed from: https://thespinoff.co.nz/atea/20-03-2018/you-cant-copyright-culture-but-damn-i-wish-you-could/.
13. Wilson, S. (2020). A boat above the water: New museum proposed or Auckland waterfront, in New Zealand Herald, Accessed from: https://www.nzherald.co.nz/nz/news/article.cfm?c_id=1&objectid=12302292.
14. Ibid.

"inspiration", and no, it's not acceptable to "have a go at it yourself" and then check with mana whenua [kinship group/tribe of a particular place] afterwards to see if it's okay.

In conversation with Timmah Ball, a First Nations planner based in Melbourne/Birrarung-Ga, she talked of the move towards "sexy black imagery" whereby white designers were seeking to make their designs "edgy and decolonial" with superficial Indigenous motifs or patterning with no real understanding of the politics of place that sits behind design in a colonised land.

Come on designers! Design is supposed to be a sophisticated practice.

Conclusion

The above sets out six dick moves that highlight the fact that colonisation doesn't just include land grabs or the stamping out of Indigenous languages. Colonisation is also found in the detail of everyday architectural practice. This is, of course not an exhaustive list and I would encourage readers, both Indigenous and non-Indigenous to think about other "dick moves" that showcase these often mini colonial acts that you've come across. Conversely, keep an eye out for any "cool moves" that showcase decoloniality in the detail of the academy and everyday architecture and design practice. They needn't be sexy, big or showy but acts by designers and scholars that represent a more inclusive and therefore more effective design world.

In the meantime:

1. Engage Indigenous groups early on in projects
2. Don't forget to put their names in your applications for architectural awards
3. Consider whether you're best to lead on an Indigenous project or kaupapa
4. Don't claim Indigenous genealogy links if they're not yours personally to claim and don't claim speaking rights on behalf of Indigenous people
5. Think carefully about your rationale for involving Indigenous practitioners or scholars in your projects and the respect you afford their contributions
6. In your bid to celebrate Indigeneity, ensure this doesn't tip over into appropriation

Colonisation, and also decolonisation is in the detail.

mop pe dike *[talk at end]*: Conclusion

The preceding texts have outlined the de-colonial project as four contestable frontiers. The first contest is between the Indigenous body and the space of the colonial city. That the colour of one's skin, or the wearing of identifying clothing, or gathering in groups in public spaces still provides reasonable grounds to be accosted by security and police alike confirms that there is still a long way to go on this front. That Indigenous people, especially children, can be homeless in their own home due to intergenerational trauma and socio-economic exclusion suggests that this frontier is much wider than expected. That Indigenous communities in the city, the suburbs, the regions, and even in discrete remote locations are attempting to achieve cultural relevancy through political involvement and participatory design, indicates that there are real opportunities for change. Changes that directly confront the legacy of colonial rule by promoting Indigenous leadership and agency.

The second contest and one that has really gained momentum since our entry into the 21st century is the relationship between architecture and Indigenous culture. Is architecture the leader, or the servant? Or is what we design and build nothing more than the result of a combination of expediency and existential necessity? Is "Indigenous architecture" no more than a commercial category ripe for perverse exploitation? These questions aside, architecture does carry an obligation to engage with culture, programme and energy. All too often, this meta-relationship is measured only through the lens of aesthetics. It is very rare that room is given to demonstrate how indigeneity informs spatial, technical and performative resolutions. These considerations broaden this frontier further.

The third contest is between the city and the land. In the Australian context, Country can be considered as a synthesis of the two, together with emotional connections that bind people to place. Where the economics of the city is a matter of ownership, the holistic notion of Country is a matter of belonging. Even so, productivity and spirituality are not exclusive realms, and should be considered complementary and necessary for a sustainable and connected society. This is an exciting frontier that requires a full-frontal assault on the assumptions of privilege that prop up the colonial city. We should expect that the removal of some parts of the city will be necessary to recover places of cultural significance, settings of shared contact experience, and natural systems and cycles that have been long buried under bitumen and concrete.

The fourth contest is the intellectual field. Here, and as evidenced throughout this publication (and the prior publication), there is a broad spectrum of experience and opinion that suggests this field will be well contested for some time to come. All too often, mainstream academia and media falls into the trap of setting a stereotype or singular definition to capture all things Indigenous. "Indigenous architecture" is but one contribution to this nomenclature. Herein lies the need for the *Our Voices* publications and other Indigenous led endeavours in building critical mass, contributing to an ongoing debate, producing durable records, and fortifying our collective ability to affect change at all levels. If we do not continue, we will lose ground and again be spoken for by non-Indigenous voices.

Furthermore, the strength of this book is in the leadership and weight of our collective Indigenous voices. From the publisher, through the co-editors and contributing authors, a safe cultural space has been built that enables a genuine offering to calmly evolve our thoughts and ideas. In terms of the built environment and those factors that express the Indigenous experience within it, this second *Our Voices* publication builds upon the learnings of the first and ensures there is always space for our voices to be heard.

In co-editing this publication, an opportunity to connect with not just previous authors but also new authors, meant that the reach of the first publication has grown and gained traction. As a larger co-editing group, the intention has always been to produce at least three publications. The first was in Aotearoa New Zealand, the second in Australia, and with great enthusiasm we now look towards Turtle Island Canada to produce the third. We again look forward to welcoming new authors to join us in future publications.

Acknowledgements

This is the second publication under the *Our Voices* banner and many people have contributed their valuable time and belief in this ongoing project.

In the first instance, this would simply not be possible without the support and understanding of ORO Editions. It is with great warmth that we acknowledge and profusely thank Gordon Goff, Kirby Anderson, Karen Gao, and all the team at ORO Editions for their extensive generosity and flexibility.

We are also eternally grateful for the financial support to cover the cost of this publication donated by:

- ORO Editions, USA
- BVN Architecture, Australia
- InFocus Management Consultants, Canada
- Sydney School of Architecture, Design and Planning, the University of Sydney, Australia
- Monash Art Design and Architecture, Monash University, Australia
- Tumu Ahurei – Deputy Vice-Chancellor (Māori) and the Ahurei and the Pro Vice Chancellor– Faculties of Science, Architecture and Design Innovation, Te Herenga Waka – Victoria University of Wellington, New Zealand

In signing off, we again thank all authors for their contributions. We trust that this publication continues to grow confidence in our collective voices and that the friendships we have generated to date strengthen our platform for the future.

Kevin, Rebecca, and Patrick.